COLLECTED WORKS OF

James Wilson

JAMES WILSON

COLLECTED WORKS OF

James Wilson

James Wilson

Edited by Kermit L. Hall and Mark David Hall
with an Introduction by Kermit L. Hall
and a Bibliographical Essay by Mark David Hall
Collected by Maynard Garrison

VOLUME 2

This book is published by Liberty Fund, Inc., a foundation established to encourage study of the ideal of a society of free and responsible individuals.

The cuneiform inscription that serves as our logo and as a design element for Liberty Fund books is the earliest-known written appearance of the word "freedom" (*amagi*), or "liberty." It is taken from a clay document written about 2300 B.C. in the Sumerian city-state of Lagash.

Cover art: James Wilson, etching by Max Rosenthal, 1890.
From Library of Congress, Prints and Photographs Division, James Wilson Biographical File, LC-USZ62-6065.
Frontispiece portrait of James Wilson by James Barton Longacre, after an original by J. P. H. Elouis, c. 1825, by permission of the National Portrait Gallery, Smithsonian Institution.

4th printing (2023),
printed on demand by Lightning Source, Inc.

Library of Congress Cataloging-in-Publication Data
Wilson, James, 1742–1798.
[Works]
Collected works of James Wilson/edited and with an introduction by Kermit L. Hall with a Bibliographical Essay by Mark David Hall; collected by Maynard Garrison.
p. cm.
Includes bibliographical references and index.
ISBN-13: 978-0-86597-682-5 (hardcover—set)
ISBN-13: 978-0-86597-684-9 (hardcover—vol 1)
ISBN-13: 978-0-86597-685-6 (hardcover—vol 2)
ISBN-13: 978-0-86597-683-2 (pbk.—set)
[etc.]
1. Law—United States. I. Hall, Kermit. II. Title.
KF213.W5H35 2007
349.73—dc22 2006102965

Liberty Fund, Inc.
11301 North Meridian Street
Carmel, Indiana 46032
libertyfund.org

LECTURES ON LAW,

DELIVERED IN THE

College of Philadelphia,

IN THE YEARS ONE THOUSAND SEVEN HUNDRED AND NINETY,
AND ONE THOUSAND SEVEN HUNDRED AND NINETY ONE.

CONTENTS OF THE SECOND VOLUME

LECTURES ON LAW.

Part 1

Part 2

Part 3

PART I.

Lectures on Law.

CHAPTER XII.
Of the Common Law.

"Sapientissima res tempus," says the profound Lord Bacon,[a] in one of his aphorisms concerning the augmentation of the sciences—Time is the wisest of things. If the qualities of the parent may, in any instance, be expected in the offspring; the common law, one of the noblest births of time, may be pronounced the wisest of laws.

This law has, at different times, and for different reasons, been denominated by different appellations. It is sometimes called, by way of eminence, the law of the land, "lex terrae." At other times, it is called the law of England. At other times again, it is called the law and custom of the kingdom. But its most general and best known appellation is, the common law. Various are the reasons, which have been assigned for this appellation: the best seems to be this—that it is the common municipal law or rule of justice;[b] the law which is described in the code of king Edward the elder, as expressing the same equal right, law, or justice, due to persons of all degrees.[c]

The term *common law* is not confined to the law of England: It is not, says Sir Henry Finch,[1] a word new and strange, or barbarous, and proper to ourselves, and the law, which we profess, as some unlearnedly would have it: it is the proper term for other laws also. Euripides[2] mentions the common laws of Greece; and Plato defines common law in this manner: that which, being taken up by the common consent of a country, is called

a. 1. Ld. Bacon. 252. Aph. 32.
b. Hale. Hist. 55.
c. El. Jur. (4to.) 94.
1. Sir Henry Finch (1558–1625) was a famed jurist and member of parliament from Canterbury. He is most famous now for his writings concerning Zionism.
2. Euripides (480–406 B.C.) was a great Grecian playwright.

law. In another place, he names it, the golden and sacred rule of reason, which we call common law.

This place, continues the same author, in his discourse of law,[d] is very notable: it opens the original and first beginning of the common law: it shows the antiquity of the name; it teaches common law to be nothing else but common reason—that refined reason, which is generally received by the consent of all.

The antiquity of the common law of England is unquestionably very high. It is worth while to listen to what may be deemed the prejudices—certainly the pardonable ones—of its fond admirers, upon a point so interesting to their partiality.

The realm of England, says Lord Chancellor Fortescue,[e] was first inhabited by the Britons; it was afterwards ruled and civilized under the government of the Romans: then the Britons prevailed again: next it was possessed by the Saxons: afterwards the Danes lorded it over us: the Saxons were successful a second time: at last, the Norman conquest took place. But, during all that time, England has been constantly governed by the same customs, by which it is governed at present. Neither the laws of the Romans, which are celebrated beyond all others for their antiquity; nor yet the laws of the Venetians; nor, in short, the laws of any other kingdom in the world are so venerable for their antiquity. So that there is no pretence to insinuate to the contrary, but that the laws and customs of England are not only good, but the very best.—Thus far from the predilection of the chancellor.

But, in truth, it is extremely difficult, if not altogether impracticable, to trace the common law of England to the era of its commencement, or to the several springs, from which it has originally flowed. For this difficulty or impossibility, several reasons may be assigned. One may be drawn from the very nature of a system of common law. As it is accommodated to the situation and circumstances of the people, by whom it is appointed; and as that situation and those circumstances insensibly change; so, especially in a long series of time, a proportioned variation of the laws insensibly takes place; and it is often impossible to ascertain the precise period, when

d. Finch. 74. 75.
e. De Laud. c. 17.

the change began, or to mark the different steps of its progress. Another reason may be drawn from the great number of different nations, which, at different successive periods, and sometimes even at the same period, possessed the government, or the divided governments of England. These added, undoubtedly, to the richness and variety of the common law; but they added likewise to the difficulty of investigating the origin of its different parts.

If this investigation is difficult, there is one consolation, that it is not of essential importance. For at whatever time the laws of England were introduced, from whatever person or country they were derived; their obligatory force arises not from any consideration of that kind, but from their free and voluntary reception in the kingdom.

Several writers, some of them very ingenious and learned, think they can discover, in the common law, features, which strongly indicate, that it is of a Grecian extraction. Without adopting implicitly the authenticity of this high descent, it may be well worth our while to examine the particulars, on which the opinion is founded. If they lead us not to this conclusion, they may, perhaps, lead us to something else, which will be, at least, equally valuable and instructive.

The similarity between the idiom of our language and that of the Grecians has persuaded some very sensible men to believe, that the inhabitants of Great Britain were, in a very remote age, connected, in some manner, with the inhabitants of Greece. This similarity is, indeed, very striking. No one, I believe, who is acquainted with the Greek, the Latin, and the English languages, will hesitate to declare, that there is a closer affinity of idiom between the Greek and the English, than between the English and the Latin, or between the Latin and the Greek.

The very idea of a traditionary law, transmitted from generation to generation merely by custom and memory, may be considered as derived, in part at least, from the practice of the Druids, who considered it as unlawful to commit their religious instructions to writing. But we are informed by the penetrating and intelligent Caesar, that, in other business, whether of a publick or of a private nature, they used the Grecian letters—"*Gaecis literis utuntur.*"[f]

f. De bel. Gal. l. 6. c. 13.

Pliny[3] conjectures that the name of *Druid* was derived from the Greek word δρυζ, quercus, an oak, because they performed their solemn ceremonies in the deep recesses of groves formed by oaks; and because, in their sacrifices, they used the leaves of those trees.[g] The missletoe, it is well known, was of sacred import in their religious mysteries.

Nathaniel Bacon,[4] a gentleman of Gray's inn,[5] wrote a historical and political discourse of the laws and government of England, particularly during the early periods of its history. This discourse, we are informed, was collected from manuscript notes of Mr. Selden,[6] so famed for his various and extensive erudition. To the notes of an antiquarian, so celebrated and so profound, attention will be expected in an investigation of the present kind.

In that discourse we are told, that, though it be both needless and fruitless to enter the lists concerning the original of the Saxons; yet, about the time of Tiberius, their government was, in general, so suitable to that of the Grecians, as if not by the remains of Alexander's army, which was supposed to emigrate into the north, nevertheless, by the neighbourhood of Greece, much of the Grecian wisdom was disseminated among them, before the Roman glory was mounted up to the full pitch; and because this wisdom could never be thus imported but in vessels of men's flesh, rigged according to the Grecian guise, it may well be supposed that there is some, consanguinity between the Saxons and the Grecians, although the degrees be not known.[h]

Their country, continues he, they divided into counties or circuits, all under the government of twelve lords, like the Athenian territory under the archontes. These had the judicial power of distributive justice committed to them, together with one hundred of the commons out of each division. The election of these princes with their commission was concluded

3. Likely refers to Pliny the Elder (23–79), a Roman author, scientist, and historian who died in the eruption of Mount Vesuvius.

g. 3. Rep. Pref. 9 b.

4. Nathaniel Bacon (1593–1660) was an English attorney and politician.

5. Gray's Inn is one of the four Inns of Court (Lincoln's Inn, Middle Temple, and Inner Temple being the other three), a place where barristers receive legal training and supervision.

6. John Selden (1584–1654) was an English jurist, scholar, and politician.

h. Bac. on Gov. 9.

inter majora,[7] by the general assembly, and they executed their commission in circuits, like unto the Athenian heliastick or subdial court, which was rural, and for the most part kept in the open air. In brief, their judicial proceedings were very suitable to the Athenian, but their military more like the Lacedaemonian, whom, above all others, in their manners, they most resembled.[i]

Austin[8] is generally considered as the apostle of the Saxons, who converted them to christianity: but our author suggests, that he was an apostle of another kind—to reconcile them to the see of Rome. To prove this, he adduces a remarkable fact, that the Saxons kept Easter "more Asiatico;" and, against Austin's will, retained that custom fifty years after Austin began his mission among them.[j]

In enumerating the different manners of trial among the Saxons, he says, that the last and most usual one was by witnesses, before the jurors, and their votes thereupon: this made the verdict, and it determined the matter in fact. In former time, questionless, it was a confused manner of trial, by votes of the whole multitude; which made the votes hard to be discerned. But time taught them better advice, to bring the voters to a certain number, according to the Grecian way, who determined controversies by the suffrages of four and thirty, or the major part of them.[k]

Speaking of a certain regulation concerning dower, which was derived from the Latins, he says; "but the Germans learned from the Greeks otherwise: for the laws both of Solon and Lycurgus forbade it, lest marriages should be made for reward, and not grounded on affection."[l]

After having described, in detail, a number of particulars relative to the Saxon government and laws, he makes this general remark: "Nor did the fundamentals alter, either by the diversity and mixture of people of several nations in the first entrance, nor from the Danes or Normans in their survenue; not only because in their original they all breathed one air of the

7. Between the powerful.

i. Id. 10.

8. Austin is the anglicized name of St. Augustine (?–604), the first Archbishop of Canterbury.

j. Bac. on Gov. 12.

k. Id. 56.

l. Id. 64.

laws and government of Greece; but also they were no other than the common dictates of nature, refined by wise men, which challenge a kind of awe, in the sense of the most barbarous."[m]

He concludes his observations concerning the Saxon commonwealth in this expressive manner. "It was a beautiful composure; mutually dependent in every part from the crown to the clown; the magistrates being all choice men; and the king the choicest of the chosen: election being the birth of esteem, and that of merit: this bred love and mutual trust; which made them as corner stones, pointed forward to break the wave of danger.

"Lastly, it was a regular frame in every part, squared and made even by laws, which, in the people, ruled as *lex loquens,*[9] and, in the magistrate, as *lex intelligens;*[10] all of them being grounded on the wisdom of the Greeks, and the judicials of Moses."[n]

The history, says an inquisitive writer, of the constitutions of the different European nations may be much elucidated by institutions, ascertained to have existed in their sister countries, during the corresponding periods of their progress. The rise of the constitutions of the Greek and Italian states will derive light from what is known of the Gaulick, German, and Scandinavian tribes.[o]

Dr. Pettingal,[11] in his very learned inquiry concerning the use and practice of juries, differs from Mr. Bacon with regard to the channel, through which the Grecian customs flowed into the Saxon commonwealths: but he admits that those customs were originally derived from Greece. "The likeness," says he, "of the Greek and Saxon government, supposed to be owing to the neighbourhood of Greece and Saxony, proceeded from a different cause. For, as the Romans took their laws and institutions from Greece, and particularly in the instance of the heliastick court, which was a court of trial by jury, and on which the Romans formed their *judicium* or jury;

m. Bac. on Gov. 68.
9. A speaking law.
10. Understood law.
n. Id. 70.
o. 3. Edin. Phil. Trans. 10.
11. John Pettingal (1708–1781) was an English scholar who wrote a book on juries in the ancient world.

so when they sent their colonies into Germany, they sent also their laws and usages along with them, and by these means the wisdom of Greece and the practice of the heliastick court got among the Saxons in the shape of the Roman *judicia;* and the plan of the Greek government, through the channel of the Roman jurisprudence, laid the foundation of many customs that had a resemblance to the Greek, but in fact were no other than an imitation of the Roman polity, which originally was derived from Athens: so that the jury among the Saxons and northern nations was derived from the Roman *judicia,* as the *causa proxima,*[12] but both of them drew their origin from the court of δικασαί, or jury, among the Greeks. This was the manner, in which the resemblance between the Saxons and Greeks, spoken of by Bacon, was produced."[p]

With regard to the institution of juries, he afterwards observes; "where shall we go, with so much propriety, to look for its origin, as among those who, of all mankind, were the depositaries and patrons of equal law and liberty, and which they themselves had learned from the wisdom and good government established in Athens by Solon? For nothing can be so absurd as to imagine, that such a noble political structure, as had distinguished the only two civilized nations of Europe, and whose legal limitations of power and obedience had done honour even to human nature, should, in times future, be the fortuitous result of a tumultuous deliberation, and that of Scythians and barbarians, rather than an imitation of the wisdom of those customs, which had been introduced among them by their conquerors."[q]

The particular history of juries will find its proper place elsewhere. Suffice it to mention them now among the group of institutions said to be derived from the Grecians to the Saxons either immediately, or through the intermediate channel of the Romans.

The laws and institutions of Greece flowed into Italy, and were conveyed to the many different states there, through a vast variety of channels.

The first inhabitants of this "terra potens virorum"[13] were composed

12. Immediate cause.
p. Pett. on Jur. 154. 155.
q. Pett. on Jur. 159.
13. Land of strong honor.

of Grecian tribes, the overflowings of their native habitations, who migrated, in early days, into the southern parts of the Italian continent; from this circumstance, it was denominated Magna Graecia.[14] These colonists brought with them their own laws and customs.[r] These laws and customs were incorporated into one general body, and made a part of the unwritten or customary law of Rome. "The law of the ancient Romans," says Dr. Burn,[15] in the preface to his book on ecclesiastical law,[s] "had its foundation in the Grecian republicks."

It is well known, that the Roman system of jurisprudence was much indebted to the wise and peaceful institutions of Numa. There was one, which produced strong, and extensive, and lasting consequences in the Roman republick; and which seems to have furnished an example for later times—the establishment of *pagi* or villages. The conquered and vacant lands he distributed among the citizens. These he divided into districts, and placed over each a superintendant, in order to induce them to improve in the arts of agriculture. The consequence of this wise regulation was, that the functions of war and peace were frequently discharged by one and the same person. The farmer, the soldier, and the magistrate were often united in the same character; and reflected on each other reciprocal ornament. The respected citizen stepped from the plough to the consulship without being elated; and, without being mortified, returned from the consulship to the plough: Thus the Cincinnati were formed.

Towards the latter end of the third century of Rome, a solemn deputation, consisting of three commissioners, was despatched to Athens, with instructions to obtain a transcript of the celebrated laws of Solon, and to make themselves fully acquainted with the regulations, the manners, and the institutions of the other states of Greece.[t]

The constitution of Athens had lately received great improvements under the administration of some of her most illustrious citizens, Aristides,[16]

14. Literally "Great Greece," but the reference is to the Greek colonies in southern Italy.

r. Bever. 2.

15. Richard Burn (1709–1785) was an English legal scholar.

s. P. 1.

t. Livy. l. 3. c. 31.

16. Aristides (530–468 B.C.) was a great Athenian strategist and statesman. He fell from political grace because of his opposition to Themistocles, but later returned to a position of power.

Themistocles, and Cimon;[17] and, at this very time, the splendid Pericles was at the head of her government.

After an absence of about two years, the commissioners returned, with copies of the Athenian laws. The decemvirs, of whom the commissioners were three, were then appointed, with full powers to form and propose a digest of laws for Rome. With much alacrity and zeal they entered upon the execution of the very important trust, with which they were invested by their confiding country. In the arduous business, they received the most valuable assistance from a wise Ephesian, who had been driven, by the hand of envy, from his native country; and who, during his exile, had opportunities of personally observing the principles and characters of men, and the establishments and forms of society. His accumulated treasures of observation and reflection were imparted liberally to the decemvirs. The name of Hermodorus[18] was gratefully transmitted to posterity, by a statue erected to his honour in the forum.

The code, which the decemvirs composed, consisted partly of entire laws transcribed from the Grecian originals; partly of such as were altered and accommodated to the constitution and manners of the Romans; and partly of the former laws received and approved in Rome. It was engraved on ten tables, and fixed up in the most conspicuous part of the forum; that the whole people might have an opportunity of perusing and examining it at their conveniency and leisure. When sufficient time had been allowed for those purposes, an assembly of the people was convened. In that assembly, after invocations that what might be done should prove happy and auspicious to the commonwealth, the proposed laws were read. The decemvirs declared, that they had provided, as far as their abilities could provide, that the laws should be equal and impartial to the high and to the low; but that on the counsels and deliberations of the citizens at large, more reliance could be placed; for that the Roman people should have no laws, but such as were ratified as well as ordered by the consent of all.[u] The ten tables received the solemn ratification of the people. Two more were afterwards added in a second decemvirate. All these formed the celebrated code of the

17. Cimon (c. 507–449 B.C.) was a great Athenian soldier and statesman.
18. Recounted by Pomponius (*de Orig Jur.* Dig. 1. tit. 2. s. 4.), and Pliny (*H. N.* xxxiv. 11).
u. Livy. l. 3. c. 34.

twelve tables; the fountain, as Livy[19] honourably denominates them, of all publick and private law. They constituted the foundation of that immense fabrick of jurisprudence, which has extended the influence and the glory of Rome, far beyond the limits and existence of the Roman power.

To the twelve tables, after some time, the *responsa prudentum*[20] began to be superadded. These were the commentaries of lawyers, who accommodated them to the successive practice and proceedings of the courts of justice. This part of the law was denominated, in contradistinction to the laws of the twelve tables, the *jus non scriptum,* or unwritten law; and having no other name, began then to be called the *civil* law. By Justinian, it is styled the *jurisprudentia media;* because it intervened between the laws of the twelve tables, and the imperial constitutions.[v]

In the free and happy periods of the Roman commonwealth, great regard was paid to customary law. We have already seen,[w] on another occasion, that it was thought immaterial whether a law received the sanction of the people by their formal suffrage, or by the uniform course of their conduct and manners. Thus did Romans speak and reason while they enjoyed the blessings of liberty. Nor did the spirit of their law change immediately with the spirit of their government. Long after the impure air of despotism tainted the latter, the vital principles of freedom continued the former in a tolerable state of internal health and soundness. Even under the emperours, the opinions of the Roman lawyers, and the decisions of the Roman courts, with regard to property, and to the rights of private persons, seem not to have been vitiated by the principles of their government. The rules of justice among individuals could not prejudice, in the most remote degree, the power or the interest of the emperour, placed above the reach of all private regards; their rights were, therefore, investigated and enforced with a balanced impartiality.[x]

I have observed, that, in the free and happy periods of the Roman commonwealth, great regard was paid to customary law. Even so late as the time

19. Titus Livius, or Livy (c. 59 B.C.–A.D. 17), wrote a magisterial history of Rome.
20. Letter of wisdom.
v. Burn's Ecc. Law. Pref. 1.
w. Ante. vol. 1. p. 469. 470.
x. Consult Gibbon's Rom. Emp. c. 44. vol. 8. p. 19. and the authorities cited in his notes.

of Justinian, the unwritten law constituted one of the two great divisions, into which the system of Roman jurisprudence was thrown. "Constat,"[y] says the emperour, "autem jus nostrum, quo utimur, aut scripto, aut sine scripto; ut apud Graecos των νομων όι μεν εγγαρφοι, όι δε αγραφοι." "Our law, which we use, consists, like the law of the Grecians, of what is written, and of what is unwritten." This passage, by the by, strongly intimates, in the Institutes, a principle of attachment and imitation operating in favour of the Grecian system. This principle appears, in the most explicit manner, from what we find in the next section of the Institutes. "Et non ineleganter in duas species jus civile distributum esse videtur; nam origo ejus ab institutis duarum civitatum, Athenarum scilicet et Lacedaemoniorum, fluxisse videtur. In his enim civitatibus ita agi solitum erat, ut Lacedaemonii quidem ea quae pro legibus observabant, memoriae mandarent: Athenienses vero ea qae in legibus scripta comprehendissent, custodirent." "The civil or municipal law is divided, with some degree of elegance, into two kinds. For its origin seems to be derived from the institutions of two states—that of the Athenians, and that of the Lacedaemonians. In those states, the manner of transacting their legislative business was such, that the Lacedaemonians trusted to memory for the preservation of their laws; whereas the laws of the Athenians were committed to writing."

Concerning unwritten or customary law, Justinian thus expresses himself. "Sine scripto jus venit, quod usus approbavit; nam *diuturni* mores, consensu utentium comprobati, legem imitantur." "The unwritten law supervenes upon the approbation of usage; for long customs, approved by the consent of those who use them, acquire the qualities of a law." By the way, it deserves to be remarked here, that the expression, which, on a former occasion,[y] I cited from an act of parliament as characteristick of the common law of England, is the literal translation of the expression used by Justinian to characterize the unwritten law of the Roman empire—diuturnus—long. The epithet *immemorial* is used by neither of those very high authorities.

If unwritten law possessed such a dignified rank in the system of Roman jurisprudence so late as even the reign of Justinian; we may be well

y. Just. Ins. l. 1. t. 2. s. 3.
y. Ante. vol. 1. p. 570. [Footnote letter repeated in original.]

justified in supposing that this species of law was entitled to a still greater proportion of regard, four or five centuries before that time. Four or five centuries before that time, it was extended to the island of Great Britain.

The jurisprudence, which had been grossly adapted to the wants of the first Romans, was polished and improved, towards the latter years of the commonwealth, by the infusion and operation of the Grecian philosophy. The Scaevolas[21] had been taught by precedents and experience. But Servius Sulpicius[22] was the first civilian, who established his art on certain and general principles. For the discernment of truth and falsehood, he applied, as an infallible rule, the logick of Aristotle and the Stoicks, reduced particular cases to general principles, and diffused, over the dark and shapeless mass, the light of order, and the graces of eloquence.

The jurisprudence of Rome was adorned and enriched by the exquisite genius of Cicero, which, like the touch of Midas, converts every object into gold. In imitation of Plato, he composed a republick: and for the use of his republick, formed a system of laws. In this system, he expatiates on the wisdom and excellency of the Roman constitution.[z]

Julius Caesar was the first Roman who visited the island of Great Britain; and, perhaps, he had no great reason to exult in the success of his visit. His own account of his retreat is unfurnished with a decent apology. The poet, whose republican spirit was unbroke to the pliant arts of flattery, says in explicit terms.

Territa quaesitis ostendit terga Britannis.[23]

The first foundations of an effective conquest and a permanent settlement, which were laid in Britain under the auspices of Rome, were those, which were begun in the reign of the emperour Claudius.[24]

The character of his administration may be thus described. From the general tenour of his conduct it is plain, that he contemplated the senate as the sovereign power of the whole empire. He made many attempts to

21. A famous family of ancient Rome.

22. Servius Sulpicius Rufus (c. 106–43 B.C.) was a Roman orator, jurist, and statesman.

z. Consult Gib. Rom. Emp. c. 44. vol. 8. p. 26. 27. and the authorities cited.

23. He showed his frightened back to the Britons he had pursued.

24. Tiberius Claudius Drusus Nero Germanicus (10 B.C.–54) was the Roman emperor (41–54) who subdued Britannia.

introduce an improvement of the constitution, by reviving or reforming antiquated laws, and by enacting salutary new ones: but these attempts he meditated and prosecuted by the advice and with the concurrence of the senate. So far, therefore, as the establishments in Britain were carried on during the administration of Claudius, it is not likely that they were marked by circumstances of uncommon rigour or oppression. Indeed, the acquisitions made in the island during that and some succeeding reigns were both very limited and very precarious.

Julius Agricola,[25] who governed it in the reign of Vespasian, Titus, and Domitian,[26] was the first who formed a regular plan for completing the conquest, and rendering the acquisition useful to the conquerors. Among the Britons he introduced the Roman civility and laws; he reconciled them to the Roman manners and language; he instructed them in learning and the arts; he taught them to know and to covet all the conveniences and delicacies of life; he employed every soothing contrivance to render their fetters easy, and even fashionable. The inhabitants, taught, by direful experience, how disproportioned their military strength and military skill were to the military strength and military skill of the Romans, and lulled by the flattering scenes of ease and elegance, which were exhibited to their views and wishes, acquiesced in the splendid dominion of their masters, and were gradually incorporated as a portion of the mighty empire of Rome.[a]

Agricola disseminated the modes of Roman education among the sons of the British nobility; and improved them so well, that, in a short time, those who had most despised the Roman language, applied with ardour, to the study and the profession of Roman eloquence. An affectation of the Roman dress was the natural consequence; and the gown was considered in Britain as a splendid distinction. Luxury succeeded splendour and refinement; and the Britons were Romanised, without reflecting that the arts and

25. Gnaeus Julius Agricola (37–93) was a brilliant Roman general and statesman who was the father-in-law of Tacitus. He was governor of Britannia for just a brief time, but proved himself most capable of reconciling the native inhabitants to Roman rule and customs.

26. Imperator Caesar Vespasianus Augustus, referred to in English as Vespasian (9–79), was Roman Emperor from 69 to 79. His two sons, Titus and Domitian, were subsequently emperors (Titus: 79–81 and Domitian: 81–96).

a. 1. Guth. Eng. 40.

accomplishments which were liberal in a Roman, were, in a Briton, servile; and that what they viewed as the accompaniments of politeness, were, in reality, nothing better or nobler than the instruments of subjection.[b]

The Romans held the possession and the government of the most considerable part of Britain near four hundred years. During that long period, a very frequent and intimate intercommunication of marriages, manners, customs, and laws must have taken place.

In the whole province there are said to have been about one hundred and fifty Roman stations.[c] These were connected by inferiour fortresses, erected at proper distances, and garrisoned by regular troops. Each of those garrisons attracted the neighbouring inhabitants; a town or village was begun; and a settlement was formed indiscriminately by Roman and by native families. As military service was often rewarded with possessions in land, the example of the Roman officers and soldiers must have spread the knowledge and practice of agriculture, while their industry in the management of their estates contributed to beautify and improve the face of the country.

The connexion with Britain, which the soldiers of the Roman army formed by living in the country, was seldom dissolved, even when they were discharged from the service. They had gradually acquired an attachment to the places where they had long resided, and chose to continue that residence where their attachment was now formed. Their offspring became natural inhabitants; and Britain, in this manner, received fresh accessions of Romans, to supply the place of such natives as were drawn from it, in order to recruit the army in other provinces of the empire.

It was the policy of Rome to extend her jurisprudence wherever she had extended her dominion. This policy promoted her influence and her interest among the vanquished people; and, at the same time, established among them tranquillity and order. This policy was peculiarly necessary in Britain, to prevent the private wars, and restrain the mutual acts of violence and outrage, to which the inhabitants were remarkably addicted. The introduction and establishment of the Roman laws was unavoidably, however, a work of time. For a considerable period, the Roman magistrates confined their operations to the publick administration of the province;

b. Tac. Agric. c. 21—Millar. 16. 17.
c. Millar. 10.

while the British chiefs were permitted to retain their ancient jurisdiction in matters of private property, and to determine the controversies of their tenants and dependents.

Some writers are of opinion, that this jurisdiction was gradually circumscribed, and, at last, entirely annihilated; and that, during the long government of the Romans, the original laws and customs of the Britons were disused and forgotten. Perhaps the more probable opinion is, that, during this extended succession of time, the two nations became blended together in their laws and customs, as well as by their intermarriages; so as to be neither wholly Roman, nor wholly British. Those laws, indeed, which related to government and the administration of publick affairs, were, it may be presumed, altogether Roman.

Accordingly, when the exhausted empire was obliged to collect her last expiring efforts around the immediate seat of life and existence; the departure of the Romans from Britain was fatal to all the institutions of government which had been formed, ripened, and established during the long lapse of time, which we have already mentioned. The officers, who directed and managed the administration of the province, and the judges, who, at least in matters relating to publick law, had acquired a complete jurisdiction, retired from a country, abandoned by its master. The courts of justice were shut: government, and the order attendant on government, were dissolved. The rudder of the state knew no hand, which had a right to hold it: the vessel was, therefore, tossed at the pleasure of the winds and waves.

Time, however, and necessity gradually introduced some form of government, though a very simple one. The country was broken into districts, and placed under chiefs. A general of their united forces was appointed. Voltigern[27] was the last, who was promoted to that high dignity.

From the foregoing deduction, it is highly probable, that, at the period to which we have now brought our remarks, the system of law in Britain, if, at that period, any kind of law deserved the name of a system, was a motley mixture of Roman and British institutions. The language, at that time used in Britain, was, as we have every reason to believe, a composition of the Roman and British tongues.

27. Voltigern (Vortigern) was a warlord of the Britons in the mid-fifth century, and gets the blame for inviting the Anglo-Saxons into Britain to settle.

Sir William Blackstone mentions three instances,[d] in which the British jurisprudence bears a great resemblance to some of the modern doctrines of the English law. One is, the very notion itself of an oral unwritten law, delivered down from age to age, by custom and tradition merely. This seems derived from the practice of the Druids, who never committed any of their instructions to writing. This observation suggests a claim, unquestionably, to the notion of a common law subsisting among the Britons. But it, by no means, authorizes an exclusive claim. We have seen that, in the pure times of the Roman commonwealth, a customary law was known and highly respected at Rome. At the time when the Roman law was translated to Britain, it retained its customary qualities in their full vigour and extent.

The second instance mentioned by Sir William Blackstone is, the partible quality of lands by the custom of gavelkind, which still obtains in many parts of England, and, till the reign of Henry the eighth, prevailed universally over Wales. This, says he, is undoubtedly of British original. But the partible quality of lands, if not entirely, yet nearly on the same principles, prevailed among the Romans, as well as among the Britons. Nor was it confined even to those two nations. The Greeks, the Romans, as we are informed in the Commentaries, the Britons, the Saxons, and even originally the feudists divided the lands equally; some among all the children at large, some among the males only.[e]

The third instance, mentioned by Sir William Blackstone as of British original, is, the ancient division of the goods of an intestate between his widow and children, or next of kin; which has since been revived by the statute of distributions. But it is well known, that the statute of distributions is moulded in the form of Roman as well as of ancient British jurisprudence.[f]

Well known is the event of the invitation, which Voltigern gave to a body of the Saxons to aid him against his northern enemies.[g] As it has happened on other occasions, the allies became the masters of those whom they engaged to assist.

d. 4. Bl. Com. 401.
e. 2. Bl. Com. 215.
f. 2. Bl. Com. 516. 517. Bever. 482.
g. 2. Whitak. 545.

We have no complete account of the circumstances which attended the settlement of the Saxons in Britain. From the doleful representations of some early and passionate annalists, our historians, in general, have been led to suppose, that all the Britons, who were not reduced to captivity, were massacred by their barbarous enemies, or, disdaining submission, retreated among the mountains of Wales, or withdrew into the country of Armorica in France; to which country, the name of Bretagne is said to have been derived from those unfortunate refugees. A bold and industrious antiquarian has lately shown, however, that this extraordinary supposition is without any solid foundation. It is, indeed, highly probable, that many of the Britons were subjected to very great hardships, and were obliged even to abandon their native soil. But it appears hard to believe, that the Saxons should be stimulated by barbarity to proceed so far as, contrary to their own interests, to exterminate the ancient inhabitants. There is even complete evidence, that, in some parts of the island, the Britons were so far from being destroyed or obliged to fly their country, that they were permitted to retain a certain proportion of their landed property. This proportion, a third part of the whole, was the same with that allotted to the ancient inhabitants, in some of those provinces on the continent of Europe, which were conquered by the other German tribes.

The language, which spread itself among the Saxons after their settlement in Britain, contained a great proportion of the Latin and British tongues. This large infusion of those different ingredients into the same language, is, of itself, a strong proof, that the inhabitants were compounded of the different nations, by whom those tongues were originally spoken.[h]

The victorious Saxons were less civilized than the conquered Britons. The latter gradually communicated to the former a portion of that refinement, which had not been entirely effaced from themselves. At last, after a lapse of near two centuries, the two nations, by habits, treaties, commerce, and intermarriages, were entirely blended together; and their union produced such a compound system of manners and customs, as might be expected to arise from the declining state of one, and the improving state of the other. This blending principle would have its effect upon the laws,

h. 2. Whitak. 235. 236.

as well as upon the manners and habits of both nations. The conquerors and the conquered would be incorporated into one people, and compose, as the antiquarian[i] before mentioned expresses himself, a mingled mass of Saxon Britons and British Saxons.

We are told of three kinds of laws used in England during the government of the Saxons: the Mercian law,[28] which contained the local constitutions of the kingdom of Mercia; the Dane law, which comprised the customs introduced by those, whose name it bore; and the West Saxon law, a system compiled by Alfred the Great; whose elevated and extensive talents were employed, in the most vigorous manner, for the improvement of the laws and constitution of his country.

These three systems of law were different, rather in unessential forms, than in important principles. For this we have the authority of the very learned Spelman. "Our Saxons, though divided into many kingdoms, yet were they all one, in effect, in manners, laws, and language: so that the breaking of their government into many kingdoms, or the reuniting of their kingdoms into a monarchy, wrought little or no change among them, touching laws. For though we talk of the West Saxon law, the Mercian law, and the Dane law, whereby the west parts of England, the middle parts, and those of Suffolk, Norfolk, and the north were severally governed; yet held they all a uniformity of substance, differing rather in their mulcts, than in their canon, that is, in the quantity of fines and amerciaments, than in the course and frame of justice."[j]

These distinct codes were afterwards reduced into one uniform digest, for the use and observance of the whole kingdom. This digest was undertaken and commenced by King Edgar:[29] it was completed by his grandson, King Edward; and has been since well known and distinguished by the appellation of the Confessor's laws. It is conjectured to have been chiefly a revival of the code of the great Alfred, accompanied with such improvements as were suggested by subsequent experience.

i. 2. Whitak. 111.

28. The laws of Mercia, one of the kingdoms in the Anglo-Saxon heptarchy. Mercia was located in the present-day Midlands region of England.

j. 2. Henry. 277. 278. cites Spel. Rel. p. 49.

29. King Edgar the Peaceful (c. 942–975) consolidated the Anglo-Saxon kingdoms. Edgar's reign was the height of Anglo-Saxon rule of England.

We have now brought the history of the common law down to the period of the Norman conquest. We have seen its rise taking place, by slow degrees, in ages very remote, and in nations very different from one another. We have seen it, in its converging progress, run into one uniform system, mellowed by time and improved by experience. In every period of its existence, we find imprinted on it the most distinct and legible characters of a customary law—a law produced, extended, translated, adopted, and moulded by practice and consent.

The period through which we have gone is, indeed, peculiarly interesting. "The whole period of our national history before the conquest," says an English writer, "is the most important and momentous in our annals. It most forcibly lays hold upon the passions by the quick succession and active variety of incidents, and by the decisive greatness of its revolutions. And, what is much more, it is that period of our history, which gives the body and the form to all the succeeding centuries of it. It contains the actual commencement of every part of our publick and private economy."[k]

Here we make a pause in the history of the common law. To pursue it minutely from the Norman conquest to the accession of the Stuart line would be a tedious, a disagreeable, but, fortunately, it is an unnecessary task.

The common law, as now received in America, bears, in its principles, and in many of its more minute particulars, a stronger and a fairer resemblance to the common law as it was improved under the Saxon, than to that law, as it was disfigured under the Norman government. How much it was disfigured, and why we should not receive it in its disfigured state, will appear from the following very interesting part of Sir William Blackstone's Commentaries.

> The last and most important alteration, introduced by the Norman conquest, both in our civil and military polity, was the ingrafting on all landed estates, a few only, excepted, the fiction of feodal tenure; which drew after it a numerous and oppressive train of servile fruits and appendages; aids, reliefs, primer seisins, wardships, marriages, escheats, and fines for alienation; the genuine consequences of the maxim then adopted, that all the lands in England were derived from, and holden, mediately or immediately, of the crown.

k. 1. Whitak. Pref. 7.

The nation, at this period, seems to have groaned under as absolute a slavery, as it was in the power of a warlike, an ambitious, and a politick prince to create. The consciences of men were enslaved by sour ecclesiasticks, devoted to a foreign power, and unconnected with the civil state under which they lived; who now imported from Rome, for the first time, the whole farrago of superstitious novelties, which had been engendered by the blindness and corruption of the times, between the first mission of Augustin, the monk, and the Norman conquest.

The ancient trial by jury gave way to the impious decision by battle. The forest laws totally restrained all rural pleasures and manly recreations. And in cities and towns, the case was no better; all company being obliged to disperse, and fire and candle to be extinguished, by eight at night, at the sound of the melancholy curfew.

The ultimate property of all lands, and a considerable share of the present profits, were vested in the king or by him granted out to his Norman favourites; who, by a gradual progression of slavery, were absolute vassals to the crown, and as absolute tyrants to the commons. Unheard of forfeitures, talliages, aids, and fines were arbitrarily extracted from the pillaged landholders, in pursuance of the new system of tenure. And, to crown all, as a consequence of the tenure by knight service, the king had always ready at his command an army of sixty thousand knights, or *milites;* who were bound, upon pain of confiscating their estates, to attend him in time of invasion, or to quell any domestick insurrection.

Trade, or foreign merchandise, such as it then was, was carried on by the Jews and Lombards; and the very name of an English fleet, which king Edgar had rendered so formidable, was utterly unknown to Europe: the nation consisting wholly of the clergy, who were also the lawyers; the barons, or great lords of the land; the knights or soldiery, who were the subordinate landholders; and the burghers, or inferiour tradesmen, who, from their insignificancy, happily retained, in their socage and burgage tenure, some points of their ancient freedom. All the rest were villains or bond men.

From so complete and well concerted a scheme of servility, it has been the work of generations for our ancestors, to redeem themselves and their posterity into that state of liberty, which we now enjoy: and which, therefore, is not to be looked upon as consisting of mere encroachments on the crown, and infringements of the prerogative, as some slavish and narrow minded writers in the last century endeavoured to maintain; but as, in general, a gradual restoration of that ancient constitution, whereof our Saxon forefathers had been unjustly deprived, partly by the policy, and partly by the force, of the Norman.[1]

From the deduction, which we have made, it appears, I think, in a satisfactory manner, that the rich composition of the common law is formed from all the different ingredients, which have been enumerated; yet, when we descend to particular principles and rules, it is very difficult, it is often impossible, to ascertain the particular source, from which such rules and principles have been drawn. That some of our customs have been derived from the Grecians, though probably through the intermediate channel of the Romans; that others of them have been derived immediately from the Romans, others from the Britons, others from the Saxons, and others, in fine, from the Normans, seems to be evinced by the reasonable rules of historical credibility. But to say that such or such a particular custom has descended to us from such and such a particular origin, would be often to hazard too much upon uncertain conjecture. It may, however, be done sometimes, upon facts and arguments, which are clear and convincing: and whenever it can be done, it will amply repay all the care and trouble of the investigation. As has been already mentioned, the most proper way to teach and to study the common law is to teach and to study it as a historical science. Under many titles, we shall have an opportunity of pursuing this method.

Besides those particular instances; of which notice will be taken afterwards; there is one pretty general distribution of the common law, according to which, different parts of it may be referred to different nations, by whom, in all probability, they were introduced.

The original frame of the British constitution, different, indeed, in many important points, from what it now is, and bearing, to some of the constitutions which have lately been formed, and established in America, a degree of resemblance, which will strike and surprise those who compare them together—this venerable frame may be considered as of Saxon architecture. To a Saxon origin may also be ascribed much of that part of the common law, which relates to crimes and punishments. One lovely feature, in particular, we have the pleasure to recognise. The ancient

1. 4. Bl. Com. 411–413.

Germans, of whom the Saxons composed a part, discriminated punishments, as we are informed by Tacitus,[m] according to the kind, and proportioned them according to the measure of the crime. "Liberty," says the celebrated Montesquieu,[n] "is in its highest perfection, when criminal laws derive each punishment from the particular nature of the crime." With regard to this very interesting part of the law, very wide deviations from Saxon principles have been made in the English criminal code, since the period of the Norman conquest.

The common law, as it respects contracts and personal property, discovers evident traces of the Roman jurisprudence. It has been the opinion of some, that those parts of the common law have been borrowed from the civil law, subsequent to the great legislative era,[o] when the pandects of Justinian were discovered at Amalfi: I suggest, merely for consideration at present, a conjecture, that many of those parts were incorporated into the common law, during the long period of near four centuries, when the Roman jurisprudence predominated in England.

Much of the common law respecting real estates, as it has been received in England since the time of William the Conqueror; and a considerable part of it, as it is still received in that kingdom, particularly the feudal principles and policy, should be referred to a Norman extraction.

Concerning the period, at which the feudal system was introduced into England, there has been long and learned controversy among lawyers and antiquarians. "At the close of the first century," says Whitaker in his History of Manchester, "our tenures in Britain appear undeniably to have been purely military in their design, and absolutely feudal in their essence. The primary institution of feuds is unanimously deduced, by our historical and legal antiquarians, from the northern invaders of the Roman empire; and the primary introduction of them into this island is almost as unanimously referred to the much more recent epocha of the Norman conquest. But they certainly existed among us before, and even formed the primitive establishment of the Britons." "They must have existed coeval with the first

m. De mor. Germ. c. 12.
n. Spir. Laws. b. 12. c. 4.
o. About the year 1130.

plantation of the island. They were plainly the joint result of a colonizing and a military spirit. The former providentially animated the first ages of the Noachidae was constantly prosecuted under the discipline of regular order, and the control of regal authority, and had whole regions to partition among the members of the colony. The latter was excited by the frequent migrations of colonists and the numerous invasions of settlements in the same ages, and naturally provided for the security of the colony, by the institution of a military establishment."[p]

From Mr. Whitaker's[30] own account, it appears that he is singular in his sentiments with regard to the antiquity of the feudal system. Indeed, if his sentiments are well founded, that system must have been coeval and coextensive with society itself. But from the account which we have already[q] given of the origin and first principles of society, the inference, we apprehend, may be fairly made, that its first ages were ages of equality, perhaps of some culpable degree of license. The opinion is indeed singular—that rule and subordination in the extreme, in other words, tyranny and slavery, should be necessarily extended with the extension of the human race.

It is remarkable, however, that this very writer makes, with regard to the Saxons, a peculiar exception from this general and almost universal system. "No traces," says he, "of the primitive feuds appear visible among the Saxons; and they seem to have been the only nation of Germany that did not plant them in their conquests."[r] His conjecture, therefore, is, that the Saxons had adopted this improvement from the Britons. He represents the whole Saxon system, in consequence of this adoption, as informed with one strong principle of subordination, which diffused its influence through every part, and formed a scale of dependence from the sovereign to the villain. Thus, one continued chain of subordination was carried regularly from the villain to the monarch; the higher link of the whole being fastened to the foot of the throne, and keeping the whole machine of national power steadily dependent from it.[s]

p. 1. Whitak. 262. 264.
30. John Whitaker (1735–1808) was a British historian.
q. Ante. vol. 1. p. 636.
r. 2. Whitak. 153.
s. Id. 157. 158.

Others inform us, and apparently on better grounds, that in the early ages of society, estates in land were free; that they were held in propriety, and not by tenure; that they were hereditary as well as free; that such were the real estates of the Greeks, of the Romans, and particularly of the Saxons; that, among the latter, they were alienable likewise at the pleasure of the owner, and devisable by will. The Saxons were absolutely masters of their land; and were not obliged to transmit it to the blood which the donor intended to favour. It was still, however, considered as the property of a citizen; and, therefore, subjected its owner to the general obligation of taking arms in defence of his country.

The differences between estates in land under the Saxon government, and those which were held under that of the conqueror, will be plain and striking by a short enumeration and contrast. Before the conquest, lands were the absolute proprieties of the owners; they could be devised and transferred at pleasure. No wardship or marriage was due or exacted. In all these things, an alteration was made on the introduction of the feudal tenures. Lands could not be alienated without the consent of the superiour: they could not be devised by will. The heir had no right to enter into the inheritance of his ancestor, until he had paid a relief, and had been admitted by his lord. As to landed estates, therefore, the law introduced by the conqueror might well be denominated a new, a Norman law.

At common law, too, all inheritances were estates in fee simple; of different kinds indeed, qualified and conditional, as well as absolute.[t]

"When all estates were fee simple," says my Lord Coke, "then were purchasers sure of their purchases, farmers of their leases, creditors of their debts: and for these, and other like causes, by the wisdom of the common law, all estates of inheritance were fee simple: and what contentions and mischiefs have crept into the quiet of the law by these fettered inheritances, daily experience teacheth us."[u]

"Out of all the books and reports of the common law," says the same very experienced judge, "I have observed, that though sometimes by acts of parliament, and sometimes by invention and contrivance of men, some points of the ancient common law have been diverted from its proper

t. 2. Ins. 333.
u. 1. Ins. 19b.

channel; yet, in the revolutions of time, it has been, with much publick satisfaction, and to avoid many great inconveniences, been restored to its proper and ancient course. For example; the wisdom of the common law was, that all estates of inheritance should be fee simple, so that one man might safely alien, demise, and contract to and with another. But the statute of Westminster the second created an estate tail, and made a perpetuity by act of parliament, restraining tenant in tail from aliening or demising, but only for his own life. This, in process of time, introduced such trouble and mischief, that, after two hundred years, necessity discovered a method, by law, for a tenant in tail to alien.

"In like manner, by the ancient common law, freeholds could not pass from one to another but by matter of record, or solemn livery of seisin. Against this, however, uses were invented, and grew common and almost universal, in destruction of the ancient common law in that point. But, in time, the numerous inconveniences of this being found by experience, the statute of 27. H. VIII. c. 10. was made to restore the ancient common law, in this particular, as expressly appears by the preamble of the statute itself. Of the same truth, an infinity of other examples might be produced; but these shall, at present, suffice."[v]

We have mentioned the common law, as a law which is unwritten. When we assign to it this character, we mean not that it is merely oral, and transmitted from age to age merely by tradition. It has its monuments in writing; and its written monuments are accurate and authentick. But though, in many cases, its *evidence* rests, yet, in all cases, its *authority* rests not, on those written monuments. Its authority rests on reception, approbation, custom, long and established. The same principles, which establish it, change, enlarge, improve, and repeal it. These operations, however, are, for the most part, gradual and imperceptible, partial and successive in a long tract of time.

It is the characteristick of a system of common law, that it be accommodated to the circumstances, the exigencies, and the conveniencies of the people, by whom it is appointed. Now, as these circumstances, and exigencies, and conveniencies insensibly change; a proportioned change, in time and in degree, must take place in the accommodated system. But though

v. 3. Rep. Pref. 18.

the system suffer these partial and successive alterations, yet it continues materially and substantially the same. The ship of the Argonauts became not another vessel, though almost every part of her materials had been altered during the course of her voyage.

Again; we are taught both by observation and by experience, that the farther laws reach from their original institutions, the more extensive and the more numerous they become. In the first association of a community, their prospect is not enlarged, their wants are comparatively few: but as the society increases, their views expand, and their wishes multiply: what is the consequence? New laws and provisions, suited to the growing multitude of successive exigencies, must be made. The system, of course, becomes larger and more complex.

The same principle of accommodation in a system of common law, will adjust its improvement to every grade and species of improvement made by the people, in consequence of practice, commerce, observation, study, and refinement. As the science of legislation is the most noble, so it is the most slow and difficult of sciences. The jurisprudence of a state, willing to avail itself of experience, receives additional improvement from every new situation, to which it arrives; and, in this manner, attains, in the progress of time, higher and higher degrees of perfection, resulting from the accumulated wisdom of ages. The illustrious legislators, who have illuminated the political world, such as Solon, Numa, Lycurgus, collected the customs which they found already adopted, and disposed them regularly, with the necessary amendments and illustrations.

The same principle of accommodation, which we have already traced in so many directions, may be traced in still one direction more. It silently and gradually introduces; it silently and gradually withdraws its customary laws. Disuse may be justly considered as the repeal of custom. Laws, which are long unobserved in practice, become laws, which are antiquated in theory. "On strong grounds this rule is received, that laws may be abrogated, not only by the express declaration of the legislature, but, through desuetude, by the tacit consent of all."[w] A law ought not, indeed, to be presumed obsolete upon slight pretences; but, on the other hand, a total disuse, for a long period of time, may be justly considered as a suf-

w. D. l. 1. t. 3. l. 32. p. 1.

ficient reason for not carrying into effect a disrespected and neglected ordinance.

"It has happened to the law, as to other productions of human invention, particularly those which are closely connected with the transactions of mankind, that the changes wrought by a series of years have been gradually rendering many parts of it obsolete; so that the systems of one age have become the objects of mere historick remembrance in the next. Of the numerous volumes that compose a lawyer's library, how many are consigned to oblivion by the revolutions in opinions and practice; and what a small part of those, which are still considered as in use, is necessary for the purposes of common business!"[x]

There are some great eras, when important and very perceptible alterations take place in the situation of men and things: at such eras, the accommodating principle, which we have so often mentioned, will introduce similar and adequate alterations in the rules and practice of the common law. Such considerable changes, together with their extensive influences, diffuse, over many parts of the system, a new air and appearance. At some of those eras, the improvement is as rapid as the change is great. Why should not the present age in America, form one of those happy eras?

During many—very many revolving centuries, the common law has been the peculiar and the deserved favourite of the people of England. It suffered much, as we have seen, from the violence of the Norman conquest; but it still continued the theme of their warmest praise, and the object of their fondest hopes. Its complete restoration was the burthen of every memorial, and the prayer of every petition. The knowledge of this law formed a considerable part of the little learning of the early and unenlightened ages.

Those, who had received the best education, says Selden, in his dissertation on Fleta,[y][31] applied themselves assiduously to the study of the ancient English laws and manners, which related to government and the administration of civil affairs. From such characters judges and licensed advocates were selected. These laws and manners were taught in the private families

x. 1. Reeve. Pref. 1. Roll. Pref. 3–5.

y. c. 7. s. 7.

31. *Fleta* refers to a legal commentary written in England c. 1290 by an unknown author in Fleet prison. Seldon first published it in 1647.

of the most illustrious characters of the kingdom, in monasteries, in colleges, in universities. They had no acquaintance with the Theodosian[32] or Justinian codes. They taught only the manners of our ancestors, and that law, which, even before the period of which we speak, and down to our own times, is known by the name of the common law of England.

The affectionate manner, in which the great and good Lord Chief Justice Hale speaks of this law, recommends it and him with equal warmth. He introduces it—as the common municipal law of the kingdom—as the superintendent of all the particular laws known in any of the courts of justice—as the common rule for the administration of publick affairs in that great kingdom—as the object, of which that great kingdom had been always tender; and with great reason; not only because it is a very just and excellent law in itself; but also because it is singularly accommodated to the frame of the English government, and to the disposition of the English nation. As such, it is by a long experience, incorporated into their very temperament, and has become the constitution of the English commonwealth.[z]

In the natural body, diseases will happen; but a due temperament and a sound constitution will, by degrees, work out those adventitious and accidental diseases, and will restore the body to its just state and situation. So is it in the body politick, whose constitution is animated and invigorated by the common law. When, through the errours, or distempers, or iniquities of men or times, the peace of the nation, or the right order of government have received interruption; the common law has wrought out those errours, distempers, and iniquities; and has reinstated the nation in its natural and peaceful state and temperament.

The best kings of England have been always jealous and vigilant to reform what has, at any time, been found defective in that law; to remove all obstacles, which could obstruct its free course; and to support, countenance, and encourage it, as the best, the safest, and the truest rule of justice in all matters, criminal as well as civil.[a]

We have seen how much the common law has been loved and revered by individuals, by families, and by the different seminaries of education

32. The Roman legal code as set down by Theodosius II (401–450), who was emperor of the East from 408 to 450.

z. Hale. Hist. 44.

a. Hale. Hist. 44. 45.

throughout England: let us now see how much it has been respected by even the legislative power of the kingdom.

On a petition to parliament for redress, in the thirteenth year of Richard the second,[33] the following remarkable judgment of parliament is entered—It appears to the lords of parliament, that the petition is not a proper petition to parliament; since the matter contained in it ought to be determined by the common law: and, therefore, it was awarded, that the party petitioning should take nothing by his suit in parliament; because he might sue at common law, if he thought proper.[b]

We have viewed, in a number of instances, the accommodating spirit of the common law. In other instances its temper is decided and firm. The means are varied according to times and circumstances; but the great ends of liberty are kept steadily and constantly in view.

Its foundations, laid in the most remote antiquity, have not been overturned by the successive invasions, or migrations, or revolutions which have taken place. The reason has been already hinted at: it contains the common dictates of nature, refined by wisdom and experience, as occasions offer, and cases arise.

In all sciences, says my Lord Bacon,[c] they are the soundest, that keep close to particulars. Indeed a science appears to be best formed into a system, by a number of instances drawn from observation and experience, and reduced gradually into general rules; still subject, however, to the successive improvements, which future observation or experience may suggest to be proper. The natural progress of the human mind, in the acquisition of knowledge, is from particular facts to general principles. This progress is familiar to all in the business of life; it is the only one, by which real discoveries have been made in philosophy; and it is the one, which has directed and superintended the instauration of the common law. In this view, common law, like natural philosophy, when properly studied, is a science founded on experiment. The latter is improved and established by carefully and wisely attending to the phenomena of the material world; the former, by attending, in the same manner, to those of man and society. Hence, in both, the most regular and undeviating principles will be found,

33. Richard II (1367–1400) was King of England from 1377 to 1399.
b. Hale. Hist. 46. 47.
c. 4. Ld. Bac. 5.

on accurate investigation, to guide and control the most diversified and disjointed appearances.

How steadily and how effectually has the spirit of liberty animated the common law, in all the vicissitudes, revolutions, and dangers, to which that system has been exposed! In matters of a civil nature, that system works itself pure by rules drawn from the fountain of justice: in matters of a political nature, it works itself pure by rules drawn from the fountain of freedom.

It was this spirit, which dictated the frequent and formidable demands on the Norman princes, for the complete restoration of the Saxon jurisprudence: it was this spirit, which, in magna charta, manifested a strict regard to the rights of the commons, as well as to those of the peerage: it was this spirit, which extracted sweetness from all the bitter contentions between the rival houses of Lancaster and York: it was this spirit, which preserved England from the haughtiness of the Tudors, and from the tyranny of the Stuarts: it was this spirit, which rescued the States of America from the oppressive claims, and from all the mighty efforts made to enforce the oppressive claims, of a British parliament.

The common law of England, says my Lord Coke,[d] is a social system of jurisprudence: she receives other laws and systems into a friendly correspondence: she associates to herself those, who can communicate to her information, or give her advice and assistance. Does a question arise before her, which properly ought to be resolved by the law of nations? By the information received from that law, the question will be decided: for the law of nations, is, in its full extent, adopted by the common law, and deemed and treated as a part of the law of the land. Does a mercantile question occur? It is determined by the law of merchants. By that law, controversies concerning bills of exchange, freight, bottomry, and ensurances receive their decision. That law is indeed a part of the law of nations; but it is peculiarly appropriated to the subjects before mentioned. Disputes concerning prizes, shipwrecks, hostages, and ransombills, are, under the auspices of the common law, settled and adjudged by the same universal rule of decision. Does a contract, in litigation, bear a peculiar reference to the local laws of any particular foreign country? By the local laws of that foreign country, the common law will direct the contract to be interpreted and ad-

d. Rep. 28. Calvin's Case.

justed. Does a cause arise within the jurisdiction of the admiralty? Within that jurisdiction the civil law is allowed its proper energy and extent.

But, while she knows and performs what is due to others, the common law knows also and demands what is due to herself. She receives her guests with hospitality; but she receives them with dignity. She liberally dispenses her kindness and indulgence;—but, at the same time, she sustains, with becoming and unabating firmness, the preeminent character of *gravior lex*.[34]

There is much truth and good sense, though there is some quaintness of expression, in the following encomium of the common law, which I take from my Lord Coke.[e] "If all the reason, that is dispersed into so many several heads, were united into one, yet could he not make such a law as the law of England is; because by many successions of ages it has been fined and refined by an infinite number of grave and learned men, and by long experience grown to such a perfection for the government of this realm, as the old rule may be justly verified of it, neminem oportet esse sapientiorem legibus: no man ought to be wiser than the law, which is the perfection of reason." Indeed, what we call human reason, in general, is not so much the knowledge, or experience, or information of any one man, as the knowledge, and experience, and information of many, arising from lights mutually and successively communicated and improved.

To those, who enjoy the advantages of such a law as has been described, I may well, address myself in the words of Cicero,[f] "Believe me, a more inestimable inheritance descends to you from the law, than from those who have left, or may leave you fortunes. A farm may be transmitted to me by the will of any one: but it is by the law alone that I can peacefully hold what is already my own. You ought, therefore, to retain the publick patrimony of the law, which you have received from your ancestors, with no less assiduity than you retain your private estates; not only because these

34. Serious law.

e. 1. Ins. 97. b.

f. Mihi credite: major haereditas venit, unicuique vestrum, a jure et a legibus, quam ab ils, a quibus bona relicta sunt. Nam, ut perveniat ad me fundus, testamento alicujus fieri potest: ut retineam quod meum factum sit, sine jure civili non potest. Quapropter non minus diligenter ea, quae a majoribus accepists, publica patrimonia juris, quam privatae rei vestrae retinere debetis; non solum quod haec jure civili septa sunt; sed etiam quod patrimonium unius incommodo demittitur; jus amitti non potest sine magno incommodo civitatis. Cic. pro Coec. c. 26.

are fenced and protected by the law; but for this further reason, because the loss of a private fortune affects only an individual, whereas the loss of the law would be deeply detrimental to the whole commonwealth."

Does this inestimable inheritance follow the person of the citizen; or is it fixed to the spot, on which the citizen first happened to draw the breath of life? On this great question, it will be proper to consider what the law of England, and, also, what the law of reason says. Perhaps both will speak substantially the same language.

By the common law, every man may go out of the realm to carry on trade, or on any other occasion, which he thinks a proper one, without the leave of the king; and for so doing no man shall be punished.[g]

We are told, however, that if the king, by a writ of ne exeat regnum, under his great or privy seal, thinks proper to prohibit any one from going abroad; or sends a writ to any man, when abroad, commanding his return; and, in either case, the subject disobeys; it is a high contempt of the king's prerogative, for which the offender's lands shall be seized, till he return; and then he is liable to fine and imprisonment.[h]

The discussion of this prerogative, and the cases, in which it may be justly and usefully exerted, it is unnecessary, for my present purpose, to undertake, or enumerate; because if this prerogative was admitted in the fullest extent, in which it has ever been claimed, it would weaken neither the principles nor the facts, on which my observations shall be grounded.

A citizen may leave the kingdom: an alien may enter it. Does the former lose?—does the latter acquire the rights of citizenship? No. Neither climate, nor soil, nor time entitle one to those rights: neither climate, nor soil, nor time can deprive him of them. Citizens, who emigrate, carry with them, in their emigration, their best and noblest birthright.[i]

It is remarkable, however, that, in the charters of several of the American colonies, there is this declaration, "that the emigrants and their posterity shall still be considered as English subjects." Whether the solicitude of the colonists obtained, or the distrust of the reigning sovereigns imposed this clause, it would be superfluous to inquire; for the clause itself was equally unnecessary and inefficient. It was unnecessary, because, by

g. F.N.B. 85. Jenk. 88.

h. 1. Bl. Com. 266. Chal. 26. 27.

i. The law is the birthright of every subject; so wherever subjects go, they carry their laws with them. 2. P. Wms. 75.

the common law, they carried with them the rights of Englishmen; it was inefficient; because, if such had not been the operation of the common law, the right of citizenship could not have resulted from any declaration from the crown. A king of England can neither confer nor take away the rights of his subjects. Accordingly, the charter of Pennsylvania, perhaps the most accurate of all the charters, contains no such declaration. When the charter of Massachusetts, soon after the revolution of 1688, was renewed by king William, he was advised by his law council, that such a declaration would be nugatory.[k]

As citizens, who emigrate, carry with them their laws, their best birthright; so, as might be expected, they transmit this best birthright to their posterity. By the statute 25. Edw. III. says my lord Bacon, which, if you believe Hussey,[35] is but a declaration of the common law, all children, born in any part of the world, if they be of English parents, continuing, at that time, as liege subjects to the king, and having done no act to forfeit the benefit of their allegiance, are, ipso facto, naturalized. If divers families of English men and women plant themselves at Lisbon, and have issue, and their descendants intermarry among themselves, without any intermixture of foreign blood; such descendants are naturalized to all generations; for every generation is still of liege parents, and therefore naturalized; so as you may have whole tribes and lineages of English in foreign countries. And therefore it is utterly untrue that the law of England cannot operate, but only within the bounds of the dominions of England.[l]

This great man, whose keen and comprehensive genius saw and understood so much, seems to have viewed the principles of colonization and the situation of colonists, with his usual penetration and sagacity. It was his sentiment, that the American colonies should be guided and governed by the common law of England.[m]

It has been already observed, that there are some great eras, when important and very perceptible alterations take place in the situation of men and things; and that, at such eras, the accommodating spirit of the common law will introduce, into its practice and rules, corresponding and ad-

k. Chal. 14. 15.
35. Possibly William Hussey (1443–1495), an English politician and judge.
l. 4. Ld. Bac. 192.
m. 3. Ld. Bac. 581.

equate alterations. To the situation of the American colonists, this observation may be applied with singular propriety and force. The situation, in which they found themselves in America, was, in many important particulars, very different from that, in which they had been before their departure from England. The principles of that law, under whose guidance the emigration was made, taught them, that the system, in its particular parts, must undergo changes proportioned to the changes in their situation. This sentiment was understood clearly and in its full extent. By alterations, which, after their emigration, might be made in England, the obligatory principle of the common law dictated, that they should in no manner be affected; because to such alterations they had now no means of giving their consent. Hence the rule, that acts of parliament, made after the settlement of a colony, have, in that colony, no binding operation.

It is highly requisite, that these great truths should be stated, and supported, and illustrated in all their force and extent.

The emigrants, who in the year 1620 landed near Cape Cod, at a place, which they afterwards called New Plymouth, had the honour of planting the first permanent colony in New England. Before they landed, they entered into a political association, which, on many accounts, deserves to be noticed in the most particular manner. It is in these words. "In the name of God. Amen. We, whose names are hereunder written, the loyal subjects of our dread sovereign lord king James, by the grace of God, of Great Britain, France, and Ireland king, defender of the faith, &c. having undertaken, for the glory of God and advancement of the Christian faith, and honour of our king and country, a voyage, to plant the first colony in the northern parts of Virginia, do by these presents, solemnly and mutually, in the presence of God and of one another, covenant and combine ourselves together into a civil body politick, for our better ordering and preservation, and furtherance of the ends aforesaid; and by virtue hereof, do enact, constitute, and frame such just and equal laws and ordinances, from time to time, as shall be thought most meet for the general good of the colony, unto which we promise all due subjection and obedience. In witness whereof, we have subscribed our names at Cape Cod, 11th November, 1620."[n]

n. Chal. 102.

In this manner was a civil society formed, by an original compact, to which every one consented, and, of consequence, by which every one was bound. During the infancy of the colony, we are told, the legislature consisted of the whole body of the male inhabitants. In the year 1639 they established a house of representatives, composed of deputies from the several towns. These representatives, in the true spirit of the principles, which we have been delineating, determined to make the laws of England the general rule of their government. "To these laws," says their ancient historian, Hubbard, "they were willing to be subject, though in a foreign land; adding some municipal laws of their own, in such cases, where the common and statute laws of England could not well reach, and afford them help in emergent cases."[o] Under the foregoing compact and the principles of legislation, which have been mentioned, this colony long enjoyed all the blessings of a government, in which prudence and vigour went hand in hand.[p]

In Virginia we see the same principles adopted and ratified by practice. In the month of March 1662, the assembly of that ancient dominion met: with the most laudable intentions, it reviewed the whole body of the laws of the colony. In this review, their object was, "to adhere to the excellent and often refined customs of England, as nearly as the capacity of the country would admit."[q]

In Maryland we behold a repetition of the same scene. In the month of April of the same year, the legislature of this colony, with a spirit congenial to that of the common law, declared, that, in all cases where the usages of the province were silent, justice should be administered according to the customs and statutes of England; "so far as the court shall judge them not inconsistent with the condition of the colony."[r]

The foregoing principles were recognised even under the arbitrary government of James the second. When he passed a commission—the legality of which is not the present subject, to carry on a temporary administration in Massachussetts, New Hampshire, Maine, Narraghanset, the commissioners were created a court of record for administering affairs civil and

o. Chal. 87. 88.
p. Id. 89.
q. Id. 245.
r. Id. 360.

criminal, so that the forms of proceedings and judgments be consonant to the English laws, as near as the circumstances of the colony will admit.[s]

It has been already remarked, that as the rules of the common law are introduced by experience and custom; so they may be withdrawn by discontinuance and disuse. Numerous instances of the conduct of the colonies settled in America evince the force and extent of this remark. Many parts of the common law as received in England, a kingdom populous, ancient, and cultivated, could receive no useful application in the new settlements, inconsiderable in respect both of numbers and improvement.

This principle is fully recognised by the learned Author of the Commentaries on the laws of England. "It hath been held," says he, "that if an uninhabited country be discovered and planted by English subjects; all the English laws then in being, which are the birthright of every subject, are immediately there in force. But this must be understood with very many and very great restrictions. Such colonists carry with them only so much of the English law, as is applicable to their own situation and the condition of an infant colony. The artificial refinements and distinctions incident to the property of a great and commercial people, the laws of police and revenue (such especially as are enforced by penalties) the mode of maintenance for the established clergy, the jurisdiction of spiritual courts, and a multitude of other provisions, are neither necessary nor convenient for them; and, therefore, are not in force."[t]

It has been often a matter of some difficulty to determine what parts of the law of England extended to the colonies, and what parts were so inapplicable to their situation as not to be entitled to reception. On this, as on many other subjects, those who felt had a right to judge. The municipal tribunals in the different colonies decided the question in the controverted instances, which were brought before them; and their decisions and practice were deemed authoritative evidence on the points, to which they related.

The advocates for the legislative power of the British parliament over the American colonies remind us, that the colonists were liable to the *duties* as well as entitled to the *rights* of Englishmen; and that, as Englishmen, they owed obedience to their ancient legislature; according, as it is

s. Chal. 417.
t. 1. Bl. Com. 107.

said, to a principle of universal equity; that he who enjoys the benefit shall submit patiently to all its inconveniences.[u]

It is always proper to guard against verbal equivocation; the source of the grossest errours both in opinion and practice. That it is the duty of some Englishmen to pay obedience to the legislature of England, is admitted very readily. The principles, on which this obedience is due, have been amply illustrated in a former part of our lectures.[v] Acts of parliament have been shown to be binding, because they are made with the consent or by the authority of those, whom they bind. Such Englishmen, therefore, as have had an opportunity of expressing this consent, or of exercising this authority, are certainly bound to pay obedience to those acts of parliament. But is this the case with all Englishmen? Let us know what is meant by the term. Is it confined to those, who are represented in parliament? In that confined sense, it is conceded that they owe obedience to that legislature. Is it extended to all those, who are entitled to the benefits of the common law of England? In that extended sense, no such concession will or ought to be made: such a concession would destroy the vital principle of all their rights—that of being bound by no human laws, except such as are made with their own consent. It never is the duty of an Englishman, of one entitled to the common law as his inheritance—it never is the duty of such a one to surrender the animating principle of all his rights.

He who enjoys the benefit, it is said, shall submit patiently to all its inconveniences. True: but do Englishmen who are not and cannot be represented in parliament, enjoy the benefit? Unquestionably, they do not. To the inconveniences, then, they are under no obligation of submitting. This is the true inference. The opposite inference burthens the colonists with the inconveniences separated from the benefit: it does more—it burthens the colonists with the inconveniences, augmented in consequence of this very separation. When the benefit of representation is lost; the inconveniences will be increased in a dreadful proportion. This reasoning seems to be just in theory. Let us apply to it the touchstone of fact.

In the journals of the house of commons, we find some short notes taken of a parliamentary debate, in the year 1621, concerning tobacco. The

u. Chal. 15. 28.
v. Ante. vol. 1. p. 191. et seq. [p. 558]

result of this debate was a bill, which was afterwards passed into a law, for preventing the inordinate use of tobacco. Among other short notes on this subject, is the following one, very instructive and interesting—"Mr. Solicitor—loveth England better than Virginia."[w] To every claim of obedience to the parliament without representation there, the standing answer and objection ought to be, in reference to the spirit of Mr. Solicitor's honest, and, indeed, natural declaration—the members of parliament love England better than America.

This important subject deserves to be pursued further. Citizens, who emigrate, carry with them their rights and liberties. When to these rights and liberties, duties and obligations are inseparably annexed, the latter should be performed wherever the former can be enjoyed. But, in some instances, the enjoyment of the former becomes, from the nature and circumstances of things, altogether impracticable. The question, which we now consider, presents to us one of those instances. Obedience to acts of parliament is, as we have seen at large, founded on the principle of consent. That consent is expressed either personally or through the medium of representation. That it cannot be given personally is evident from the case supposed: the citizen has emigrated to another country. The same reason shows, that it cannot be given through the medium of representation. The right of representing is conferred by the act of electing: elections for members of parliament are held within the kingdom: at those elections, the citizen, who has emigrated into another country, cannot vote. The result, then, is unavoidably this: if by the emigration of the citizen, the enjoyment of his right of representation is necessarily lost; the duty of obedience, the consequence of enjoying that right, cannot possibly arise. When the cause is removed, the effect must cease to operate.

In this plain and simple manner, from the principles, which we have traced and established as the foundation of the obligatory force of law, we prove incontestably, that the colonists, after their emigration, were under no obligations of obedience to the acts of the English or British parliament. Principles, properly and surely laid, are eminently useful both for detecting and confuting errour, and for elucidating and confirming truth.

w. Chal. 72.

The history as well as the principles of this momentous question ought to be fully developed and known. It is an instructive, and it is an interesting one. It has engaged the attention of the civilized world. It has employed the treasures and the force of the most respectable nations. America, both North and South, almost all the European powers, either as parties or as neutrals, acted or waited in arms for the important and final decision. On one side, it was worth all that it has cost. The auspicious event we have seen and experienced. Its rise, its progress, and its merits, every citizen, certainly every lawyer and statesman, in the United States, should accurately know.

The dependence of the colonies in America on the parliament of England seems to have been a doctrine altogether unknown and even unsuspected by the colonists who emigrated, and by the princes with whose consent their emigrations were made. It seems not, for a long time, to have been a doctrine known to the parliament itself.

Those, who launched into the unknown deep, in search of new countries and habitations, still considered themselves, it is true, as subjects of the English monarchs, and behaved suitably and unexceptionably in that character; but it no where appears, that they still considered themselves as represented in an English parliament, or that they thought the authority of the English parliament extended over them. They took possession of the country in the king's name: they treated, or made war with the Indians by his authority: they established governments under his prerogative, as it was then understood, or, as it was also then understood, by virtue of his charters. No application, for those purposes, was made to the parliament: no ratification of the charters or letters patent was solicited from that assembly, as is usual in England, with regard to grants and franchises of much less importance.

My Lord Bacon's sentiments on this subject ought to have great weight with us. His immense genius, his universal learning, his deep insight into the laws and constitution of England, are well known and much admired. Besides; he lived at that very time when the settlement and the improvement of the American plantations began to be seriously pursued, and successfully to be carried into execution. Plans for the government and regulation of the colonies were then forming; and it is from the first general idea of those plans that we can best unfold, with precision and accuracy, all the more minute and intricate parts of which they afterwards consisted. "The settlement of colonies," says he, "must proceed from the option of those who will settle them, else it sounds like an exile: they must be raised by the leave and not by the command of the king. At their setting out, they must have their commission or letters patent from the king, that so they may acknowledge their dependency upon the crown of England, and under his protection." "They must still be subjects of the realm." "In order to regulate all the inconveniences, which will insensibly grow upon them," he proposes, that the king should erect a subordinate council in England, whose care and charge shall be, to advise and put in execution all things, which shall be found fit for the good of these new plantations; who, upon all occasions, shall give an account of their proceedings to the king or to the council board, and from them receive such directions as may best agree with the government of that place.[x] It is evident from these quotations, that my Lord Bacon had no conception, that the parliament would or ought to interpose, either in the settlement or in the government of the colonies.

We have seen the original association of the society, who made the first settlement in New England. In that instrument, they acknowledge themselves the loyal subjects of the king; and promise all due subjection and obedience to the colony: but we hear nothing concerning the parliament. Silence is sometimes expressive: it seems to be strongly so in this instance.

About sixty years afterwards, and during the reign of Charles the second, the general court of that colony exhibit the following natural account of the principles, on which the first settlement was made. "The first comers here," say they, "having first obtained leave of king James, of happy memory, did adventure, at their own proper costs and charges, through many foreseen and afterwards felt sufferings, to break the ice, and settle the first English plantation in this then uncultivated remote part of your dominions. We have had now near about sixty years lively experience of the good consistency of the order of these churches with civil government and order, together with loyalty to kingly government and authority, and the tranquillity of this colony. May it therefore please your most excellent majesty to favour us with your gracious letters patent for our incorporation into a body politick, with singular the privileges as your majesty has been accustomed to grant to other colonies, so to your majesty's colony of

x. 1. Ld. Bac. 725. 726.

Connecticut."[y] Still no mention is made of parliament: still no application is made to that body. These omissions could not have been owing to accident: they must have been intentional. Before this time, the pretensions of parliament, during the existence of the commonwealth, had been both known and felt; and, at this time, must have been remembered.

By the charter of Rhode Island, granted in the fourteenth year of Charles the second, the king grants and confirms all that part of *his* dominions in New England in America, containing the Narraghanset Bay, and countries and parts adjacent, &c. Here, also, no notice is taken of the parliament.

The following transactions relating to Virginia, exhibit, in a very striking point of view, the sentiments both of the king and of the colonists, concerning the interference of parliament with the business of colonial administration. Sir William Berkely,[36] who, in the year 1639, was appointed governour of that colony, was, among other things, directed to summon the burgesses of all the plantations, who, with the governour and council, should constitute the grand assembly, with power to make acts for the government of the colony, as near as may be to the laws of England.

A discontented party in Virginia contrived, in what particular manner is not mentioned, to have a petition presented, in the name of the assembly to the house of commons, praying a restoration of the ancient patents and corporation government. The governour, the council, and the burgesses no sooner heard of a transaction so contrary to truth and their wishes, than they transmitted an explicit disavowal of it to England; and, at the same time, sent an address to the king, acknowledging his bounty and favour towards them, and earnestly desiring to continue under his immediate protection. In that address, they desired that the king would, under his royal signet, confirm their declaration and protestation against the petition presented, in their names, to the house of commons, and transmit that confirmation to Virginia. The king expresses strong satisfaction with this address; declares that their so earnest desire to continue under his immediate protection is very acceptable to him; and informs them, that he had not before the least intention to consent to the introduction of any company over the colony; but that he was much confirmed in his former

y. Chal. 106. 107.

36. William Berkeley (1605–1677) served as governor of Virginia from 1642 to 1652 and from 1660 to 1677.

resolutions by the address; since he would think it very improper to change a form of government, under which his subjects there received so much content and satisfaction. He transmits to them, under his royal signet, his approbation of their petition and protestation.[z]

In the colony of Massachussetts, the famous navigation act, made by the English parliament, met with a strong and steady opposition. It was not enforced by the governour annually chosen by the people, whose interest it was that it should not be observed. Of consequence, no custom house was established. The colony carried on the greater part of the trade of the plantations to every quarter of the globe: and vessels from every European country, from France, from Spain, from Italy, from Holland, were crowded together in the harbour of Boston. This prosperous situation excited the envy and the jealousy of the mercantile and manufacturing interests in England. These principles produced, from the merchants and manufacturers, a representation to Charles the second; in which they prayed, that the colonies might receive no supplies but from England; and that the subjects of New England might be compelled to trade according to law. When information of these measures was transmitted to Massachussetts by her agents in England; the general court avowed the conduct of the colony; justified that conduct in point of legality; and stated the sacrifice which it was willing to make of its interests, though not of its rights. It acknowledged that no regard had been paid to the laws of navigation. It urged that those laws were an invasion of the rights and privileges of the subjects of his majesty in that colony, they not being represented in the parliament; because, according to the usual sayings of the learned in the law, the laws of England were bounded within the four seas, and did not reach America; but that, as his majesty had signified his pleasure, that those laws should be observed, it had made provision, by an ordinance of the colony, which obliged masters of vessels to yield faithful obedience, and commanded officers to see them strictly observed.[a]

A letter written in the year 1698 from governour Nicholson of Maryland[37] to the board of trade shows that the sentiments of the colony of

z. Chal. 121. 122. 133. 134.

a. Chal. 400. 407. 408.

37. Francis Nicholson (1655–1728) was a governor of several colonies, including New York (1689–1690), Virginia (1699–1705), Nova Scotia (1712–1717), and South Carolina (1721–1725).

Massachussetts, with regard to the authority of acts of parliament, had, when the letter was written, become general in the colonies. "I have observed that a great many people in *all* these provinces and colonies, especially in those under proprietaries, and the two others under Connecticut and Rhode Island, think that no law of England ought to be in force and binding to them without their own consent: for they foolishly say they have no representatives sent from themselves to the parliament of England: and they look upon all laws made in England, that put any restraint upon them, to be great hardships."[b]

b. Chal. 442. 443.

CHAPTER XIII.

Of the Nature and Philosophy of Evidence.

Evidence is a subject of vast and extensive importance in the study and practice of the law: it is of vast and extensive importance, likewise, in the business and general management of human affairs.

"Experience," says Sir William Blackstone, "will abundantly show, that above a hundred of our law suits arise from disputed facts"—and facts are the objects of evidence—"for one where the law is doubted of. About twenty days in the year are sufficient, in Westminster Hall, to settle, upon solemn argument, every demurrer or other special point of law, that arises throughout the nation. But two months are annually spent in deciding the truth of facts, before six distinct tribunals, in the several circuits of England, exclusive of Middlesex and London, which afford a supply of causes much more than equivalent to any two of the largest circuits."[a]

But evidence is not confined, in its operation and importance, to the courts of justice. Its influence on the human mind, human manners, and human business is great and universal. In perception, in consciousness, in remembrance, belief always forms one ingredient. But belief is governed by evidence. In every action which is performed with an intention to accomplish a particular purpose, there must be a belief that the action is fitted for the accomplishment of the purpose intended. So large a share has belief in our reasonings, in our resolutions, and in our conduct, that it may well be considered as the main spring, which produces and regulates the movements of human life.

In a subject of so great use and extent, it is highly necessary that our first principles be accurate and well founded. It is, however, matter of just and deep regret, that very little has been said, and that still less has been satis-

a. 3. Bl. Com. 330.

factorily said, concerning the sound and genuine sources and principles of evidence. "An inquiry," says Eden, in his Principles of penal law, "into the general rules and maxims of evidence, is a field still open to investigation. For the considerations of some very ingenious writers on this subject have been too much influenced by their acquiescence in personal authority, and we are furnished rather with sensible and useful histories of what the law of evidence actually is, than with any free and speculative disquisition of what it ought to be."[b] The truth is, I may add, that the philosophy, as well as the law of evidence is a field, which demands and which is susceptible of much cultivation and improvement.

"Evidence, in legal understanding," says my Lord Coke, "doth not only contain matters of record, as letters patent, fines, recoveries, enrollments, and the like; and writings under seal, as charters and deeds; and other writings without seal, as court rolls, accounts, which are called evidences, *instrumenta;* but, in a larger sense, it containeth also *testimonia,* the testimony of witnesses, and other proofs to be produced and given to a jury, for the finding of any issue joined between the parties. And it is called evidence, because thereby the point in issue is to be made evident to the jury. Probationes debent esse evidentes (id est) perspicuae et faciles intelligi."[c1]

The learned Author of the Commentaries on the Laws of England describes evidence as signifying that, which demonstrates, makes clear, or ascertains the truth of the very fact or point in issue, either on the one side or on the other.[d]

When we are informed that it is called evidence, because thereby the point in issue is to be made evident to the jury; we are informed of little, if any thing, more than an identical proposition; and, consequently, are not enabled by it to make any considerable progress in the attainment of science.

To say that evidence demonstrates, makes clear, and ascertains the truth of a fact, is rather to describe its effects than its nature. Its effects, too, are described in a manner, neither very accurate nor precise; as I shall afterwards have occasion to show more particularly.

b. Eden 164. 165.
c. 1. Ins. 283.
1. Proofs ought to be evident; that is, they ought to be plain and easily understood.
d. 3. Bl. Com. 367.

But the truth is, that evidence is much more easily felt than described. We experience, though it is difficult to explain, its operations and influence. A man may have a good eye, and may make a good use of it, though he cannot unfold the theory of vision.

These reflections naturally lead us to one illustrious source of the propriety of a jury to decide on matters of evidence. "It is much easier," says the Marquis of Beccaria, "to feel the moral certainty of proofs, than to define it exactly. For this reason I think it an excellent law, which establishes assistants to the principal Judge, and those chosen by lot: For that ignorance which judges by its feelings is little subject to errour."[e]

Perhaps there is no more unexceptionable mode of expressing what we feel to be evidence, than to say—it is that which produces belief.

Belief is a simple operation of the mind. It is an operation, too, of its own peculiar kind. It cannot, therefore, be defined or described. The appeal for its nature and existence, must be made to the experience, which every one has of what passes within himself. This experience will, probably, inform him, that belief arises from many different sources, and admits of all possible degrees, from absolute certainty down to doubt and suspicion.

The love of system, and of that unnatural kind of uniformity to which system is so much attached, has done immense mischief in the theory of evidence. It has been long the aim and labour of philosophers to discover some common nature, to which all the different species of evidence might be reduced. This was the great object of the schools in their learned lucubrations concerning the criterion of truth. This criterion they endeavoured to find from a minute and artificial analysis of the several kinds of evidence; by means of which they expected to ascertain and establish some common quality, which might be applied, with equal propriety, to all. Des Cartes placed this criterion of truth in clear and distinct perception,[f] and laid it down as a maxim, that whatever we clearly and distinctly perceive to be true, is true. The meaning, the truth, and the utility of this maxim seem to be all equally problematical.

e. Bec. c. 14. p. 39.

f. We give the name of evidence to a clear and distinct view of things and of their relations. 1. Burl. 8.

This criterion of truth was placed by Mr. Locke in a perception of the agreement or disagreement of our ideas. This, indeed, is the grand principle of his philosophy, and he seems to consider it as a very important discovery. "Knowledge," says he, "seems to me to be nothing but the perception of the connexion and agreement, or disagreement and repugnancy of any of our ideas. In this alone it consists. For since the mind, in all its thoughts and reasonings, hath no other immediate object but its own ideas, which it alone does or can contemplate; it is evident, that our knowledge is only conversant about them."[g] "We can have no knowledge farther than we have ideas. We can have no knowledge farther than we have perception of that agreement or disagreement."[h]

In order to perceive whether two ideas agree or disagree, they must be compared together: According to this hypothesis, therefore, all knowledge must arise from the comparison of ideas.

Let us try this hypothesis by applying it minutely and carefully to a principle of knowledge allowed by all philosophers—and the only one allowed by all philosophers—to be sound and unexceptionable: I mean the principle of consciousness:—I mean, farther, the most clear and simple appeal, which can possibly be made to that clear and simple principle, *I think.* This has always been admitted to form a principle and a part of knowledge. According to the hypothesis of Mr. Locke, this knowledge must be nothing but the perception of the agreement—for disagreement cannot enter into the question here—between ideas. What are the ideas to be compared, in order that the agreement may be discovered? *I* and *thought*? Let us grant every indulgence, and suppose, for a moment, that existence and thought are nothing more than *ideas;* and then let us see how the comparison of ideas, and how their agreement in consequence of their comparison, will stand.

How is the knowledge of this truth—"I think"—drawn from the perception of any agreement between the idea of *me* and the idea of *thought*? When I think, I am conscious of thinking; and this consciousness is the clearest and most intimate knowledge. But does this consciousness arise from the perception of agreement between the idea of *me* and the idea of

g. Locke on Und. b. 4. c. 1.
h. Id. b. 4. c. 3.

thought? No. From Mr. Locke's own system, no such knowledge can arise from the perception of any such agreement: because the agreement does not, at all times, take place.

"The mind" says he, "can sensibly put on, at several times, several degrees of thinking, and be sometimes, even in a waking man, so remiss, as to have thoughts dim and obscure to that degree, that they are very little removed from none at all; and, at last, in the dark retirements of sound sleep, loses the sight, perfectly, of all ideas whatsoever.[i] The knowledge, then, of this truth, that *I think,* does not arise from the perception of any agreement between the idea *me* and the idea of *thought;* since, according to Mr. Locke's own account of the matter, that agreement does not always subsist.

Let us try this hypothesis—that knowledge is the perception of the agreement or disagreement of our ideas—by another instance; and let us attend to the result. I perceive a small book in my hand. My faculty of seeing gives me not merely a simple apprehension of the book; it gives me, likewise, a concomitant belief or knowledge of its existence; of its shape, size, and distance. By the perception of the agreement of what ideas, is this knowledge or belief acquired? This belief is inseparably connected with the perception of the book; and does not arise from any perception of agreement between the idea of the book, and the idea of myself.

I remember to have dined a few days ago with a particular company of friends. This remembrance is accompanied with clear and distinct belief or knowledge. How does this belief or knowledge arise? Is it from the perception of agreement between ideas? Between what ideas? Between the idea of *me,* and the idea of my *friends*? This agreement, I presume, would have been the same, whether we had dined together or not. Is it from the agreement between the idea of *me* and the idea of *dining*? But how, from this agreement, will the knowledge of dining with *my friends* arise? On this state of the supposition, I might have dined with strangers or with enemies.

Let us examine the future, as we have examined the past. If a certain degree of cold freezes water now, and has been known to freeze it in all times past; we believe, nay, we rest assured, that the same degree of cold will continue to freeze the water while the cold continues; and returning, will be attended with the same effect, in all times future. But whence does

i. Locke on Und. b. 2. c. 19. s. 4.

this belief or assurance arise? Does it arise from the comparison of ideas—from the perception of their agreement? When I compare the idea of *cold* with that of *water hardened into a transparent solid body,* I can perceive no connexion between them: no man can show the one to be the necessary effect of the other: no one can give a shadow of reason why nature has conjoined them. But from experience we learn that they have been conjoined in times past; and this experience of the past is attended with a belief and assurance, that those connexions, in nature, which we have observed in times past, will continue and operate in times to come.[k]

We now see, that our knowledge, which proceeds from consciousness, from the senses, from memory, and from anticipation of the future occasioned by experience of the past, arises not from any perception of the agreement or disagreement of our ideas. These are important parts of our knowledge: the evidence, upon which these parts of our knowledge is founded, is an important part of the system of evidence. All, however, rests on principles, very different from that which is assigned by Mr. Locke, as the sole principle of knowledge. We may go farther still, and say, if knowledge consists solely in the perception of the agreement or disagreement of ideas, there can be no knowledge of any proposition, which does not express some agreement or disagreement of ideas; consequently, there can be no knowledge of any proposition, which expresses either the existence, or the attributes, or the relations of things; which are not ideas. If, therefore, the theory of ideas be true, there can be no knowledge of any thing else: if we have knowledge of any thing else, the theory of ideas must be unfounded. For the knowledge of any thing else than ideas must arise from something else than the perception of the agreement or disagreement of ideas.[l]

This principle, assigned by Mr. Locke, that knowledge is nothing but a perception of the agreement or disagreement of our ideas, is founded upon another—the existence of ideas or images of things in the mind. This theory I have already had an opportunity of considering, and I shall not now repeat what I then delivered at some length. I then showed, I hope, satisfactorily, that this theory has no foundation in reason, in consciousness, or

k. Reid's Inq. 437. 438.
l. Reid's Ess. Int. 552.

in the other operations of our minds; but that, on the contrary, it is manifestly contradicted by all these, and would, in its necessary consequences, lead to the destruction of all truth, and knowledge, and virtue; though those consequences were, by no means, foreseen by Mr. Locke, and many succeeding philosophers, who have adopted, and still adopt, his theory concerning the existence of ideas or images of things in the mind.

If this theory has, as we have shown it to have, no foundation—if these ideas have, as we have shown them to have, no existence; then Mr. Locke's great principle, which represents knowledge and belief, and consequently evidence, upon which knowledge and belief are grounded, as consisting in the perception of the agreement or disagreement of those ideas, must tumble in ruins, like a superstructure, whose basis has been undermined and removed.

It is nevertheless true, that, in our law books, the general principles of evidence, so far as any notice is taken of general principles on this subject, are referred, for their sole support, to the theory of Mr. Locke. This will appear obvious to any one who is acquainted with that theory, and peruses the first pages of my Lord Chief Baron Gilbert's Treatise upon Evidence. This unfolds the reason why I have employed so much pains to expose and remove the sandy and unsound foundation, on which the principles of the law of evidence have been placed.

Let us now proceed to erect a fabrick on a different and a surer basis—the basis of the human mind.

I am, by no means, attached to numerous and unnecessary distinctions; but, on some occasions, it is proper to recollect the rule, "qui bene distinguit, bene docet."[2] It is possible to blend, as well as to distinguish, improperly. Nature should always be consulted. We are safe, when we imitate her in her various, as well as when we imitate her in her uniform appearances. By following her as our guide, we can trace evidence to the following fourteen distinct sources.

I. It arises from the external senses: and by each of these, distinct information is conveyed to the mind.

II. It arises from consciousness; or the internal view of what passes within ourselves.

2. Who distinguishes well, teaches well.

III. It arises from taste; or that power of the human mind, by which we perceive and enjoy the beauties of nature or of art.

IV. It arises from the moral sense; or that faculty of the mind, by which we have the original conceptions of right and wrong in conduct; and the original perceptions, that certain things are right, and that others are wrong.

V. Evidence arises from natural signs: by these we gain our knowledge of the minds, and of the various qualities and operations of the minds, of other men. Their thoughts, and purposes, and dispositions have their natural signs in the features of the countenance, in the tones of the voice, and in the motions and gestures of the body.

VI. Evidence arises from artificial signs; such as have no meaning, except that, which is affixed to them by compact, or agreement, or usage: such is language, which has been employed universally for the purpose of communicating thought.

VII. Evidence arises from human testimony in matters of fact.

VIII. Evidence arises from human authority in matters of opinion.

IX. Evidence arises from memory, or a reference to something which is past.

X. Evidence arises from experience; as when, from facts already known, we make inferences to facts of the *same* kind, unknown.

XI. Evidence arises from analogy; as when, from facts already known, we make inferences to facts of a *similar* kind, not known.

XII. Evidence arises from judgment; by which I here mean that power of the mind, which decides upon truths that are selfevident.

XIII. Evidence arises from reasoning: by reasoning, I here mean that power of the mind, by which, from one truth, we deduce another, as a conclusion from the first. The evidence, which arises from reasoning, we shall, by and by, see divided into two species—demonstrative and moral.

XIV. Evidence arises from calculations concerning chances. This is a particular application of demonstrative to ascertain the precise force of moral reasoning.

Even this enumeration, though very long, is, perhaps, far from being complete. Among all those different kinds of evidence, it is, I believe, impossible to find any common nature, to which they can be reduced. They agree, indeed, in this one quality—which constitutes them evidence—that they are fitted by nature to produce belief in the human mind.

It will be proper to make some observations concerning each of the enumerated kinds of evidence. In the business of life, and, consequently, in the practice of a lawyer or man of business, they all occur more frequently than those unaccustomed to consider them are apt to imagine.

I. The truths conveyed by the evidence of the external senses are the first principles, from which we judge and reason with regard to the material world, and from which all our knowledge of it is deduced.

The evidence furnished even by any of the several external senses seems to have nothing in common with that furnished by each of the others, excepting that single quality before mentioned. The evidence of one sense may be corroborated, in some instances; and, in some instances, it may be corrected, by that of another sense, when both senses convey information concerning the same object; but still the information conveyed by each is clearly perceived to be separate and distinct. We may be assured that a man is present, by hearing and by seeing him; but the evidence of the eye is nevertheless different from the evidence of the ear.

In the sacred history of the resurrection, a beautiful and emphatical reference is had to this distinct but corresponding and reciprocally corroborating evidence of the senses, by him, by whom our nature was both made and assumed. "*Behold,*" says he, to his trembling and doubting disciples, who supposed they had seen a spirit, "*Behold* my hands and my feet, that it is I myself; *handle* me, and see; for a spirit has not flesh and bones as you see me have: And when he had thus spoken, he showed them his hands and his feet."[m] To the unbelieving Thomas, he is still more particular in his appeal to the evidence of the senses, and in the manner, in which the appeal should be made. "Reach hither thy finger and *behold* my hands; and reach hither thy hand, and *thrust it* into my side; and be not faithless, but believing."[n]

Many philosophers of high sounding fame, deeming it inconsistent with their character to believe, when they could not furnish an argument for belief, have endeavoured, with much learned labour, to suggest proofs for the doctrine—that our senses ought to be trusted. But their proofs are defective, and shrink from the touch of rigid examination. Other philosophers, of no less brilliant renown, have clearly and unanswerably discovered and exposed the fallacy of those pretended proofs: so far they have

m. Luke XXIV. 39. 40.
n. John XX. 27.

done well: but very unwisely they have attempted to do more: they have attempted to overturn our belief in the evidence of our senses, because the arguments adduced on the other side to prove its truth were shown to be defective and fallacious. From human nature an equal departure is made on both sides. It appeals not to reason for any argument in support of our belief in the evidence of our senses: but it determines us to believe them.

II. Consciousness furnishes us with the most authentick and the most indubitable evidence of every thing which passes within our own minds. This source of evidence lays open to our view all our perceptions and mental powers; and, consequently, forms a necessary ingredient in all evidence arising from every other source. There can be no evidence of the objects of the senses, without perception of them by the mind: there can be no evidence of the perception of them by the mind, without consciousness of that perception. When we see, and feel, and think, consciousness gives us the most certain information that we thus see, and feel, and think. This, as has been observed on a former occasion, is a kind of evidence, the force and authenticity of which has never been called in question by those, who have been most inclined to dispute every thing else, except the evidence of reasoning.

III. I mentioned taste, or that power of the mind by which we perceive and enjoy the beauties of nature and art, as one of the sources from which evidence arises. This faculty, in its feeling and operations, has something analogous to the impressions and operations of our external senses; from one of which, it has, in our own and in several other languages, derived its metaphorical name.

With the strictest propriety, taste may be called an original sense. It is a power, which furnishes us with many simple perceptions, which, to those who are destitute of it, cannot be conveyed through any other channel of information. Concerning objects of taste, it is vain to reason or discourse with those who possess not the first principles of taste. Again; taste is a power, which, so soon as its proper object is exhibited to it, receives its perception from that object, immediately and intuitively. It is not in consequence of a chain of argument, or a deductive process of our reasoning faculties, that we discover and relish the beauties of a poem or a prospect. Both the foregoing characters belong evidently to consciousness and to the external senses. All the three are, therefore, considered, with equal propriety, as distinct and original sources of information and evidence.

That it is fruitless to dispute concerning matters of taste has been so often said, that it has now acquired the authority and notoriety of a proverb; and its suggestions are consequently supposed, by some, to be dictated only by whim and caprice. Nothing, however, can be farther from the truth. The first and general principles of taste are not less uniform, nor less permanent, than are the first and general principles of science and morality. The writings of Cicero present him to us in two very different characters—as a philosopher, and as a man of taste. His philosophical performances are read, and ought to be read, with very considerable grains of allowance; the beauties of his oratory have been the subjects of universal and uninterrupted admiration. The fame of Homer has obtained an undisputed establishment of near three thousand years. Has a reputation equally uniform attended the philosophical doctrines of Aristotle or Plato? The writings of Moses have been admired for their sublimity by those, who never received them as the vehicles of sacred and eternal truth.

The first and most general principles of taste are universal as well as permanent: it is a faculty, in some degree, common to all. With youth, with ignorance, with savageness, its rudiments are found to dwell. It seems not less essential to man to have some discernment of the beauties both of art and nature, than it is to possess, in some measure, the faculties of speech and reason. "Let no one," says Cicero, in his excellent book de oratore, "be surprised that the most uncultivated mind can mark and discern these things: since, in every thing, the energy of nature is great and incredible. Without education or information, every one, by a certain tacit sense, is enabled to judge and decide concerning what is right or wrong in the arts. If this observation is true with regard to pictures, statues, and other performances, in the knowledge of which they have less assistance from nature; it becomes much more evident and striking with regard to the judgments, which they form concerning words, harmony, and pronunciation: for concerning these there is a common sense implanted in all, of which Nature intended that no one should be entirely devoid."[o]

IV. As a fourth source of evidence, I mentioned the moral sense, or that faculty of the mind, by which we have the original conceptions that there is a right and a wrong in conduct; and that some particular actions are

o. Cic. de Orat. l. 3. c. 50.

right, and others wrong. Without this last power of applying our conceptions to particular actions, and of determining concerning their moral qualities, our general and abstract notions of moral good and evil would be of no service to us in directing the conduct and affairs of human life.

The moral sense is a distinct and original power of the human mind. By this power, and by this power solely, we receive information and evidence of the first principles of right and wrong, of merit and demerit. He, who would know the colour of any particular object, must consult his eye: in vain will he consult every other faculty upon the point. In the same manner, he, who would learn the moral qualities of any particular action, must consult his moral sense: no other faculty of the mind can give him the necessary information.

The evidence given by our moral sense, like that given by our external senses, is the evidence of nature; and, in both cases, we have the same grounds for relying on that evidence. The truths given in evidence by the external senses are the first principles from which we reason concerning matter, and from which all our knowledge of the material world is drawn. In the same manner, the truths given in evidence by our moral faculty are the first principles, from which we reason concerning moral subjects, and from which all our knowledge of morality is deduced. The powers, which Nature has kindly bestowed upon us, are the only channels, through which the evidence of truth and knowledge can flow in upon our minds.

Virtuous demeanour is the duty, and should be the aim, of every man: the knowledge and evidence of moral truth is, therefore, placed within the reach of all.

Of right and wrong there are many different degrees; and there are also many different kinds. By the moral faculty we distinguish those kinds and degrees. By the same faculty we compare the different kinds together, and discover numerous moral relations between them.

Our knowledge of moral philosophy, of natural jurisprudence, of the law of nations, must ultimately depend, for its first principles, on the evidence and information of the moral sense. This power furnishes to us the first principles of our most important knowledge. In dignity, it is far superiour to every other power of the human mind.

V. The fifth kind of evidence, of which I took notice, is that, which arises from natural signs. By these, we gain information and knowledge of the minds, and of the thoughts, and qualities, and affections of the minds of men. This kind of evidence is of very great and extensive importance.

We have no immediate perception of what passes in the minds of one another. Nature has not thought it proper to gratify the wish of the philosopher, by placing a window in every bosom, that all interiour transactions may become visible to every spectator. But, although the thoughts, and dispositions, and talents of men are not perceivable by direct and immediate inspection; there are certain external signs, by which those thoughts, and dispositions, and talents are naturally and certainly disclosed and communicated.

The signs, which naturally denote our thoughts, are the different motions of the hand,[p] the different modulations or tones of the voice, the different gestures and attitudes of the body, and the different looks and features of the countenance, especially what is termed, with singular force and propriety, the expression of the eye. By means of these natural signs, two persons, who never saw one another before, and who possess no knowledge of one common artificial language, can, in some tolerable degree, communicate their thoughts and even their present dispositions to one another: they can ask and give information: they can affirm and deny: they can mutually supplicate and engage fidelity and protection. Of all these we have very picturesque and interesting representations, in the first interviews between Robinson Crusoe and his man Friday; they are interesting, because we immediately perceive them to be natural. Two dumb persons, in their intercourse together, carry the use of these natural signs to a wonderful degree of variety and minuteness.

We acquire information, not only of the thoughts and present dispositions and affections, but also of the qualities, moral and intellectual, of the minds of others, by the means of natural signs. The eloquence or skill of another man cannot, themselves, become the objects of any of our senses, either external or internal. His skill is suggested to us by the signs of it, which appear in his conduct: his eloquence, by those which appear in his speech. In the same manner, and by the same means, we receive evidence concerning his benevolence, his fortitude, and all his other talents and virtues.

p. To this the evidence arising from the similitude of hands may be referred.

This evidence, however, of the thoughts, and dispositions, and passions, and talents, and characters of other men, conveyed to us by natural signs, is neither less satisfactory, nor less decisive upon our conduct in the business and affairs of life, than the evidence of external objects, which we receive by the means of our senses. It is no less a part, nor is it a less important part, of our constitution, that we are enabled and determined to judge of the powers and the characters of men, from the signs of them, which appear in their discourse and conduct, than it is that we are enabled and determined to judge, by our external senses, concerning the various corporeal objects, which we have occasion to view and consider.

The variety, the certainty, and the extent of that evidence, which arises from natural signs, may be conceived from what we discover in the pantomime entertainments on the theatre; in some of which, the whole series of a dramatick tale, and all the passions and emotions to which it gives birth, are represented, with astonishing address, by natural signs. By natural signs, likewise, the painters and statuaries infuse into their pictures and statues the most intelligible, and, sometimes, the most powerful expression of thought, of affections, and even of character.

Among untutored nations, the want of letters is supplied, though imperfectly, by the use of visible and natural signs, which fix the attention, and enliven the remembrance of private or publick transactions. The jurisprudence of the first Romans exhibited the picturesque scenes of the pantomime entertainment. The intimate union of the marriage state was signified by the solemnities attending the celebration of the nuptials. The contracting parties were seated on the same sheep skin; they tasted of the same salted cake of *far* or rice. This last ceremony is well known by the name of *confarreatio.* A wife, divorced, resigned the keys, by the delivery of which she had been installed into the government of domestick affairs. A slave was manumitted by turning him round, and giving him a gentle stroke on the cheek. By the casting of a stone, a work was prohibited. By the breaking of a branch, prescription was interrupted. The clenched fist was the emblem of a pledge. The right hand was the token of faith and confidence. A broken straw figured an indenture of agreement. In every payment, weights and scales were a necessary formality. In a civil action, the party touched the ear of his witness; the plaintiff seized his reluctant adversary by the neck, and implored, by solemn solicitation, the assistance of his fellow citizens. The two competitors grasped each other's hand, as if they stood prepared for combat, before the tribunal of the pretor. He commanded them to produce the object of the dispute. They went; they returned, with measured steps; and a turf was cast at his feet, to represent the field, for which they contended, and the property of which he was to decide.[q]

In more enlightened ages, however, the use and meaning of these natural and primitive signs became gradually obliterated. But a libel may still be expressed by natural signs, as well as by words; and the proof of the intention may be equally convincing and satisfactory in cases of the first, as in those of the last kind.

VI. But evidence arises frequently from artificial as well as from natural signs; from those which are settled by agreement or custom, as well as from those which are derived immediately from our structure and constitution. Of these artificial signs there are many different species, contrived and established to answer the demands and emergencies of human life. The signals used by fleets at sea, form a very intricate and a very interesting part of naval tacticks.

But language presents to us the most important, as well as the most extensive, system of artificial signs, which has been invented for the purpose of giving information and evidence concerning the thoughts and designs of men. I mean not that language is altogether an invention of human art; for I am of opinion, that, if the first principles of language had not been natural to us, human reason and ingenuity could never have invented and executed its numerous artificial improvements. But of every language, at least of every refined language now in use, the greatest part consists of signs that are purely artificial. The evidence of language may, therefore, with sufficient propriety, be arranged under that kind of evidence, which arises from artificial signs.

Natural signs, though, as we have seen, susceptible of very considerable extent and variety, yet, when compared with the almost boundless variety and combinations of our conceptions and thoughts, have been found, in every country, and in every period of society, altogether inadequate to the communication of them in such a degree, as to accomplish, with toler-

q. Consult Gib. Rom. Emp. c. 44. vol. 8. p. 22. and the authorities cited.

able conveniency, the necessary ends and purposes of human life. Hence the invention and improvement of language; which, as has been already observed, consists chiefly of artificial signs, contrived, at first, in all probability, only to supply the deficiencies of such signs as were natural; but afterwards, as language became refined and copious substituted almost entirely in their place.

But even language, however copious and refined, is, on examination and trial, found insufficient for conveying precisely and determinately all our conceptions and designs, consisting of numberless particulars, combined into numberless forms, and related by numberless connexions. Hence the necessity, the use, and the rules of interpretation, which has been introduced into all languages and all laws. A most extensive field now opens before us. But I cannot go into it. I am confined, at present, to the mere outlines of the philosophy of evidence. Let us therefore proceed.

VII. A seventh kind of evidence arises from human testimony in matters of fact.

Human testimony is a source of evidence altogether original, suggested by our constitution, and not acquired, though it is sometimes corroborated, and more frequently corrected, by considerations arising from experience.

"This is very plain," says my Lord Chief Baron Gilbert, "that when we cannot see or hear any thing ourselves, and yet are obliged to make a judgment of it, we must see and hear from report of others; which is one step farther from demonstration, which is founded upon the view of our own senses: and yet there is that faith and credit to be given to the honesty and integrity of credible and disinterested witnesses, attesting any fact under the solemnities and obligation of religion, and the dangers and penalties of perjury, that the mind equally acquiesces therein as in knowledge by demonstration; for it cannot have any more reason to be doubted than if we ourselves had heard or seen it. And this is the original of trials, and all manner of evidence."[r]

I shall not, at present, make any remarks upon the position—that demonstration is founded on the view of our own senses. It will be examined when I come to consider that kind of evidence which arises from reasoning—probable and demonstrative. But, at present, it is material to

r. Gilb. Ev. 4.

observe, that, in the sentiments, which the very learned Judge, whose character and talents I hold in the highest estimation, seems to entertain concerning the source of our belief in testimony, the *restraints* which are wisely calculated, by human regulations, to *check,* are mistaken for the *causes* intended to *produce* this belief. The true language of the law, addressed to the native and original sentiments of the human mind concerning testimony, is not to this purport—If you find a witness to be honest and upright, credible and disinterested: if you see him deliver his testimony under all the solemnities and obligation of religion, and all the dangers and penalties of perjury; you must then believe him. Belief in testimony springs not from the precepts of the law, but from the propensity of our nature. This propensity we indulge in every moment of our lives, and in every part of our business, without attending, in the least, to the circumspect precautions prescribed by the law.

Experience has found it necessary and useful, that, at least in legal proceedings, the indulgence of this natural and original propensity should be regulated and restrained. For this purpose, the law has said, that, unless a witness appears, as far as can be known, to be honest and upright, credible and disinterested; and unless he delivers his testimony under all the solemnities and obligations of religion, and all the dangers and penalties of perjury; you shall not—It does not say, you shall not *believe* him. To prevent this act or operation of the mind might be impracticable on hearing the witness: but it says—you shall not *hear* him. Accordingly, every gentleman, in the least conversant about law proceedings, knows very well, that the qualifications and solemnities enumerated by the learned Judge, are requisite to the competency, not to the credibility, of the witness—to the admission, not to the operation, of his testimony.

The proceedings of the common law are founded on long and sound experience; but long and sound experience will not be found to stand in opposition to the original and genuine sentiments of the human mind. The propensity to believe testimony is a natural propensity. It is unnecessary to encourage it; sometimes it is impracticable to restrain it. The law will not order that which is unnecessary: it will not attempt that which is impracticable. In no case, therefore, does it order a witness to be believed; for jurors are triers of the credibility of witnesses, as well as of the truth of facts. The positive testimony of a thousand witnesses is not conclusive as to the verdict. The jury retain an indisputable, unquestionable right to acquit the person accused, if in their private opinions, they disbelieve the accusers.[s] In no case, likewise, does the law order a witness not to be believed; for belief might be the unavoidable result of his testimony. To prevent that unavoidable, but sometimes improper result, the law orders, that, without the observance of certain precautions, which experience has evinced to be wise and salutary, the witness shall not be heard. This I apprehend to be the true exposition and meaning of the regulations prescribed by the law, before a witness can be admitted to give his testimony.

It will be pleasing and it will be instructive to trace and explain the harmony, which subsists between those regulations, thus illustrated, and the genuine sentiments of the mind with regard to testimony. To discover an intimate connexion between the doctrines of the law and the just theory of human nature, is peculiarly acceptable to those, who study law as a science founded on the science of man.[t]

In a former part of these lectures,[u] I had occasion to take notice of the quality of veracity, and of the corresponding quality of confidence; and to show the operation and the importance of those qualities in promises, which relate to what is to come. It is material to illustrate the connexion, the importance, and the operation of the same corresponding qualities in testimony, which relates to what is past.

By recalling to our remembrance what we have experienced, we find, that those, with whom we have conversed, were accustomed to express such and such particular things by such and such particular words. But, in strictness, experience conveys to us the knowledge only of what is past: can we be assured, that, in future, those who have it in their power to express different things by the same words, and the same things by different words, will, in neither manner, avail themselves of that power? We act, and we cannot avoid acting, as if we were so assured. On what foundation do we so act? Whence proceeds this belief of the future and voluntary behaviour of those, with whom we converse? Have they come under any

s. Eden's Pen. Law. 169. 170.

t. Parum est jus nosse, says Justinian in his institutes (l. 1. t. 2. s. 12.) si personae, quarum causa constitutum est, ignorentur. It is to little purpose to know the law, if we are ignorant concerning the persons, for whose sake the law was constituted.

u. Ante vol. 1. p. 627.

engagements to do what we believe they will do? They have not; and if they had, what assurance could engagements convey to those, who possessed no previous reliance on the faith of promises?

There is, in the human mind, an anticipation, an original conviction, that those, with whom we converse, will, when, in future, they express the same sentiments, which they have expressed in time past, convey those sentiments by the same language which, in time past, they have employed to convey them. There is, in the human mind, a farther anticipation and conviction, that those, with whom we converse, will, when they express to us sentiments in the same language, which they have formerly employed to express them, mean, by those sentiments, to convey to us the truth.

The greatest and most important part of our knowledge, we receive by the information of others. We are, accordingly, endowed with the two corresponding principles, which I have already mentioned, and which are admirably fitted to accomplish the purpose, for which they were intended. The first of them, which is a propensity to speak the truth, and to use language in such a manner as to convey to others the sentiments, which we ourselves entertain, is a principle, degenerate as we are apt to think human nature to be, more uniformly and more universally predominant, than is generally imagined. To speak as we think, and to speak as we have been accustomed to speak, are familiar and easy to us: they require no studied or artificial exertion: a natural impulse is sufficient to produce them. Even the most consummate liar declares truths much more frequently than falsehoods. On some occasions, indeed, there may be inducements to deceive, which will prove too powerful for the natural principle of veracity, unassisted by honour or virtue: but when no such inducements operate, our natural instinct is, to speak the truth. Another instinct, equally natural, is to believe what is spoken to be true. This principle is a proper and a useful counterpart to the former.

A very different theory has been adopted by some philosophers. No species of evidence, it is admitted by them, is more common, more useful, and even more necessary to human life, than that which is derived from testimony. But our reliance, it is contended, on any evidence of this kind is derived from no other principle than our observation of the veracity of human testimony, and of the usual conformity of facts to the reports of witnesses. If it were not discovered by experience, that the memory is tenacious to a certain degree; that men have commonly a principle of probity and an inclination to truth; and that they have a sensibility to shame, when detected in a falsehood—If it were not discovered by experience, that these qualities are inherent in human nature; we should never repose the least confidence in human testimony.[v]

If belief in testimony were the result only of experience; those who have never had experience would never believe; and the most experienced would be the most credulous of men. The fact, however, in both instances, is precisely the reverse; and there are wise reasons, why it should be so. The propensity which children, before they acquire experience, discover to believe every thing that is told to them, is strong and extensive. On the contrary, experience teaches those who are aged, to become cautious and distrustful.

"Oportet discentem credere"[3] has acquired, and justly, the force and the currency of a proverb. How many things must children learn and believe, before they can try them by the touchstone of experience! The infant mind, conscious, as it should seem, of its want of experience, relies implicitly on whatever is told it; and receives, with assurance, the testimony of every one, without attempting and without being able to examine the grounds, upon which that testimony rests. As the mind gradually acquires experience and knowledge, it discovers reasons for suspecting testimony, in some cases, and for rejecting it, in others. But unless some reasons appear for suspicion or disbelief, testimony is, through the whole of life, considered and received as sufficient evidence to form a foundation both of opinion and conduct.

The reasons for suspecting or rejecting testimony may generally be comprised under the following heads. 1. When the witness testifies to something, which appears to us to be improbable or incredible. 2. When he shows himself to be no competent judge of the matter, of which he gives testimony. 3. When, in former instances, we have known him to deliver testimony, which has been false. 4. When, in the present instance, we discover some strong inducement or temptation, which may prevail on him to deceive.

While experience and reflection, on some occasions, diminish the force and influence of testimony, they, on other occasions, give it assistance, and

v. 2. Hume's Ess. 119. 120.

3. It is necessary to the learner to believe.

increase its authority. The reputation of the witness, the manner in which he delivers his testimony, the nature of the fact concerning which his testimony is given, the peculiar situation in which he stands with regard to that fact, the occasion on which he is called to produce his testimony, his entire disinterestedness as to the matter in question—each of these taken singly may much augment the force of his evidence—all of these taken jointly may render that force irresistible.

In a number of concurrent testimonies, there is a degree of probability superadded to that, which may be termed the aggregate of all the probabilities of the separate testimonies. This superadded probability arises from the concurrence itself. When, concerning a great number and variety of circumstances, there is an entire agreement in the testimony of many witnesses, without the possibility of a previous collusion between them, the evidence may, in its effect, be equal to that of strict demonstration. That such concurrence should be the result of chance, is as one to infinite; or, to vary the expression, is a moral impossibility.

To this important kind of evidence we are indebted for our knowledge of history, of criticism, and of many parts of jurisprudence; for all that acquaintance with nature and the works of nature, which is not founded on our own personal observations and experience, but on the attested experience and observations of others; and for the greatest part of that information concerning men and things, which is necessary, if not to the mere animal support, yet certainly to the ease, comfort, improvement, and happiness of human life.

In the profession of the law, and in the administration of justice, this kind of evidence acquires an importance very peculiar indeed. To examine, to compare, and to appreciate it, forms much the greatest part of the business and duty of jurors, and a very great part of the business and duty of counsel and judges. It is, therefore, highly interesting to society, that the genuine and unsophisticated principles of this kind of evidence should be generally known and understood. From the very cursory view which we have taken of them, it appears that the rules observed by the common law, in admitting and in refusing testimony, are conformable to the true theory of the human mind, and not to the warped hypotheses of some philosophical systems.

VIII. The eighth source of evidence, which I mentioned, is human authority in matters of opinion.

"Cuilibet in sua arte perito est credendum"[4] is one of the maxims of the common law. Like many other of its maxims, it is founded in sound sense, and in human nature.

Under the former head we have seen, that the infant mind, inexperienced and unsuspicious, trusts implicitly to testimony in matters of fact. It trusts, in the same implicit manner, to authority in matters of opinion. In proportion as the knowledge of men and things is gradually obtained, the influence of authority as well as of testimony becomes less decisive and indiscriminate. By the most prudent, however, and the most enlightened, it is, at no period of life, suffered to fall into desuetude or disrepute; even in subjects and sciences, which seem the most removed from the sphere of its operations.

Let us suppose, that, in mathematicks, the science in which authority is justly allowed to possess the least weight, one has made a discovery, which he thinks of importance: let us suppose that he has ascertained the truth of this discovery by a regular process of demonstration, in which, after the strictest review, he can find no defect or mistake: will he not feel an inclination to communicate this discovery to the inspection of a mathematical friend, congenial in his studies and pursuits? Will this inclination be prompted merely by the pride or pleasure of making the communication? Will it not arise, in some degree, from a very different principle—a latent but powerful desire to know the sentiments of his friend, not only concerning the merits, but also concerning the certainty of the discovery? Will not the sentiments of his friend, favourable or unfavourable, greatly increase or diminish his confidence in his own judgment? A man must possess an uncommon degree of self-sufficiency, who feels not an increased reliance on the justness of his discoveries, when he finds the truth of them fortified by the sentiments of those, who, with regard to the same subjects, are conspicuous for their penetration and discernment.

The evidence arising from authority, as well as that arising from testimony, other circumstances being equal, becomes strong in proportion to

4. Any expert in his own art is credible therein.

the number of those, on whose voice it rests. An opinion generally received in all countries and all ages, acquires such an accumulation of authority in its favour, as to entitle it to the character of a first principle of human knowledge.

IX. The ninth kind, into which we have distinguished evidence, is that, which arises from memory. The senses and consciousness give us information of those things only which exist at present. The memory conveys to us the knowledge of those things which are past. The evidence of memory, therefore, forms a necessary link in every chain of proof, by which the past is notified. This evidence is not less certain than if it was founded on strict demonstration. No man hesitates concerning it, or will give his assent to any argument brought to invalidate it. On it depends, in part, the testimony of witnesses, and all the knowledge which we possess, concerning every thing which is past.

The memory, as well as other powers of the mind which we have already mentioned, is an original faculty, and an original source of evidence, bestowed on us by the Author of our existence. Of this faculty we can give no other account, but that such, in this particular, is the constitution of our nature. Concerning past events we receive information from our memory; but how it gives this information, it is impossible for us to explain.[w]

"All our other original faculties, as well as memory, are unaccountable. He only, who made them, comprehends fully how they are made, and how they produce in us not only a conception, but a firm belief and assurance of things, which it concerns us to know."[x]

Remembrance, however, is not always accompanied with full assurance. To distinguish by language, those lively impressions of memory, which, produce indubitable conviction, from those fainter traces, which occasion an inferiour degree of assent, or, perhaps, diffidence and suspense, is, we believe, an impracticable attempt. But every one is, in fact, competent to distinguish them in such a manner, as to direct his own judgment and conduct.

X. Evidence arises from experience; as when from facts already known, we make inferences to facts of the *same* kind, unknown.

w. Reid. Ess. Int. 308.
x. Reid's Ess. Int. 310.

This branch of our subject is of great extent, of much practical utility, and highly susceptible of curious and instructive investigation. But it cannot, on this occasion, be treated as fully as it deserves to be treated.

The sources, from which experience flows, are—the external senses, consciousness, memory. The senses and consciousness give information to the mind of the existing facts, which are placed within the sphere of their operation. These articles of intelligence, when received, are committed to the charge of the memory. From all these faculties, however, there results only the knowledge of such facts as have come, or now come under our notice. But, in order to render this knowledge of service to us in directing our own conduct, and in discovering the nature of things, a further process of the mind becomes necessary. From the past, or the present, or from both, inferences must be made to the future: those inferences form that kind of evidence, which arises from experience.

If an object is remembered to have been frequently, still more, if it is remembered to have been constantly, succeeded by certain particular consequences; the conception of the object naturally associates to itself the conception of the consequences; and on the actual appearance of the object, the mind naturally anticipates the appearance of the consequences also. This connexion between the object and the frequent or constant consequences of the object, is the foundation of those inferences, which, as we have observed, form the evidence arising from experience.

If the consequences have followed the object constantly, and the observations of this constant connexion have been sufficiently numerous; the evidence, produced by experience, amounts to a moral certainty. If the connexion has been frequent, but not entirely uniform; the evidence amounts only to probability; and is more or less probable, in proportion as the connexions have been more or less frequent. That cork will float on the surface of water, and that iron will sink in it, are truths, of which we are morally certain; because these inferences are founded on connexions both sufficiently numerous and sufficiently uniform. We are not morally certain whether oak timber will float or sink in water; because, in some circumstances, it sinks, and, in other circumstances, it floats. But, if the circumstances uniformly attending the contrary effects are specified; then, under that specification, we can tell, with moral certainty, whether the timber will sink or swim.

This evidence, by which we infer what the future will be from what the past has been, is the effect of an original principle, implanted in the human mind. This principle appears in our most early infancy. The child, who is burnt, is soon taught to dread the fire. A great and necessary part of our knowledge is drawn from this source, before we are able to exercise the reasoning faculty. It is an instinctive prescience of the operations of nature, very similar to that prescience of human actions, by which we are made to rely upon the testimony of our fellow men. Without the latter, we could not receive information, by the means of language, concerning the sentiments of those, with whom we converse: without the former, we could not, by means of experience, acquire knowledge concerning the operations of nature. When we arrive at the years of discretion and are capable of exercising our reasoning power, this instinctive principle retains in us all its force; but we become more cautious in its application. We observe, with more accuracy, the circumstances attending the appearance of the object and its consequences, and learn to distinguish those which are regularly, from those which are only occasionally, to be discovered.

On this principle is built the whole stupendous fabrick of natural philosophy; and if this principle were removed, that fabrick, solid and strong as it is, would tumble in ruins to the very foundation. "That natural effects of the same kind are produced by the same causes," is a first principle laid down by the great Newton, as one of his laws of philosophizing.

On the same principle depends the science of politicks, which draws its rules from what we know by experience concerning the conduct and character of men. From this experience we conclude, that they will bestow some care and attention on themselves, on their families, and on their friends; that, without some temptation, they will not injure one another; that, on certain occasions, they will discover gratitude, and, on others, resentment. In the science of politicks, we consider not so much what man ought to be, as what he really is; and from thence we make inferences concerning the part which he will probably act, in the different circumstances and situations, in which he may be placed. From such considerations we reason concerning the causes and consequences of different governments, customs, and laws. If man were either better or worse, more perfect or less perfect, than he is, a proportioned difference ought to be adopted in the systems formed, and the provisions made, for the regulation of his conduct.

The same principle is the criterion, at least, if it is not the foundation, of all moral reasoning whatever. It is the basis of prudence in the management of the affairs and business of human life. Scarcely can a plan be formed, whether of a publick or even of a more private nature, which depends solely on the behaviour of him who forms it: it must depend also on the behaviour of others; and must proceed upon the supposition, that those others will, in certain given circumstances, act a certain given part.

XI. Evidence arises from analogy, as well as from experience. The evidence of analogy is, indeed, nothing more than a vague experience, founded on some remote similitude. When the circulation of the blood in one human body was verified by experiment, this was certainly a sufficient evidence, from experience, that, in every other human body, the blood, in like manner, circulates. When we reflect on the strong resemblance which, in many particulars, the bodies of some other animals, quadrupeds, for instance, bear to the human body; and especially on that resemblance, which is discovered in the blood vessels, in the blood itself, and in the pulsation of the heart and arteries; we discover evidence, from analogy, of the circulation of the blood in those other animals; for instance, in quadrupeds. In this application of the experiment, however, the evidence is unquestionably weaker than in that, which is transferred from one to another man. Yet, when the analogies are numerous, and evidence of a closer and more direct application is not to be obtained, the evidence from analogy is far from being without its operation and its use.

Its use, we acknowledge, appears more in answering objections, than in furnishing direct proofs. It may, for this reason, be considered as the defensive rather than the offensive armour of a speaker. It rarely refutes; but it repels refutations: it cannot kill the enemy; but it wards off his blows.

Much of the evidence in natural philosophy rises not higher, than that which is derived from analogy. We learn from experience, that there is a certain gradation in the scale of certain animals: we conclude from analogy, that this gradation extends farther than our experience reaches. Upon the foundation of analogy, the systems of ancient philosophy concerning the material world were entirely built. My Lord Bacon first delineated, and, in some instances, applied the strict and severe method of induction from experiment. Since his time, this has been employed in natural philosophy, with the greatest success.

To the common lawyer, the evidence of analogy is a subject of very great extent and importance.

In speaking of judicial decisions, my Lord Chief Justice Hale distinguishes them into two kinds: one consists of such as have their reasons singly in the laws and customs of the kingdom. In these the law gives an express decision; and the judge is only the instrument, which pronounces it. The other kind consists of decisions, which are framed and deduced, as his Lordship says, by way of deduction and illation upon those laws.

A competition between opposite analogies is the principle, into which a very great number of legal controversies may be justly resolved. When a particular point of law has been once directly adjudged; the adjudication is deemed decisive as to that question, and to every other which, in all its circumstances, corresponds completely with that question. But questions arise, which resemble the decided question only in some parts, in certain circumstances, and in certain indirect aspects; and which, it is contended, bear, in other aspects, in other circumstances, and in other parts, a much closer and stronger resemblance to other cases, which have been likewise adjudged. To stating, to comparing, and to enforcing those opposite analogies, on the opposite sides, much of the business of the bar is appropriated. In discerning the force and extent of the distinctions which are taken; in framing an adjudication in such a manner, as to preserve unimpeached the various former decisions, from which the contending analogies have been drawn; or, if all cannot be so preserved, yet so as that the weaker may be given up to the stronger—in this, much of the wisdom and sagacity of the court are employed and displayed.

The late celebrated dispute concerning literary property will place this subject, and the remarks which have been made concerning it, in a very striking point of view. On one hand, the time which an author employs, the pains which he takes, and the industry which he exerts, in the production of his literary performance, bear the nearest and the most marked resemblance to the industry exerted, to the pains taken, and to the time employed, in the acquisition of property of every other kind. This resemblance, so striking and so strong, between the labour bestowed in this, and the labour bestowed in any other way, justifies the inference and the claim, that he, who bestowed the labour in this way, should be entitled to the same perpetual, assignable, and exclusive right in the production of the labour thus bestowed; and should receive the same protection of the law in the enjoyment of this perpetual, assignable, and exclusive right, as is given and decreed to those who bestow their labour in any other manner. This is the analogy on one side. On the other hand, a book, considered with respect to the author's right in it, has a peculiar resemblance to any other invention of art; the discovery, for instance, of a new medicine, or of a new machine. Now, in these instances, unless an exclusive right is secured to the inventor by a patent, the law permits the machine or medicine to be used or imitated. Why should not the same liberty be enjoyed in the publication and sale of books? This is the analogy on the other side.

XII. Evidence arises from judgment. By judgment I here mean that power of the mind, which decides upon selfevident truths. This is a much more extensive power than is generally imagined. It is, itself, a distinct and original source of evidence; and its jurisdiction is exercised in all the other kinds of evidence, which have been already enumerated.

"There are conceptions, which ought to be referred to the faculty of judgment as their source: because, if we had not that faculty, they could not enter into our minds; and to those who have that faculty, and are capable of reflecting on its operations, they are obvious and familiar.

"Among these, we may reckon the conception of judgment itself; the notions of a proposition, of its subject, predicate, and copula; of affirmation and negation; of true and false; of knowledge, belief, disbelief, opinion, assent, evidence. From no source could we acquire these conceptions, but from reflecting on our judgments. Relations of things make one great class of our notions or ideas; and we cannot have the idea of any relation without some exercise of judgment."[y]

By our senses, we have certain sensations and perceptions. But to furnish us with these, is not the only, nor is it, indeed, the principal office of our senses. They are powers, by which we judge, as well as feel and perceive. A man, who has become blind, may, nevertheless, retain very distinct conceptions of the several colours; but he cannot, any longer, judge concerning colours; because he has lost the sense, the immediate operation of which is necessary in order to enable him to form such judgment. By our ears, we have the ideas of sounds of different kinds, such as acute

y. Reid. Ess. Int. 500, 501.

and grave, soft and loud. But this sense enables us not only to hear, but to judge of what we hear. We perceive one sound to be loud, another to be soft. When we hear more sounds than one, we perceive and judge that some are concords, and that others are discords. These are judgments of the senses.[z]

Judgment exercises its power concerning the evidence of consciousness, as well as concerning the evidence of the senses. The man, who is conscious of an object, believes that it exists, and is what he is conscious it is; not is it in his power to avoid such judgment. Whether judgment ought to be called a necessary concomitant, or rather an ingredient, of these operations of the mind, it is not material to inquire; but one thing is certain; they are accompanied with a determination that something is true or false, and with a consequent belief. This determination is not simple apprehension; it is not reasoning; it is a mental affirmation or negation; it may be expressed by a proposition affirmative or negative; and it is accompanied with the firmest belief. These are the characteristicks of judgment.[a] This name is sometimes given to every determination of the mind concerning what is true or what is false.[b] Under this head, I apply it, and confine it to that degree of judgment, which is commensurate with what is sometimes called common sense: for, in truth, common sense means common judgment.[c]

Further; judgment is implied in every operation of taste. When we say a statue or a poem is beautiful; we affirm something concerning that poem or statue: but every affirmation or denial expresses judgment. Our judgment of beauty is not, indeed, dry and uninteresting, like that of a mathematical truth. It is accompanied with an agreeable feeling or emotion, for which we have no appropriated term. It is called the sense of beauty.

Judgment is exerted also in the operations of our moral sense. When we exercise our moral powers concerning our own actions or those of others, we judge as well as feel. We accuse and excuse; we acquit and condemn, we assent and dissent; we believe and disbelieve. These are all acts of judgment.[d]

z. Reid Ess. Act. 237, 239.
a. Reid. Ess. Int. 501, 503.
b. Id. 504, 533. 534.
c. Id. 523, 530, 531.
d. Reid's Ess. Act. 474.

In short, we judge of the qualities of bodies by our external senses; we judge concerning what passes in our minds by our consciousness; we judge concerning beauty and deformity by our taste; we judge concerning virtue and vice by our moral sense: but, in all these cases, we judge; in most of them, our judgment is accompanied by feeling. Judgment accompanied by feeling forms that complex operation of the mind, which is denominated sentiment.

This train of investigation might be carried much farther; but, at present, we stop here.

Judgment, in the sense in which we here use it, is an original and an important source of knowledge, common to all men; and, for this reason, is frequently denominated common sense, as has been already intimated. In different persons, it prevails, indeed, with different degrees of strength; but none, except idiots, have been found originally and totally without it.

The laws, we believe, of every civilized nation distinguish between those who are, and those who are not, endowed with this gift of heaven. This gift is easily discerned by its effects, in the actions, in the discourse, and even in the looks of a man. When it is made a question, whether one is or is not possessed of this power, the courts of justice can usually determine the question with much clearness and certainty.

The same degree of understanding, which enables one to act with common prudence in the business of life, enables him also to discover self-evident truths concerning matters, of which he has distinct apprehension.

Selfevident truths, of every kind, and in every art and science, are the objects of that faculty, which is now under our consideration. Such truths, or axioms, as they are distinguished by way of excellence, are the foundation of all mathematical knowledge. There are axioms, too, in matters of taste. The fundamental rules of poetry, and painting, and eloquence, have always been, and, we may venture to add, always will be the same. The science of morals is also founded on axioms; many of which are accompanied with intuitive evidence, not less strong than that which is discovered in the axioms of mathematicks. Mathematical axioms can never extend their influence beyond the limits of abstract knowledge. But with axioms in other branches of science, the whole business of human life is closely and strongly connected.

XIII. Evidence arises from reasoning.

One observation, which I made concerning judgment, may be made, with the same propriety, concerning reasoning. It is, itself, a distinct and original source of evidence; and its jurisdiction is exercised also in evidence of every other kind. This suggests a very probable account why reason has been considered by many philosophers as the only source and criterion of evidence: for the powers both of judgment and of reasoning have been frequently blended under the name of reason.

As the conception of judgment should be referred to the faculty of judgment; so the conception of reasoning should be referred to the reasoning faculty, as its source. The ideas of demonstration, of probability, and of all the different modes of reasoning, take their origin from the faculty of reason. Without this faculty, we could not be possessed of those ideas.

The power of reasoning is somewhat allied to the power of judging. Reasoning, as well as judgment, must be true or false: both are accompanied with assent or belief. There is, however, a very material distinction between them. Reasoning is the process, by which we pass from one truth to another as a conclusion from it. In all reasoning, there must be a proposition inferred, and one or more, from which the inference is drawn. The proposition inferred is called the conclusion: the name of premises is given to the proposition or propositions, from which the conclusion is inferred. When a chain of reasoning consists of many links, it is easily distinguished from judgment. But when the conclusion is connected with the premises by a single link, the distinction becomes less obvious; and the process is sometimes called by one name; sometimes by the other.

In a series of legitimate reasoning, the evidence of every step should be immediately discernible to those who have a distinct comprehension of the premises and the conclusion.

The evidence, which arises from reasoning, is divided into two species—demonstrative and moral. The nature, the difference, and the uses of these two species of evidence, it is of great importance clearly and fully to understand.

Demonstrative evidence has for its subject abstract and necessary truths, or the unchangeable relations of ideas. Moral evidence has for its subject the real but contingent truths and connexions, which take place among things actually existing. Abstract truths have no respect to time or place; they are universally and eternally the same.

If these observations are just—and they are agreeable to the sentiments of those who have written most accurately on this subject—we may see the impropriety of my Lord Chief Baron Gilbert's remark, when he says, that "all demonstration is founded on the view of a man's proper senses." From hence we may see likewise the inaccuracy of Sir William Blackstone's description of evidence, when he mentions it as demonstrating the very fact in issue. The objects of our senses are objects of moral, but not of demonstrative evidence.

By writers on the civil law, the scientifick distinction, upon this subject, is accurately observed. Truths alone, say they,[e] which depend on abstract principles, are susceptible of demonstrative evidence: truths, that depend on matters of fact, however complete may be the evidence by which they are established, can never become demonstrative.

In a series of demonstrative evidence, the inference, in every step, is necessary; for it is impossible that, from the premises, the conclusion should not flow. In a series of moral evidence, the inference drawn in the several steps is not necessary; nor is it impossible that the premises should be true, while the conclusion drawn from them is false.

In demonstrative evidence, there are no degrees: one demonstration may be more easily comprehended, but it cannot be stronger than another. Every necessary truth leaves no possibility of its being false. In moral evidence, we rise, by an insensible gradation, from possibility to probability, and from probability to the highest degree of moral certainty.

In moral evidence, there not only may be, but there generally is, contrariety of proofs: in demonstrative evidence, no such contrariety can take place. If one demonstration can be refuted, it must be by another demonstration: but to suppose that two contrary demonstrations can exist, is to suppose that the same proposition is both true and false: which is manifestly absurd. With regard to moral evidence, there is, for the most part, real evidence on both sides. On both sides, contrary presumptions, contrary testimonies, contrary experiences must be balanced. The probability, on the whole, is, consequently, in the proportion, in which the evidence on one side preponderates over the evidence on the other side.

e. Encyc. Tit. Jurisprudence. vol. part 2. p. 752. (French.)

Demonstrative evidence is simple: in it there is only one coherent series, every part of which depends on what precedes, and suspends what follows. In demonstrative reasoning, therefore, one demonstration is equal to a thousand. To add a second would be a tautology in this kind of evidence. A second, it is true, is sometimes employed; but it is employed as an exercise of ingenuity, not as an additional proof. Moral evidence is generally complicated: it depends not upon any one argument, but upon many independent proofs, which, however, combine their strength, and draw on the same conclusion.

In point of authority, demonstrative evidence is superiour: moral evidence is superiour in point of importance. By the former, the understanding is enlightened, and many of the elegant and useful arts are improved. By the latter, society is supported; and the usual but indispensable affairs of life are regulated. To the acquisitions made by the latter, we owe the knowledge of almost every thing, which distinguishes the man from the child.

XIV. Evidence arises from calculations concerning chances. This kind of evidence does not occur very frequently. I take particular notice of it, because it is of much importance in some commercial transactions; especially in those relating to ensurances.

Chance furnishes materials for calculation, only when we know the remote cause, which will produce some one event of a given number; but know not the immediate cause, which will determine in favour of any one particular event of that given number, in preference to any other particular event. In calculating chances, it is necessary that a great number of instances be taken into consideration; that the greatest exactness and impartiality be used in collecting them on the opposite sides; and that there be no peculiarity in any of them, which would render it improper for becoming a part of the basis of a general conclusion.

I have now finished the long, I will not say, the complete enumeration of the different sources and kinds of evidence. Between several of them something will be found to be analogous. But, upon the most careful review, it will, I think, appear, that no one of them can be resolved into any other. Hence the propriety of considering and treating them separately and distinctly. Much advantage will, I believe, be reaped from acquiring and exercising a habit of considering them in this separate and distinct manner. For this purpose, it will be proper, when a trial of much variety and importance is perused or heard, to digest, at leisure, those things which are given or which appear in evidence, and refer them to their several sources and kinds. After this has been done, it will be of great use carefully to arrange the different sorts and parts of the evidence, and compare them together in point of solidity, clearness, and force. A habit of analyzing, combining, methodising, and balancing evidence, in this manner, will be a constant and a valuable resource in the practice of the law. Every one, who has observed or experienced that practice, must be sensible, that a lawyer's time and attention are more employed, and his talents are more severely tried, by questions and debates on evidence, than by those on all the other titles of the law, various, intricate, and extensive as they are.

To wield the weapons of evidence forms an important article in a lawyer's art. To wield them skilfully evinces a good head: to wield them honestly as well as skilfully evinces, at once, a good head and a good heart; and reflects equal honour on the profession and on the man.

I have, on this occasion, said nothing concerning the artificial rules of evidence, which are framed by the law for convenience in courts of justice. These, unquestionably, ought to be studied and known. Concerning these, much learning may be found in the several law books. Particular rules may be seen, adapted to particular cases. An intimate acquaintance with those rules will be of great practical utility in what I may call the retail business of the law; a kind of business by no means to be neglected; a kind of business, however, which should not be suffered to usurp the place of what is far more essential—the study and the practice too of the law, as a science founded on principle, and on the nature of man. The powers and the operations of the human mind are the native and original fountains of evidence. Gaudy, but scanty and temporary cascades may sometimes be supplied by art. But the natural springs alone can furnish a constant and an abundant supply. He, too, who is in full possession of these, can, with the greatest facility, and to the greatest advantage, display their streams, on proper occasions, in all the forms, and with all the ornaments, suggested and prepared by the most artificial contrivances.

It is generally supposed—and, indeed, our law books, so far as I recollect, go upon the supposition—that the evidence, which influences a court and jury, depends altogether upon what is said by the witnesses, or read from the papers. This, however, is very far from being the case. Much depends on the pleadings of the counsel. His pleadings depend much on a masterly knowledge and management of the principles of evidence. Evidence is the foundation of conviction: conviction is the foundation of persuasion: to convey persuasion is the end of pleading. From the principles of evidence, therefore, must be drawn that train and tenour of reasoning, which will accomplish the aim of the pleader, and produce the perfection of his art.

A rich and an immense prospect opens to my view; but I cannot now attempt to describe it.

THE END OF THE FIRST PART.

PART 2.

Lectures on Law.

CHAPTER I.

Of the Constitutions of the United States and of Pennsylvania—Of the Legislative Department.

In my plan, I mentioned, that I would consider our municipal law under two great divisions; that, under the first, I would treat of the law, as it relates to persons; and that, under the second, I would treat of it, as it relates to things. I pursue those two great divisions; and begin with persons.

Persons are divided into two kinds—natural and artificial. Natural persons are formed by the great Author of nature. Artificial persons are the creatures of human sagacity and contrivance; and are framed and intended for the purposes of government and society.

When we contemplate the constitution and the laws of the United States and of the commonwealth of Pennsylvania; the mighty object, which first arrests our attention, is—the people. In the laws of England, as they have been imposed or received during the last seven centuries, the "people" is a title, which has scarcely found a place, or, if it has found a place occasionally, it has attracted but a very disproportionate degree of notice or regard. Of the prerogative of the king, frequent and respectful mention is made: he is considered and represented as the fountain of authority, of honour, of justice, and even of the most important species of property. Of the majesty of the people, little is said in the books of our law. When they are introduced upon the legal stage, they are considered as the body, of which the king is the head, and are viewed as the subjects of his crown and government.

This has not been the case in all countries; it has not been the case in England at all times. It has, indeed, been the case too often and too generally; but the pages of literature will furnish us with a few brilliant exceptions. Of one permit me to take a very particular notice; for of a very particular notice it is highly deserving.

At the mention of Athens, a thousand refined and endearing associations rush immediately into the memory of the scholar, the philosopher, the statesman, and the patriot. When Homer, one of the most correct, as well as the oldest and one of the most respectable, of human authorities, enumerates the other nations of Greece, whose forces acted in the siege of Troy; he arranges them under the names of their different kings: but when he comes to the Athenians, he distinguishes them by the peculiar appellation of "the people"[a] of Athens.

Let it not surprise you, that I cite Homer as a very respectable authority. That celebrated writer was not more remarkable for the elegance and sublimity, than he was for the truth and precision, of his compositions. The geographer, who could not relish the exquisite beauties of his poetry, felt, however, uncommon satisfaction in ascertaining, by the map, the severe accuracy of his geographical descriptions. But let me mention what is still more to my present purpose and justification. From one of the orations of Aeschines[1] it appears highly probable,[b] that in the Athenian courts of justice, the poems of Homer, as well as the laws of Athens, were always laid upon the table before the judges; and that the clerk was frequently applied to, by the orator, to read passages from the former, as well as from the latter. On the authority of two lines from Homer's catalogue of the Grecian fleet, was determined a controversy between the Athenians and the inhabitants of Salamis. His immortal poems, like a meteor in the gloom of night, brighten the obscure antiquities of his country?[c]

By some of the most early accounts, which have been transmitted to us concerning Britain, we are informed, that "the people held the helm of government in their own power."[d] This spirit of independence was a ruling principle among the Saxons likewise. Concerning their original, it is both needless and fruitless—I use the expressions of the very learned Selden[e]—to enter the lists; whether they were natives from the northern parts of Germany, or the relicks of the army under Alexander. But their

a. Δημος. Pot. 12. Iliad l. 2. v. 547.

1. Aeschines (389–314 B.C.) was an Athenian statesman and orator.

b. 1. Gill. 26.

c. 1. Gill. 3.

d. Bac. on Gov. 2.

e. Id. 9.

government, adds he, was, in general, so suitable to that of the Grecians, that it cannot be imagined but much of the Grecian wisdom was derived into those parts. The people were a free people, governed by laws which they themselves made; and, for this reason, they were denominated free. This, he subjoins, was like unto the manner of the Athenians.

The Saxons were called freemen, because they were born free from all yoke of arbitrary power, and from all laws of compulsion, except those which were made by their voluntary consent: for all freemen have votes in making and executing the general laws.[f] The freedom of a Saxon consisted in the three following particulars. 1. In the ownership of what he had. 2. In voting upon any law, by which his person or property could be affected. 3. In possessing a share in that judiciary power, by which the laws were applied.[g]

By this time, we clearly perceive the exquisite propriety, historical as well as political, with which the people appear in the foreground of the national constitution and of that of Pennsylvania. "We, the people of the United States, ordain and establish this constitution for the United States of America." "We, the people of the commonwealth of Pennsylvania, ordain and establish this constitution for its government."

In free states, the people form an artificial person or body politick, the highest and noblest that can be known. They form that moral person, which, in one of my former lectures,[h] I described as a complete body of free natural persons, united together for their common benefit; as having an understanding and a will; as deliberating, and resolving, and acting; as possessed of interests which it ought to manage; as enjoying rights which it ought to maintain; and as lying under obligations which it ought to perform. To this moral person, we assign, by way of eminence, the dignified appellation of *state.*

In discussing the rights and duties of a state, I observed, that it is its right, and that, generally, it is its duty, to form a constitution, to institute civil government, and to establish laws. The general principles, on which constitutions should be formed, government should be instituted,

f. Bac. on Gov. 34.
g. Id. 84.
h. Ante. vol. 1. p. 635. 636.

and laws should be established, were treated at large then, and will not be repeated now. It is my present business to trace the application of those principles, as that application has been practically made by the people of the United States, and, in particular, by the people of Pennsylvania.

I mention the people of Pennsylvania in particular; because, in discussing this system, it is necessary that I should select the constitution, and government, and laws of some one of the states in the Union; and because it is natural, for many reasons, that Pennsylvania should be the state, whose constitution, and government, and laws are selected for this discussion. The observations, however, which I shall have occasion to make with regard to Pennsylvania, will, in the greatest number of instances, apply to her sister states, with an equal degree of propriety. Whenever any very striking difference or coincidence shall occur to me, I shall distinguish it by an especial notice.

The people of the United States must be considered attentively in two very different views—as forming one nation, great and united; and as forming, at the same time, a number of separate states, to that nation subordinate, but independent as to their own interiour government. This very important distinction must be continually before our eyes. If it be properly observed, every thing will appear regular and proportioned: if it be neglected, endless confusion and intricacy will unavoidably ensue.

The constitution of the United States is arranged, as we have formerly seen it ought to be, under three great divisions—the legislative department, the executive department, and the judicial department.

The legislative power is divided between two different bodies, a senate, and a house of representatives. The reasons and the importance of this division were explained in a former part of my lectures.[i]

In discoursing farther concerning the legislature of the United States, I shall regulate myself by the following order. I shall treat, I. of the election of its members; II. of their number; III. of the term, for which they are elected; IV. of the laws, and rules, and powers of the two houses; V. of the manner of passing laws; VI. of the powers of congress.

I. I am first to treat concerning the election of members of congress. Many of the remarks, which I shall make on this subject, will be applicable

i. Ante, vol. 1. p. 696. &c.

to the election of members of the general assembly of this commonwealth; for the assembly of Pennsylvania, like the congress of the United States, consists of two bodies, a senate and a house of representatives. Some important articles of discrimination will be noticed in their proper places.

The constitution of the United States and that of Pennsylvania rest solely, and in all their parts, on the great democratical principle of a representation of the people; in other words, of the moral person, known by the name of the state. This great principle necessarily draws along with it the consideration of another principle equally great—the principle of free and equal elections. To maintain, in purity and in vigour, this important principle, whose energy should pervade the most distant parts of the government, is the first duty, and ought to be the first care, of every free state. This is the original fountain, from which all the streams of administration flow. If this fountain is poisoned, the deleterious influence will extend to the remotest corners of the state: if this fountain continues pure and salubrious, the benign operation of its waters will diffuse universal health and soundness.

Let me, by the way, be indulged with repeating a remark, which was made and fully illustrated in a former lecture[j]—that government, founded solely on representation, made its first appearance on this, and not on the European side of the Atlantick.

Of the science of just and equal government, the progress, as we have formerly seen, has been small and slow. Peculiarly small and slow has it been, in the discovery and improvement of the interesting doctrines of election and representation. If, with regard to other subjects, government may be said, as it has been said, to be still in its infancy; we may, with regard to this subject, consider it as only in its childhood. And yet this is the subject, which must form the basis of every government, that is, at once, efficient, respectable, and free.

The pyramid of government—and a republican government may well receive that beautiful and solid form—should be raised to a dignified altitude: but its foundations must, of consequence, be broad, and strong, and deep. The authority, the interests, and the affections of the people at large

j. Ante. Vol. 1. p. 721.

are the only foundation, on which a superstructure, proposed to be at once durable and magnificent, can be rationally erected.

Representation is the chain of communication between the people and those, to whom they have committed the exercise of the powers of government. If the materials, which form this chain, are sound and strong, it is unnecessary to be solicitous about the very high degree, to which they are polished. But in order to impart to them the true republican lustre, I know no means more effectual, than to invite and admit the freemen to the right of suffrage, and to enhance, as much as possible, the value of that right. Its value cannot, in truth, be enhanced too highly. It is a right of the greatest import, and of the most improving efficacy. It is a right to choose those, who shall be intrusted with the authority and with the confidence of the people: and who may employ that authority and that confidence for the noblest interests of the commonwealth, without the apprehension of disappointment or control.

This surely must have a powerful tendency to open, to enlighten, to enlarge, and to exalt the mind. I cannot, with sufficient energy, express my own conceptions of the value and the dignity of this right. In real majesty, an independent and unbiassed elector stands superiour to princes, addressed by the proudest titles, attended by the most magnificent retinues, and decorated with the most splendid regalia. Their sovereignty is only derivative, like the pale light of the moon: his is original, like the beaming splendour of the sun.

The benign influences, flowing from the possession and exercise of this right, deserve to be clearly and fully pointed out. I wish it was in my power to do complete justice to the important subject. Hitherto those benign influences have been little understood; they have been less valued; they have been still less experienced. This part of the knowledge and practice of government is yet, as has been observed, in its childhood. Let us, however, nurse and nourish it. In due time, it will repay our care and our labour; for, in due time, it will grow to the strength and stature of a full and perfect man.

The man, who enjoys the right of suffrage, on the extensive scale which is marked by our constitutions, will naturally turn his thoughts to the contemplation of publick men and publick measures. The inquiries he will make, the information he will receive, and his own reflections on both, will afford a beneficial and amusing employment to his mind. I am far from insinuating, that every citizen should be an enthusiast in politicks, or that the interests of himself, his family, and those who depend on him for their comfortable situation in life, should be absorbed in Quixote speculations about the management or the reformation of the state. But there is surely a golden mean in things; and there can be no real incompatibility between the discharge of one's publick, and that of his private duty. Let private industry receive the warmest encouragement; for it is the basis of publick happiness. But must the bow of honest industry be always bent? At no moment shall a little relaxation be allowed? That relaxation, if properly directed, may prove to be instructive as well as agreeable. It may consist in reading a newspaper, or in conversing with a fellow citizen. May not the newspaper convey some interesting intelligence, or contain some useful essay? May not the conversation take a pleasing and an improving turn? Many hours, I believe, are every where spent, in talking about the unimportant occurrences of the day, or in the neighbourhood; and, perhaps, the frailties or the imperfections of a neighbour form, too often, one of the sweet but poisoned ingredients of the discourse. Would it be any great detriment to society or to individuals, if other characters, and with different views, were more frequently brought upon the carpet?

Under our constitutions, a number of important appointments must be made at every election. To make them is, indeed, the business only of a day. But it ought to be the business of much more than a day, to be prepared for making them well. When a citizen elects to office—let me repeat it—he performs an act of the first political consequence. He should be employed, on every convenient occasion, in making researches after proper persons for filling the different departments of power; in discussing, with his neighbours and fellow citizens, the qualities, which ought to be possessed by those, who enjoy places of publick trust; and in acquiring information, with the spirit of manly candour, concerning the manners and characters of those, who are likely to be candidates for the publick choice.

A habit of conversing and reflecting on these subjects, and of governing his actions by the result of his deliberations, would produce, in the mind of the citizen, a uniform, a strong, and a lively sensibility to the interests of his country. The same causes will effectuate a warm and enlightened attachment to those, who are best fitted, and best disposed, to support and promote those interests. By these means and in this manner, pure and genuine patriotism, that kind, which consists in liberal investigation and disinterested conduct, is produced, cherished, and strengthened in the mind: by these means and in this manner, the warm and generous emotion glows and is reflected from breast to breast.

Investigations of this nature are useful and improving, not to their authors only; they are so to their objects likewise. The love of honest and well earned fame is deeply rooted in honest and susceptible minds. Can there be a stronger incentive to the operations of this passion, than the hope of becoming the object of well founded and distinguishing applause? Can there be a more complete gratification of this passion, than the satisfaction of knowing that this applause is given—that it is given upon the most honourable principles, and acquired by the most honourable pursuits? To souls truly ingenuous, indiscriminate praise, misplaced praise, flattering praise, interested praise have no bewitching charms. But when publick approbation is the result of publick discernment, it must be highly pleasing to those who give, and to those who receive it.

If the foregoing remarks and deductions be just; and I believe they are so; the right of suffrage, properly understood, properly valued, and properly exercised, in a free and well constituted government, is an abundant source of the most rational, the most improving, and the most endearing connexion among the citizens.

All power is originally in the people; and should be exercised by them in person, if that could be done with convenience, or even with little difficulty. In some of the small republicks of Greece, and in the first ages of the commonwealth of Rome, the people voted in their aggregate capacity. Among the ancient Germans also, this was done upon great occasions. "De minoribus consultant principes," says Tacitus,[k] "de majoribus omnes:"[2] From their practices, some of the finest principles of modern governments are drawn.

But in large states, the people cannot assemble together. As they cannot, therefore, act by themselves, they must act by their representatives. And, indeed, in point of right, there is no difference between that which

k. De mor. Germ. c. 11.

2. In matters of less importance, rulers take counsel, in those of greater import, the people.

is done by the people in their own persons, and that which is done by their deputies, acting agreeably to the powers received from them. In point of utility, there is as little difference; for there is no advantage, which may not be obtained from a free and adequate representation, in as effectual a manner, as if every citizen were to deliberate and vote in person.

To the legitimate energy and weight of true representation, two things are essentially necessary. 1. That the representatives should express the same sentiments, which the represented, if possessed of equal information, would express. 2. That the sentiments of the representatives, thus expressed, should have the same weight and influence, as the sentiments of the constituents would have, if expressed personally.

To accomplish the first object, all elections ought to be free. If a man is under no external bias, when he votes for a representative, he will naturally choose such as, he imagines, will, on the several subjects which may come before them, speak and act in the same manner as himself. Every one, who is not the slave of voluntary errour, supposes that his own opinions and sentiments are right: he must likewise suppose, that the sentiments and opinions of those who think with him are right also. Every other man, equally free from bias, will vote with similar views. When, therefore, the votes generally or unanimously centre in the same representatives, it is a satisfactory proof, that the sentiments of the constituents are generally or altogether in unison, with regard to the matters, which, they think, will be brought under the consideration of their representatives; and also, that the sentiments of the representatives will be, with regard to those matters, in unison with those of all, or of a majority of their constituents.

To accomplish the second object, all elections ought to be equal. Elections are equal, when a given number of citizens, in one part of the state, choose as many representatives, as are chosen by the same number of citizens, in any other part of the state. In this manner, the proportion of the representatives and of the constituents will remain invariably the same.

If both the requisites are established and preserved, such counsels will be given, such resolutions will be taken, and such measures will be pursued, by the representative body, as will receive the concurrence, the approbation, and the support of the community at large.

In a free government, it is of essential importance to ascertain the right of suffrage, and those inhabitants who are entitled to the exercise of that right. To vote for members of a legislature, is to perform an act of original sovereignty. No person unqualified should, therefore, be permitted to assume the exercise of such preeminent power. We are told, that, among the Athenians, exquisitely sensible to all the rights of citizenship, a stranger who interfered in the assemblies of the people, was punished with death. Such dangerous interference was considered as a species of treason against their rights of sovereignty.

A momentous question now occurs—who shall be entitled to suffrage? This darling privilege of freemen should certainly be extended as far as considerations of safety and order will possibly admit. The correct theory and the true principles of liberty require, that every citizen, whose circumstances do not render him necessarily dependent on the will of another, should possess a vote in electing those, by whose conduct his property, his reputation, his liberty, and his life, may be all most materially affected.

By the constitution of the United States,[1] the members of the house of representatives shall be chosen by the people of the several states. The electors, in each state, shall have the qualifications requisite for electors of the most numerous branch of the state legislature.

This regulation is generous and wise. It is generous; for it intrusts to the constitutions or to the legislatures of the several states, the very important power of ascertaining and directing the qualifications of those, who shall be entitled to elect the most numerous branch of the national legislature. This unsuspicious confidence evinces, in the national constitution, the most friendly disposition towards the governments of the several states. For how can such a proper disposition be evinced more strongly, than by providing that its legislature, so far as respects the most numerous branch of it, should stand upon the same foundation with theirs; and by providing farther, that this foundation should be continued or altered by the states themselves?

This regulation is wise as well as generous. An attention to its genuine principle and tendency must have a strong effect, in preventing or destroying the seeds of jealousy, which might otherwise spring up, with regard to the genius and views of the national government. It has embarked itself on the same bottom with the governments of the different states: can a

1. Art I. s. 2.

stronger proof be given of its determination to sink or swim with them? Can proof be given of a stronger desire to live in mutual harmony and affection? This is an object of the last importance; for, to adopt an expression used by my Lord Bacon, "the uniting of the hearts and affections of the people is the life and true end of this work."[m]

The remarks which I have made on this subject place, in a clear and striking point of view, the propriety, and indeed the political necessity, of a regulation made in another part of this constitution. In the fourth section of the fourth article it is provided, that, "the United States shall guaranty to every state in this Union a republican form of government." Its own existence, as a government of this description, depends on theirs.

As the doctrine concerning elections and the qualifications of electors is, in every free country, a doctrine of the first magnitude; and as the national constitution has, with regard to this doctrine, rested itself on the governments of the several states; it will be highly proper to take a survey of those provisions, which, on a subject so interesting, have been made by the different state constitutions: for every state has justly deemed the subject to be of constitutional importance.

In the constitution of Pennsylvania, the great principle, which animates and governs this subject, is secured by an explicit declaration, that "elections shall be free and equal."[n] This is enumerated among the great points, which are "excepted out of the general powers of government, and shall for ever remain inviolate."[o] The practical operation of this great and inviolable principle is thus specified and directed: "In elections by the citizens, every freeman of the age of twenty one years, having resided in the state two years next before the election, and within that time paid a state or county tax, which shall have been assessed at least six months before the election, shall enjoy the rights of an elector."[p]

It well deserves, in this place, to be remarked, how congenial, upon this great subject, the principles of the constitution of Pennsylvania are to those adopted by the government of the Saxons. The Saxon freemen, as we

m. 4. Ld. Bac. 220.
n. Art. 9. s. 5.
o. Art. 9. s. 26.
p. Cons. Penn. Art. 3. s. 1.

have already seen, had votes in making their general laws.[q] The freemen of Pennsylvania, as we now see, enjoy the rights of electors. This right, it has been shown, is equivalent, and, in a state of any considerable extent, must, on every principle of order and convenience, be substituted to the other. This is far from being the only instance, in which we shall have the pleasure of finding the old Saxon maxims of government renewed in the American constitutions. Particular attention will be paid to them, as they present themselves.

By the constitution of New Hampshire, "every male inhabitant, with town privileges, of twenty one years of age, paying for himself a poll tax, has a right to vote, in the town or parish wherein he dwells, in the election of representatives."[r]

In Massachussetts, this right is, under the constitution, enjoyed by "every male person, being twenty one years of age, and resident in any particular town in the commonwealth for the space of one year next preceding, having a freehold estate within the same town, of the annual income of three pounds, or any estate of the value of sixty pounds." Every one so qualified may "vote in the choice of a representative for the said town."[s]

The right to choose representatives in Rhode Island is vested in "the freemen of the respective towns or places." This regulation is specified in the charter of Charles the second. The state of Rhode Island and Providence Plantations has not assumed a form of government different from that, which is contained in the abovementioned charter.[t]

The qualifications requisite, in the state of Connecticut, to entitle a person to vote at elections, are, maturity in years, quiet and peaceable behaviour, a civil conversation, and forty shillings freehold, or forty pounds personal estate: if the selectmen of the town certify a person qualified in those respects, he is admitted a freeman, on his taking an oath of fidelity to the state.[u]

It ought to be observed, by the way, that this power to admit persons to be freemen, or to exclude them from being freemen, according to the

q. Bac. on Gov. 34.
r. Cons. N. H. p. 11. 14.
s. Cons. Mass. c 1. s. 3. a. 4.
t. Char. R.I. p. 41. 51.
u. Cons. Con. p. 54.

sentiments which others entertain concerning their conversation and behaviour, is a power of a very extraordinary nature; and is certainly capable of being exercised for very extraordinary purposes.

The constitution of New York ordains, "that every male inhabitant of full age, who shall have personally resided within one of the counties of the state, for six months immediately preceding the day of election, shall, at such election, be entitled to vote for representatives of the said county in assembly; if during the time aforesaid he shall have been a freeholder, possessing a freehold of the value of twenty pounds, within the said county, or have rented a tenement therein of the yearly value of forty shillings; and been rated and actually paid taxes to the state."[v]

"All inhabitants of New Jersey, of full age, who are worth fifty pounds, proclamation money, clear estate within that government, and have resided within the county, in which they shall claim a vote, for twelve months immediately preceding the election, shall be entitled to vote for representatives in assembly."[w]

The right of suffrage is not specified in the constitution of Delaware; but it is provided, that, in the election of members of the legislature, it "shall remain as exercised by law at present."[x]

In Maryland, "all freemen above twenty one years of age, having a freehold of fifty acres of land in the county, in which they offer to vote, and residing therein; and all freemen having property in the state above the value of thirty pounds current money, and having resided in the county, in which they offer to vote, one whole year next preceding the election, shall have a right of suffrage in the election of delegates for such county."[y]

We find, in the constitution of Virginia, no specification of the right of suffrage: it is declared, however, that this right shall remain as it was exercised at the time when that constitution was made.[z]

It is provided by the constitution of North Carolina, "that all freemen of the age of twenty one years, who have been inhabitants of any county within the state twelve months immediately preceding the day of any

v. Cons. N. Y. c. 7. p. 58.
w. Cons. N. J. c. 4. p. 70. 71.
x. Cons. Del. c. 5. p. 95.
y. Cons. Mar. c. 2. p. 109.
z. Cons. Vir. p. 126.

election, and shall have paid publick taxes, shall be entitled to vote for members of the house of commons, for the county in which they reside."[a]

According to the constitution of South Carolina, "every free white man, of the age of twenty one years, being a citizen of the state, and having resided in it two years previous to the day of election, and who has a freehold of fifty acres of land, or a town lot, of which he hath been legally seized and possessed at least six months before such election, or, not having such freehold or lot, has resided within the election district, in which he offers to give his vote, six months before the election, and has, the preceding year, paid a tax of three shillings sterling towards the support of government, shall have a right to vote for members of the house of representatives for the election district, in which he holds such property, or is so resident."[b]

I am not possessed of the present constitution of Georgia. By its late constitution, it was provided, that "all male white inhabitants, of the age of twenty one years, and possessed, in their own right, of ten pounds value, and liable to pay tax in the state, or being of any mechanick trade, and shall have been a resident six months in the state, shall have a right to vote at all elections for[c] representatives."[d]

a. Cons. N. C. c. 8. p. 134.

b. Cons. S. C. art. 1. s. 4.

c. Cons. Georg. c. 9. p. 158.

d. Alterations have been made by several of the states in their constitutional provisions on this subject.

According to the present constitution of Delaware, "every white freeman of the age of twenty one years, having resided in the state two years next before the election, and within that time paid a state or county tax; which shall have been assessed at least six months before the election, shall enjoy the right of an elector." Art. 4. s. 1.

By an amendment of the constitution of Maryland, confirmed in the year one thousand eight hundred and two, it is provided that every free white male citizen of the state, and no other, above twenty one years of age, having resided twelve months next preceding the election in the city or county at which he offers to vote, shall have a right of suffrage. Constitutions, p. 174.

The present constitution of Georgia directs that the electors of members of the general assembly shall be citizens and inhabitants of the state, and shall have attained the age of twenty one years, and have paid all publick taxes which may have been required of them, and which they have had an opportunity of paying agreeably to law, for the year preceding the election, and shall have resided six months within the county. Art. 4. s. 1.

In order to complete the view taken of this subject in the text, it will proper to state the provisions made by the constitutions of the new states admitted into the Union respecting the qualifications of electors.

From the foregoing enumeration—its length and its minuteness will be justified by its importance—from the foregoing enumeration of the provisions, which have been made, in the several states, concerning the right of suffrage, we are well warranted, I think, in drawing this broad and general inference—that, in the United States, this right is extended to every freeman, who, by his residence, has given evidence of his attachment to the country, who, by having property, or by being in a situation to acquire property, possesses a common interest with his fellow citizens; and who is not in such uncomfortable circumstances, as to render him necessarily dependent, for his subsistence, on the will of others.

By the same enumeration, we are enabled, with conscious pleasure, to view and to display the close approximation, which, on this great subject, the constitutions of the American States have made, to what we have already seen to be the true principles and the correct theory of freedom.

Again; the same enumeration places in the strongest and most striking light, the wisdom and the generous confidence, which rested one of the principal pillars of the national government upon the foundation prepared for it by the governments of the several states.

With this sentiment I began—with this sentiment I conclude my remarks concerning the qualifications required from those, who elect the house of representatives of the United States.

In Vermont, "every man of the full age of twenty one years, having resided in the state for the space of one whole year next before the election of representatives, and who is of a quiet and peaceable behaviour, and will take the following oath or affirmation, shall be entitled to all the privileges of the state.—'You do solemnly swear (or affirm) that whenever you give your vote or suffrage, touching any matter that concerns the state of Vermont, you will do it so as in your conscience you shall judge will most conduce to the best good of the same, as established by the constitution, without fear or favour of any man.'" Cons. Ch. 2. s. 21.

By the constitution of Tennessee, every freeman of the age of twenty one years and upwards, possessing a freehold in the county wherein he may vote, and being an inhabitant of the state, and every freeman, being an inhabitant of any one county in the state six months immediately preceding the day of election, shall be entitled to vote for members of the general assembly, for the county in which he shall reside. Art. 3. s. 1.

The constitution of Kentucky provides, that in all elections for representatives, every free male citizen (negroes, mulattoes, and Indians excepted) who at the time being hath attained to the age of twenty one years, and resided in the state two years, and the county or town in which he offers to vote one year next preceding the election, shall enjoy the right of an elector. Art. 2. s. 8.

In the state of Ohio, the rights of electors are enjoyed by all white male inhabitants above the age of twenty one years, having resided in the state one year next preceding the election, and who have paid or are charged with a state or county tax. Cons. Art. 4. s. 1. *Ed.*

We now proceed to examine the qualifications required from those, who are elected to that dignified trust.

1. A representative must have attained the age of twenty five years.[e]

It is amusing enough to consider the different ages, at which persons have been deemed qualified or disqualified for different purposes, both in private and in publick life.

A woman, as we learn from my Lord Coke and others, has seven ages for several purposes appointed to her by the law. At seven years of age, her father, if a feudal superiour, was entitled to demand from his vassals an aid to marry her: at nine, she may have dower: at twelve, she may consent to marriage: at fourteen, she may choose a guardian: at sixteen, marriage might be tendered to her by her lord: at seventeen, she may act as executrix: at twenty one, she may alienate her lands and goods.[f] A man, also, has different ages assigned to him for different purposes. At twelve years of age, he was formerly obliged to take the oath of allegiance: at fourteen, he can consent to marriage: at the same age he can choose his guardian: at twenty one, he may convey his personal and real estate.[g]

The foregoing are the different ages allowed for different purposes in private life. In publick life, there has, with regard to age, been a similar variety of assignments; the reasons of some of which it is hard to conjecture; for the propriety of others, it is equally hard to account.

In the government of the United States, it is supposed, that no one is fit to be a member of the house of representatives, till he is twenty five years of age; to be a senator, till he is thirty;[h] to be a president, till he is thirty five.[i]

The duration assigned by nature to human life is often complained of as very short: that assigned to it by some politicians is much shorter. For some political purposes, a man cannot breathe before he numbers thirty five years: as to other political purposes, his breath is extinguished the moment he reaches sixty. By the constitution of New York,[j] "the chan-

e. Cons. U.S. art. 1. s. 2.
f. 1. Ins. 78. b.
g. Id. ibid.
h. Cons. U.S. art. 1. s. 3.
i. Id. art. 2. s. 1.
j. C. 24. p. 63.

cellor, the judges of the supreme court, and the first judge of the county court in every county, hold their offices—until they shall respectively have attained the age of sixty years."

How differently is the same object viewed at different times and in different countries! In New York, a man is deemed unfit for the first offices of the state *after* he is sixty: in Sparta, a man was deemed unfit for the first offices of the state *till* he was sixty. Till that age, no one was entitled to a seat in the senate, the highest honour of the chiefs.[k] How convenient it would be, if a politician possessed the power, so finely exercised by the most beautiful of poets! Virgil[3] could, with the greatest ease imaginable, bring Aeneas and Dido together; though, in fact, some centuries elapsed between the times, in which they lived. Why cannot some politician, by the same or some similar enchanting art, produce an ancient and a modern government as cotemporaries? The effect would be admirable. The moment that a gentleman of sixty would be disqualified from retaining his seat as a judge of New York, he would be qualified for taking his seat as a senator of Sparta.

2. Before one can be a representative, he must have been seven years a citizen of the United States.[l]

Two reasons may be assigned for this provision. 1. That the constituents might have a full and mature opportunity of knowing the character and merit of their representative. 2. That the representative might have a full and mature opportunity of knowing the dispositions and interests of his constituents.

3. The representative must, when elected, be an inhabitant of that state, in which he is chosen.[m]

The qualification of residence we have found to be universally insisted on with regard to those who elect: here the same qualification is insisted on with regard to those who are elected. The same reasons, which operated in favour of the former qualification, operate with equal, indeed, with greater force, in favour of this. A provision, almost literally the same with the present one, was made in England three centuries and a half ago. By a statute

k. 1. Gil. c. 3. p. 107. 8. War. Bib. 29.
3. Publius Vergilius Maro, or Virgil (70–19 B.C.), was a Roman poet.
l. Cons. U. S. art. 1. s. 2.
m. Cons. U. S. art. 1. s. 2.

made in the first year of Henry the fifth, it was enacted, that "the knights of the shires, which from henceforth shall be chosen in every shire, be not chosen, unless they be resident within the shire where they shall be chosen, the day of the date of the writ of the summons of the parliament"—"And moreover it is ordained and established, that the citizens and burgesses of the cities and boroughs be chosen men, citizens and burgesses, resiant, dwelling, and free in the same cities and boroughs, and no other in any wise."[n] To this moment, this statute continues unrepealed—a melancholy proof, how far degenerate and corrupted manners will overpower the wisest and most wholesome laws. From Sir Bulstrode Whitlocke[4] we learn, that, above a century ago, noncompliance with this statute was "connived at."[o] The statute itself has been long and openly disregarded. The consequences of this disregard may be seen in the present state of the representation in England.

Thus far concerning the election of the house of representatives, and the qualifications of the members and of the electors. It remains to speak concerning the election and the qualifications of the senators.

The senators are chosen by the legislatures of the several states. Every senator must have attained to the age of thirty years; he must have been nine years a citizen of the United States; and he must, when elected, be an inhabitant of that state, for which he shall be chosen.[p]

Some have considered the senators as immediately representing the sovereignty, while the members of the other house immediately represent the people, of the several states. This opinion is founded on a doctrine which I considered and, I believe, refuted very fully in a former lecture:[q] the doctrine is this—that the legislative power is the supreme power of the state. The supreme power I showed to reside in the people.

By the constitution of the United States, the people have delegated to the several legislatures the choice of senators, while they have retained in their own hands the choice of representatives. It would be unwise, how-

n. St. 1. Hen. 5. c. 1. Bar. 380.
4. Sir Bulstrode Whitelocke (1605–1675) was an English author and member of parliament.
o. 1. Whitl. 496.
p. Cons. U.S. art. 1. s. 3.
q. Ante. vol. 1. ch. 5.

ever, to infer from this, that either the dignity or the importance of the senate is inferiour to the dignity or the importance of the house of representatives. One may intrust to another the management of an equal or even superiour business, while he chooses to transact personally a business of an equal or even an inferiour kind.

Between the senate of the United States, and that of Pennsylvania, there is one remarkable point of difference, of which it will be proper, in this place, to take particular notice. According to the constitution of the United States, two senators are chosen by the legislature of each state: while the members of the house of representatives are chosen by the people. According to the constitution of Pennsylvania,[r] the senators are chosen by the citizens of the state, at the same time, in the same manner, and at the same place where they shall vote for representatives.

To choose the senators by the same persons, by whom the members of the house of representatives are chosen, is, we are told, to lose the material distinction, and, consequently, all the benefits which would result from the material distinction, between the two branches of the legislature.

If this, indeed, should be the necessary consequence of electing both branches by the same persons; the objection, it is confessed, would operate with a force irresistible. But many and strong reasons, we think, may be assigned, why all the advantages, to be expected from two branches of a legislature, may be gained and preserved, though those two branches derive their authority from precisely the same source.

A point of honour will arise between them. The esprit du corps will soon be introduced. The principle, and direction, and aim of this spirit will, we presume, be of the best and purest kind in the two houses. They will be rivals in duty, rivals in fame, rivals for the good graces of their common constituents.

Each house will be cautious, and careful, and circumspect, in those proceedings, which, they know, must undergo the strict and severe criticism of judges, whose inclination will lead them, and whose duty will enjoin them, not to leave a single blemish unnoticed or uncorrected. After all the caution, all the care, and all the circumspection, which can be employed, strict and severe criticism, led by inclination and enjoined by duty, will

r. Art. 1. s. 5.

find something to notice and correct. Hence a double source of information, precision, and sagacity in planning, digesting, composing, comparing, and finishing the laws, both in form and substance. Every bill will, in some one or more steps of its progress, undergo the keenest scrutiny. Its relations, whether near or more remote, to the principles of freedom, jurisprudence, and the constitution will be accurately examined: and its effects upon the laws already existing will be maturely traced. In this manner, rash measures, violent innovations, crude projects, and partial contrivances will be stifled in the attempt to bring them forth. These effects of mutual watchfulness and mutual control between the two houses, will redound to the honour of each, and to the security and advantage of the state.

The very circumstance of sitting in separate houses will be the cause of emulous and active separate exertion. The era, when the commons of England met in an apartment by themselves, is, with reason, considered, by many writers, as a memorable era in the history of English liberty. "After the formation of the two houses of parliament," says Mr. Millar,[5] in his historical view of the English constitution,[s] "each of them came to be possessed of certain peculiar privileges; which, although probably the objects of little attention in the beginning, have since risen to great political importance. The house of commons obtained the sole power of bringing in money bills." This subject will, by and by, come under our more immediate view.

Rivals for character, as we have seen the two houses to be, they will be rivals in all pursuits, by which character can be acquired, established, and exalted. To these laudable pursuits the crown of success will best be obtained, by vigour and alacrity in the discharge of the business committed to their care.

A difference in the posts assigned to the two houses, and in the number and duration of their members, will produce a difference in their sense of the duties required and expected from them. The house of representatives, for instance, form the grand inquest of the state. They will diligently inquire into grievances, arising both from men and things. Their commissions will commence or be renewed at short distances of time. Their sentiments, and

5. John Millar (1735–1801) was a historian of the English government.
s. P. 396 (4to.)

views, and wishes, and even their passions, will have received a deep and recent tincture from the sentiments, and views, and wishes, and passions of their constituents. Into their counsels, and resolutions, and measures, this tincture will be strongly transfused. They will know the evils which exist, and the means of removing them: they will know the advantages already discovered, and the means of increasing them. As the term of their commission and trust will soon expire, they will be desirous, while it lasts, of seeing the publick business put, at least, in a train of accomplishment. From all these causes, a sufficient number of overtures and propositions will originate in the house of representatives. These overtures and propositions will come, in their proper course, before the senate. Those, which shall appear premature, will be postponed till a more convenient season. Those, which shall appear crude, will be properly digested and formed. Those, which shall appear to be calculated upon too narrow a scale, will be enlarged in their operation and extent. Those, which shall appear to be dictated by local views, inconsistent with the general welfare, will be either rejected altogether, or altered in such a manner, as that the interest of the whole shall not be sacrificed, or rendered subservient, to the interest of a part.

Articles of information, detached and seemingly unconnected, introduced by the house of representatives, at different times, from different places, with different motives, and for different purposes, will, in the senate, be collected, compared, methodised, and consolidated. Under their plastick hands, those materials will be employed in forming systems and laws, for the prosperity and happiness of the commonwealth.

If, at any time, the passions or prejudices of the people should be ill directed or too strong; and the house of representatives should meet, too highly charged with the transfusion; it will be the business and the duty of the senate to allay the fervour; and, before it shall give a sanction to the bills or resolutions of the other house, to introduce into them the requisite ingredients of mildness and moderation.

Extremes, on one hand, are often the forerunners of extremes on the other. If a benumbing torpor should appear in the body politick, after the effects of violent convulsions have subsided; and if the contagious apathy should spread itself over the house of representatives; it will then become the business and the duty of the senate, to infuse into the publick councils and publick measures the proper portion of life, activity, and vigour.

In seasons of prosperity, it will become the care of the senate to temper the extravagance, or repress the insolence, of publick joy. In seasons of adversity, the senate will be employed in administering comfort and cure to the publick despondency.

In fine; the senate will consider itself, and will be considered by the people, as the balance wheel in the great machine of government; calculated and designed to retard its movements, when they shall be too rapid, and to accelerate them, when they shall be too slow.

These reflections, which seem to arise naturally from the subject before us, will, we hope, be sufficient to convince you, that the most beneficial purposes may be rationally expected from the senate of Pennsylvania, though the senators, as well as the members of the house of representatives, be elected immediately by the citizens of the commonwealth.

Another circumstance, not yet mentioned, deserves to be added to this account. The districts for the election of senators, are to be formed by the legislature. In forming those districts, the legislature are empowered to include in them such a number of taxable inhabitants as shall be entitled to elect four senators.[t] An enlarged and judicious exercise of this power will have a strong tendency to increase the dignity and usefulness of the senate. It may, I believe, be assumed as a general maxim, of no small importance in democratical governments, that the more extensive the district of election is, the choice will be the more wise and enlightened. Intrigue and cunning are the bane of elections by the people, who are unsuspicious, because they are undesigning: but intrigue and cunning are most dangerous, because they are most successful, in a contracted sphere.

II. I am now to consider the number of members of which the legislature of the United States consists.

The representatives are apportioned among the several states according to their numbers. The number of representatives shall not exceed one for every thirty thousand.[u] The senate shall be composed of two senators from each state.[v]

t. Cons. Penn. art. 1. s. 7.
u. Cons. U. S. art. 1. s. 2.
v. Id. art. 1. s. 3.

The Union consists now of fourteen, and will soon consist of fifteen states. Of consequence, the senate is composed now of twenty eight, and will be composed soon of thirty members.

A census of the United States has been taken, agreeably to the constitution, and the returns of that census are nearly completed. By these it appears, that, allowing one representative for every thirty thousand returned on the census, the house of representatives will consist of one hundred and twelve members.[w]

Every one has heard of the saying of the famous Cardinal de Retz[6]—that every publick assembly, consisting of more than one hundred members, was a mere mob. It is not improbable, that the Cardinal drew his conclusion from what he had seen and experienced. He lived in a turbulent season; and, in that turbulent season, was distinguished as a most turbulent actor. Of consequence, he was much conversant with mere mobs. But surely no good reason can be given, why the number one hundred should form the precise boundary, on one side of which, order may be preserved, and on the other side of which, confusion must unavoidably prevail. The political qualities of publick bodies, it is, in all likelihood, impossible to ascertain and distinguish with such numerical exactness. Besides; the publick bodies, most celebrated for the decency and dignity, as well as for the importance, of their proceedings, have far exceeded, in number, the bounds prescribed by the Cardinal for the existence of those respectable qualities: witness the senate of Rome, and the parliament of Great Britain.

w. After the census mentioned in the text, the representatives were apportioned among the states, by an act of congress passed on the fourteenth day of April, 1792, agreeably to a ratio of one member for every thirty three thousand persons in each state, computed according to the rule prescribed by the constitution. The number of representatives, agreeably to that ratio, amounted to one hundred and five.

A second enumeration was made in the year one thousand eight hundred; and the representatives were, by an act of congress passed on the fourteenth day of January, 1802, apportioned among the states agreeably to the same ratio. Their number amounted to one hundred and forty one. The state of Ohio has since been admitted into the Union, and is entitled to one member. This last apportionment is still in force.

The senate of the United States, at present, consists of thirty four members. *Ed.*

6. Jean François Paul de Gondi, Cardinal de Retz (1614–1679), was a French clergyman and political agitator.

There is, however, with regard to this point, an extreme on one hand, as well as on the other. The number of a deliberative body may be too great, as well as too small. In a great and a growing country, no precise number could, with propriety, be fixed by the constitution. A power, in some measure discretionary, was, therefore, necessarily given to the legislature, to direct that number from time to time. If the spirit of the constitution be observed in other particulars, it will not be violated in this.

III. I proceed, in the third place, to treat of the term, for which the members of the national legislature are chosen.

In the greatest part of the states, the members of the most numerous branch of their legislature are chosen annually; in some, every half year. The members of the least numerous branch are generally chosen for a longer term. By the constitution of the United States,[x] the members of the house of representatives are chosen "every second year."

When we consider the nature and the extent of the general government, we shall be satisfied, I apprehend, that biennial elections are as well proportioned to it, as annual elections are proportioned to the individual states, and half yearly elections to some of the smallest of them.

The senators of the United States are chosen for six years; but are so classed, that the seats of one third part of them are vacated at the expiration of every second year; so that one third part may be chosen every second year.[y]

In Pennsylvania, the senators are chosen for four years; but are so classed, that the seats of one fourth part of them are vacated at the expiration of every year; so that one fourth part may be chosen every year.[z]

The intention, in assigning different limitations to the terms, for which the members of the different houses are chosen, and in establishing a rotation in the senate, is obviously to obtain and secure the different qualities, by which a legislature ought to be distinguished. These qualities are, stability, consistency, and minute information. All these qualities may be expected, in some degree, from each house; but not in equal proportions. For minute information, the principal reliance will be placed on the house

x. Art. 1. s. 2.
y. Cons. U. S. art. 1. s. 3.
z. Cons. Penn. art. 1. s. 5. 9.

of representatives; because that house is the most numerous; and because its members are most frequently chosen. The qualities of stability and consistency will be expected chiefly from the senate; because the senators continue longer in office; and because only a part of them can be changed at any one time.

IV. I proceed to treat concerning the laws, and rules, and powers of the two houses of congress.

The parliament of Great Britain has its peculiar law; a law, says my Lord Coke,[a] with which few are acquainted, but which deserves to be investigated by all. The maxims, however, upon which the parliament proceeds, are not, it seems, defined and ascertained by any particular stated law: they rest entirely in the breast of the parliament itself. The dignity and independence of the two houses, we are told, are preserved, in a great measure, by keeping their privileges indefinite.[b]

Very different is the case with regard to the legislature of the United States, and to that of Pennsylvania. The great maxims, upon which our law of parliament is founded, are defined and ascertained in our constitutions. The arcana of privilege, and the arcana of prerogative, are equally unknown to our system of jurisprudence.

By the constitution of the United States,[c] each house of the legislature shall be the judge of the qualifications and returns, and also of the elections, of its own members. By the constitution of Pennsylvania,[d] each house shall judge of the qualifications of its members: but contested elections shall be determined by a committee to be selected, formed, and regulated in such manner as shall be directed by law. With regard to this subject, the constitution of Pennsylvania has, I think, improved upon that of the United States. Contested elections, when agitated in the house itself, occasion much waste of time, and, too often, a considerable degree of animosity among the members. These inconveniences will be, in a great measure, avoided by the proceedings and decision of a committee, directed and governed by a standing law.

a. 1. Ins. 11 b.
b. 1. Bl. Com. 163. 164.
c. Art. 1. s. 5.
d. Art. 1. s. 12.

It is proper, in this place, to take notice, that the house of representatives in congress have appointed a standing committee of elections. It is the duty of this committee, to examine the certificates of election, or other credentials of the members returned; to take into their consideration every thing referred to them concerning returns and elections; and to report their opinions and proceedings to the house.[e]

In the United States and in Pennsylvania, the legislature has a right to sit upon its own adjournments: but neither house shall, without the consent of the other, adjourn for more than three days, nor to any other place, than that in which the two houses shall be sitting.[f] In England, the sole right of convening, proroguing, and dissolving the parliament forms a part, and, obviously, a very important part, of the prerogative of the king.[g] Here we discover, in our new constitutions, another renovation of the old Saxon customs. The original meetings of the wittenagemote in England were held regularly at two seasons of the year; at the end of spring, and at the beginning of autumn.[h] Afterwards there came to be two sorts of wittenagemote; one held by custom, and at the stated periods; the other called occasionally,[i] and by a special summons from the king. Under the princes of the Norman and Plantagenet lines, the ancient and regular meetings of the national legislature were more and more disregarded. The consequence was, that, in progress of time, the whole of the parliamentary business was transacted in extraordinary meetings, which were called at the pleasure of the sovereign.[j] *Principiis obsta.*[7] In consequence of acquiring the power to call the parliament together, that of putting a negative upon its meetings, in other words, of proroguing or dissolving it, was, in all cases, vested in the crown.[k]

e. Jour. Rep. 13th April, 1789.

f. Cons. U. S. art. 1. s. 5. Cons. Penn. art. 1. s. 16.

g. 1. Bl. Com. 187. 188.

h. Bac. on Gov. 36. Millar. 146. 242.

i. A similar distinction between stated and occasional assemblies was observed by the Athenians. The times of the former were appointed by law: the latter were summoned by those at the head of the civil or of the military department of the government; as emergencies in those different departments arose. 1. Pot. Ant. 91. 92.

j. Millar. 242. 244.

7. Resist the beginnings.

k. Id. 311.

The constitution of the United States provides,[l] that the senators and representatives shall, in all cases, except treason, felony, and breach of the peace, be privileged from arrest during their attendance at the session of their respective houses, and in going to and returning from them. The constitution of Pennsylvania[m] contains a similar provision, excepting in one particular. The members are not entitled to privilege, if their conduct has been such, as to give reasonable cause of fear that they will break the peace; in the same manner as they are not entitled to it, if, by their conduct, the peace has been actually broken. This necessary privilege has continued substantially the same, since the time of the Saxons. The grand assembly of the wittenagemote, as we are told by Mr. Selden, was holden sacred; and all the members were under the publick faith, both in going and coming, unless the party were *fur probatus.*[8] This privilege of safe pass, being thus ancient and fundamental, and not by any law taken away, resteth still in force.[n]

The members of the national legislature, and those also of the legislature of Pennsylvania, shall not, for any speech or debate in either house, be questioned in any other placed.[o] In England, the freedom of speech is, at the opening of every new parliament, particularly demanded of the king in person, by the speaker of the house of commons.[p] The liberal provision, which is made, by our constitutions, upon this subject, may be justly viewed as a very considerable improvement in the science and the practice of government. In order to enable and encourage a representative of the publick to discharge his publick trust with firmness and success, it is indispensably necessary, that he should enjoy the fullest liberty of speech, and that he should be protected from the resentment of every one, however powerful, to whom the exercise of that liberty may occasion offence.

When it is mentioned, that the members shall not be questioned in any *other* place; the implication is strong, that, for their speeches in either house, they may be questioned and censured by that house, in which they are spoken. Besides; each house, both in the United States and in Penn-

l. Art. 1. s. 6.
m. Art. 1. s. 17.
8. A proved thief.
n. Bac. on Gov. 38.
o. Cons. U. S. art. 1. s. 6. Cons. Penn. art. 1. s. 17.
p. 1. Bl. Com. 164.

sylvania, has an express power given it to "punish its members for disorderly behaviour."[q] Under the protection of privilege, to use indecency or licentiousness of language, in the course of debate, is disorderly behaviour, of a kind peculiarly base and ungentlemanly.

Each house may not only punish, but, with the concurrence of two thirds, it may expel a member.[r] This regulation is adopted by the constitution of Pennsylvania:[s] "but," it is added, "not a second time for the same cause." The reason for the addition evidently is—that the member, who has offended, cannot be an object of a second expulsion, unless, since the offence given and punished by the first expulsion, he has been either re-elected by his former constituents, or elected by others. In both cases, his election is a proof, that, in the opinion of his constituents, he either has not offended at all, or has been already sufficiently punished for his offence. The language of each opinion is, that he ought not to be expelled again: and the language of the constituents is a law to the house.

Each house may determine the rules of its proceedings. This power is given, in precisely the same terms, by the constitution of the United States, and by that of Pennsylvania.[t] Its propriety is selfevident.

The constitution of the United States directs,[u] that each house shall keep a journal of its proceedings, and, from time to time, publish them, except such parts as may require secrecy: it directs further, that the yeas and nays of the members of either house, on any question, shall, at the desire of one fifth of those present, be entered on the journal. The constitution of Pennsylvania[v] goes still further upon these points: it directs, that the journals shall be published weekly; that the yeas and nays shall be entered on them, at the desire of any two members; and that the doors of each house, and of committees of the whole, shall be open, unless when the business shall be such as ought to be kept secret.

That the conduct and proceedings of representatives should be as open as possible to the inspection of those whom they represent, seems to be, in

q. Con. U. S. art. 1. s. 5. Cons. Penn. art. 1. s. 23.
r. Cons. U. S. art. 1. s. 5.
s. Art. 1. s. 13.
t. Cons. U. S. art. 1. s. 5. Cons. Penn. art. 1. s. 13.
u. Art. 1. s. 5.
v. Art. 1. s. 14, 15.

republican government, a maxim, of whose truth or importance the smallest doubt cannot be entertained. That, by a necessary consequence, every measure, which will facilitate or secure this open communication of the exercise of delegated power, should be adopted and patronised by the constitution and laws of every free state, seems to be another maxim, which is the unavoidable result of the former. For these reasons, I feel myself necessarily and unavoidably led to consider the additional regulations made, upon this subject, by the constitution of Pennsylvania, as improvements upon those made by the constitution of the United States. The regulation—that the doors of each house, and of committees of the whole, shall be open—I view as an improvement highly beneficial both in its nature and in its consequences—both to the representatives and to their constituents. "In the house of commons," says Sir William Blackstone, "the conduct of every member is subject to the future censure of his constituents, and therefore should be openly submitted to their inspection."[w] But I forbear to enter more largely into this interesting topick.

The house of representatives in congress shall choose their speaker and other officers.[x] The like provision is made by the constitution of Pennsylvania,[y] with respect to both houses of the general assembly.

The speaker of the house of commons cannot give his opinion, nor can he argue any question in the house.[z] From this view of the matter, one would be apt to imagine, that as the Latins assigned to a grove the name of *lucus, a non lucendo*,[9] so the English distinguished the first officer of the house of commons by the appellation of speaker, because, by the rules of that house, he could say neither yes nor no. But if we trace things to their origin, we shall be led to discover the reason of this denomination.

The first mode of passing a bill through parliament was by a petition to the king. This petition represented the grievance or inconvenience, concerning which complaint was made, and requested that it should be removed. When a petition was offered by the commons, after they sat in a separate house, it was necessary to appoint some person to intimate their

w. 1. Bl. Com. 181.
x. Cons. U. S. Art. 1. s. 2.
y. Art. 1. s. 11.
z. 1. Bl. Com. 181.
9. It is called a grove because it is not light.

views and wishes to the king. This person, chosen by themselves, and approved by the king, whom they would not address by the mouth of a person disagreeable to him, was denominated their speaker.[a]

To discharge this part of his duty in the dignified, and, at the same time, in the respectful manner, in which it ought to be discharged, was frequently considered as a business of a very arduous nature. It will not be unentertaining, to learn, from one of the speakers of the house of commons, the qualities, which, in his opinion, were necessary for the proper performance of the speaker's office.

"Whence," said Serjeant Yelverton,[10] "your unexpected choice of me to be your mouth or speaker should proceed, I am utterly ignorant. Neither from my person nor nature doth this choice arise: for he that supplieth this place ought to be a man big and comely, stately and well spoken, his voice great, his carriage majestical, his nature haughty. But, contrarily, the stature of my body is small, myself not so well spoken, my voice low, my carriage lawyerlike and of the common fashion, my nature soft and bashful. If Demosthenes, being so learned and so eloquent as he was, trembled to speak before Phocion[11] at Athens; how much more shall I, being unlearned and unskilful, supply this place of dignity, to speak before the unspeakable majesty and sacred personage of our dread and dear sovereign, the terrour of whose countenance" (he speaks of Queen Elizabeth) "will appal and abase even the stoutest heart."[b]

All bills for raising revenue shall originate in the house of representatives; but the senate may propose amendments as in other bills. This provision is common to the United States and Pennsylvania.[c]

In a former lecture,[d] this subject was considered under one aspect, under which it then made its appearance. It now claims consideration in other respects: and ought to be examined with a greater degree of minuteness.

a. Millar 414.

10. Sir Christopher Yelverton (1536–1612) was serjeant-at-law in 1589 and queen's serjeant from 1598 to 1602. This passage comes from remarks he made upon being elected Speaker of the House of Commons in 1597. Serjeants held the highest and most ancient degree at the English bar.

11. Phocion (c. 402–c. 318 B.C.) was an Athenian general, a statesman, and, late in life, a student of Plato.

b. 4. Parl. Hist. 411, 412.

c. Cons. U. S. art. 1. s. 7. Cons. Penn. art. 1. s. 20.

d. Ante Vol. 1. p. 731.

In England, all grants of aids by parliament begin in the house of commons. Of that house, this is an ancient,[e] and, now, an indisputable privilege. With regard to it, the commons are so jealous, that, over money bills, they will not suffer the other house to exert any powers, except simply those of concurrence or rejection. From the lords, no alteration or amendment will be received on this delicate subject. The constitutions of the United States and Pennsylvania have, on this head, adopted the parliamentary law of England in part; but they have not adopted it altogether. They have directed, that money bills shall originate in the house of representatives; but they have directed also, that the senate may propose amendments in these, as well as in other bills. It will be proper to investigate the reasons of each part of the direction. This will best be done by tracing the matter historically, and attending to the difference between the institution of the house of lords in England, and that of the senates of the United States and Pennsylvania.

During a considerable time after the establishment of the house of commons as a separate branch of the legislature, it appears, that the members of that house were, with regard to taxes and assessments, governed altogether by the instructions, which they received from their constituents. Each county and borough seems to have directed its representatives, concerning the amount of the rates to which they might give their assent. By adding together the sums contained in those particular directions, it was easy to ascertain, in the house of commons, the sum total, which the commonalty of the kingdom were willing to grant. To the extent of this sum, the commons conceived themselves empowered and directed to go; but no farther.

According to this mode of proceeding, the imposition of taxes produced no interchange of communication between the two houses of parliament. To introduce a money bill, or an amendment to a money bill, into the house of lords—to deliberate upon the bill or amendment in that house—after agreeing to it there, to submit it to the deliberation of the house of commons—all this would have been perfectly nugatory. Let us suppose, that the bill or amendment had undergone the most full and careful examination in the house of lords, who, acting only for themselves, could examine it under every aspect, unfettered by exteriour direction and con-

e. 4. Ins. 29.

trol: let us suppose it then transmitted to the house of commons, for their concurrence: what could the house of commons do? They could not deliberate upon the bill or the amendment: they could only compare it with their instructions: if they found it consistent with them, they could give, if inconsistent, they must refuse, their consent. The only course, therefore, in which this business could be transacted, was, that the commons should begin by mentioning the sum, which they were empowered to grant, and that what they proposed should be sent to the house of lords, who, upon all the circumstances, might deliberate and judge for themselves.[f]

In this manner, and for these reasons, the house of commons became possessed of this important privilege, which is now justly regarded by them, as one of the strongest pillars of their freedom and power. Once possessed of this privilege, they were far from relinquishing it, when the first reasons for its possession had ceased. Other reasons, stronger than the first, succeeded to them. In the flux of time and things, the revenue and influence of the crown became so great, and the property of the peerage, considered with relation to the general property of the kingdom, became comparatively so small, that it was judged unwise to permit that body to model, or even to alter, the general system of taxation. This is the aspect, under which this subject was viewed in the lecture, to which I have alluded; and I will not repeat now what was observed then.

From this short historical deduction, it appears, that the provision, which we now consider, is far from being so important here, as it is in England. In the United States and in Pennsylvania, both houses of the legislature draw their authority, either immediately, or, at least, not remotely, from the same common fountain. In England, one of the houses acts entirely in its private and separate right.

But though this regulation is by no means so necessary here, as it is in England; yet it may have its use, so far as it has been adopted into our constitutions. Our houses of representatives are much more numerous than our senates: the members of the former are chosen much more frequently, than are the members of the latter. For these reasons, an information more local and minute may be expected in the houses of representatives, than can be expected in the senates. This minute and local

f. Millar. 398.

information will be of service, in suggesting and in collecting materials for the laws of revenue. After those materials are collected and prepared, the wisdom and the patriotism of both houses will be employed in forming them into a proper system.

The house of representatives shall have the sole power of impeaching. All impeachments shall be tried by the senate. These regulations are found both in the constitution of the United States[g] and in that of Pennsylvania.[h]

The doctrine of impeachments is of high import in the constitutions of free states. On one hand, the most powerful magistrates should be amenable to the law: on the other hand, elevated characters should not be sacrificed merely on account of their elevation. No one should be secure while he violates the constitution and the laws: every one should be secure while he observes them.

Impeachments were known in Athens. They were prosecuted for great and publick offences, by which the commonwealth was brought into danger. They were not referred to any court of justice, but were prosecuted before the popular assembly, or before the senate of five hundred.[i]

Among the ancient Germans also, we discover the traces of impeachments: for we are informed by Tacitus, in his masterly account of the manners of that people,[j] that it was allowed to present accusations, and to prosecute capital offences, before the general assembly of the nation.

An impeachment is described, by the law of England, to be, a presentment to the most high and supreme court of criminal jurisdiction, by the most solemn grand inquest of the kingdom.[k]

It is evident that, in England, impeachments, according to this description, could not exist before the separation of the two houses of parliament. Previous to that era, the national council was accustomed to inquire into the conduct of the different executive officers, and to punish them for malversation in office, or what are called high misdemeanors. The king himself was not exempted from such inquiry and punishment: for it had not yet become a maxim—that the king can do no wrong.

g. Art. 1. s. 2, 3.
h. Art. 4. s. 1. 2.
i. 1. Pot. Ant. 125.
j. Ch. 12.
k. 2. Hale. P. C. *150. 4. Bl. Com. 256.

Prosecutions of this nature were not, like those of ordinary crimes, intrusted to the management of an individual: they were conducted by the national council themselves; who acted, improperly enough, in the double character of accusers and judges. Upon the separation of the two houses, it became an obvious improvement, that the power of trying those high misdemeanors should belong to the house of lords, and that the power of conducting the prosecution should belong to the house of commons. In consequence of this improvement, the inconsistent characters of judge and accuser were no longer acted by the same body.[l]

We find the commons appearing as the grand inquest of the nation, about the latter end of the reign of Edward the third. They then began to exhibit accusations for crimes and misdemeanors, against offenders who were thought to be out of the reach of the ordinary power of the law. In the fiftieth year of that reign, they preferred impeachments against many delinquents. These impeachments were tried by the lords.[m]

In the United States and in Pennsylvania, impeachments are confined to political characters, to political crimes and misdemeanors, and to political punishments. The president, vice president, and all civil officers of the United States; the governour and all other civil officers under this commonwealth, are liable to impeachment; the officers of the United States, for treason, bribery, or other high crimes and misdemeanors; the officers of this commonwealth, for any misdemeanor in office. Under both constitutions, judgments, in cases of impeachment, shall not extend further than to removal from office, and disqualification to hold any office of honour, trust, or profit.[n]

Thus much concerning the laws, and rules, and powers of the two houses of the congress of the United States, and concerning those of the two houses of the general assembly of Pennsylvania.

V. I next consider the manner of passing laws.

To laws properly made, the following things are of indispensable necessity—information—caution—perspicuity—precision—sagacity—conciseness. For obtaining those valuable objects, different states have adopted

l. Millar. 403.
m. 2. Reeve. 85.
n. Cons. U. S. art. 2. s. 4. art. 1. s. 3. Cons. Penn. art. 4. s. 3.

different regulations. It will be worth while to bestow some attention upon the most remarkable among them.

At Athens, laws were made according to the following very deliberate process. When any citizen had conceived any plan, which, he thought, would promote the interests of the commonwealth, he communicated it to certain officers, whose duty it was to receive information of every thing which concerned the publick. These officers laid the plan before the senate. If it appeared to the senate to be pernicious or useless, they rejected it. If otherwise, they agreed to it; and it then became what we may call a bill, or overture. It was written on a white tablet, and fixed up in a publick place, some days before the meeting of the general assembly of the people. This was done, that the citizens might have an opportunity of reading and forming a deliberate judgment, concerning what was to be proposed to them for their determination. When the assembly met, the bill was read to them; and every citizen had a right to speak his sentiments with regard to it. If, after due consultation, it was thought inconvenient or improper, a negative was put upon it: if, on the contrary, the people approved of it, it was passed into a law.

We are informed, that no one, without much caution and a perfect acquaintance with the constitution and former laws, would presume to propose a new regulation; because the danger was very great, if it proved unsuitable to the customs and inclinations of the people.[o]

With all these numerous precautions, so many obscure and contradictory laws were gradually introduced into the Athenian code, that a special commission was established to make a selection among them. The labour even of the special commissioners was, however, fruitless.[p]

Peculiarly rigid was the constitution of the Locrians, with regard to propositions for making a law. The citizen, who proposed one, appeared in the assembly of the people, with a cord round his neck. Encircled by that solemn monitor, he laid before them the reasons, on which his proposal was founded: if those reasons were unsatisfactory, he was instantly strangled.[q]

o. 1. Pot. Ant. 140.
p. 2. Anac. 271.
q. 1. Pot. Ant. 140.

Among the Romans, legislation, as it might be expected, was considered as a science: it was cultivated with the most assiduous industry, and was enriched with all the treasures of reason and philosophy. The mistress of the world had laws to instruct her how to make laws. In digesting the original plan of a bill, the magistrate, who proposed it, used every possible precaution, that it might come before the people in a form, the most perfect and unexceptionable. He consulted, in private, with his friends, upon its form and matter. The object was, that it might contain no clause contrary to the interests of the commonwealth; no provision inconsistent with former laws, not intended to be repealed or altered; and no regulation, which might produce a partial advantage to the connexions or relations of the proposer, or to the proposer himself.

As unity and simplicity are essential perfections of every good law; every thing foreign to the bill immediately in contemplation was strictly prohibited. By incoherent assemblages, the people might be induced to receive as law what they might dislike; or to reject what they might desire.

A bill, after all the precautions before mentioned, was submitted to the examination of the senate. On being approved there, it was fixed up publickly in some conspicuous part of the forum, that every citizen might understand fully what it contained. A meeting of the "comitia" was appointed by proclamation at the end of twenty seven days. When this time was elapsed, the people assembled. The bill proposed was proclaimed by the publick crier; and the person who proposed it was expected to speak first in its support. After this, any other member of the assembly was at liberty to deliver his sentiments; and, to prevent any improper influence, a private citizen, had always the privilege of speaking before a magistrate, except the magistrate who was the proposer of the law.

When the debates concerning the bill were finished, preparation was made for voting upon it. The names of the centuries were thrown promiscuously into an urn, and being blended together by the hand of the presiding magistrate, they were drawn out, one by one. The century first drawn was called the "prerogative century." After these preparatory steps were taken, the magistrate, who proposed the law, commanded proclamation to be made for every one to repair to his respective century. The prerogative century was called out first, and afterwards the others, as their lots directed.

In the early times of the republick, the votes were given "viva voce;" but that mode being productive of much confusion, and having a tendency to subject the lower orders of citizens to the influence of their superiours, the more secret and independent method by ballot was introduced. It is to be remembered, that the citizens voted in their own right, and not by representation. To vote by ballot, in such a situation, was unquestionably a great improvement in a free system of government, such as that of Rome then was; and accordingly we find that Cicero[r] denominates the tablet, "the silent assertor of liberty."

In this solemn, deliberate, circumspect manner, what was called "lex," a law, in its strict and proper sense, was enacted. It was passed at the instance of a senatorial magistrate, by the whole aggregate body of the people (senators and patricians, as well as plebeians) in whom alone the majesty of the commonwealth resided.[s]

The general preamble to a capitulary of laws made in the reign of Edward the first, gives us an intimation of the course, which, in England, was observed, at that period, in passing laws. It mentions, that, "in the presence of certain reverend fathers, bishops of England, and others of the council of the realm of England, the underwritten constitutions were recited; and afterwards they were heard and published before the king and his council, who all agreed, as well the justices as others, that they should be put into writing for a perpetual memory, and that they should be stedfastly observed."[t]

In Great Britain, laws are now passed in the following manner. All bills, except those of grace, originate in one of the two houses; and all other bills, except those for raising a revenue, may originate in either house of parliament. A bill may be brought in upon motion made to the house; or the house may give directions to bring it in. It is read—suppose in the house of commons—a first, and, at a convenient distance, a second time. After each reading, the speaker opens the substance of it, and puts the question, whether farther proceedings shall be had upon it. When it has had the second reading, it is referred to a selected committee, or to a

r. De leg. agr. II. 2. De leg. III. 17

s. Bever. 71–77.

t. 4. Edw. 1. st. 3.

committee of the whole house. In these committees, paragraph after paragraph is debated, blanks are filled up, and alterations and amendments are made. After the committee have gone through it, they report it with these amendments: the house then consider it again, and the question is put upon every clause and amendment. When it is agreed to by the house, it is then ordered to be engrossed for a third reading. On being engrossed, it is read a third time; amendments are sometimes made to it; and a new clause, which, in this late stage of its progress, is called a rider, is sometimes added. The speaker, again, opens the contents of the bill; and, holding it up in his hand, puts the question—Shall this bill pass? If this is agreed to, the title is then settled; and one of the members is directed to carry it to the lords, and desire their concurrence.

In that house, it passes through the same numerous stages, as in the house of commons. If it is rejected, the rejection passes *sub silentio;*[12] and no communication takes place concerning it, between the two houses. On agreeing to it, the lords send a message, notifying their agreement; and the bill remains with them, if they have made no amendments. If they make amendments, they send them, with the bill, for the concurrence of the house of commons. If the two houses disagree with regard to the amendments; a conference usually takes place between members deputed by them, respectively, for this purpose. In this conference, the matters, concerning which the two houses differ in sentiment, are generally adjusted: but if each house continue inflexible, the bill is lost. If the commons agree to the amendments made by the lords to the bill, it is sent back to them with a message communicating their agreement.

Similar forms are observed, when a bill originates in the house of lords.[u]

We see, with what cautious steps, the business proceeds from its commencement to its conclusion. Each house acts repeatedly as a court of review upon itself: each house acts repeatedly as a court of review upon the other also. Could one believe it?—Notwithstanding all these proofs and instances of circumspection and care, which are constantly exhibited by the legislature of Great Britain, when it passes laws, precipitancy in passing them is frequently a well grounded cause of complaint. "Perhaps," says a sensible and humane writer upon the criminal jurisprudence of England,

12. Under silence; without any notice being taken.

u. 1. Bl. Com. 181–184.

"the great severity of our laws has been, in some degree, owing to their having been made *flagrante ira*,[13] on some sudden occasion, when a combination of atrocious circumstances, attending some particular offence, inflamed the lawgivers."[v]

In the house of representatives in congress, every bill must be introduced by motion for leave, or by an order of the house on the report of a committee: in either case, a committee to prepare the bill shall be appointed. When it is intended to introduce a bill of a general nature by motion for leave, one day's notice, at least, of the motion shall be given: every such motion may be committed.

Every bill must receive three several readings in the house, previous to its passage; and no bill shall be read twice on the same day, without a special order of the house.

The first reading of a bill shall be for information; and, if opposition be made to it, the question shall be, "Shall the bill be rejected?" If no opposition be made, or if the question to reject be determined in the negative, the bill shall go to its second reading without a question.

When a bill is read the second time, the speaker shall state it as ready for commitment or engrossment: if committed, a question shall be, whether to a select committee, or to a committee of the whole house. If the bill be ordered to be engrossed, a day shall be appointed, when it shall receive the third reading. After commitment and report of a bill, it may, notwithstanding, be recommitted, even at any time before its passage.

In forming a committee of the whole house, the speaker shall leave his chair; and a chairman to preside in the committee shall be appointed.

A bill, committed to a committee of the whole house, shall be first read throughout by the clerk, and shall be then read again and debated by clauses. The body of the bill shall not be defaced or interlined; but all amendments, as they shall be agreed to, shall be duly entered, by the clerk, on a separate paper, noting the page and line, to which they refer; and, in this manner, shall be reported to the house. After being reported, it shall again be subject to be debated and amended by clauses, before a question to engross it be taken.[w]

13. With anger.
v. 1. Dagge. 274.
w. Jour. Rep. 7th April, 1789.

In the senate of the United states, one day's notice, at least, shall be given of an intended motion for leave to bring in a bill.

Every bill shall receive three readings previous to its being passed: these readings shall be on three different days, unless the senate unanimously direct otherwise: and the president shall give notice at each reading, whether it be the first, or the second, or the third.

No bill shall be committed or amended until it shall have been read twice: it may then be referred to a committee.[x]

The senate never go into a committee of the whole house. A committee of the whole house is composed of every member; and to form it, the speaker leaves the chair, and may sit and debate as any other member of the house. The vice president of the United States is, *ex officio,* president of the senate; but he has no vote, unless they be equally divided.[y] That this high officer might not be placed in a situation in which he could neither preside nor vote, is, I presume, the reason, why the senate do not resolve themselves into a committee of the whole. It is a rule, however, in the senate, that all bills, on a second reading, shall, unless otherwise ordered, be considered in the same manner, as if the senate were in a committee of the whole, before they shall be taken up and proceeded on by the senate, agreeable to the standing rules.[z]

Such, so numerous, and so wise, are the precautions used by our national legislature, before a bill can pass through its two different branches. But all these precautions, wise and numerous as they are, are far from being the only ones directed by the wisdom and care of our national constitution.

After a bill has passed, in both houses, through all the processes, which we have minutely enumerated, still, before it becomes a law, it must be presented to the president of the United States for his scrutiny and revision. If he approve, he signs it; but if not, he returns it, with his objections, to the house, in which it has originated. That house enter the objections, at large, on their journal, and proceed to reconsider the bill. If, after such reconsideration, two thirds of the members agree to pass it, it is sent, with the objections, to the other house, by which also it is reconsidered; and if

x. Jour. Sen. 1789. p. 15.
y. Cons. U. S. art. 1. s. 3.
z. Jour. Sen. 1789. p. 39.

approved by two thirds of that house, it shall become a law. In all such cases, the votes of both houses shall be determined by yeas and nays; and the names of the persons voting for and against the bill shall be entered on the journal of each house respectively.[a]

I have already illustrated,[b] at large, the nature, the political advantages, and the probable consequences, of the qualified negative vested in the president of the United States. I now consider it merely as an excellent regulation, to secure an additional degree of accuracy and circumspection in the manner of passing the laws.

The observations, which I have made on this subject, have a relation to the constitution and legislature of this commonwealth, as close as to those of the national government. A negative, similar to that of the president of the United States, is lodged in the governour of Pennsylvania;[c] and the rules of proceeding, adopted by the two houses which compose the legislature of this state, are substantially the same with the rules framed by the two houses which compose the legislature of the Union. It is, therefore, unnecessary, and it would be tedious, to make, to the former, a formal application of what has been mentioned concerning the latter.

By both constitutions, and in both legislatures, provision has been made, as far as, by human contrivance, it would seem, provision can be made, in order to prevent or to check precipitancy and intemperance, in the exercise of the all-important power of legislation, And yet, after all, there is, perhaps, too much reason to apprehend that the *cacoethes legisferundi*[14] will be but too prevalent in both governments. This is an imperfection—in the present state of things, the very best institutions have their imperfections—this is an imperfection incident to governments, which are free. In such governments, the people, at once subjects and sovereigns, are too often tempted to alleviate or to alter the restraints, which they have imposed upon themselves.

We have already seen, that, in Athens, the number and intricacy of the laws were productive of great inconveniences, and were considered and felt

a. Cons. U. S. art. 1. s. 7.
b. Ante. vol. 1. p. 734.
c. Cons. Penn. art. 1. s. 22.
14. Malignant law.

as a grievance of the most uneasy and disagreeable kind. Livy, whose eloquence is marked as conspicuously by its justness as by its splendour, gives us a strong representation of the unwieldiness of Roman laws. He[d] describes them as "immensus aliarum super alias acervatarum legum cumulus"—an immense collection of piles of laws, heaped upon one another in endless confusion. The description of the energetick Tacitus is still more concise and expressive—"legibus laborabatur"[15]—the state staggered under the burthen of her laws.[e] As to Pennsylvania, I will, as it becomes me, simply state the fact. Within the last fifteen years, she has witnessed and she has sustained an accumulation of acts of legislation, in number eight hundred and seventy one.

Far be it from me to avail myself of the abuse, and to urge it against the enjoyment, of freedom. But while I prize the inestimable blessing highly as I do, I surely ought, in every character which I bear, to suggest, to recommend, and to perform every thing in my power, in order to guard its enjoyment from its abuse.

VI. I come now to the last head, under which I proposed to treat concerning the legislative department: this was, to consider the powers vested in congress by the constitution of the United States.

On this subject, we discover a striking difference between the constitution of the United States and that of Pennsylvania. By the latter,[f] each house of the general assembly is vested with every power necessary for a branch of the legislature of a free state. In the former, no clause of such an extensive and unqualified import is to be found. The reason is plain. The latter institutes a legislature with general, the former, with enumerated, powers. Those enumerated powers are now the subject of our consideration.

One great end[g] of the national government is to "provide for the common defence." Defence presupposes an attack. We all know the instruments by which an attack is made by one nation upon another. We all, likewise, know the instruments necessary for defence when such an attack is made. That nation, which would protect herself from hostilities, or

d. L. 3. c. 34.
15. Labored law.
e. Tac. Ann. l. 3.
f. Art. 1. s. 13.
g. Cons. U. S. Pream.

maintain peace, must have it in her power—such is the present situation of things—to declare war. The power of declaring war, and the other powers naturally connected with it, are vested in congress. To provide and maintain a navy—to make rules for its government—to grant letters of marque and reprisal—to make rules concerning captures—to raise and support armies—to establish rules for their regulation—to provide for organizing, arming, and disciplining the militia, and for calling them forth in the service of the Union—all these are powers naturally connected with the power of declaring war. All these powers, therefore, are vested in congress.[h]

As the law is now received in England, the king has the sole prerogative of making war.[i] On this very interesting power, the constitution of the United States renews the principles of government, known in England before the conquest. This indeed, as we are told by a well informed writer,[j] may be accounted the chief difference between the Anglo-Saxon and the Anglo-Norman government. In the former, the power of making peace and war was invariably possessed by the wittenagemote; and was regarded as inseparable from the allodial condition of its members. In the latter, it was transferred to the sovereign: and this branch of the feudal system, which was accommodated, perhaps, to the depredations and internal commotions prevalent in that rude period, has remained in subsequent ages, when, from a total change of manners, the circumstances, by which it was recommended, have no longer any existence.

There is a pleasure in reflecting on such important renovations of the ancient constitution of England. We have found, and we shall find, that our national government is recommended by the antiquity, as well as by the excellence, of some of its leading principles.

Another great end of the national government is, "to ensure domestick tranquillity." That it may be enabled to accomplish this end, congress may call forth the militia to suppress insurrections.

Again; the national government is instituted to "establish justice." For this purpose, congress is authorized to erect tribunals inferiour to the supreme court; and to define and punish offences against the law of nations,

h. Cons. U. S. Art. 1. s. 8.
i. 1. Bl. Com. 257.
j. Millar. 30.

and piracies and felonies committed on the high seas. These points will be more fully considered under the judicial department.

It is an object of the national government to "form a more perfect union." On this principle, congress is empowered to regulate commerce among the several states, to establish post offices, to fix the standard of weights and measures, to coin and regulate the value of money, and to establish, throughout the United States, a uniform rule of naturalization.

Once more, at this time: the national government was intended to "promote the general welfare." For this reason, congress have power to regulate commerce with the Indians and with foreign nations, and to promote the progress of science and of useful arts, by securing, for a time, to authors and inventors, an exclusive right to their compositions and discoveries.

An exclusive property in places fit for forts, magazines, arsenals, dock yards and other needful buildings; and an exclusive legislation over these places, and also, for a convenient distance, over such district as may become the seat of the national government—such exclusive property, and such exclusive legislation, will be of great publick utility, perhaps, of evident publick necessity. They are, therefore, vested in congress, by the constitution of the United States.

For the exercise of the foregoing powers, and for the accomplishment of the foregoing purposes, a revenue is unquestionably indispensable. That congress may be enabled to exercise and accomplish them, it has power to lay and collect taxes, duties, imposts, and excises.

The powers of congress are, indeed, enumerated; but it was intended that those powers, thus enumerated, should be effectual, and not nugatory. In conformity to this consistent mode of thinking and acting, congress has power to make all laws, which shall be necessary and proper for carrying into execution every power vested by the constitution in the government of the United States, or in any of its officers or departments.

And thus much concerning the first great division of the national government—its legislative authority. I proceed to its second grand division—its executive authority.

CHAPTER II.
Of the Executive Department.

In a former part of my lectures,[a] it was shown, that the powers of government, whether legislative or executive, ought to be restrained. But there is, it was observed, a remarkable contrast between the proper modes of restraining them; for that the legislature, in order to be restrained, must be divided; whereas the executive power, in order to be restrained, should be one. The reasons of this remarkable contrast were, on that occasion, traced particularly, and investigated fully.

We have seen, in our remarks on the congress of the United States, that it consists of two branches—that it is formed on the principle of a divided legislature. We now see, that, in the executive department, the principle of unity is adopted. "The executive power shall be vested in a president of the United States of America."[b]

In treating of the executive department of the United States, I shall consider, 1. The title of the president. 2. His powers and duties.

1. I am to consider the title of the president of the United States. His title is by election.

The general preference which has been given, by statesmen and writers on government, to a hereditary before an elective title to the first magistracy in a state, was the subject of full discussion in a former lecture.[c] I then, I hope, showed, that this preference, however general, and however favoured, is, in truth and upon the genuine principles of government, ill founded. My remarks on this subject I will not, at this time, repeat.

It will probably occasion surprise, when I state the elective title of our

a. Ante. vol. 1. p. 700. 701.
b. Cons. U. S. art. 2. s. 1.
c. Ante vol. 1. p. 728.

first executive magistrate as a renewal, in this particular, of the ancient English constitution. Without hesitation, however, I state this elective title as such.

Well aware I am, that, with regard to this point, I differ in my opinion from the Author of the Commentaries on the laws of England. He thinks it clearly appears, from the highest authority England is acquainted with, that its crown has ever been a hereditary crown.[d] The best historical evidence, however, speaks, I apprehend, a language very different from that, which Sir William Blackstone considers as the highest authority.

A king among the old Saxons, says Selden, was, in probability, a commander in the field, an officer *pro tempore.* His title rested upon the good opinion of the freemen; and it seemeth to be one of the best gems of his crown, for that he was thereby declared to be most worthy of the love and service of the people.[e]

The sheriff, says he, in another place, was chosen by the votes of the freeholders, and, as the king himself, was entitled to his honour by the people's favour.[f] The magistrates, he tells us, in the same spirit, were all choice men; and the king the choicest of the chosen; election being the birth of esteem, and this of merit.[g]

The dignity and office of the king, says Mr. Millar, though higher in degree, was perfectly similar to those of the tithing man, the hundreder, and the earl; and he possessed nearly the same powers over the whole kingdom, which those inferiour officers enjoyed in their particular districts.[h]

King Offa,[1] in an address to his people, speaks of his elective title, and of the great purpose for which he was elected, in the following very remarkable and unequivocal terms—[i] "electus ad libertatis tuae tuitionem, non meis meritis, sed sola liberalitate vestra."

d. 1. Bl. Com. 210.
e. Bac. on Gov. 29. 30.
f. Id. 41.
g. Id. 70.
h. Millar. 153.
1. King Offa (?– 796) was the Mercian king from 757 until his death. "I have been elected to safeguard your liberty not through any merits of my own, but solely through your liberality."
i. Sulliv. 244. (4to.)

It appears from history, says a very accurate inquirer,[j] that all the kings of the Saxon race were elected to their kingly office.

Even the mighty Conqueror, says the learned Selden,[k] stooping under the law of a Saxon king, became a king by leave; wisely foreseeing, that a title gotten by election is more certain than that which is gotten by power. Henry the third brought in with him the first precedent in point, of succession by inheritance in the throne of England.

Sir William Blackstone himself, in one place in his Commentaries, speaking of the Saxon laws, mentions, among others, the election of their magistrates by the people, originally even that of their kings. He adds, indeed, that dear bought experience afterwards evinced the convenieuce and necessity of establishing a hereditary succession to the crown.[l]

If an elective title is a distemper in the body politick; the history and experience of England would lead us to conclude, that a hereditary title is a remedy still worse than the disease. Henry the third is stated as the first fair instance of a prince ascending the throne by virtue of a hereditary claim. How soon was this claim transmitted, in crimson characters, to his posterity, by the fatal and factious war of the *roses* concerning the right of succession! How long and how destructively did that war rage! How pernicious were its consequences, for ages after its immediate operations had ceased! How few and how short have been the lucid intervals, during which the madness of a contested claim to the succession or to the enjoyment of the English or the British crown has not disturbed the peace and serenity of the nation!

The intrigues, and cabals, and tumults, and convulsions, which are assumed as necessarily annexed to the election of a first magistrate, are perpetually urged against this mode of establishing a title to the office. It is well worth our while to mark the sedulous attention, with which intrigues, and cabals, and tumults, and convulsions, in the election of our first magistrate, are avoided, nay, we trust, rendered impracticable, by the wise provisions introduced into our national constitution.

j. Id. 245.
k. Bac. on Gov. 72.
l. 4. Bl. Com. 406.

To avoid tumults and convulsions, the president of the United States is chosen by electors, equal, in number, to the whole number of senators and representatives, to which all the states are entitled in congress. These, as we shall find by referring to one part of the constitution, cannot much exceed the number of one for every thirty thousand citizens. These, as we shall find by referring to another part of the constitution, are only equal to the number, which compose the two deliberative bodies of the national legislature. If they are not too numerous to transact, with decency and with tranquillity, the legislative business of the Union, in two places; surely they are not too numerous to perform, with decency and with tranquillity, a single act; in as many places as there are states: for, in their respective states, the electors are obliged to meet.

In the appointment of the electors, there is not reason for the least apprehension of convulsions and tumults. They are to be appointed by each state; and they are to be appointed in such a manner as the legislature of each state shall direct. They will, in all probability, be appointed in one of the two following modes—by the citizens—or by the legislature. If the former; the business will be managed in the same manner as the election of representatives in each state. If the latter; it will be managed by those to whom the different states have intrusted their legislative authority—that kind of authority, the exercise of which requires the greatest degree of coolness and caution. Of either mode, can tumults and convulsions be the apprehended result?

To intrigue and cabal, the election of the president is rendered equally inaccessible, as to convulsions and tumults. Those, who appoint the electors, have a deep interest, or represent such as have a deep interest, in the consequences of the election. This interest will be best promoted by far other arts than those of cabal and intrigue. Such electors, we may, therefore, presume, will be appointed, as will favour and practise those other arts. Some reliance, consequently, may be placed on the characters of the electors.

But this is, by no means, the only circumstance, on which the expectations of the United States rest for candour and impartiality in the election of a president. Other circumstances ensure them. 1. The electors must vote by ballot. Ballot has been called the silent assertor of liberty: with equal justness, it may be called the silent assertor of honesty. 2. The electors must give their votes on the same day throughout the United States. How can cabal and intrigue extend or combine their influence at the same time, in many different places, separated from one another by the distance of hundreds or thousands of miles? 3. Each elector must vote for two persons, without distinguishing which of the two he wishes to be the president. The precise operation of his vote is not known to himself at the time when he gives it. By this regulation, simple but sagacious, cabal and intrigue, could they even be admitted, would be under the necessity of acting blindfold at the election. The sinister plans, formed separately in every part, might and often would be defeated by the joint and unforeseen effect of the whole. For it is the unforeseen effect of the whole, which must finally determine, or furnish materials for finally determining, the election of the president.

His election shall be finally determined in this manner. The person, in whose favour the greatest number of votes is given, provided that number shall be a majority of the whole number of electors, shall be the president. If more than one person have a majority, and, at the same time, an equal number of votes; the house of representatives shall immediately choose one of them for president, by ballot. If no person have a majority of votes of the electors; the house of representatives shall choose, by ballot, a president from the five highest on the list.

After the choice of the president, the person having the greatest number of votes of the electors shall be the vice president. But if there remain two or more having equal votes; the senate shall choose from them the vice president by[m] ballot.[n]

m. Cons. U. S. art. 2. s. 1.

n. By an alteration of the constitution recommended by congress in December, 1803, and which, having received the approbation of three fourths of the states in the Union, has now become a part of the constitution, the regulations mentioned in the text have been changed in the following particulars. The electors are directed to name, in their ballots, the person voted for as president, and, in distinct ballots, the person voted for as vice president, and to transmit to the seat of government distinct lists of the persons so voted for. The person having the greatest number of votes for president, shall be the president, if such number be a majority of the whole number of electors appointed; and if no person have such majority, then from the persons having the highest numbers, not exceeding three on the list of those voted for as president, the house of representatives shall choose immediately, by ballot, the president. If the house do not make a choice before the fourth day of March then next following, the vice president shall act as president, as in case of the death or constitutional disability of the president. The person, having the greatest number of votes as vice president, shall be the vice president, if such number be a

Thus much concerning the title of the president of the United States.

2. I am, in the next place, to consider his powers and duties.[o]

He is to take care that the laws be faithfully executed; he is commander in chief of the army and navy of the United States, and of the militia, when called into their actual service. In the Saxon government, the power of the first executive magistrate was also twofold. He had authority to lead the army, as we are informed by Selden, to punish according to demerits and according to laws, and reward according to discretion. The law martial and that of the sea were branches of the positive law, settled by the general vote in the wittenagemote, and not left to the will of a lawless general or commander: so tender and uniform were those times both in their laws and liberties.[p] The person at the head of the executive department had authority, not to make, or alter, or dispense with the laws, but to execute and act the laws, which were established: and against this power there was no rising up, so long as it gadded not, like an unfeathered arrow, at random. On the whole, he was no other than a *primum mobile*,[2] set in a regular motion by laws, which were established by the whole body of the nation.[q]

The president has power to nominate, and, with the advice and consent of the senate, to appoint ambassadours, judges of the supreme court, and, in general, all the other officers of the United States. On this subject, there is a very striking and important difference between the constitution of the United States and that of Pennsylvania. By the latter, the first executive magistrate possesses, uncontrolled by either branch of the legislature, the power of appointing all officers, whose appointments are not, in the constitution itself, otherwise provided for.[r] On a former occasion[s] I noticed a maxim, which is of much consequence in the science of government—that

majority of the whole number of electors appointed; and if no person have a majority, then from the two highest numbers on the list, the senate shall choose the vice president. A quorum for the purpose shall consist of two thirds of the whole number of senators, and a majority of the whole number shall be necessary to a choice. No person constitutionally ineligible to the office of president, shall be eligible to that of vice president of the United States—*Ed.*

o. Cons. U. S. Art. 2. s. 2, 3.

p. Bac. on Gov. 40.

2. First moving thing.

q. Id. 32, 33.

r. Cons. Penn. art. 2. s. 8.

s. Ante. vol. 1. p. 701, 705.

the legislative and executive powers be preserved distinct and unmingled in their exercise. This maxim I then considered in a variety of views: and, in each, found it to be both true and useful. I am very free to confess, that, with regard to this point, the proper principle of government is, in my opinion, observed by the constitution of Pennsylvania much more correctly, than it is by the constitution of the United States. In justice, however, to the latter, it ought to be remarked, that, though the *appointment* of officers is to be the concurrent act of the president and senate, yet an indispensable prerequisite—the *nomination* of them—is vested exclusively in the president.

The observations which I have delivered concerning the appointment of officers, apply likewise to treaties; the making of which is another power, that the president has, with the advice and consent of the senate.

The president has power to fill up all vacancies that may happen, in offices, during the recess of the senate, by granting commissions, which shall expire at the end of their next session.

He has no stated counsellors appointed for him by the constitution. Their inutility, and the dangers arising from them, were before[t] fully shown. He may, however, when he thinks proper, require the opinion, in writing, of the principal officer in each of the executive departments, upon any subject relating to the duties of their offices.

On extraordinary occasions, he may convene both houses of the legislature, or either of them: and, in case of disagreement between them, with respect to the time of adjournment, he may adjourn them to such time as he shall think proper.

It is his duty, from time to time, to lay before congress information of the state of the Union; and to recommend to their consideration such measures, as he shall judge necessary and expedient.

He has power to grant reprieves and pardons for offences against the United States, except in cases of impeachment.

To prevent crimes, is the noblest end and aim of criminal jurisprudence. To punish them, is one of the means necessary for the accomplishment of this noble end and aim.

t. Ante. vol. I. p. 729.

The certainty of punishments is of the greatest importance, in order to constitute them fit preventives of crimes. This certainty is best obtained by accuracy in the publick police, by vigilance and activity in the executive officers of justice, by a prompt and certain communication of intelligence, by a proper distribution of rewards for the discovery and apprehension of criminals, and, when they are apprehended, by an undeviating and inflexible strictness in carrying the laws against them into sure and full execution.

All this will be readily allowed. What should we then think of a power, given by the constitution or the laws, to dispense with accuracy in the publick police, and with vigilance, vigour, and activity in the search and seizure of offenders? Such a power, it must be admitted, would seem somewhat extraordinary.

What, it will next be asked, should we think of a power, given by the constitution or the laws, to dispense with their execution upon criminals, after they have been apprehended, tried, convicted, and condemned? In other words—can the power to pardon be admissible into any well regulated government? Shall a power be given to insult the laws, to protect crimes, to indemnify, and, by indemnifying, to encourage criminals?

From this, or from a similar view of things, many writers, and some of them very respectable as well as humane, have been induced to conclude, that, in a government of laws, the power of pardoning should be altogether unknown.

Would you prevent crimes? says the Marquis of Beccaria: let the laws be clear and simple: let the entire force of the nation be united in their defence: let them, and them only, be feared. The fear of the laws is salutary: but the fear of man is a fruitful and a fatal source of crimes. Happy the nation, in which pardons will be considered as dangerous! Clemency is a virtue which belongs to the legislator, and not to the executor of the laws; a virtue, which should shine in the code, and not in private judgment. The prince, in pardoning, gives up the publick security in favour of an individual: and, by his ill judged benevolence, proclaims an act of impunity.[u]

With regard, says Rousseau, to the prerogative of granting pardon to

u. Bec. c. 41. 46.

criminals, condemned by the laws of their country, and sentenced by the judges, it belongs only to that power, which is superiour both to the judges and the laws—the sovereign authority. Not that it is very clear, that even the supreme power is vested with such a right, or that the circumstances, in which it might be exerted, are frequent or determinate. In a well governed state, there are but few executions; not because many are pardoned, but because there are few criminals. Under the Roman republick, neither the senate nor the consuls ever attempted to grant pardons: even the people never did this, although they sometimes recalled their own sentence.[v]

In Persia, when the king has condemned a person, it is no longer lawful to mention his name, or to intercede in his favour. Though his majesty were drunk and beside himself; yet the decree must be exectued; otherwise he would contradict himself; and the law admits of no contradiction.[w]

"Extremes, in nature, equal ends produce;" so in politicks, as it would seem.

The more general opinion, however, is, that in a state, there ought to be a power of pardoning offences. The exclusion of pardons, says Sir William Blackstone, must necessarily introduce a very dangerous power in the judge or jury, that of construing the criminal law by the spirit instead of the letter; or else it must be holden, what no man will seriously avow, that the situation and circumstances of the offender (though they alter not the essence of the crime) ought to make no distinction in the punishment.[x]

I cannot, upon this occasion, enter into the discussion of the great point suggested and decided, in a very few words, by the learned Author of the Commentaries—that judges and juries have no power of construing the criminal law by the spirit instead of the letter. But I cannot, upon any occasion, suffer it to pass under my notice, without entering my caveat against implicit submission to this decision. I well know the humane rule, that, in the construction of a penal law, neither judge nor jury can extend it to facts equally criminal to those specified in the letter, if they are not contained in the letter. But I profess myself totally ignorant of any rule—I think it would be an inhuman one—that the letter of a penal law may be carried

v. Rous. Or. Com. 54. l. 2. c. 5.
w. Mont. Sp. L. b. 3. c. 10.
x. 4. Bl. Com. 390.

beyond the spirit of it; and it may certainly be carried by the letter beyond the spirit, if judges and juries are prohibited, in construing it, from considering the spirit as well as the letter. But to return to our present subject.

The most general opinion, as we have already observed, and, we may add, the best opinion, is, that, in every state, there ought to be a power to pardon offences. In the mildest systems, of which human societies are capable, there will still exist a necessity of this discretionary power, the proper exercise of which may arise from the possible circumstances of every conviction. Citizens, even condemned citizens, may be unfortunate in a higher degree, than that, in which they are criminal. When the cry of the nation rises in their favour; when the judges themselves, descending from their seats, and laying aside the formidable sword of justice, come to supplicate in behalf of the person, whom they have been obliged to condemn; in such a situation clemency is a virtue; it becomes a duty.

But where ought this most amiable prerogative to be placed? Is it compatible with the nature of every species of government? With regard to both these questions, different opinions are entertained.

With regard to the last, the learned Author of the Commentaries on the laws of England declares his unqualified sentiment—"In democracies, this power of pardon can never subsist; for there nothing higher is acknowledged than the magistrate, who administers the laws: and it would be impolitick for the power of judging and of pardoning to centre in one and the same person. This would oblige him (as the President Montesquieu observes) very often to contradict himself, to make and unmake his decisions: it would tend to confound all ideas of right among the mass of the people; as they would find it difficult to tell, whether a prisoner were discharged by his innocence, or obtained a pardon through favour. In Holland, therefore, if there be no stadtholder, there is no power of pardoning lodged in any other member of the state.

"But in monarchies, the king acts in a superiour sphere; and though he regulates the whole government as the first mover, yet he does not appear in any of the disagreeable or invidious parts of it. Whenever the nation see him personally engaged, it is only in works of legislature, magnificence, or compassion."[y]

y. 4. Bl. Com. 390. 391.

Let us observe, by the way, the mighty difference between the person described by Selden, as the first magistrate among the Saxons, and him described by Sir William Blackstone, as the monarch of England since that period. The former was set in regular motion by the laws: the latter is the first mover, who regulates the whole government.

Let me also repeat here, what has been mentioned in another place. One of the most enlightened writers on English jurisprudence imagines, that the power of pardoning is a power incommunicable to the democratical species of government. For the western world new and rich discoveries in jurisprudence have been reserved. We have found, that this species of government—the best and the purest of all—that, in which the supreme power remains with the people—is capable of being formed, arranged, proportioned, and organized in such a manner, as to exclude the inconveniences, and to secure the advantages of all the others.

Why, according to Sir William Blackstone, can the power to pardon never subsist in a democracy? Because, says he, there, nothing higher is acknowledged, than the magistrate, who administers the laws. By pursuing the principle of democracy to its true source, we have discovered, that the law is higher than the magistrate, who administers it; that the constitution is higher than both; and that the supreme power, remaining with the people, is higher than all the three. With perfect consistency, therefore, the power of pardoning may subsist in our democratical governments: with perfect propriety, we think, it is vested in the president of the United States.

The constitution, too, of Pennsylvania, animated by the wise and powerful recommendation, conveyed, by innumerable channels, to the convention, which proposed and framed it, "that they should imitate, as far as it applies, the excellent model exhibited in the constitution of the United States"—the constitution of Pennsylvania[z] vests the power of pardoning in the governour of the commonwealth.

It is by no means, however, a unanimous sentiment, if we collect the publick sentiment from the constitutions of the different states of the Union, that the power of pardoning criminals should be vested *solely* in the supreme executive authority of the state.

z. Art. 2. s. 9.

By the constitution of New York,[a] the governour, in cases of treason or murder, can only suspend the execution of the sentence, until it shall be reported to the legislature, at their subsequent meeting; and they shall either pardon, or direct the execution of the criminal, or grant a further reprieve.

In the state of Delaware the governour possesses the power of granting pardons, except where the law shall otherwise direct.[b] A similar legislative control is imposed on the governours of Maryland, Virginia, and North Carolina, by the constitutions[c] of those states.[d]

In the states of New Hampshire, Massachussetts and South Carolina, pardons can be granted only after a conviction.[e]

The president and vice president hold their offices during the term of four years.

The president shall, at stated times, receive, for his services, a compensation, which shall neither be increased nor diminished during the period, for which he is elected; and he shall not receive, within that period, any other emolument from the United States, or any of them.

I here finish what I propose to say concerning the second great division of the national government—its executive authority.

a. S. 18.

b. Cons. Del. s. 7.

c. Cons. Mar. s. 33. Cons. Vir. p. 127. Cons. N. C. s. 19.

d. By the present constitution of Delaware, this legislative control over the power of the governour to grant pardons is destroyed—Art. 3. s. 9. In Vermont, the power of the executive to grant pardons is restrained in cases of treason and murder; in which they have power "to grant reprieves, but not to pardon, until after the end of the next session of assembly." Cons. c. 2. s. 11. By the constitution of Kentucky, the power of pardoning is, in cases of treason, vested in the general assembly, but the governour may grant reprieves until the end of their next session. Art. 3. s. 11. In Tennessee and Ohio, pardons can be granted only after conviction. Cons. Ten. art. 2. s. 6. Cons. Ohio, art. 2. s. 5. In Georgia likewise, according to her present constitution, the governour can grant pardons only after conviction; and in cases of treason and murder, he can only respite the execution, and make report thereof to the next general assembly, by whom a pardon may be granted. Cons. Geor. art. 2. s. 7. *Ed.*

e. Cons. N. H. p. 18. 19. Cons. Mas. c. 2. s. 1. a. 8. Cons. S. C. art. 2. s. 7.

CHAPTER III.
Of the Judicial Department.

The judicial power of the United States is vested in one supreme court, and in such inferiour courts as are established by congress.[a]

A court, according to my Lord Coke,[b] is a place where justice is judicially administered.

To Egypt, where much wisdom, we are assured, was to be learned, we trace the first institution of courts of justice. Concerning its administration, the Egyptians were remarkably vigilant and exact; for they believed, that on it depended entirely the support or the dissolution of society. Their highest tribunal was composed of thirty judges.[c] At the head of it was placed the person, who, at once, possessed the greatest share of wisdom, of probity, and of the publick esteem.

The trials, it is said, were carried on in writing; and, to avoid unnecessary delay, the parties were allowed to make only one reply on each side. When the evidence was closed, the judges consulted together concerning the merits of the cause. When they were fully understood and considered, the president gave the signal for proceeding to a judgment, by taking in his hand a small image, adorned with precious stones. When the sentence was pronounced, the president touched, with the image, the party, who had gained his cause. The image was without eyes; and was the symbol, by which the Egyptians were accustomed to represent Truth. It is probably from this circumstance, that Justice has been painted blind.

The judges of this court received from government what was necessary for their support; so that the people paid them nothing for obtaining justice.

a. Cons. U. S. art. 3. s. 1.
b. 1. Ins. 58.
c. 1. Gog. Or. L. 55.

We are told, that no advocates were admitted in this tribunal; but that the parties themselves drew up their own processes. This, however, must probably be understood with some limitation; for we cannot reasonably imagine, that all the inhabitants of Egypt were not only taught to write, but were also possessed of a degree of legal skill, sufficient to qualify them for composing their own defences. It is not unlikely, that the regulation went no farther than one, which we have seen adopted in another state—Every one has a right to be heard by himself and his counsel.

On the model of this high tribunal of Egypt, was formed the celebrated court of the Areopagus at Athens.[1] This court was instituted, one thousand and five hundred years before the Christian era, by Cecrops,[2] who was originally of Sais, a city of the lower Egypt, and to whom Athens, the seat of literature and politeness, of eloquence and patriotism, owed its foundation and first establishments.

This excellent man relinquished the fertile banks of the Nile, in order to avoid the tyranny, under which his native country, at that time, groaned. After a tedious voyage, he reached the shores of Attica: and was received in the most friendly manner by its inhabitants. Placed, after some time, at the head of their affairs, he conceived the noble design of bestowing happiness on his adopted country. For this purpose, he introduced among his new compatriots many valuable and memorable institutions, of which, indeed, he was not strictly the author—if he had, he would have been the first of legislators and the greatest of mortals—but which he brought, probably with his own judicious improvements, from a nation, who had been attentive to carry them to perfection during a long series of ages. Some of his institutions—in all of them wisdom and humanity shone conspicuous—will claim our future attention. At present, it is directed to the court of the Areopagus.

Aristides—well qualified to decide upon this subject; for he was distinguished by the appellation of the just—informs us, that this court was the most sacred and venerable tribunal in all Greece. From its first establishment, it never pronounced a sentence, which gave reasonable cause of complaint. Strangers, even sovereigns, solicited and submitted to its decisions;

1. The Areopagus was the chief homicide court of ancient Athens.
2. Cecrops I was the mythical Greek king who founded Athens.

which contributed, more than any thing else, to disseminate the principles of justice first among the Grecians.[d]

The proceedings in this tribunal were, in some instances, very solemn and striking. In a prosecution for murder, the prosecutor was obliged to swear, that he was related to the person deceased—for none but near relations could prosecute—and that the prisoner was the cause of his death. The prisoner swore, that he was innocent of the crime, of which he was accused. Each confirmed his oath with the most direful imprecations; wishing that, if he swore falsely, himself, his family, and his houses might be utterly destroyed and extirpated by the divine vengeance.[e]

In early times, it is said, the parties were obliged to plead their causes themselves. But this severity was afterwards relaxed. Those, who were accused, might avail themselves of the assistance of counsel. The counsel, however, were never permitted, in pleading, to wander from the merits of the cause. This close and pertinent manner of speaking gave the tone to the bar of Athens, and extended itself to the speeches, which were delivered in other assemblies.[f] In this manner, we may naturally account for the condensed vehemence so remarkable in the orations of Demosthenes.

Let me conclude this account of the Areopagus by mentioning an incident, seemingly of slight importance, but which will not be related without producing, in my hearers, feelings in proper unison with those, which the incident occasioned. A little bird, pursued by its enemy, took refuge in the bosom of one of the judges. Instead of protecting, he stifled it. For this instance of cruelty he received punishment; and was thus taught that he, whose heart is callous to compassion, should not be suffered to have the lives of the citizens at his mercy.

You will not, after this, be surprised, when you are told, that the decisions of the Areopagus were deemed the standards of humanity, as well as of wisdom.[g]

In order to understand, fully and in their true spirit, the juridical institutions of the United States and of Pennsylvania, it will be of the greatest use to take a minute and historical view of the judicial establishments of

d. 2. Gog. Or. L. 16. 21. 1. Anac. 11.
e. 1. Pot. Ant. 106.
f. 2. Gog. Or. L. 23.
g. 2. Anac. 290.

England; especially those which were formed under the government of the Saxons.

Civil governments, in their first institutions, are nothing more than voluntary associations for the purposes of society. When the Saxons first settled in Britain, they found themselves obliged, by the disorders of the times, to associate, in their different settlements, for their mutual security and protection. Families, connected by consanguinity or other ties, found it agreeable, as well as necessary, to live together in the same neighbourhood, in order to enjoy the social pleasures of peace, as well as to give and receive assistance in the time of war. These societies were known by the appellation of vills or towns.[h] On some occasions, an association of the same kind was necessary, and it was therefore gradually introduced, between the inhabitants of a larger district. Those larger districts were distinguished by the name of hundreds.[i] The connexions and the exigencies of society becoming, on great emergencies, still more important and extensive, the members of different hundreds also associated together, and formed districts larger still, which were denominated shires. The officer who presided over them was called alderman or earl. Hundreders and tythingmen, as their names import, presided over the lesser associations.[j]

This establishment of tythings, and hundreds, and shires, though, at first, intended chiefly for the mutual defence of the inhabitants, was soon rendered subservient to other purposes, salutary and important.[k] The same motives which induced them to associate for their security against foreign danger, induced them also to take measures for preventing or composing internal differences or animosities. In this manner, a judicial authority was gradually assumed by every tything over the members, of which it was formed. In the same manner and upon the same principles, the hundred exercised the power of determining the controversies, which arose within the bounds of its larger district. In the same manner and upon the same principles still, the shire established a similar jurisdiction over the different hundreds comprehended within its still more extensive territory.[l]

h. Millar. 113.
i. Millar. 117.
j. Id. 117. 114.
k. Id. 121.
l. Id. 122.

These courts took cognizance of every cause, civil and criminal; and as, in the first instance, they enjoyed respectively the sole jurisdiction within the boundaries of each, they soon and naturally became subordinate, one to another: from the sentence of the tything, an appeal lay to the hundred, and from the sentence of the hundred, an appeal lay to the shire.

It deserves also to be known—for it is important to know—that, besides the defence of the country and the decision of law suits, the Saxon tythings, hundreds, and shires were accustomed to deliberate upon matters of still greater consequence. They received complaints concerning the grievances or abuses in administration, which happened within their respective districts, and applied a remedy by introducing new regulations. Thus the heads of families in every tything exercised a legislative power, within their own limits: but were liable to be controlled by the meetings of the hundred, which enjoyed the same power in a larger district: both of these were subordinate to the assemblies of the shire, which possessed a legislative authority over all the hundreds in that extensive division.[m] Unto the county court, says Selden,[n] all the freemen of the county assembled, to learn the law, to administer justice, and to provide remedy for publick inconvenience.[o]

As the freemen of a tything, of a hundred, and of a shire determined the common affairs of their several districts: so the union of people belonging to different shires produced a greater assembly, consisting of all the freemen of a kingdom. This national council was called the wittenagemote. The king presided. During the heptarchy, each of the Saxon kingdoms had a wittenagemote of its own: but when they were all reduced into one, a greater wittenagemote was formed, whose authority extended over the whole English nation.[p] Those who could not attend the wittenagemote in

m. Millar. 130.

n. Bac. on Gov. 42.

o. A striking analogy will sometimes be found where it is least to be expected. The empire of Peru was divided into small districts, each consisting of ten families: five of these constituted a higher class: two of these composed a third class, called a hundred; ten hundreds formed the great class of a thousand. Over each of these a superintending officer was appointed to administer justice, and to provide, that those committed to his care should be furnished with the means of industry and the necessaries of life.

Between two governments, so remote from each other in time and place, this analogy could not have been the effect of imitation: it must have been the native result of similar states and circumstances of society. Bever. 7, 8.

p. Millar. 132.

person, had always the right of appointing a procurator to represent them in their absence.[q]

The wittenagemote exercised powers of a judiciary, as well as of a legislative kind. They heard complaints concerning great quarrels and enormities, which could not be adjusted or redressed by the ordinary courts; and they endeavoured, by their superiour authority, either to reconcile the parties, or to decide their controversies. By frequent interpositions of this nature, the great council was formed into a regular court of justice, and became the supreme tribunal of the kingdom. In this tribunal, appeals from the courts of every shire, as well as original suits between the inhabitants of different shires, were finally determined.[r]

The original meetings of the wittenagemote were held regularly at two seasons of the year: but the increase of business, especially of that which regarded the administration of justice, rendered it afterwards necessary that its meetings should be more frequent. Occasional meetings were, therefore, convened by the king. At those occasional meetings, the nobility, who resided at a distance, seldom gave themselves the trouble of appearing. Of consequence, the business devolved on those members who happened to be at court, or who might be said to compose the privy council of the king. For this reason, they seldom undertook matters of general legislation; but confined themselves chiefly to the hearing of appeals. These smaller and occasional meetings of the wittenagemote seem to have suggested the idea of the aula regis.[s]

After the conquest, appeals to parliament multiplied: the members of that assembly became daily less disposed to execute this part of their duty: a regular tribunal was, therefore, formed, in order to discharge it. Of this tribunal, the great officers of the crown became the constituent members. To these were added such as, from their knowledge of the law, were thought qualified to give the best assistance.[t] This court received, from the place in which it was commonly held, the appellation of the *aula regis*.[3] In

q. Id. 143, 144.
r. Id. 150.
s. Millar. 242. 243.
t. Id. 316.
3. King's hall or palace.

its constitution, it corresponded exactly with the *cour de roy*,[4] which, after the accession of Hugh Capet,[5] was gradually formed out of the ancient parliament of France; and with the aulick council,[6] which, after the time of Otho the Great,[7] arose, in the same manner, out of the diet of the German empire.[u]

For some time after its first formation, the king, whenever he thought proper to sit as a judge, presided in the aula regis: but he, at length, ceased to discharge the ordinary functions of a judge; and the grand justiciary became, in a manner, the sole magistrate of the court.[v]

The institution of this court was a great improvement in the system of judicial policy. It was always in readiness to determine every controversy, criminal and civil. The reparation of injuries was secured; the expenses of litigation were diminished; and justice pervaded the remotest parts of the kingdom. It had the power of reviewing the sentences of inferiour jurisdictions; and, by that means, produced a consistency and even a uniformity of decision, in the judiciary system of the nation.[w]

From circumstances, however, which were the natural consequences of the introduction and progress of the feudal system in England, this court began and continued to make ambitious and unnecessary encroachments on the inferiour jurisdictions. Soon after the conquest, too, a complete separation of the ecclesiastical from the temporal courts took place. The bishop no longer sat as a judge in the court of the county; nor the archdeacon in that of the hundred. From the moment of this separation, the clergy were zealous, and they were successful, in extending their own jurisdiction, and invading that of the subordinate temporal tribunals.[x] By the gradual and strong operation of these causes and circumstances, the county courts, in particular, dwindled into a state of insignificance; their power was, at length, exercised only on matters of an inconsiderable value;

4. The royal court of France.
5. Hugh Capet (938–996) was the King of France from 987 to 996.
6. The Aulic Council was one of two supreme courts for the Holy Roman Empire.
7. Otto I the Great (912–973) was emperor of the Holy Roman Empire.
u. Id. 317.
v. Millar. 318.
w. Id. 324. 325.
x. Id. 331.

and the greatest part of causes, civil, criminal, and fiscal, were drawn into the vortex of the aula regis, or into that of the ecclesiastical courts.[y]

So far as these changes related to the aula regis, the consequence of them was, that this court, at first admirably accommodated to the arrangements of the juridical system then existing in vigour, became, afterwards, defective, unwieldy, and inconvenient. It followed the king, wherever the political state of the kingdom required his presence. A court, thus ambulatory, was inconsistent with the leisure and deliberation, which are necessary for judges in forming their decisions; and it was still more incompatible with the interest of the parties, who, with their witnesses, were obliged to travel about from place to place, before they could obtain a final determination of their suits.[z] Besides, the great increase of judicial business, which now crowded into the aula regis, rendered the proper despatch of that business an object altogether unattainable: from this cause, therefore, as well as from the other, the administration of justice became tedious, burthensome, and expensive.

The remedies for these grievances seem to have been natural and easy—to establish the aula regis as a stationary court—and to remand a great proportion of the original causes to those tribunals, which were best fitted, in the first instance, to decide them. These remedies, however, though easy and natural, were not applied. The county jurisdictions had ceased to be objects of favour at court: and the splendour of a retinue, composed of the officers of the judicial as well as the executive department, was a gratification too fascinating to be easily relinquished.

One of the remedies, indeed, it was found necessary to adopt in part; and the remedy, even in that part, was obtained with difficulty, and was soon abridged by ingenious and favourite fictions of law. When magna charta was demanded of King John, one of the articles inserted in the important instrument was—"that common pleas should no longer follow the court of the king, but should be held in some certain and appropriated place." When we see this regulation forming a part of that great transaction between the king and the nation, we may be fully satisfied, that it was much wished for, but could not be easily obtained. In consequence of this

y. Millar. 326. 331.
z. Id. 421. 422.

regulation, a court of common pleas, detached from the aula regis, was erected, and was appointed, for the future, to have a fixed and permanent residence. But though the court of common pleas obtained, in this manner, a separate establishment, and was held by separate judges, yet it was deemed inferiour in rank to the aula regis held by the grand justiciary, and in which the king still continued to sit sometimes in person; and, for this reason, was considered as subject to its decisions of review.[a]

There is much reason to believe, that the other remedy, so natural and easy, for lessening or removing the inconveniences, which arose from the crowd of business in the aula regis—that of reinstating the inferiour jurisdictions in their original degree of respectability—was, by no means, suffered to escape the attention of those, who obtained the great charter. One of the articles of their demand was—"that the king should promise to appoint justiciaries, constables, sheriffs, and bailiffs of such as knew the law of the land, and were well disposed to observe it."[b] With this demand the king literally complied, and engaged to appoint men only of such characters.[c] Had this engagement continued and been fulfilled, the subordinate, and, in particular, the county establishments for the administration of justice—for to the county establishments I wish to direct your particular attention—would have gradually regained, as they gradually lost, their original dignity and importance. The uniform and uninterrupted appointment of judges, intelligent, upright, and independent—men, who, in the language of magna charta, "knew and would observe the law of the land"—would, without any farther or more explicit provision, have been amply sufficient to have attracted and secured the confidence of suitors, and, by a necessary consequence, to recover and retain the usefulness and the respectability of the courts. This engagement, however, was neither continued nor fulfilled. In the instrument confirmed by Henry the third, this, among many other important regulations of the magna charta of John, was unfortunately omitted. The county establishments, from that period to the present moment, have been despised or disregarded in England; and other establishments, less natural and less convenient to the nation, have been substituted in their place. To the view of those other establishments we now proceed.

a. Millar. 424.
b. Bl. 8. art. 42.
c. Id. 18. art. 45.

When we consider the administration of justice in theory, it seems very susceptible of an arrangement in three great divisions. Prosecutions for crimes are easily distinguished from suits concerning property: and, in suits concerning property, the demands of government are as easily distinguished from demands of individuals. On the foundation of this specious theory, a triple division was made, in England, of the unwieldy jurisdiction accumulated in the aula regis. We have already seen, that "common pleas," or demands of property made by individuals, were detached from that court by an article of the great charter. In the reign of Edward the first, a farther division was made of its powers; the court of exchequer was erected to decide in matters regarding the publick revenue. The cognizance of crimes was the only division now remaining to the original court. To an alteration, so material, in its jurisdiction and power, an alteration, equally material, in its establishment and name was added, and the aula regis now subsided into the court of king's bench. This court is still, in its constitution, ambulatory; and may attend the person of the king in whatever part of the kingdom he shall be. The process of this court is in the king's name, and must be returned before him "ubicunque fuerimus in Anglia."[d8]

We now see, clearly and fully, the origin of the three great courts of common law, which, during a series of centuries, have been the ornaments of Westminster hall; and we now see, clearly and fully, the distinct principles, on which those three courts were separately erected. To the king's bench was allotted the jurisdiction of offences and crimes: decisions concerning the property of individuals—meum and tuum, as our books express it—were committed to the court of common pleas: the enforced collection of the publick revenue was intrusted to the court of exchequer.

I conclude my inquiries respecting the juridical history of England, at a period, at which others generally begin theirs.

To the jurists of Pennsylvania, this investigation, though minute, concerning the distribution of the powers and the jurisdiction of the aula regis, is deeply interesting; nay, it is of indispensable necessity; for, by the constitution and laws of Pennsylvania, a jurisdiction, similar to the combined jurisdiction of that court, is reunited in the supreme court of this com-

d. 3. Bl. Com. 41.
8. Wherever we may be in England.

monwealth. But along with that reunion, the measures proper for avoiding its inconveniences have been adopted. The supreme court is stationary; and juridical establishments, highly respectable, are formed in every county. These, in due course, will become the objects of particular attention.

By the historical deduction which we have made, we are now properly prepared to examine, by a particular survey, the judicial departments of the United States and this commonwealth; and to estimate, with correctness, the numerous jurisdictions, supreme and subordinate, of which those departments are composed, and upon the qualities and proportions of which, the declining or the flourishing state of those departments, and of every thing connected with those departments, must ultimately depend.

The judicial power of the national government extends—to all cases, in law or equity, arising under the constitution, the laws, or the treaties of the United States; to all cases affecting publick ministers and consuls; to all cases of admiralty and maritime jurisdiction; to controversies, to which the United States shall be a party; to controversies between two or more states; between a state and citizens of another state; between citizens of different states; between citizens of the same state, claiming lands under grants of different states; and between a state, or the citizens thereof, and foreign states, citizens, or[e] subjects.[f]

Besides the supreme court established by the constitution, the judicial power of the United States is, at present, vested in circuit and in district courts.

The supreme court has original jurisdiction in all cases, to which a state shall be party, and in all cases affecting publick ministers and consuls. In all the other cases before mentioned, it has appellate jurisdiction, both as to law and fact; but with such exceptions, and under such regulations, as are made by congress.[g] It consists of a chief justice and five associate jus-

e. Cons. U. S. art. 3. s. 2.

f. The supreme court of the United States, in the case of Chisholm *v.* the state of Georgia (2 Dall. 419.) decided, that under the clause of the constitution which extends the judicial power of the United States to controversies "between a state and citizens of another state," a state was liable, *as defendant*, to a suit commenced by such citizens. But by the eleventh article of the amendments to the constitution, it is declared that "the judicial power of the United States shall not be construed to extend to any suit in law or equity, commenced or prosecuted against one of the United States by citizens of another state, or by citizens or subjects of any foreign state." Vide post. ch. 4. *Ed.*

g. Cons. U. S. Art. 3. s. 2.

tices; and holds annually two sessions at the seat of the national government. One session commences on the first Monday of February; the other, on the first Monday of August. Four judges are a[h] quorum.[i]

The judges, both of the supreme and inferiour courts, hold their offices during good behaviour; and, at stated times, receive, for their services, a compensation, which cannot be diminished during their continuance in office.[j]

The supreme court has power to issue writs of prohibition to the district courts, when they proceed as courts of admiralty and maritime jurisdiction; and writs of mandamus, in cases warranted by the principles and usages of law, to any courts appointed, or persons holding office, under the authority of the United States.[k]

Final judgments and decrees of a circuit court, where the matter in dispute exceeds two thousand dollars, may be reexamined and reversed or affirmed in the supreme court,[l] upon a writ of errour.[m]

h. Laws. U. S. 1. con. 1. sess. c. 20. s. 1.

i. By an act of congress passed 29th April, 1802, the supreme court is to hold but one session annually, commencing on the first Monday in February. Four of the justices form a quorum. If four shall not attend within ten days after the time appointed for the commencement of the session, the business shall be continued to the next stated session; but any one or more of the justices may make all necessary orders preparatory to the hearing, trial, or decision of any case returned to or depending in the court. The August session is abolished; but one of the justices is directed to attend at the seat of government on the first Monday of August annually, and has power to make all necessary orders in any case returned to or depending in the court, preparatory to the hearing, trial, or decision. Writs and process may be returnable on the first Monday in August, in the same manner as to the February session, and may also bear *teste* on that day, as though a session of the court was holden. Laws. U.S. 7. con. 1. sess. c. 31. s. 1. 2. *Ed.*

j. Cons. U. S. art. 3. s. 1.

k. Laws. U. S. 1. con. 1. sess. c. 20. s. 13.

l. Laws. U. S. 1. con. 1. sess. c. 20. s. 22.

m. See the case of Wiscart et al. *v.* Dauchy, (3. Dall. 321. 327) in which the supreme court of the United States decided, that causes of admiralty and maritime jurisdiction and suits in equity, as well as other civil actions, could be removed from the circuit into the supreme court by writ of errour only, and not by appeal; and that therefore nothing was removed for reexamination but the law. By an act of congress since, passed (7. con. 2. sess. c. 93. s. 2.) it is provided that an appeal shall be allowed to the supreme court of the United States from final judgments or decrees rendered in the circuit court in cases of equity, of admiralty and maritime jurisdiction, and of prize or no prize; where the matter in dispute, exclusive of costs, shall exceed the value of two thousand dollars. No new evidence, however, can be received in the supreme court on the hearing of the appeal, except in admiralty and prize causes. *Ed.*

If the validity of a statute or treaty of the United States, or of an authority exercised under them, be drawn in question, in any suit in the highest court of law or equity of a state, in which a decision of the suit could be had; and a decision is against their validity—if the validity of a statute of any state, or of an authority exercised under that state, is, in any suit in such court, drawn in question, as repugnant to the constitution, treaties, or laws of the United States; and a decision is in favour of their validity—if the construction of any clause of the constitution, of a treaty, of a statute of the United States, or of a commission held under them, is, in any suit in such court, drawn in question; and a decision is against the title, right, privilege, or exemption, specially set up or claimed by either party under such clause—a final judgment or decree, in all these cases, may, upon a writ of errour, be reexamined and affirmed or reversed in the supreme court of the United States.[n]

The United States are divided into circuits and districts.

The districts are, in number, sixteen: one consists of that part of the state of Massachussets, which lies easterly of the state of New Hampshire, and is called Maine district: one consists of the state of New Hampshire, and is called New Hampshire district: one consists of the remaining part of the state of Massachussetts, and is called Massachussetts district: one consists of the state of Rhode Island and Providence Plantations, and is called Rhode Island district: one consists of the state of Connecticut, and is called Connecticut district: one consists of the state of New York, and is called New York district: one consists of the state of New Jersey, and is called New Jersey district: one consists of the state of Pennsylvania, and is called Pennsylvania district: one consists of the state of Delaware, and is called Delaware district: one consists of the state of Maryland, and is called Maryland district: one consists of the state of Virginia, and is called Virginia district: one consists of the state of North-Carolina, and is called North Carolina district: one consists of the state of South Carolina, and is called South Carolina district: one consists of the State of Georgia, and is called Georgia district:[o] one consists of the state of Vermont, and is

n. Laws. U. S. 1. con. 1. sess. c. 20. s. 25.
o. Id. 1. con. 1. sess. c. 20. s. 2.

called Vermont district:[p] one consists of Kentucky, and is called Kentucky district.

These districts, except Maine and Kentucky, are divided into three circuits, the eastern, the middle, and the southern. The eastern circuit consists of the districts of New Hampshire, Massachussetts, Rhode Island, Connecticut, New York, and Vermont: the middle circuit consists of the districts of New Jersey, Pennsylvania, Delaware, Maryland, and Virginia: the southern circuit consists of the districts of North Carolina, South Carolina, and Georgia.[q]

In each district, there is a district court, consisting of one judge,[r] who resides in the district, and holds four sessions annually.[s]

In each district of the three circuits, two courts, called circuit courts, are annually held. These courts consist of any two justices of the supreme court, and of the district judge of the district, any two of whom constitute a quorum.[tu]

Over crimes and offences, committed upon the high seas, or within the respective districts, and cognizable under the authority of the United States, the district courts have jurisdiction; provided the punishment exceed not whipping with thirty stripes, a fine of one hundred dollars, or imprisonment for six months. From jurisdiction over such crimes or offences, the courts of the several states are excluded.[v]

p. Laws U. S. 1. con. 3. sess. c. 12. s. 2.

q. Id. 1. con. 1. sess. c. 20. s. 4.

r. Id. s. 3.

s. For the alterations which have been made in the distribution of the United States into districts and circuits, and in the sessions of the district courts, the number of which now varies in different districts, see Laws U. S. 3. cong. 1. sess. c. 54. 7. cong. 1. sess. c. 31. 7. cong. 2. sess. c. 60. *Ed.*

t. Laws U. S. 1. con. 1. sess. c. 20. s. 4.

u. The circuit courts now consist of one of the judges of the supreme court and the judge of the district; either of whom may hold the court. In cases removed from a district to a circuit court by appeal or writ of errour, judgment shall be rendered in conformity to the opinion of the judge of the supreme court. In other cases, if the opinions of the judges shall be opposed, the question respecting which they disagree shall, during the same term, at the request of either party or their counsel, be stated under the direction of the judges, and certified to the supreme court, by whom it shall be finally decided; and their decision and order shall be remitted to the circuit court, and be then entered of record, and shall have effect according to the nature of the decision or order. No punishment shall, in any case, be inflicted, when the judges are divided in opinion on the question respecting it—Laws U. S. 7. cong. 1. sess. c. 31. s. 4. 5. 6. *Ed.*

v. Laws U. S. 1. con. 1. sess. c. 20. s. 9.

The district courts have, in the first instance, exclusive cognizance of all causes of admiralty and maritime jurisdiction,[w] and of seizures under laws of impost, navigation, or trade; provided the seizures be made on the high seas, or within their respective districts, on waters navigable from the sea by vessels of ten or more tons burthen. But the right of a common law remedy is saved to suitors in all cases, in which the common law is competent to give it.[x] Of seizures on land, or on waters, other than as above described, and of all suits for penalties and forfeitures incurred under the laws of the United States, the district courts have, likewise, in the first instance, exclusive cognizance.

Of all causes, in which an alien sues for a tort only in violation of the law of nations or of a treaty of the United States, the district courts have cognizance, concurrent, as the case may be, with the circuit courts, or with the courts of the several states. They have a similar concurrent cognizance of all suits at common law, in which the United States sue, and the matter in dispute, exclusive of costs, amounts to the value of one hundred dollars. They have, exclusively of the courts of the several states, jurisdiction of all suits against consuls or vice consuls, except for offences above the description before mentioned.[y]

The circuit courts have concurrent jurisdiction with the district courts of the crimes and offences cognizable in the latter, and they have exclusive cognizance of all other crimes and offences cognizable under the authority of the United States, except where provision is or shall be otherwise made.

They have, concurrent with the courts of the several states, original cognizance of all civil suits at common law or in equity, where the matter in dispute, exclusive of costs, exceeds the value of five hundred dollars, and where the United States are plaintiffs, or an alien is a party, or a suit is between a citizen of the state, in which it is brought, and a citizen of another state.[z]

The final decrees and judgments of a district court in civil actions, where the matter in dispute, exclusive of costs, exceeds the value of fifty dollars,

w. Every district court in the United States possesses all the powers of a court of admiralty, whether considered as an instance or as a prize court. 3. Dall. 16. *Ed.*

x. Laws U. S. 1. con. 1. sess. c. 20. s. 9.

y. Id. ibid.

z. Laws U. S. 1. con. 1. sess. c. 20. s. 11.

may, upon a writ of errour, be reexamined, and reversed or affirmed in a circuit court, holden in the same district.[a][b]

From the foregoing detail, which was necessary, though not entertaining, we find, that as yet, only three species of courts are known to the constitution and laws of the United States; and that even to one of those species no appropriate order of judges is assigned; for the judges of the circuit courts are drawn together, in opposite directions, from the supreme court and the district. This very uncommon establishment may become the subject of some future remarks.

I proceed to take a view of the courts of Pennsylvania.

The first, which attracts our notice, is "the high court of errours and appeals." This court was constituted by a late law. A court of the same name and of much the same kind was known in Pennsylvania, before the present constitution. This court, as at present established, consists of the judges of the supreme court, of the presidents of the courts of common pleas, and of three other persons, appointed during good behaviour, and removable in the same manner as the judges of the supreme court. Five judges form a quorum. It is empowered to decide on writs of errour from the supreme court, and on appeals from the register's courts in the several counties of the commonwealth.[c]

The supreme court has been long known in Pennsylvania, though not always by the same name. By consulting the records of our laws, we shall find "an act for erecting a provincial court," passed as early as the year one thousand six hundred and eighty four. It had power to try titles of land, to try all causes civil and criminal, both in law and equity, not determinable in the county courts, and to decide appeals from inferiour jurisdictions.[d] This law was continued, according to a general regulation in force at that time, from one session of the general assembly to another, till the year one

a. Id. s. 22.

b. By the 21st. section of the same act, an *appeal* to the circuit court was allowed from final decrees in a district court *in causes of admiralty and maritime jurisdiction,* where the matter in dispute exceeded the value of three hundred dollars exclusive of costs. By a later act (7. cong. 2. sess. c. 93. s. 2.) it is provided that from *all final judgments or decrees* in any of the district courts of the United States, an appeal, where the matter in dispute, exclusive of costs, shall exceed the value of fifty dollars, shall be allowed to the circuit court for the same district. *Ed.*

c. 3. Laws Penn. 97. s. 17.

d. R. O. book A. p. 71.

thousand six hundred and ninety. From that year to the year one thousand seven hundred, there is a chasm in the laws of Pennsylvania. To those, who are conversant in the general history of the province, the reasons of this chasm are well known.

In the year one thousand seven hundred and one, a new act was passed for establishing a provincial court. By this act, the court had jurisdiction in equity by bill and answer, such as is necessary in courts of chancery, and *proper in these parts.*[e] This law was, in the year one thousand seven hundred and five, repealed by the queen in council.

In the year one thousand seven hundred and fifteen, another law was passed "for erecting a supreme or provincial court of law and equity."[f] This experienced the fate of the former—it was repealed by the king in council in the year one thousand seven hundred and nineteen.

I may be permitted to remark, by the way, that such was the fate of many of the most valuable laws, which were passed in the early periods of Pennsylvania. They well deserve the attention of every one, who wishes to become a master of her juridical history. They disclose, in the most striking as well as the most authentick manner, how soon and how strongly a spirit of jealousy began to operate in the administration of the colonies.

Will it be believed, that the benefit of the great palladium of liberty—the writ of habeas corpus—was refused to be imparted to the plantations? Will it be believed, that the name of Somers[9]—a name, in Europe, so dear to liberty—stands first in the list of those, by whom the tyrannick refusal was given? These things ought not to be believed without the most irrefragable testimony: if the most irrefragable testimony of their authenticity can be produced, these things ought to be both believed and published. They show how dangerous it is for freedom to depend upon her best friends for a *foreign* support.

In December one thousand six hundred and ninety five, the committee of plantations wrote, to the governour and council of Massachussetts, a letter on the subject of a variety of laws passed by the legislature of that

e. R. O. book A. vol. 1. p. 110.

f. R. O. book A. vol. 2. p. 109.

9. John Somers (1651–1716), the first Baron Somers, was a prominent English legal author and statesman.

colony. Many of those laws were favourable to liberty; and, among others of this spirit, there was one concerning the writ of habeas corpus. With regard to this law, the committee expressed themselves in the following manner, truly remarkable. "Whereas by the act for securing the liberty of the subject, and preventing illegal imprisonments, the writ of habeas corpus is required to be granted, in like manner as is appointed by the statute of 31. Charles II. in England; which privilege has not as yet been granted in any of his majesty's plantations: it was not thought fit in his majesty's absence, that the said act should be continued in force; and, therefore, the same hath been repealed." My Lord Somers signed the letter![g]

I return to the supreme court of this commonwealth.

By a law, made in the year one thousand seven hundred and twenty two, and which is still in force, a court of record was established, and styled the supreme court of Pennsylvania. To that court power is given to issue writs of habeas corpus, certiorari, and writs of errour, and all remedial and other writs and process, in pursuance of the powers given to it.[h] Its judges are authorized to minister justice to all persons, and exercise the jurisdictions and powers granted by law, as fully and amply as the justices of the court of king's bench, common pleas, and exchequer, at Westminster, or any of them, can do.[i] It was made a doubt, whether, under the authority of this law, the supreme court could exercise original jurisdiction, and take cognizance of causes at their commencement. A law, passed a few years ago, gives it expressly original jurisdiction in enumerated cases.[j]

By the constitution of Pennsylvania,[k] the jurisdiction of the supreme court shall extend over the state; and the judges of it shall, by virtue of their offices, be justices of oyer and terminer and general gaol delivery in the several counties.

Besides the powers formerly and usually exercised by it, it has now the powers of a court of chancery so far as relates to the perpetuating of testimony, the obtaining of evidence from places not within the state, and the care of the persons and estates of those, who are *non compotes mentis*.[l]

g. Chal. 74.
h. 1. Laws Penn. 179. s. 11.
i. Id. 180. s. 13.
j. 2. Laws Penn. 472. s. 4. 5.
k. Art. 5. s. 3.
l. Cons. Penn. art. 5. s. 6.

The judges of this court hold their offices during good behaviour; but, for any reasonable cause, which shall not be ground of impeachment, the governour may remove any of them, on the address of two thirds of each branch of the legislature.[m] They shall, at stated times, receive, for their services, an adequate compensation, to be fixed by law; which shall not be diminished during their continuance in office.

By a law passed during the present year, the supreme court is established in the same manner, and with the same powers, as it has been heretofore established by the laws of the state, consistently with the provisions contained in the constitution.[n] It holds three terms in the year; one, on the first Monday in January; another, on the first Monday in April; and the third, on the first Monday in[o] September.[p]

By the constitution of Pennsylvania,[q] a court of common pleas, an orphans' court, a register's court, and a court of quarter sessions of the peace are established for each county. Before I consider these jurisdictions separately, it will be proper to premise some observations, equally applicable to them all.

Among the dispositions and arrangements of judicial power, the institution of counties has long made a conspicuous figure. The division of England into counties is generally ascribed to the legislative genius of the great Alfred. His genius was unquestionably equal to the task; but part of it was performed before his reign. A country so large as some of the kingdoms of the heptarchy could not, according to the policy and the exigencies of the times, enjoy the administration of justice without a division into subordinate districts. Accordingly, in the old laws, before the union of England under Egbert,[10] we find the mention of sheriffs and shires.[r] But though Alfred did not commence, he undoubtedly extended the county

m. Cons. Penn. art. 5. s. 2.

n. 3. Laws Penn. 92. s. 1.

o. Id. ibid.

p. The terms of the supreme court now commence on the first Mondays in March, September, and December. March term continues three weeks; September term, two weeks; and December term four weeks. The first and last days of each term are return days. 5. Laws Penn. 166. *Ed.*

q. Art. 5. s. 1.

10. King Egbert of Wessex (c. 770–839) was king from 802 to 839 and oversaw Wessex's rise to become the most powerful of the Anglo-Saxon kingdoms.

r. Sulliv. 245.

establishments of England. Before his reign, the Danes had made extensive settlements in the northern parts of the kingdom. During some years after the commencement of his reign, they confined him within very narrow limits, and ravaged the rest according to their savage pleasure. At last, however, this great man, whom so many embarrassments surrounded, and who surmounted so many embarrassments, obliged those, who had viewed him with supercilious contempt, to acknowledge him as their superiour and lord. After his conquest over the Danes, he then settled the boundaries of the counties through every part of England. In the southern parts of the kingdom, they were, probably, laid out according to the former limits. In the northern parts, which were less fertile and more uncultivated, they were laid out on a larger scale. Hence, to this day, we find the largest counties in the north of England.

In every county, justice was administered to the inhabitants near their places of residence, without the delay and expense of resorting to Westminster.

Each of the counties or shires had, as we are told by Selden, their two chief governours for distributive justice: of these, the sheriff was the more ancient and worthy; being, in certain cases, aided by the power of the county. His office was partly judicial and partly ministerial. In the last character, he was the king's servant to execute his writs: in the first, he regulated the courts of justice within the county. The other officer was the coroner, whose duty it was to inquire of homicide upon the view, to seize escheats and forfeitures, to receive appeals of felony, and to keep the rolls of criminal proceedings. He was chosen, as was the sheriff, from among the men of the first rank in the county.[s]

In those times, the county court was surrounded with numerous and respectable attendants: it was considered as the great theatre, on which the justice and the power of the county were displayed.[t] In those times, justice was administered principally in the county establishments; and it was only in cases of uncommon magnitude or difficulty, that recourse was had to that judicial tribunal, whose jurisdiction extended over the whole kingdom. In those times, the proceedings and decisions of the courts were simple and unembarrassed—an advantage, as a learned writer

s. Bac. on Gov. 40, 41.

t. Forum plebeiae justitiae, et theatrum comitivae potesatis. Spel. Gloss. v. comitatus.

says,[u] which always attends the infancy of laws—an advantage, as I will venture to say, which always attends their perfection. Such have been, and such will be the true character and native consequences of county establishments, properly instituted and properly organized.

Let us now trace their origin and their progress in Pennsylvania.

In the second session of her legislature, it was enacted, that "all actions of debt, account, slander, and trespass, shall be first tried by the court of the county, in which the cause of action arises."[v] In a subsequent session, it was constituted a court of equity as well as of law.[w] Soon afterwards the sphere of the county jurisdictions was enlarged. It was enacted, that trials of titles of lands, actions of debt, account, and slander, and all actions civil or criminal whatever (excepting treason, murder, manslaughter, and other enormous crimes) shall be first heard and determined in the proper counties by the respective justices; and that the county courts shall be held quarterly, and oftener, if there be occasion.[x]

These institutions fell at the chasm of legislation, which I have already mentioned; but their spirit was afterwards revived, continued, and invigorated. They received, it is true, some checks, similar to those, which were experienced by the supreme court. In the year one thousand seven hundred and fourteen, an act was passed for establishing the several courts of common pleas within the province.[y] It met its fate at the same time and in the same manner as the law for establishing the supreme court.

By a subsequent law, more fortunate, a court of record, styled the county court of common pleas, was established in every county, with power to hear and determine all pleas and causes, civil, personal, real, and mixed, according to the laws and constitutions of the province.[z] Here appears a plain separation of the civil from the criminal jurisdiction, both of which were, before this time, vested in the county courts. The criminal jurisdiction was, by the same law, transferred to a court instituted at the same time,[a] and styled "the general quarter sessions of the peace and gaol delivery."[b]

u. 4. Bl. Com. 407.
v. R. O. Book A. p. 32.
w. Id. p. 70.
x. Id. p. 84.
y. Id. vol. 2. p. 112.
z. 1. Laws Penn. 182. s. 21.
a. See R. O. Book A. vol. 2. p. 90.
b. 1. Laws Penn. p. 176. s. 3.

By the constitution,[c] the judges of the courts of common pleas shall hold their offices during good behaviour.

I am next to consider the establishment and the jurisdiction of orphans' courts in Pennsylvania. These are institutions of the last importance to the welfare of the commonwealth.

Among the ancients, those who studied and practised the sciences of jurisprudence and government with the greatest success, were convinced, and, by their conduct showed their conviction, that the fate of states depends on the education of youth.

History, experience, and philosophy combine in declaring—that the best and most happy of countries is that country, which is the most enlightened.

"It was a leading principle with our ancestors," says Isocrates in his oration on reforming the government of Athens, "not to limit the education of the citizens to any particular period of life. Great pains were employed upon them during their youth; and, as they advanced to the years of maturity, they were watched with an attention still more sedulous than before. Their manners were an object of such high concern, that the Areopagus seemed instituted with no other view but to preserve them."[d] It was the business of this court to appoint tutors and governours for the youth; and to take care that they were educated in a manner corresponding to their situation and circumstances.[e]

A similar degree of watchfulness and assiduity was bestowed upon education, in other parts of Greece. Epaminondas,[11] we are told, in the last year of his life, said, heard, beheld, and performed the very same things, as at the age in which he received the first principles of his education.[f]

Nothing, indeed, can be of greater importance, than to conduct our children in the same manner, in which we ought to conduct ourselves.

"Custom," says my Lord Bacon, "is the principal magistrate of man's life. But custom is certainly most perfect, when it beginneth in young

c. Art. 5. s. 2.

d. Gil. Lys. & Isoc. 487.

e. 1. Pot. Ant. 104.

11. Epaminondas (c. 418–362 B.C.) was a brilliant Theban general who overthrew Spartan dominance in the Peloponnese.

f. Mont. Sp. L. b. 4. c. 4.

years. This we call education; which, in effect, is but an early custom. But if the force of custom, simple and segregate, be great; the force of custom, copulate and conjoined and collegiate, is far greater. For there, example teacheth, company comforteth, emulation quickeneth, glory raiseth. Certainly the great multiplication of virtues upon human nature resteth upon societies well ordained and disciplined."[g]

Things are sometimes best displayed by the side of their contraries. It has been the benign aim of patriot legislators to disseminate knowledge: it has been the infernal wish of despots and the minions of despots to extinguish it. The political principles of Mr. Hobbes are well known. Such an abhorrence he contracted for popular government, and the principles of freedom, that he was anxious to see both extirpated from the face of the earth. In order to obtain this consummation, in his perverted judgment so devoutly to be wished, he recommends it to princes to destroy the Greek and Latin authors. "By reading them," says he, "men have, under a false show of liberty, acquired a habit of favouring tumults, and of licentiously controlling the conduct of their sovereigns."[h] In France, during a late reign, a minister was heard to say—"I will put an end to all schools;" and another is said to have declared—"I am tired with these publications; if I continue ten years longer in office, I am determined that no books, except the court calender, shall be printed in Paris."[i] But in France, that late reign is now passed.

The same savage and tyrannick maxims have, in former times, been avowed in America. But those times are now also passed. It will not, however, be unuseful to turn our eyes back upon them; and, with the mingled emotions of disdain and conscious joy, to trace the striking contrast between the views of government in a past, and those in the present age.

In the reign of Charles the second, the lords of the committee of plantations transmitted to Virginia a series of inquiries concerning the condition of the colony. Among the answers returned by Sir William Berkeley, who was then its governour, we find the following one, too extraordinary to be passed without particular notice. "I thank God, there are no free schools, nor printing; and, I hope, we shall not have, these hundred

g. 3. Ld. Bac. 357. 358.
h. Lev. P. 2. c. 21. 1. Shaft. Char. 88.
i. Fr. Rev. 266.

years. For learning has brought disobedience, and heresy, and sects into the world; and printing has divulged them and libels against the best government: God keep us from both!"[j] By the court of Charles, this prayer was received most graciously; and, agreeably to its principle, a succeeding governour was ordered "to allow no person to use a printing press on any occasion whatsoever."[k]

Very different were the principles, which animated the genius of the immortal Alfred. He considered learning and the sciences as the glory and the felicity of his reign. He founded and endowed schools: difficult as the task was in that unenlightened age, he provided those schools with proper instructors. Still farther to diffuse a taste for knowledge, and to transmit its blessings to posterity, he made a law, obliging all freeholders, possessing two hides of land or upwards, to send their sons to school, and give them a liberal education. By his own example—for he was the most accomplished scholar of his age—by his powerful recommendations of learning—for he made it the great road to preferment—he introduced among his people the most ardent pursuits after intellectual acquirements. The old bewailed their unhappiness in being ignorant; some, at a very advanced age, applied themselves to study; and all took care to procure proper instruction for their children, and their other young relations.[l]

According to the theory of Plato[m] and the institutions of Lycurgus,[n] the care and education of children were taken entirely out of the hands of their parents. The propriety of this regulation I will not, at present, examine. Suffice it to say, that the laws ought to give every possible encouragement and assistance to the education of children; but particularly of those, who are unfortunately deprived of their parents.

We now see the reasons and the importance of establishing orphans' courts. The first object of their jurisdiction is the education of orphans: their property is the second.

So early as the second session of the legislature of Pennsylvania, orphans' courts were established in every county to inspect the estates, us-

j. Chal. 328.
k. Id. 345.
l. 2. Henry 356.
m. 4. Anac. 341.
n. Id. 163.

age, and employment of orphans; "that care," says the law, "may be taken for those, that are not able to take care for themselves."[o] Their education is more immediately the object of a subsequent law, which was made in the same session.[p] "That poor as well as rich may be instructed in commendable learning," it was enacted, "that all persons having children, and the guardians or trustees of orphans, shall cause them to be instructed in reading and writing; and to be taught some useful trade or profession; that the poor may work to live, and the rich, if they become poor, may not want."

By a law still in force, orphans' courts appoint guardians over such orphans as the court shall judge incapable, according to the rules of the common law, of choosing guardians for themselves; admit orphans, of the proper age, to choose their own guardians; and direct the binding of orphans to be apprentices to trades or other employments. But it is provided, that no orphan shall be bound an apprentice to any person, or be placed under the guardianship of any person, whose religious persuasion is different from that of the orphan's parents.[q]

You will probably be surprised, that the regulations known to our laws for the education of orphans here close. You have reason for your surprise. Those regulations are, indeed, defective. To parental affection the care of education may, in most instances, be safely intrusted. But in no other principle ought the laws to repose an implicit confidence, concerning an object of the greatest magnitude, immediately to orphans, and eventually to the publick. In Sparta, one of the most respectable members of the state was placed at the head of all the children. Would not some similar institution be eligible with regard to such of them as are deprived of their parents?

The jurisdiction of the orphans' courts, as it respects the property of orphans, will be discussed with more propriety, when we come to the second great division of the law—that, which relates to things.

By the constitution of Pennsylvania,[r] the judges of the court of common pleas of each county compose its orphans' court.

I proceed to the consideration of the register's court.

o. R. O. Book A. p. 34.
p. Id. p. 46.
q. 1. Laws. Penn. 101. s. 7. 102. s. 12.
r. Art. 5. s. 7.

In England, the probate of wills and the granting of letters of administration belong to the jurisdiction of the ecclesiastical courts. In Pennsylvania, this jurisdiction is turned into a very different channel.

In the first session of the legislature of Pennsylvania, a registry was established for wills, for letters of administration, and for the names of guardians and executors.[s]

A law passed in the year one thousand seven hundred and five directed, that an officer, called register general, should be appointed for the probate of wills, and granting letters of administration. He was directed to keep his office at Philadelphia, and to constitute a deputy in each county of the province. The deputies were empowered to take probates and grant letters of administration, as amply as the register general himself could do. A will proved, or letters of administration granted, in any one county, superceded the necessity of another probate or other letters of administration in any other county.[t]

When objections were made, or caveats entered against the proving of any will, or granting letters of administration; and when there was occasion to take the final accounts of executors or administrators, or to make distribution of decedents' estates, the register general and his deputies were respectively obliged to call to their assistance two or more of the justices of the court of common pleas, who were empowered and required to give their assistance, accordingly, to do all judicial acts concerning the matters before mentioned. This was the register's court.[u]

The office of register general is now abolished; and, by the constitution, a register's office for the probate of wills and granting letters of administration shall be kept in each county.[v]

The register of wills, together with the judges of the court of common pleas, or any two of them, compose the register's court.[w]

The court of quarter sessions of the peace is the last of those courts, which, by the constitution of Pennsylvania, form the juridical establishment for every county in the commonwealth.

s. R. O. Book. A. p. 18.
t. 1. Laws. Penn. 56. s. 8.
u. R. O. book A. vol. 2. p. 43.
v. Cons. Penn. art. 5. s. 11.
w. Id. art. 5. s. 7.

In England, the general or quarter sessions of the peace is a court of record held, in every county, once in every quarter of the year. It is held before two or more justices of the peace, for the execution of that authority, which is conferred on them by the commission of the peace, and a great variety of acts of parliament.

By the statute of 34 Ed. III. c. 1. the court of general quarter sessions have authority to hear and determine all felonies and trespasses whatever done in the county in which they sit. But they seldom try any greater offences than small felonies; remitting crimes of a heinous nature to the assizes, for a more publick and solemn trial and decision. There are many offences, which ought to be prosecuted in the quarter sessions, as belonging particularly to the jurisdiction of that court. Of this kind are the smaller misdemeanors, not amounting to felony; such as offences relating to the highways, taverns, vagrants, and apprentices. It has cognizance also of controversies relating to the settlement and provision for the poor, and orders for their removal. It cannot try any newly created offence, without an express authority given by the statute, which creates it.[x]

In Pennsylvania, the courts of quarter sessions of the peace are formed upon the model, and exercise jurisdiction according to the practice of the courts of the same denomination in England. In one important particular, however, there is a very material difference between them. The courts of quarter sessions in England are composed of the justices of the peace, who hold their commissions only during the pleasure of the crown: those in Pennsylvania are composed of the judges of the court of common pleas, who hold their commissions during their good behaviour.[y]

Thus much concerning the court of quarter sessions.

In each county, and in such convenient districts as are directed by law, the governour of Pennsylvania appoints a competent number of justices of the peace.[z]

To the common law, the conservation of the peace has always been an object of the most particular attention and regard. Long before the institution of justices of the peace was known, many officers were, ex offi-

x. Wood. Ins. 499. 4. Bl. Com. 268.
y. Cons. Penn. art. 5. s. 7. 2.
z. Cons. Penn. art. 5. s. 10.

cio, or by election, or by particular appointment, guardians of the publick tranquillity—conservatores pacis.[a]

When quarrels suddenly arise—when violence is committed—when riots and tumults are likely to ensue, it is vain to wait for the interposition of the ordinary courts of justice. That cannot be obtained soon enough for preventing or suppressing the disorders. It is highly important, therefore, that men of character and influence, to whom, upon any emergency, application may be easily made, should be invested with sufficient power to arrest disorderly persons, to confine them, and to preserve or restore the quiet of the country.

The *peace,* in the most extensive sense of the term, comprehends the whole of the criminal law. "Against the peace," all crimes are laid to be committed. Whoever, therefore, had authority to take cognizance of crimes was, from the nature of his office, considered as a conservator of the peace. The king himself was styled its great conservator through all his dominions. His judges and his ministers of justice were also official conservators of the peace. Others were conservators by tenure or prescription. Others, again, were elected in the full county court, in pursuance of a writ directed to the sheriff. Besides all these, extraordinary conservators of the peace were appointed by commission from the king, as occasion required. They were to continue, says my Lord Bacon, for the term of their lives, or at the king's pleasure. For this service, adds the same great authority, choice was made of the best men of calling in the county, and but few in the shire. They might bind any man to keep the peace, and be of the good behaviour; and they might send for the party, directing their warrant to the sheriff or constable to arrest the party and bring him before them.

This it was usual to do, when complaint was made, upon oath, by any one, that he stood in fear of another; or when the conservator himself saw the disposition of any man inclined to a breach of the peace, or to misbehave himself in some outrageous manner. In such cases, the conservator might, by his own discretion, send for such a fellow, and, as he should see cause, oblige him to find sureties for the peace, or for his good behaviour. If he refused to find them, a commitment to gaol would be the unavoidable consequence.

a. Millar, 433.

Those, who were conservators of the peace by virtue of their offices, still retain the character and power: those, who became so by election or appointment, are superseded by the justices of the peace.[b]

Of this institution, says my Lord Coke,[c] it is such a form of subordinate government for the tranquillity and quiet of the realm, as no part of the christian world hath; provided it be duly executed.

The power of the justices of the peace arises from two different sources—their commission, and acts of parliament, which have created the objects of their jurisdiction.

By his commission, every justice is appointed a conservator of the peace, and is vested with a separate power to suppress riots and affrays, to take securities for the peace or good behaviour; and for defect of sureties may commit to the common gaol or house of correction. For treason, felony, or breach of the peace, he may commit even a fellow-justice.[d]

The powers, which, by acts of parliament, have been conferred, from time to time, upon one, two, or more justices of the peace, are accumulated to such a degree as to form a jurisdiction of immense variety and importance. They are so many and so great that, as Sir William Blackstone observes,[e] the country is greatly obliged to any worthy magistrate, who, without sinister views of his own, will engage in this troublesome service. For this reason, he is protected, by many statutes, in the honest discharge of his office; and, for any unintentional errour in his practice, great indulgence is shown to him in the courts of law. On the other hand, tyrannical abuses of his office are punished with the merited severity; and all persons, who recover a verdict against him, for a wilful or malicious injury, are entitled to double costs.

In England, a justice of the peace holds his office only during the pleasure of the king: by the constitution of Pennsylvania, he holds it during his good behaviour. He may be removed on conviction of misbehaviour in office, or of any infamous crime, or on the address of both houses of the legislature.[f]

b. 4. Ld. Bac. 59. 99. 1. Bl. Com. 349. 2. Reev. 122.
c. 4. Ins. 170.
d. Wood. Ins. 80.
e. 1. Bl. Com. 354.
f. Cons. Penn. art. 5. s. 10.

The presidents of the courts of common pleas, within their circuits, and the other judges, within their several counties, are justices of the peace, so far as relates to criminal matters.[g]

This distinction, suggested by the constitution, brings into our view a very important branch of the power of a justice of the peace. He possesses civil as well as criminal jurisdiction in Pennsylvania, and decides concerning property as well as concerning offences. This branch of his power deserves a particular consideration.

The easy, the regular, and the expeditious administration of justice has, in every good government, been an object of particular attention and care. To the attainment of an object so interesting, the distribution of the juridical powers among convenient districts is highly conducive. Such distribution, therefore, has, in many states, been made with a degree of precision suited to its importance. Every citizen should be always under the eye and under the protection of the law and of its officers: each part of the juridical system should give and receive reciprocally an impulse in the direction of the whole.

In Athens, there was a grade of magistrates, who, in the several districts, had jurisdiction of suits, when the sum in controversy did not exceed ten drachms. They had cognizance also of actions of assault and battery.[h]

Arbitrators likewise acted a very considerable part on the juridical theatre of Athens. There were two kinds of them. One kind consisted of those, who were drawn by lot to determine controversies, in their own tribe, concerning demands, which exceeded ten drachms in value. Their sentence was not final; for if either of the contending parties thought himself injured by it, he might appeal, for redress, to a superiour court of justice.[i] Arbitrators of the other kind were such as the parties themselves chose to determine the controversy between them. From the determination of these arbitrators, the law permitted no appeal. But they took an oath to give their sentence without partiality.[j]

We have seen and traced the importance of the county establishments. But counties are too extensive for their inhabitants to meet on every occasion. Hence the propriety of inferiour divisions.

g. Id. art. 5. s. 9.
h. Gil. Lys. & Isoc. 489. 1. Pot. Ant. 122.
i. 1. Pot. Ant. 122.
j. 1. Pot. Ant. 123.

Among the Saxons, there was a magistrate called the hundredary, who presided over that division of a shire which was called a hundred. This magistrate was known to the ancient Germans, as we find, in Tacitus,[k] an express reference made to his jurisdiction. The hundredary was, in virtue of his office, empowered to appoint the times and places for the meetings of the hundred court; to preside in those meetings; and to carry the sentences of the court into full execution. All the members within the hundred were originally members of the hundred court, and obliged, under severe penalties, to attend. This, however, was discovered, by experience, to be inconvenient; and, therefore, the court was new modelled by a law of the great Alfred. It was reduced to the hundredary or his bailiff, and twelve of the hundred; and these twelve were sworn, neither to condemn the innocent, nor to acquit the guilty. It was a mixed court, possessing both civil and criminal jurisdiction. Many petty causes came before it. Its proceedings were simple and summary: but if any one thought himself aggrieved by its decision, he had the right of appealing to a superiour tribunal. In this court also, sales of land, and other important transactions between members of the same hundred were published and confirmed.[l]

We have seen, that, in Pennsylvania, a very early attention was given to the respectable establishment of county courts. In the same session, which was the second after the settlement of the province, attention was also given to districts more circumscribed. It was enacted, that, in every precinct, three persons should be chosen yearly as peace makers in that precinct. That arbitrations might be as valid as the judgments of courts, it was directed, that the parties should sign a reference of the matter in controversy to the peace makers so chosen. This reference being ratified by the county court, the award of the peace makers was as conclusive as a judgment; and was registered in court in the same manner as other judgments.[m]

A farther regulation was made, also in the same session, that speedy justice might be administered to the poor, and in matters of small value. Debts under forty shillings were ordered to be heard and determined, upon sufficient evidence, by any two justices of the peace of that county, in which the cause arose. The justices were directed to report their judgment to the next

k. De mor. Ger. c. 12.

l. Bac. on. Gov, 42, 43. 2. Henry. 241. 242.

m. R. O. Book A. p. 29.

county court. This judgment, if approved by the court, was to be recorded as good and binding.[n] Thus matters stood with regard to small debts, before the chasm of legislation, which has been repeatedly mentioned.

In the year one thousand seven hundred and five, a law was made, empowering any one justice of the peace to take cognizance of debts under the sum of forty shillings. His judgment concerning them is declared to be final and conclusive, and without appeal.[o] This law was repealed, but its principle was confirmed by another, made ten years afterwards.[p] Such is the law still with regard to debts under the sum of forty shillings.

By a law made in the year one thousand seven hundred and forty five, the jurisdiction of a single justice of the peace was extended, from sums under forty shillings, to sums not exceeding five pounds. But with regard to the exercise of the extended jurisdiction, two very salutary precautions are used. At the request of the parties, referees, named by them and approved by the justice, shall hear and examine the cause. Upon their return, the justice shall give judgment. In all cases, except those determined on the return of referees, an appeal lies from the judgment of the justice to the next court of common pleas. Upon an appeal made, the justice shall send a transcript of his judgment to the prothonotary of the court, which has the appellate, jurisdiction of the cause.[q]

Since the revolution,[r] the jurisdiction of a single justice is carried as high as debts not exceeding the sum of ten pounds.[s]

n. Id. p. 34.
o. Id. vol. 1. p. 154.
p. 1. Laws Penn. 113, 114.
q. 1. Laws Penn. 305. s. 1. 307. s. 7. 8.
r. 2. Laws Penn. 304.
s. By a law passed in the year one thousand seven hundred and ninety four (3. Laws Penn. 536.) the jurisdiction of the justices of the peace was extended to actions of debt and other demands not exceeding twenty pounds, under the regulations and exceptions contained in the act of 1745. An appeal from the judgment of the justice to the court of common pleas was allowed only in cases, where the debt or demand exceeded five pounds. Either party might, before judgment given by the justice, elect to have the cause tried in the court of common pleas, if the debt or demand exceeded ten pounds.

By the present constitution of Pennsylvania (art. 9. s.6.) it is declared, "that trial by jury shall be as heretofore, and the right thereof remain inviolate." This constitution was adopted in the year 1790. At that time, the jurisdiction of justices of the peace, (before whom a trial by jury cannot be had) was confined to cases of debt and contract not exceeding ten pounds; and even of such cases, some, in which unliquidated damages were claimed, were excepted out of their jurisdiction. In cases of torts, they possessed no jurisdiction whatever. The law of 1794 was early

From this historical deduction, it is natural to observe, that the civil jurisdiction of justices of the peace seems to have been a growing favourite with the legislature of Pennsylvania. It was introduced, at first, with

---

opposed, as repugnant to the above mentioned provision of the constitution, which, it declared, "was excepted out of the general powers of government," and should "for ever remain inviolate." (Art. 9. s.26.) A respectable minority in the house of representatives protested against the act, at the time it was passed in that house, on this, among other grounds. (Jour. H. Rep. 23d. Feb. 1793.) No judicial determination on the subject has taken place. It was once brought before the supreme court of the state; but the law, which was temporary, expiring, the judges declined pronouncing a decision.

The attachment of the legislature, however, to the jurisdiction of the justices of the peace, has continued and increased. By a law passed at their last session (March 1804.) which repeals all the prior laws above mentioned, that jurisdiction has been extended to all cases of debts, and of demands for damages on promises of whatever kind, not exceeding the amount of one hundred dollars. (s. 1.) But it is declared, that their jurisdiction shall not be construed to extend to actions of ejectment, of replevin, on real contracts for the sale or conveyance of lands or tenements, or upon promise of marriage (s. 15.) And in cases of rent not exceeding one hundred dollars, they have power to compel the landlord to defalcate or set off the just account of the tenant out of the same; but the landlord *may* then *wave* farther proceedings before the justice, and pursue the method of distress, in the usual manner, for the balance so settled. (s. 12.)

If the demand does not exceed five dollars and thirty three cents, the justice himself hears the parties, and gives judgment, which is final. If the demand is for a sum exceeding that amount, the case shall, if both parties consent, be submitted to referees, whose award shall be transmitted to the justice, and he shall enter judgment on it, which shall be final and conclusive, if for a sum not exceeding fifty three dollars. (s. 3.) If either of the parties refuse to refer, the justice may hear them and give judgment. (s. 4.)

If the cause is decided by the justice alone, and the demand exceeds the sum of five dollars and thirty three cents, either party, if dissatisfied with the judgment, may appeal to the court of common pleas; as he may likewise do, if judgment is given on the award of referees, and such award exceeds the sum of fifty three dollars. (s. 4.) No appeal lies in the case of rent: but the remedy by replevin is declared to remain as before the act passed. (s. 12.)

This act did not receive the sanction of the governour; not being returned by him, to the house in which it originated, within ten days after it was presented to him, it became a law. Acts of a similar nature passed by the two houses at the two prior sessions, had been negatived by him, on account of their being contrary to the above cited provision of the constitution (which he declared to be his decided opinion, and to be more and more confirmed by reflection) as well as of their dangerous and oppressive tendency.

From these circumstances, and those before stated in this note, the question respecting the constitutionality of the late law must be considered as *at least doubtful.* It is worthy of observation, too, that the objections apply more forcibly to the late law, than to that of 1794. For, by the former, no right is given to either party to elect, before judgment given by the justice, to have the cause tried by a jury in the court of common pleas, as was given by the latter.

The justices of the peace also possess, by an act passed 1st March, 1799, (4. Laws Penn. 351.) which was temporary, but has been revived and made perpetual, jurisdiction over actions brought for the recovery of damages for any trespass done to real or personal property, where they do not exceed twenty dollars. *Ed.*

apparent hesitation and reserve: it was confined to sums under forty shillings: it was intrusted to two magistrates, not to one: the judgment even of two magistrates was not binding till it was approved by the county court. The same jurisdiction was afterwards intrusted to a single magistrate, conclusively and without appeal. The jurisdiction of a single magistrate has been since extended from two to five, and from five to ten pounds: with the two precautions, indeed, of which I have already taken notice.

It may be observed, and the observation certainly has weight, that experience, the best test of things, must unquestionably have witnessed in favour of this jurisdiction; otherwise it would not, in this gradually progressive manner, have been intrusted and extended. But the weight of this observation ought to be compared with that of another, which is found in the opposite scale.

We have seen who are to exercise this jurisdiction: let us now see upon whom it is to be exercised—"upon the poorer sort of people," says the law, "who are unable to bear the expenses arising by the common method of prosecution."[t] Let us suppose it possible, that a magistrate, in the exercise of his final and conclusive jurisdiction, may be guilty of gross partiality or wilful injustice; how is redress to be obtained by the unhappy sufferer under his injustice or partiality? Only by a prosecution against him. But the unhappy sufferer appeared or was brought before him, only because he was unable to bear the expense of a common prosecution. Would the prosecution of a magistrate, clothed with authority, and heretofore answering before his associates in office—would such a prosecution be less expensive? Would he, who was unable to bear the former, be strengthened in such a manner as to support the burthen of the latter? That the oppressed have suffered in silence, is no proof that the oppressed have not suffered.

Before the establishment of the present constitution, this was, in Pennsylvania, a subject of well founded alarm. One half, probably, of the personal property, which, in this commonwealth, becomes, during the revolution of a year, the subject of judicial decision, is withdrawn from the trial by jury, and committed to the summary and solitary determinations of the justices of the peace. Before the establishment of the present constitution,

t. 1. Laws Penn. 304. 305.

the single magistrates, on whom this jurisdiction was conferred, were not appointed by any respectable and responsible officer, nor chosen by any considerable part of the community, or at stated and well known times: they were elected in a corner, as occasion offered, or contrivance planned. The causes, which came before a justice chosen, and anxious to be again chosen, in this manner, were frequently suits between a party, on one side, who would have a vote at his succeeding election, and a party, on the other side, who would be entitled to no such vote. The poor and friendless part of the community—those, who were soonest ruined by oppression—those, who were least able to struggle against it—were the part selected to be delivered over, bound hand and foot, to magistrates possessing such powers, and possessing them by such means, and in such a manner. Surely, this was a subject of well founded alarm.

The cause of alarm is removed by the salutary provisions, which we find in the present constitution of the commonwealth. The justices of the peace are appointed by the governour, who, by the citizens of the commonwealth, is himself elected, and who, to the citizens of the commonwealth, is himself responsible. The justices of the peace are appointed during good behaviour; and can no longer be seduced, by a dependent situation, to disgrace themselves and their offices by sinister adjudications. Farther; they are habitually controlled by the judges of the court of common pleas. Those judges have, within their respective counties, the like powers with the judges of the supreme court, to issue writs of certiorari to the justices of the peace, and to cause their proceedings to be brought before them, and the like right and justice to be done.[u]

But though the cause of alarm be now removed, the cause of considerate circumspection still subsists: for it is still true, that the property decided by justices of the peace is property withdrawn from a trial by jury. The constitution suggests, indeed, that those magistrates are to exercise a civil jurisdiction; but the terms, on which, and the extent, to which that jurisdiction is to be exercised, are left, as is proper, to be marked and ascertained by the wisdom and the experience of the legislature.

Perhaps the distant view which I have taken of the hundred courts, may not have been altogether impertinent to the present subject. Perhaps it will

u. Cons. Penn. art. 5. s. 8.

not be impracticable, after some time, to introduce them into Pennsylvania, modified, indeed, but with modifications not destructive of their principle. Such a tribunal should not be considered as a fanciful alteration, or a wild experiment; it ought rather to be deemed a close adherence to the wisdom of the ancient plan, concerted by the great Alfred, and to the spirit of his excellent and venerable institutions. To an object of this kind, the legislature is fully competent; for the constitution[v] empowers it to establish courts from time to time.

I have now made a tour through the courts of the United States, and through a number of the courts of Pennsylvania. Perhaps I ought here to make an apology for the degree of minuteness, with which I have surveyed and described them. Let me apologize by reciting an incident, which I remember to have heard in my younger years.

From the castle of Edinburgh, in Scotland, the prospect is uncommonly rich, extensive, and diversified. A young gentleman, born and educated at no very considerable distance from it, set out on his travels through Europe, with a view to notice attentively every thing, which he should find most worthy of his remark. When he was at Rome, the subject of exquisite prospects became, one day, the topick of conversation in a company of literati, to whom he had been introduced. Among others, that from the castle of Edinburgh was mentioned; and to our young traveller a reference was naturally made for a minute description of its different parts and beauties. They expressed themselves happy in so fine an opportunity of learning every particular concerning that, of which vague and general accounts had so much excited their admiration. With blushes, he was obliged to disclose the fact—that though he had resided, from his birth, near an object, which so well deserved to be known, yet he had never bestowed upon it the least share of attention, and was, therefore, totally unqualified to gratify the company by describing it. A profound silence was observed. It was not lost upon the young traveller. He returned immediately to Scotland, and acquired the knowledge of what was worthy to be known at home, before he went farther abroad in search of what was remarkable in foreign countries.

v. Art. 5. s. 1.

The institutions of other nations and of other times merit, most unquestionably, our perusal and our study. The travels of a young Anacharsis,[12] in which the governments and laws of Sparta and of Athens are so beautifully delineated, richly deserve to be read and admired. But to us, the governments, and laws, and institutions of the United States and of Pennsylvania ought to be the constant standard, with which we compare those of every other country. How can we compare them with a standard, which is unknown?

Trusting, therefore, that the interesting nature of the things which I describe will compensate for my minuteness and for my many imperfections in describing them, I proceed to give an account of some other jurisdictions known to the constitution and laws of the United States and of this commonwealth.

Circuit courts form a part, and a very valuable part, of our juridical system in Pennsylvania. These are of two kinds—courts of nisi prius, which try issues joined in civil causes—courts of oyer and terminer and general gaol delivery, which hear and determine criminal causes.

The courts of nisi prius are derived from the supreme court; and act as its auxiliaries in the exercise of its very important jurisdiction. They decide, in the several counties, all questions of fact, which arise in civil causes depending in the supreme court. They are called courts of nisi prius from the following circumstance—The causes commenced in the courts of Westminster Hall are, by the course of those courts, appointed to be tried at their bar, by a jury returned from the county, in which the cause of action arises. But in the writ, enjoining the attendance of the jury, there is this proviso—*nisi prius* justitiarii ad assisas capiendas venerint—unless, before the day prefixed, the judges of assize come into the county in question. This they do: the issue joined in the cause is tried in the proper county: the verdict is taken, and returned to the court above, on the day when the jury would otherwise have been obliged to appear and try it at bar.[w] By this means, much trouble and expense are saved to the parties, the jury, and

12. Anarchasis (sixth century B.C.) was a Greek author.
w. 4. Ld. Bac. 64.

the witnesses.[x] By this wise arrangement, the investigation of the facts—a matter frequently of the greatest consequence even in civil causes, is carried on in the county, sometimes in the very neighbourhood, in which the dispute arose; while questions of law are left to be considered by a court, which, from its permanent situation, is better qualified for deciding points of difficulty and importance.

The courts of nisi prius are held between the terms of the supreme court, at such times as the judges think most convenient for the[y] people.[z]

If it is highly expedient and convenient, that civil actions should be tried in the county, in which the causes of action arose; it is much more so, that criminal prosecutions should be tried in the county, in which the crimes were committed. A crime can seldom be proved in any other manner than by oral testimony. But of all the modes of proof, that which requires the attendance of witnesses from a great distance, is necessarily the most burthensome and expensive. In another view, too, it is very important, that every crime should be tried and every criminal should be punished near the place, where the guilt was contracted. One great design of punishment is to deter others from imitating the conduct, for which it

x. 3. Bl. Com. 59.

y. 3. Laws Penn. 92. s. 1.

z. Courts of nisi prius are now held only in the county of Philadelphia. In the other counties of the state, they have been superseded by courts, styled "circuit courts," established by an act of assembly passed in the year one thousand seven hundred and ninety nine. (4. Laws Penn. 362.)

The circuit courts are held by one or more of the justices of the supreme court, at such times and places as the justices of that court appoint, having due regard to the convenience of the people (s. 1.) In most of the counties, they are held once, and sometimes twice in the year, at the discretion of the justices.

They have no original jurisdiction; but have power to issue writs of certiorari, habeas corpus, and all other remedial and other writs and process, grantable by the justices of the supreme court by virtue of their offices (except writs of errour, and certiorari after judgments, orders, or decrees); and the writs and process so issued are returnable in the circuit court. Appeals also lie to the circuit court in each county from the register's and orphans' courts of that county. (s. 3.)

The circuit courts have power to give judgment, pass decrees, and award execution, and generally exercise similar power in any cause before them, and in which jurisdiction is given to them, in as ample a manner as if sitting in bank. They have power, though not sitting as a court of oyer and terminer, to try any capital or other criminal case removed into the circuit court, and to pronounce judgment, and award execution, as fully as the supreme court may do. (s. 4.)

If either of the parties to any suit removed from the common pleas, register's court, or orphans' court is dissatisfied with the decision of the circuit court on any demurrer, special verdict, case stated, point reserved on the trial, motion in arrest of judgment or for a new trial, or to set aside a judgment, discontinuance, or non pros. he may appeal to the supreme court. (s. 4.) *Ed.*

is inflicted. This design is most effectually accomplished, when the same persons, who have seen the law violated, are witnesses also of the dismal consequences, by which its violation is unavoidably succeeded.

In England, crimes are generally tried before judges, who sit by virtue of two commissions from the crown. One is a commission of oyer and terminer: the other is a commission of general gaol delivery. The first is directed to the judges of the circuits, and to many others of the best account within the circuits, as we are informed by my Lord Bacon. By this commission, they are authorized to hear and determine all treasons, felonies, and misdemeanors. But this commission gives them no power to proceed upon any other indictments than those found before themselves. The second commission is directed only to the judges themselves, and the clerk of the assize associate. This commission empowers them to try and deliver every prisoner in the gaol, for whatever offence he may have been committed, or before whatever judges he may have been indicted: but, by this commission, they have authority only over those who are prisoners in the gaol.[a]

By the law of the land, says my Lord Coke,[b] this commission was instituted, that men might not be detained a long time in prison; but might receive full and speedy justice.

Commissions of oyer and terminer are either general, or they are particular, in respect of the persons, of the offences, or of the places where the offences are committed.[c] Sometimes, upon urgent occasions, the king issues a special or extraordinary commission of oyer and terminer and gaol delivery, confined to those offences, which demand immediate inquiry and punishment. On these, the course of proceeding is the same as on ordinary and general commissions.[d]

The constitution of Pennsylvania declares,[e] that no commission of oyer and terminer or gaol delivery shall be issued. This power is expressly excepted out of the general powers of government. The powers granted, in England, by those commissions, are, in this commonwealth, placed much better for the security and advantage of the citizens. The judges of the

a. 4. Ld. Bac. 61.
b. 4. Ins. 168.
c. 4. Ins. 162. 163.
d. 4. Bl. Com. 267.
e. Art. 9. s. 15. 26.

supreme court are, by virtue of their offices, justices of oyer and terminer and general gaol delivery in the several counties of the state. The judges of the court of common pleas, in each county, are, in the same manner, justices of oyer and terminer and general gaol delivery for the trial of capital and other offences in such county.[f]

We have already seen that all those judges hold their offices during their good behaviour. The judges, both of the supreme and inferiour courts of the United States, hold their offices by the same tenure. The important nature of this difference between the situation of those, who exercise criminal jurisdiction in England, and that of those, who exercise it in the United States and in Pennsylvania, was fully shown in a former lecture,[g] when I was engaged in drawing a parallel between the government of the United States and that of Great Britain.

You have frequently heard of the distinction between law and equity, of courts of equity, and of equitable jurisdiction and powers.

Though no court of equity subsists separately in the United States or in Pennsylvania, yet this subject demands your closest attention. It occupies an important station in the science of law.

By Aristotle, equity is thus defined—"the correction of that, in which the law is defective, by being too general."[h] In making laws, it is impossible to specify or to foresee every case: it is, therefore, necessary, that, in interpreting them, those cases should be excepted, which the legislator himself, had he foreseen them, would have specified and excepted. Such interpretation, however, ought to be made with the greatest circumspection. By indulging it rashly, the judges would become the arbiters, instead of being the ministers of the laws. It is not to be used, unless where the strongest and most convincing reasons appear for using it. A strong reason for using it is drawn from the spirit of the law, or the motive which prevailed on the legislature to make it. When equity is taken in this sense, every court of law is also a court of equity. When equity is taken in this sense—and, applied to the interpretation of law, this is its genuine meaning—it is an expression synonimous to true and sound construction.[i]

f. Cons. Penn. art. 5. s. 3. 5.
g. Ante. vol. 1. p. 744.
h. Gro. 366.
i. 3. Bl. Com. 429.

Terms, and the relative positions of terms, are frequently too apt to mislead us. When we find a court of law and a court of equity placed in contradistinction to each other, how natural is it to conclude, that the former decides without equity, and that the latter decides without law. Such a conclusion, however, is greatly erroneous.

It has, indeed, been said, concerning a court of equity, that it determines by the spirit, and not by the letter of a rule. But ought not this to be said concerning a court of law likewise? Is not each equally bound—does not each profess itself to be equally bound—to explain the law according to the intention of those, who made it? In the interpretation of laws, whether strictly or liberally, there is not a single maxim, which is not adopted, in the same manner, and with the same force, by both courts. Hitherto, then, we find no difference between a court of law and a court of equity.

It has been supposed, that it is the peculiar and exclusive business of a court of equity to take cognizance of frauds, and accidents, and trusts. One kind of trusts, indeed—a technical, a useless, and a mischievous kind, as I shall show in the proper place—a trust created by the limitation of a second use—has been forced into the courts of equity, by the narrowness of the courts of law. But of other trusts, the courts of law take full and unreserved cognizance; particularly the very important and extensive trust of money received by one to the use of another. An action, founded on this trust, has often been compared to a bill in equity, on account of its useful and salutary influence. For accidents, too, remedy is found in a court of law: for the loss of deeds; for mistakes in payments, receipts, and accounts; for the destruction of records; and for a variety of other contingencies. For relief from other accidents, which might be specified, application to a court of law, we own, is vain; but application to a court of equity is vain also. With regard to frauds, they are as much the objects of cognizance and resentment in the courts of law, as they are in the courts of equity: a fraud in obtaining a devise of lands is always sent out of chancery to be determined at law.[j] Hitherto, again, we find no difference between a court of law and a court of equity.

A court of equity has been represented as bound by no precedents or rules, but as proceeding arbitrarily, according to the sentiments of the

j. 3. Bl. Com. 431.

chancellor, arising from the circumstances of every particular case. But, in truth, precedents and rules govern as much in chancery as they govern in courts of law. Decrees are often founded on no other principle, than a reverence for a series of former concurring determinations. Hitherto, still, again, we find no difference between a court of equity and a court of law. The rules of property, the rules of interpretation, and the rules of evidence are, in both, the same. The systems of jurisprudence in both are systems equally laboured and artificial, and founded equally on the same principles of justice and positive law.

Let it be observed farther, that the distinction between law and equity, as administered in separate courts, is not known at present, nor seems to have been known at any former period, in any country, excepting England, and those of her colonies, who, in this instance, have imitated the practice of England. Even in England, the aula regis, anciently, as we have seen, a court of supreme jurisdiction over the whole kingdom, administered equal justice, according to the rules of equity as well as of law. In none of our very ancient authors, such as Glanvil,[13] Bracton, Fleta, and Britton,[14] do we find the remotest reference or allusion to the equitable jurisdiction in the court of chancery. When the aula regis, become unwieldy and cumbersome, was divided into a number of distinct courts, a court of equity, existing separately from a court of law, did not, by any means, enter into the original plan of partition.[k]

Whence then the origin and progress of this distinct and independent equitable jurisdiction, which, in England, has become so very extensive and important? In what material or essential points, does it differ from a jurisdiction exercised according to the rules and principles of law? These questions merit full and satisfactory answers.

In very early times, the chancellor of England was nothing more than an officer merely ministerial. He was the king's secretary. In this character, he had the sole charge of writing the king's letters. In the same character, he acquired the sole power of issuing the king's writs.[l] These writs were

13. Ranulf de Glanvill (?–1190) was chief justiciar of England during the reign of Henry II. He is reputed to be the author of *Tractatus de legibus et consuetudinibus regni Anglie* (*Treatise of the Laws and Customs of England,* c. 1187–1189).

14. *Britton* likely refers to a legal text written in the late thirteenth century by an unknown author. It is the first book of English law to be written in Norman French rather than Latin.

k. 3. Bl. Com. 49.

l. Millar. 469.

necessary, not only to bring the defendant into court, but also to give the court jurisdiction over the cause. For, soon after the conquest, it became a general rule, that no plea could be held in the king's court without the king's writ.[m] As causes and the kinds of causes multiplied, the chancellor was more and more employed in issuing writs, and in framing new writs, directed to the courts of common law, in order to empower them to give remedy in cases, in which none could before be obtained.

On this subject we find an early legislative provision.[n] "When, in one case, a writ was found in the chancery; and, in a like case falling under the same right and requiring the like remedy, no precedent of a writ could be produced, the clerks in chancery were directed to form a new one. If they could not agree, it was adjourned to the next parliament, that a writ might be framed by the consent of the learned in the law." This provision was made, "lest it should happen that the court of the king should be deficient in doing justice to the suitors." Here we see the chancery fully established as the great *officina brevium*.[15] These writs, however, were all intended to be returnable in the courts of justice. At this time, the chancery itself was not considered as a court: it is always mentioned as an office merely.[o]

In the reign of Richard the second, the provision, which we have just now read, was applied to a purpose, unforeseen and unexpected. Uses of land—a species, not of property, but of an artificial and mysterious claim to the advantages of property, which I shall hereafter consider minutely—began, about that time, to be introduced. The establishment of them was, to the clergy, a lucrative and a favourite object: for it would have eluded the statutes of mortmain. To accomplish this object, John Waltham,[16] the bishop of Salisbury, and at that time chancellor, by a strained interpretation of the law, devised the writ of subpoena—the powerful instrument of chancery jurisdiction—and made it returnable before himself in chancery, in order to oblige a feoffee to uses to account for the profits of the land.[p] Successful in assuming the jurisdiction of one case, the chancellor afterwards extended it to others; and, in the time of Edward the fourth, the

m. 1. Reev. 66.

n. St. 13. Edw. 1. c. 24.

15. Short workshop.

o. 1. Reev. 43.

16. John Waltham was keeper of the privy seal from 1386–1389 and treasurer from 1391 until his death in 1395.

p. Millar. 475. 3. Bl. Com. 51.

process by subpoena was become the daily practice of the court. Such was the origin of the equitable jurisdiction of chancery.

The description which we have given of courts of equity and courts of law, and of equitable and legal jurisdictions, is conformable to the practice and proceedings of the court of chancery and of the courts of common law in England, at present, and during the last hundred years, or the greatest part of them. But this description cannot, with propriety, be applied to the practice and proceedings of those courts at periods more remote: in those remote periods, a court of equity was considered and acted as possessing a power, altogether discretionary. "Equity," says Mr. Selden,[q] "is a roguish thing. For law we have a measure: know what to trust to. Equity is according to the conscience of him that is chancellor; and as that is larger or narrower, so is equity. It is all one as if they should make the standard of measure a chancellor's foot. What an uncertain measure would this be! One chancellor has a long foot: another, a short foot; a third, an indifferent foot. 'Tis the same thing in the chancellor's conscience." Similar, though not expressed, perhaps, in a similar manner, were the sentiments of the principal lawyers of that age—of Spelman, of Coke, of Lambard,[17] and even of the great Bacon,[r] who himself held the office of chancellor, and who, of all others, appears to have been the best qualified to understand the nature of that office. This, indeed, was in the infancy, as it may be called, of the court of chancery, before its jurisdiction was settled, and when the chancellors, partly from their ignorance of law, and partly from ambition and lust of power, had arrogated to themselves such unlimited authority, as has since been totally disclaimed by their successours.

In the remote periods, which we have mentioned, while a court of equity acted and was considered as possessing powers altogether discretionary, the courts of law, on the other hand, acted upon principles, which were both narrow and unjust.[s] If the judges of the courts of common law had been as liberal then as they have been since, the court of chancery would never have swelled to its present enormous bulk. "I have always thought,"

q. Table talk.

17. William Lambard (1536–1601) was an English jurist who wrote *Archaionomia* (1568), *Eirenarcha* (1581), and *Archaion* (1591).

r. Millar. 477. 3. Bl. Com. 433.

s. 3. Bl. Com. 433.

said the very able and learned Judge,[t] whose opinion I now quote, "that formerly there was too confined a way of thinking in the judges of the courts of common law; and that courts of equity have risen, because the judges have not properly applied the principles of the common law, but, being too narrowly governed by old cases and maxims, have too much prevented the publick from having the benefit of that law." This contracted spirit, prevailing, for a long time, in the courts of common law, necessarily drove a multitude of suitors into a court of equity for relief. The doors of this court were constantly open to receive them.

I adduce an instance, familiar and striking. A double bond—a bond, with a penalty containing the double of the sum really due—is an instrument peculiar, I believe, to England, and those countries which have adopted the laws of England. It was originally contrived to evade those absurd constitutions, which interdicted the receipt or payment of interest for the use of money lent. Since interest could not be allowed by the law, as it then stood, the penalty was, in the courts of law, considered as the real debt, when the debtor did not perform his agreement at the time stipulated; and for the penalty, judgment was accordingly given. In proportion as business and trade became considerable and extended, the necessity and the propriety of paying and receiving interest became daily more apparent, and was allowed by the law; and, in the reign of Henry the eighth, it was declared, by an act of parliament, that the debt or loan itself was, "the just and true intent," for which the obligation was given. One would naturally suppose, that this legislative declaration would have been a sufficient authority for the courts of law to alter the principle, on which their former judgments had been given. The narrow minded judges of those times thought otherwise; and, adhering wilfully and technically to the letter of the settled precedents, refused to consider the payment of principal, interest, and costs as a full satisfaction for the bond. In the courts of equity, where a more liberal spirit prevailed, the instrument, according to "its just and true intent," was considered as merely a security for the money really due, and was discharged on its payment. But so pertinaciously, in this instance, did the courts of law cling to their precedents, even so late as the present century, that the parliament was obliged, at length, to interpose,

t. Lord Chief Justice Wilmot. 2. Wils. 350.

and to direct, that what had long been the practice in the courts of equity, should, in future, be the practice in the courts of law.[u]

We now see the causes of the progress, which a distinct and independent equitable jurisdiction made in England.

In many instances, however, and, indeed, in the general principles of their proceedings and adjudications, the courts of law and equity have, for a century past, gradually approximated to one another. A series of eminent lawyers, who successively filled the chancellor's chair, formed the system of equity into a regular science, which, like the science of law, cannot be acquired without the aids of study and experience. In the courts of law, a series of lawyers, equally eminent, have, by degrees, embraced the enlarged and enlightened principles, by which law as well as equity should be governed and illustrated. In chancery, it is a maxim, that equity follows the law. In the courts of law, a powerful reason for adopting a principle or rule is the consideration, that the principle or rule has been adopted in chancery. Each jurisdiction, as far as possible, follows the other, in the best and most effectual measures for attaining the great ends of certainty, peace, and justice. The suggestion, indeed, of every bill in equity, in order to give jurisdiction to the court, is still, that the complainant has no remedy at the common law. But he who views the variety and extent of the causes determined in chancery, must be satisfied that this suggestion is now a mere fiction, copied, indeed, from the realities of former times.

We are now prepared to give an answer to the second question, which was proposed some time ago—In what material or essential points, does the jurisdiction of chancery differ from a jurisdiction exercised according to the rules and principles of the common law?

They differ not, as we have seen, in the rules of property, of evidence, or of interpretation: they differ not in the principles of justice or of positive law. Still, however, they differ in some points very material, and which ought to be known.

They differ with regard to the mode of proof. By the rules of the common law, as a party cannot be a witness in his own favour, so he cannot be obliged to become a witness, or to furnish evidence, against himself.

u. 3. Bl. Com. 435.

But the views of equity, with regard to this subject, are more extensive and refined. If the defendant knows the claim made upon him to be well founded, he ought neither to conceal it, nor refuse to satisfy it. If he has done nothing improperly, he can sustain no loss by a candid declaration of what he has done. If his conduct has been fraudulent, the fraud should receive no protection: but it receives protection, if it is suffered to be concealed. For these reasons, when material facts rest only in the knowledge of the party, a court of equity examines him, on oath, with regard to the truth of the transaction.

In mercantile transactions, this mode of discovery is peculiarly reasonable and important. In such transactions, the parties are generally at a distance from one another: their contracts, therefore, cannot be made in the presence of witnesses. Of such transactions, each party keeps or ought to keep a regular diary or account. On the truth and accuracy of this account, the other party may naturally be supposed to place a very considerable degree of dependence.

As this mode of discovery is unknown to the courts of law, equity has acquired a concurrent jurisdiction with those courts in all matters of account. From the same source, it has acquired a jurisdiction in matters of fraud, and judgments at law obtained by fraud or concealment.

In the courts of common law, the trial is by a jury. This trial requires, that the witnesses should give their testimony *viva voce,* and in open court. But in courts of equity, the mode of trial is by administering interrogatories to the witnesses, and taking their depositions in writing, wherever they may happen to reside. For this reason, the chancery alone can take proofs by commission, when the witnesses are abroad, or about to go abroad, or are prevented by age or infirmity from attending.

When a contract has been made and broken, a court of law only awards damages for the breach; but a court of equity will decree a specifick performance. It will likewise set aside deeds, and order sales and conveyances of lands.[v]

These are the principal, though not the only points, in which the jurisdiction of a court of equity differs materially from that of the courts of common law. I speak of those jurisdictions as considered under the

v. Millar. 482. 3. Bl. Com. 437.

aspects, under which they have been hitherto viewed. There is a particular aspect, in which they have never, so far as I know, been viewed; but to which I shall, by and by, direct your minute attention.

In the mean time, it will be proper to consider a question, which has employed the talents of the most eminent writers on jurisprudence. Should the jurisdiction according to equity, and the jurisdiction according to law, be committed to the same court? or should they be divided between different courts?

My Lord Bacon thinks that they should be divided: my Lord Kaims thinks that they should be united. All this is very natural. My Lord Bacon presided in a divided, my Lord Kaims was a judge in a united jurisdiction. Let us attend to their arguments: the arguments of such consummate masters will suggest abundant matter of instruction, even if we cannot subscribe to them implicitly.

The reason assigned by my Lord Bacon for preferring the division of these jurisdictions between several courts is, that if they are committed to the same court, the distinction between them will soon be lost; for that the discretionary will soon draw along with it the legal power.[w]

My Lord Kaims admits, that, in the science of jurisprudence, it is undoubtedly of great importance, that the boundary between equity and common law be clearly ascertained; because, otherwise, we shall in vain hope for just decisions. A judge, adds he, who is uncertain whether the case belong to equity or to common law, cannot have a clear conception what judgment ought to be pronounced. But, on the other hand, may it not be urged, that to divide, among different courts, things intimately connected bears hard upon every man, who has a claim to prosecute; because, before he bring his action, he must, at his peril, determine a point extremely nice—whether the case is to be governed by equity, or by common law? Nor is the most profound knowledge always sufficient to prevent inconveniences upon this subject: for, though he may be perfectly acquainted with his own demand, he cannot certainly foresee the defence, nor divine whether it will be a defence at law or in equity. Weighing these different arguments, the preponderancy seems, in his opinion, to be on the side of a united jurisdiction. The sole inconvenience of a united jurisdiction—that

w. 1. Ld. Bac. 253. Aph. 45.

it tends to blend common law with equity—may admit a remedy by an institute, distinguishing, with accuracy, their boundaries: but the inconvenience of a divided jurisdiction admits not any effectual remedy.[x]

Both these great men agree in one point—that the distinction between common law and equity ought, by all means, to be preserved; and one of them recommends even an institute to distinguish their limits with accuracy. With the becoming deference to such high authority, it may be worth while to examine, whether, in the fluctuating situation of men and business, an attempt to fix permanently the line of division between law and equity would not be fruitless and impracticable. This line, I am apt to believe, will be found to change necessarily according to different circumstances—the state of property—the improvement of the arts—the experience of the judges—the refinement of the people.

In rude ages, the first decisions of judges arose, probably, from their immediate feelings; in other words, from considerations of equity. In the course of their business, many similar cases would successively occur: upon these, similar decisions would naturally be given. A number of precedents, thus introduced, would, from the power of custom, acquire authority and respect. General rules would gradually be formed; and the utility of establishing them would become an object of attention. Those rules, however, upon a little further experience, would be found, at some times, too narrow; at other times, too broad. To adhere rigidly to them, at all times, would be to commit injustice under the sanction of law. To avoid an evil so alarming, it would be thought advisable, upon extraordinary occasions, to recede from general maxims, and to decide, as originally, according to the immediate sentiments of justice. In this manner, the distinction between equity and strict law was, probably, introduced: the former comprehended the established rules: the latter comprised their exceptions.

But when the exceptions became numerous, many of them also would be found to be similar, and, consequently, to require a similar decision. Those similar decisions would, in time, produce a new rule; and this new rule would, in its turn, give birth to new exceptions.

If this account of the matter is just—and it seems to be natural—law and equity are in a state of continual progression; one occupying inces-

x. Prin. of Eq. 49.

santly the ground, which the other, in its advancement, has left. The posts now possessed by strict law were formerly possessed by equity; and the posts now possessed by equity will hereafter be possessed by strict law.

In this view of the subject—and it is an interesting one—equity may be well deemed the conductor of law towards a state of refinement and perfection.

In this view of the subject, we can find no difficulty in pronouncing, that every court of law ought also to be a court of equity; for every institution should contain in it the seeds of its perfection, as well as of its preservation.

In this view of the subject, we shall find as little difficulty in pronouncing, that every court of equity will gradually become a court of law; for its decisions, at first discretionary, will gradually be directed by general principles and rules. Thus, in England, the court of chancery has gradually devested itself of its original and arbitrary character, and has approached to that of the courts of common law. Thus, again, in England, the courts of common law, animated lately with the spirit of improvement inspired by a liberal age, have enlarged their powers of just decision, and have advanced within the precincts of equity.

The particulars, in which they still differ, are, indeed, of importance; but I see no reason why the separate powers of chancery, placed there very properly, indeed, should be thought incommunicable to the courts of common law.

A power to compel discoveries by a party may, without any incongruity, be annexed to a common law jurisdiction. This, to a certain degree, has been already done by a law of the United States. In the trial of actions at law, the courts of the national government are authorized to require the parties to produce books or writings in their power, in cases, in which they might be compelled to produce them by the ordinary rules of proceeding in chancery.[y]

The power of granting commissions to take, upon interrogatories, the depositions of foreign, removing, or infirm witnesses is familiar, in practice, to the courts both of the United States and of Pennsylvania.

The power of compelling a specifick performance is, I apprehend, strictly and originally a power at the common law. In some of its unpropitious

y. Laws U. S. 1. cong. 1. sess. c. 20. s. 15.

eras, indeed, the exercise of this part of its authority has, in most cases, fallen into disuse, and has not been revived, but anciently it subsisted in its full force and vigour; and, in one case, it is supposed to subsist in its full force and vigour to this day. I fortify my opinion by instances of the fact.

Fines, or solemn agreements acknowledged and entered of record, are well known to be of very high antiquity at the common law. It is generally, I believe, supposed, that they took place only in pleas respecting land. But the fact is unquestionably otherwise. Fines were executed in other pleas. If either of the parties violated the agreement, a suit upon it was commenced. When they both appeared in court; if they both acknowledged the writing containing the agreement; or if the agreement was stated to be such by the justices, before whom it was taken, and this was testified by their record; then the party, who had broken it, was in the king's mercy, and was attached till he gave good security to perform the concord in future—either the specifick thing agreed on, if that was possible; or otherwise, in some instances, an equivalent.[z] Can a power to adjudge a specifick performance be expressed more unequivocally or more strongly? This instance is referred to a period so ancient as the reign of Henry the second.

In the reign of Edward the first, we find that, in some cases, land could be recovered in a writ of covenant; and in such cases, it was a real action: in other cases, damages only could be recovered; and in such cases, it was a personal action. The former writ of covenant was generally that, on which fines were levied.[a] Actions of covenant for land occur likewise in the time of Edward the second. It was held, that this action was appropriated for the recovery of a fee simple or of a term.[b]

In tracing this subject down to the reign of Edward the third, we find that a writ of covenant was that, upon which fines were most commonly levied. But, by this time, the writ of covenant was usually brought upon a supposed transaction. The writ of covenant, in this instance, had the effect of actually transferring the land; and thus produced a *specifick* effect.[c] Such, with regard to fines, continues to be the practice to the present day.

z. 1. Reev. 119.
a. Id. 477.
b. 2. Reev. 33. 147.
c. Id. 173.

I think I have now proved, that the power to adjudge a specifick performance is strictly and originally a power at common law.

The power to set aside deeds, and to order sales and conveyances of land, can be considered only as branches of the power to compel a specifick performance.

In all the views which we have hitherto taken of this important part of jurisprudence, we find no reason to conclude, that a court of chancery would bestow any improvement of essential importance, on the juridical system of the United States, or of this commonwealth.

There is, however, another view, in which this subject ought to be considered. In that other view, if I mistake not, the establishment of a court of chancery will be found a matter of great moment both to the United States and to Pennsylvania.

Military power has too long governed in the affairs of men: influence of a kind more peaceful and benign is, we hope, about to assume its place. We trust that, in future, men, instead of knowing and treating one another as enemies, and as engaged in enterprises mutually destructive, will know and treat one another as friends, and as jointly operating in plans and systems for promoting the prosperity, the virtue, and the felicity of the human race.

Deeds of arms, we fondly anticipate, will not be the themes of future songs. The more delightful subjects of agriculture, of the arts, and of commerce will employ the efforts of genius the most sublime.

Commerce arrests our present attention. Its encouragement is justly a favourite object with every government, which is good and wise. The protection of commerce, and of foreign merchants engaged in commerce, forms an article in the great charter of the liberties of England. A regulation, so salutary and so humane, deserves, as it has obtained, the warmest eulogium of the eloquent Montesquieu. Upon this subject, his powers carried him away like a torrent, rapid and irresistible: my humbler aim is to glide along a smooth and gentle stream.

The law merchant as well as the law maritime forms a branch of the general law of nations. The inference is natural, that mercantile as well as maritime transactions should be the object of a separate jurisdiction; and that we should see courts of commerce as well as courts of admiralty.

Things done upon the sea are deemed worthy of peculiar cognizance: are things done beyond the sea less entitled to peculiar notice?

In the rude and barbarous times, which are past, and which, we pray, may never return—in those times, above alluded to, when nations were known to nations only by feats of hostility; even their hostile feats were subjected to the cognizance of law, and were dignified with an appropriate jurisdiction. The court of chivalry, held before the lord high constable and earl marshal of England, had cognizance of contracts and deeds of arms and of war out of the realm, and also of things which touched war within the realm.[d] When war was the general trade, this court enjoyed a high degree of consequence and reputation. My Lord Coke calls it "the honourable court." As commerce comes in the place of war, should not commercial come in the place of military institutions?

Even with regard to commerce, we shall find, in former ages, establishments expressly made and calculated for its protection and encouragement, in the manner in which it was then carried on. This was chiefly in markets and publick fairs, at which merchants attended personally with their merchandise. It was not then usual to trust property to a great amount in the hands of foreign correspondents.

So early as the reign of Henry the third, we find the delays, and what were called the solemnities, of proceedings dispensed with, where the plaintiff deserved a particular respect or privilege; as noble persons, or merchants, who were continually leaving the kingdom.[e]

Edward the first[18] has been often and deservedly styled the English Justinian. In his reign we may expect to find a proper attention paid to the interests of commerce. Our expectation will not be disappointed. In his reign the statute of merchants was made.

The pressing demands, which arise in the course of mercantile transactions, rendered the delays and the niceties of the law inconvenient, and sometimes fatal, to the credit and fortunes of the merchants. This, it is said, occasioned many to withdraw from the kingdom. Those, who re-

d. 4. Ins. 123.
e. 1. Reev. 295. 296. 300.
18. Edward I (1239–1307) was king of England from 1272 to 1307.

mained, made application that some speedy course might be appointed for recovering their debts at the stipulated times of payment. In compliance with their application, the following method of securing a ready payment of their debts was provided by parliament. The merchant was to bring his debtor before the magistrates specified in the law, to acknowledge the debt and the time of payment. This recognisance was entered on a roll. If the debtor did not make payment at the time appointed, the magistrate, before whom the recognisance was acknowledged, was, on the application of the creditor, obliged immediately to cause the chattels and devisable lands of the debtor to be sold, to the amount of the debt, by the appraisement of honest men. The money, if the property was sold, was paid instantly to the creditor: if the property could not be sold, it was delivered to him according to the appraisement. If, from partiality to the debtor, the appraisers set too high a price upon the goods, they were themselves obliged to take them at the price which they fixed, and to satisfy the creditor for the money due to him.[f]

Commerce continued to be patronised by the kings, and encouraged by the legislature, of England. In the twenty seventh year of Edward the third,[19] was made the famous statute of the staple, containing a most complete code of regulations for commercial transactions at the staple, or great mart, which was then established in certain places of England.

As this mart was intended, in its very institution, for the resort of foreign merchants, a mode, consonant to the ideas of foreigners, and fitted to the nature of mercantile transactions, was adopted for administering justice. That disputes might be decided among them according to their own conceptions, it was provided, that none of the justices of the courts of Westminster Hall, nor any other justices, if they came to the places where the mart was, should interfere with the jurisdiction of the mayor and constables of the staple. Within the town where the mart was, those officers had cognizance of people and of things touching the mart. All merchants coming to it, and their servants, were, in all things concerning it, governed by the law merchant, and not by the common law of the land, nor by the usages of cities, or boroughs, or towns; nor were they, concern-

f. 1. Reev. 405.
19. Edward III (1312–1377) was king of England from 1327 to 1377.

ing such things, to implead or be impleaded before the magistrates of such cities, boroughs, or towns. That the foreign merchants might have reason to complain of no one, and that no one might have reason to complain of them, speedy justice was administered from day to day, and from hour to hour.

That contracts made within the staple might be strictly observed, and that payments might be punctually made, a course similar to that of the statute merchant was directed. The mayor of the staple was empowered to take similar recognisances of debts; and upon those recognisances, similar proceedings were held. A recognisance of this kind has obtained the name of a statute staple.[g]

It was directed that, in every staple town, the mayor should be one well acquainted with the law merchant, that he might be qualified for the discharge of such an important trust.[h]

If we refer to the institutions of the ancient nations; we shall find that, among them too, tribunals have been established for the decision of mercantile causes. Magistrates, called ναυτοδικαι, had the jurisdiction of them in Athens.[i] The praetor peregrinus determined them in Rome.[j] Even after the fall of the western empire, the institution of courts for the trial of commercial suits subsisted in many places:[k] and fairs and markets had their peculiar jurisdictions assigned for the expeditious determination of controversies that might arise in them.

The United States have the most extensive prospects of commerce before them. The variety of their climate, the richness of their soil, the number and value of their productions furnish them with abundant materials to exchange for the manufactures and refined commodities of Europe and of Asia. The genius of their governments is favourable to trade, because it is favourable to equality and industry, the only pillars, on which trade can be supported. The long and cumbrous list of duties and customs, which publick debts, the arts of finance, and the political views of government have introduced into every country of Europe, is, in a great measure, unknown

g. 2. Reev. 71.
h. 2. Reev. 75.
i. Bouch. The. Com. 134.
j. Id. 138.
k. Id. 140.

in their ports. They possess not, indeed, the advantages of use and habit to form precedents for their transactions, publick and private, with foreign nations, and with the individuals of whom foreign nations are composed: but to compensate for this, they are disengaged from one inconvenience, with which use and habit are naturally accompanied—I mean that of confining the imagination, and damping the spirit of vigorous and enlarged enterprise. In order to improve the opportunities, with which they are favoured, and to avail themselves, as they ought, of the happy situation, in which they are placed, they should encourage commerce by a liberal system of mercantile jurisprudence.

These observations concerning the situation, the duty, and the interest of the United States, receive an easy and a strong application to the situation, the duty, and the interest of Pennsylvania.

In other countries, as we have seen, where commerce has been regarded as an object worthy of the publick attention, jurisdictions have been established for the trial and determination of commercial causes. In the United States and in Pennsylvania, commercial causes are tried in the same manner, by the same tribunals, at the same expense, and with the same delay, as other controversies relating to property. This must be often productive of the most serious disadvantages.

Before the revolution, we were strangers, in a great measure, to what is properly called foreign commerce. The same system of commercial law pervaded Great Britain and her colonies. The rules, therefore, of admitting foreign testimony, and of authenticating foreign transactions, have been but lately the objects of much consideration. They have not been fixed with the clearness and precision, which are now become requisite. But they should, as soon as possible, be ascertained, particularized, and rendered as easy as the precautions necessary to avoid fraud will admit.

Great innovations should not be made: a wise and well tempered system must owe much to experience. But the foundations should be laid betimes. They should be broad, and deep, and well compacted, that they may be sufficient to support the magnificent structure, which the present and future ages will build upon them.

The important ends, which may be attained by a court of chancery formed and organized for commercial purposes, now begin to appear in prospect before us. In this view, the establishment of courts of chancery appears to be of high importance to the United States in general, and to the commonwealth of Pennsylvania in particular.

It will not, I am sure, be supposed, that I am unfriendly to the trial by jury. I love—I admire it: but my love and my admiration spring from proper principles: I love and I admire with reason on my side. Sacrilege would be offered to the venerable institution, by profaning it to purposes, for which it was never intended. Let it be maintained in purity—let it be maintained in vigour: but if it be so maintained, it must be maintained in that spirit, and in that application, for which it was formed, and to which it is so exquisitely adjusted. Its genius should be encouraged and concentred: if it be applied to foreign and unnatural objects, its strength will soon dissolve and evaporate.

Let us attend to the nature of mercantile transactions. Accounts never were, by the course of the common law, brought to trial before a jury. To a jury, indeed, the general question—ought the party to account—was submitted for its determination. But the adjustment of the accounts was submitted to auditors, instead of being tried by a jury. If, upon any article in account, the auditors cannot agree; or, if agreeing, the parties are not satisfied; then, upon each point, so litigated, a separate and distinct issue may be taken, and that issue must be tried by a jury. In this manner, a hundred issues may be joined in the same cause, and tried separately by as many juries; but the general statement of the disputed accounts still remains before the auditors, and by them the general result from the whole must be formed and ascertained. This mode of liquidating accounts judicially at common law, is obviously exposed to many disadvantages and delays; and, for this reason, the action of account has, in a great measure, fallen into disuse. In England, the parties in unsettled and litigated accounts have recourse to chancery; in Pennsylvania, to arbitrators, or to jurors acting in the character of arbitrators.

The numerous embarrassments, which arise from the want of a proper commercial forum, are well known and severely felt both by the gentlemen of the bar, and by the gentlemen of the exchange.

Impressed with these truths, the committee who were appointed to report a draught of a constitution for the consideration of the late convention of Pennsylvania, included, in their report, the plan of a chancery establishment. The convention thought it improper to fix that establishment as a part of the constitution, but have given ample powers to the legislature to adopt that or any similar one, and to model and alter it as the sage instructions of time may direct.

Impressed with these truths, which I have both witnessed and experienced, I have thought it my duty to bring this important subject fully into your view. Viewed in a commercial light, Pennsylvania, and particularly her metropolis, attracts solicitous attention both on this and on the other side of the Atlantick. Every friend to Pennsylvania, every friend to her metropolis, every enlightened friend to the interests of commerce, must wish ardently to see her commercial establishments complete. These observations apply to the United States on a scale still more extensive; and, as applied to them, therefore, acquire still an additional degree of importance.

With these observations I conclude, at last, my minute delineation—if drawn in a more masterly manner, it would be interesting as well as minute—of the juridical establishments of the United States and of Pennsylvania.

CHAPTER IV.
Of the Nature of Courts.

The next subjects of my remarks are, the nature, and the constituent parts of courts.

That the judicial department should be independent, is a principle, which, in a former part of my lectures,[a] I had an opportunity of stating, explaining, and enforcing at large. In the review which we have now made of that department, as established in the United States and in this commonwealth, we see what a strict and uniform regard has been paid to the practical observance of this very important principle. To neither of the constitutions is a judicial magistrate known, who holds his office by a tenure less secure or less respectable than that of his own good behaviour.

All courts should be open. This is one of the rules, which, by the constitution of Pennsylvania,[b] is rendered inviolable by the legislature itself. It is a rule of the highest moment.

The place of administering justice was originally at the gates of the cities—in other words, in the presence of all the people. Such was the practice in the days of Job.[c] By Moses also, of legislators the first and wisest, the same ancient custom is mentioned.[d] Homer speaks of it as subsisting in the heroick ages.[e] In some countries, this simple and undisguised mode is still observed.[f]

Among the Saxons, as we are informed by Selden, their courts, like the heliastick court at Athens, were, for the most part, kept in the open air.[g]

a. Ante, vol. 1. p. 703.
b. Art. 9. s. 11.
c. Job xxix. 7.
d. Gen. xxiii. 18.
e. Il. l. 18. v. 497.
f. 1. Gog. Or. L. 28.
g. Bac. on Gov. 10.

By the ancient Romans, trials were held in publick, in the presence of the accused, and of all who wished to hear them. This procedure was open and noble; says the writer[h] who mentions it; it breathed Roman magnanimity.

In France, too, as appears, we are told, from some old manuscript law books, criminal processes were anciently carried on in publick, and in a form not very different from the publick judgments of the Romans. "The witnesses," says Beaumanoir, one of the oldest writers on the laws of France, "ought to give their testimony in open court."[i]

All trials, says Beccaria,[j] should be publick; that opinion, which is the best, or, perhaps, the only cement of society, may curb the authority of the powerful, and the passions of the judge; and that the people, inspired with courage, may say, "We are not slaves; we are protected by the laws."

"Let not," says my Lord Bacon,[k] in the same spirit of sound sense, "decrees issue in silence: let judges give the reasons of their judgments: let them do this openly; that what is unrestrained in point of authority, may be circumscribed by a regard to character and fame."

But why, it may be asked, are examples produced in such numbers—why do we cite authorities of so much weight, in order to establish a principle, in itself so extremely plain? Is it not selfevident, that, in a court of justice, every one is entitled to a publick trial? Why, then, refer us to instances, in Asia, in Greece, in Rome, in France, of the enjoyment of a selfevident right?

Because, in Asia, in Greece, in Rome, in France, too, till very lately, the enjoyment of this selfevident right has been lost. Liberty, indeed, says it is selfevident: but tyranny holds a contrary language; and unfortunately for the human race, the voice of tyranny has been more loud and more powerful than the voice of freedom.

To states as well as to individuals, the lesson is salutary—let those, who stand, take heed lest they fall. Asia is fallen, Greece is fallen, Rome is fallen, France is fallen—I correct myself—she rises. Let the other monitory instances suggest caution: I offer them not to your imitation.

h. Com. on Bec. c. 22.
i. Mont. Sp. L. b. 28. c. 34.
j. C. 14.
k. 1. Ld. Bac. 252. Aph. 38.

The slave who suffers, and the slave who dreads the inquisition—how would he exult to be able to say, in the irrevocable language of Pennsylvania, "all courts shall be open."

According to the rules of judicial architecture, a system of courts should resemble a pyramid. Its base should be broad and spacious: it should lessen as it rises: its summit should be a single point. To express myself without a metaphor—in every judicial department, well arranged and well organized, there should be a regular, progressive gradation of jurisdiction; and one supreme tribunal should superintend and govern all the others.

An arrangement in this manner is proper for two reasons. 1. The supreme tribunal produces and preserves a uniformity of decision through the whole judicial system. 2. It confines and it supports every inferiour court within the limits of its just jurisdiction.

If no superintending tribunal of this nature were established, different courts might adopt different and even contradictory rules of decision; and the distractions, springing from these different and contradictory rules, would be without remedy and without end. Opposite determinations of the same question, in different courts, would be equally final and irreversible. But when, from those opposite determinations, an appeal to a jurisdiction superiour to both is provided, one of them will receive a sentence of confirmation, the other, of reversal. Upon future occasions, the determination confirmed will be considered as an authority; the determination reversed will be viewed as a beacon.

Ampliare jurisdictionem[1] has been a principle avowed by some judges: it is natural, and will operate where it is not avowed. It will operate powerfully and irresistibly among a number of coordinate and independent jurisdictions; and, without a tribunal possessing a control over all, the pernicious and interfering claims could neither be checked nor adjusted. But a supreme court prohibits the abuse, and protects the exercise, of every inferiour judiciary power.

In France, before the present revolution, the establishment of a number of parliaments or independent tribunals produced, in the different provinces, a number of incongruous and jarring decisions. This has been assigned, and with much apparent reason, as the great source of that diversity

1. To enlarge the jurisdiction.

of customs and laws, which prevailed, to an uncommon degree, in the different parts of the kingdom of France, in other respects so well compacted.

In England, the principles and the rules of law are, through the whole judiciary department, reduced to a standard, uniform in an exemplary degree. In no country perhaps, does a stronger impression prevail of the advantages resulting from stability in the administration of justice. But by an unwise inattention, to say the least of it, to the inferiour establishments, the base of the exquisitely proportioned edifice, erected by Alfred, is narrowed and weakened; and its beauty and durability are consequently impaired.

In the United States and Pennsylvania—for here we must take the two constitutions in a collected view—a fine and regular gradation appears, from the justices of the peace in the commonwealth, to the supreme court of the national government. The justice of peace is, in criminal matters, assisting to the court of quarter sessions: in civil causes, his jurisdiction is subordinate to the court of common pleas. The courts of common pleas, and quarter sessions, and orphans' courts of each county are subordinate to the supreme court, whose jurisdiction extends over the commonwealth. The supreme court is, by a late law, rendered subordinate to the high court of errours and appeals. With regard to the register's court, an exception is introduced by the law just now mentioned. Though a county jurisdiction, it is not rendered subordinate to the supreme court by an appeal: that revisionary process is directed *per saltum*[2] to the high court of errours and appeals. From the highest court of a state, a writ of errour lies, in federal causes, to the supreme court of the United States. In the national government, a writ of errour lies from a district to a circuit court, and from a circuit to the supreme court.

In controversies, to which the state or nation is a party, the state or nation itself ought to be amenable before the judicial powers. This principle, dignified because it is just, is expressly ratified by the constitution of Pennsylvania.[1] It declares, that suits may be brought against the commonwealth. The manner, the courts, and the cases, in which they may be brought, are left to the direction of the legislature. It was deemed sufficient to recognise

2. By a leap.
1. Art. 9. s. 11.

the principle: its operation will be guided in such a way, as time and circumstances shall suggest. Upon the same principle, the judicial power of the national government "shall extend to controversies to which the United States are a party; and to controversies between two or more states."[m]

These provisions may be viewed by some as incompatible with the opinions, which they have formed concerning the sovereignty of the states.

In the introduction to my lectures,[n] I had an opportunity of showing the astonishing and intricate mazes, in which politicians and philosophers have, on this subject, bewildered themselves, and of evincing, that the dread and redoubtable sovereign, when traced to his ultimate and genuine source, is found, as he ought to be found, in the free and independent man. In one of my lectures,[o] I proved, I hope, that the only reason, why a free and independent man was bound by human laws, was this—that he bound himself. Upon the same principle on which he becomes bound by the laws, he becomes amenable before the courts of justice, which are formed and authorized by those laws. If one free and independent man, an original sovereign, may do all this; why may not an aggregate of free and independent men, a collection of original sovereigns, do this likewise? The dignity of the state is compounded of the dignity of its members. If the dignity of each singly is undiminished, the dignity of all jointly must be unimpaired. Is a man degraded by the manly declaration, that he renders himself amenable to justice? Can a similar declaration degrade a state?

To be privileged from the awards of equal justice, is a disgrace, instead of being an honour; but a state claims a privilege from the awards of equal justice, when she refuses to become a party, unless, in the same case, she becomes a judge.

"In any cause"—said the judge of the high court of admiralty of England, in a very late decision[p]—"In any cause where the crown is a party, it can no more withhold evidence of documents in its possession, than a private person. If the court thinks proper to order the production of any publick instrument, that order must be obeyed."

In the Mirrour of Justices, we have an account of the first constitutions

m. Cons. U. S. art. 3. s. 2.
n. Ante. vol. 1. p. 444. 445.
o. Ante. vol. 1. p. 572. et seq.
p. 1. Col. Jur. 68.

ordained by the ancient kings of England. When the writer of that book calls them ancient, they must be so indeed; for my Lord Coke[q] informs us, that most of it was written long before the conquest. Among these constitutions, we find the following very remarkable one. "It was ordained that the king's court should be open to all plaintiffs; from which they should have, without delay, remedial writs, as well against the king or the queen as against any *other* of the people."[r] You are pleased by tracing another instance, in which Saxon principles are renewed by our constitutions.

"Judges ought to know, that the poorest peasant is a man, as well as the king himself: all men ought to obtain justice; since in the eyes of justice, all men are equal; whether the prince complain of a peasant, or a peasant complain of the prince."[s] These are the words of a king—of the late Frederick of Prussia.[3] In his courts of justice, that great man stood upon his native greatness, and disdained to mount upon the artificial stilts of sovereignty.

In England, there is a noted distinction, which runs through the whole system of courts. Some are courts of record: others are courts not of record.

A court of record is one, whose proceedings and acts are entered in rolls of parchment, and whose power is to hold pleas according to the course of the common law. These rolls, being the memorials of the judges, import in them such incontrollable credit, that they admit no averment, or plea, or proof, to the contrary of what they contain. Such a record can be tried only by itself.[t] No possible kind of evidence, not even that of the senses, can shake its authenticity; if we may rely on the authority of a well known story in Westminster Hall. A party, in perfect health, was hearing his cause; but his counsel, by an unfortunate stroke of his plea, had killed him on the record. The judges could, by no means, take notice of him, though he stood before their eyes. He averred that he was alive: his averment could not be received: it was against the record.[u]

q. 10. Rep. Pref. 14.

r. 4. Cou. Ang. Norm. 437.

s. Warv. 343.

3. Frederick II (1712–1786) ruled Prussia from 1740 to 1786. He is often referred to as Frederick the Great.

t. 1. Inst. 260.

u. Bar. on st. 248.

A court, not of record, is one, whose acts are not enrolled in parchment, or whose proceedings are not according to the course of the common law.[v]

It deserves to be remarked, that the distinction between courts of record and courts not of record was unknown in England till after the Norman conquest.[w] The occasion and the cause of its introduction deserve also to be remarked. The Conqueror,[4] averse to the Saxon law of liberty, but unwilling to run the risk of an attempt to overturn it at once, formed a plan, artful and too successful, for undermining it by degrees. He appointed all the judges of the *curia regis* from among the Normans, ignorant of the Saxon laws, and fond of their own. The language of the court was altered; and all pleadings and proceedings were entered in the Norman tongue. This introduced the technical terms and, imperceptibly, the rules and maxims of that foreign jurisprudence.

This introduction of a new language, the exaltation of the aula regis, and the consequent depression of the county courts, paved the way, in the opinion of a very sensible lawyer,[x] for the distinction between courts of record and not of record. Courts of record were those, whose proceedings were duly entered in the Norman tongue, and, unless reversed, could never be questioned or contradicted. To have allowed such a privilege to the county courts, in which the Saxon suitors were judges, and whose proceedings were in the English language, would have been inconsistent with the genius of the Conqueror's plan; for it would have had a tendency to confirm, rather than to depress, the Saxon system. The county courts, therefore, were considered as courts not of record.

From any thing I have said, no inference, I hope, will be drawn, that I deem fidelity and exactness in registering and preserving the acts of courts of justice as matters of small importance: they are of the greatest. I only mean to enter my protestation against a sacrifice of the principles of common sense, to a superstitious regard for the infallibility of records.

v. Wood. Ins. 464.

w. 1. Reev. 68.

4. William of Normandy (c. 1028–1087) defeated the English at the Battle of Hastings in 1066 and ruled England as king from 1066 to 1087.

x. Sulliv. 271.

CHAPTER V.

Of the Constituent Parts of Courts.— Of the Judges.

I now proceed to consider the constituent parts of courts. The judges form one of those constituent parts. Let me introduce their character by the beautiful and correct description of the magna charta of King John. A judge should know the laws: he should be disposed to observe them.

It seems to be the opinion of some, that severity should be the striking feature in a judge's countenance. His countenance should reflect the sentiments of his heart. In his heart should be written the words of the law. If the law say, and the law does say, that, in all its judgments, justice shall be executed in mercy; on the heart of a judge will this heavenly maxim be deeply engraven; in his looks it will beam.

> —Nec supplex turba timebunt.
> Judicis ora sui; sed erunt sub judice triti.[1]
>
> *Ovid*

He ought, indeed, to be a terrour to evil doers; but he ought also to be a praise to those who do well. The more numerous as well as the more valuable part of the citizens are, we trust, of the latter description. Complacency, therefore, rather than vengeance, should habitually influence the sentiments, and habitually mark the features of a judge.

A judge is the blessing, or he is the curse of society. His powers are important: his character and conduct can never be objects of indifference.

When a judge is mentioned as the curse of society, Jefferies,[2] of infamous memory, instantly starts into view. Some circumstances, which

1. And the suppliant crowd will not fear the face of its judge, but they will be safe under the judge.

2. George Jeffreys (1645–1689) was the highly political, partial, and vindictive judge who had Algernon Sidney wrongly executed.

attended the fate of that odious man, place, in the strongest light, that deep detestation which is always entertained, and which is expressed whenever it can be expressed with safety, against the character and person of an oppressive and tyrannical judge.

When his master abdicated the throne, his own security lay only in flight. From the law, the law's worst assassin could expect no protection. That he might escape unknown, he shaved his eye brows, put on a seaman's habit, and, all alone, made the best of his way to Wapping, with a design to take shipping for a foreign country. But his countenance could not remain undiscovered under all this disguise: a man, whom, upon a trial, he had frightened almost into convulsions, no sooner got a glimpse of it, than, in a moment, he recollected all the terrours he had formerly felt. Notice was instantly given to the mob, who rushed in upon him like a herd of wolves. He was goaded on to the lord mayor: the lord mayor, seeing a man, on whom he had never looked without trembling, brought before him in this situation, fell into fits, was carried to his bed, and never rose from it. On his way to the tower, to which he was committed, he saw threatening faces on every side; he saw whips and halters held up around him; and cried out in agony, "for the Lord's sake, keep them off." I saw him, I heard him, says a cotemporary historian, and without pity too; though, without pity, I never saw any other malefactor.[a]

On the other hand—I now speak from Beccaria[b]—a man of enlightened understanding, appointed guardian of the laws, is the greatest blessing that a sovereign can bestow on a nation. Such a man is accustomed to behold truth, and not to fear it: unacquainted with the greatest part of those imaginary and insatiable necessities, which so often put virtue to the proof, and accustomed to contemplate mankind from the most elevated point of view, he considers the nation as his family, and his fellow citizens as brothers.

Patience of hearing, says the great Lord Bacon, is an essential part of justice; and an overspeaking judge is no well tuned cymbal. It is no grace to a judge, first to find that, which, in due time, he might have heard from the bar; or to show quickness of conceit in cutting witnesses or counsel

a. 4. Guth. 1063.
b. C. 42.

off too short; or to prevent information by questions, even by pertinent ones. In hearing a cause, the parts of a judge are four—to direct the evidence—to moderate length, repetition, or impertinency of speech—to recapitulate, select, and collate the material parts of that which hath been said—to give the rule or sentence.[c]

A judge, particularly a judge of the common law, should bear a great regard to the sentiments and decisions of those, who have thought and decided before him.

It may be asked—why should a point be received as law, merely because one man or a succession of men have said it is law, any more than another point should be received as reason, merely because one philosopher or a set of philosophers have said it is reason? In law, as in philosophy, should not every one think and judge for himself? *Stare decisis*[3] may prevent the trouble of investigation; but it will prevent also the pleasure and the advantages of improvement.

Implicit deference to authority, as I have declared on more occasions than one, I consider as the bane of science; and I honour the benefactors of mankind, who have broken the yoke of that intellectual tyranny, by which, in many ages and in many countries, men have been deprived of the inherent and inalienable right of judging for themselves. But how natural it is, from one extreme to vibrate with violence to its opposite one! Though authority be not permitted to tyrannise as a mistress; may she not be consulted as a skilful guide? May not respect be paid, though a blind assent be refused, to her dictates?

A man must have an uncommon confidence in his own talents, who, in forming his judgments and opinions, feels not a sensible and strong satisfaction in the concurrence of the judgments and opinions of others, equally or more conversant than himself with the subjects, on which those judgments and opinions are formed. Society of wise men in judgment is like the society of brave men in battle: each depends not merely on himself: each depends on others also: by this means, strength and courage are diffused over all. To human authority in matters of opinion, as well as to human testimony in matters of fact, a due regard ought to be paid. To rely

c. 3. Ld. Bac. 377.

3. To stand with what has been decided.

on both these kinds of evidence, is a propensity planted, by nature, in the human mind.

In certain sciences, a peculiar degree of regard should be paid to authority. The common law is one of those sciences. Judicial decisions are the principal and most authentick evidence, which can be given, of the existence of such a custom as is entitled to form a part of the common law. Those who gave such decisions, were selected for that employment, on account of their learning and experience in the common law. As to the parties, and those who represent the parties to them, their judgments continue themselves to be effective laws, while they are unreversed. They should, in the cases of others, be considered as strong evidence of the law. As such, every prudent and cautious judge will appreciate them. He will remember, that his duty and his business is, not to make the law, but to interpret and apply it.

CHAPTER VI.
The Subject Continued. Of Juries.

Juries form, with a few exceptions, another constituent part of courts: they form, especially, a constituent part of courts exercising criminal jurisdiction.

I mentioned, in a former lecture,[a] that I love and admire the trial by jury; and that my love and admiration of it spring from proper principles. Those principles I am now to unfold.

When I speak of juries, I feel no peculiar predilection for the number twelve: a grand jury consists of more, and its number is not precisely fixed.

When I speak of juries, I see no peculiar reason for confining my view to a unanimous verdict, unless that verdict be a conviction of a crime—particularly of a capital crime. In grand juries, unanimity is not required.

When I speak of juries, I mean a convenient number of citizens, selected and impartial, who, on particular occasions, or in particular causes, are vested with discretionary powers to try the truth of facts, on which depend the property, the liberty, the reputation, and the lives of their fellow citizens.

Having described what I mean when I speak of juries, it is proper that I should assign, in the fullest and clearest manner, my reasons for some parts of my description.

The first part in this description, which has drawn your most marked attention, is, probably, that which represents the powers, vested in juries, as discretionary. This part, therefore, merits the first illustration. It will be remembered all along, that the discretionary power vested in

a. Ante. p. 941.

juries is a power to try the truth of facts. "Ad quaestionem facti respondent juratores."[1]

The truth of facts is tried by evidence. The principal species of evidence, which comes before juries, is the testimony of witnesses.

In a former lecture,[b] I had occasion to observe, that human testimony is a source of evidence altogether original, suggested by our constitution; and not acquired, though it is sometimes corroborated, and more frequently corrected, by considerations arising from experience. I had occasion further to observe, that, in no case, the law orders a witness to be believed; for the testimony of a thousand witnesses may not produce belief; and that, in no case, the law orders a witness not to be believed; for belief may be the unavoidable result of his testimony. These general positions, then laid down, it is now our business to fortify and apply. If we shall be successful in fortifying and applying them; we shall see, in a new and in a very striking light, the sublime principle of the institution of juries.

It is tedious, and it is painful, to travel through all the numerous degrees, into which it has been attempted to arrange the force of evidence. Some writers on the subject have divided proofs into such as are near, and such as are remote. Others have been adventurous enough to define the precise number of each, which is necessary to superinduce the condemnation of a person, who is accused. One says, two will be sufficient: a second says, three are necessary: a third fixes upon a number different from either. They have never reflected, that evidence arises from the circumstances attending the fact: that those circumstances should be considered in a collected and not in a separate view; and that on the more or less intimate connexion which subsists between them, the strength or weakness of the evidence resulting from them depends.

The truth of this remark will sufficiently appear, if we consider separately any of the presumptions enumerated by those writers on the criminal law. There is not one of them, which may not appear favourable, or unfavourable, or indifferent to the person under trial. A man, with a bloody sword in his hand, is seen running from a house. On entering it, a person run through the body, and no other person, is found there. Would not the presumption be strong, that the man, who ran from the house was the assassin? But

1. Jurors address the question of fact.
b. Ante. p. 807. 808.

should a jury be compelled, on this evidence, to convict him? Should he not be allowed to prove, if he can, the connexion of this strong circumstance against him with another, in his favour, equally strong—that, passing the door of the house, he was drawn, by the cries of the person assassinated, to his assistance, and suddenly seized the poignard which the assassin had left in his side? The weight of any one circumstance cannot be ascertained independently of others: the number and connexion of those others cannot be specified, previously, in a didactick treatise upon the degrees of evidence.

Thus it is with regard to evidence arising from circumstances: will more success attend an attempt to ascertain systematically the degrees of evidence arising from positive testimony? This depends upon the character of him who delivers, and upon the character of him who receives it. That, which would be believed from the mouth of a witness famed for his integrity and good sense, would be disbelieved, if told by a witness remarkable for falsehood or credulity. A person, hackneyed in the ways and vices of the world, who has deceived and who has been deceived a thousand times, is slow to credit testimony. An undesigning countryman, who has never practised nor experienced the artifices of fraud, believes implicitly every thing he hears. Can the characters of witnesses—can the characters of jurors be graduated in a dissertation upon evidence? And yet, in each particular case, the force of evidence must depend upon the character both of witnesses and jurors.

For these reasons, we find, in the institutions of antiquity, no general rules prescribed concerning the force of testimony, or the weight of presumptions: the emperour Hadrian[2] expressly declares the impracticability of prescribing them. When one of his judges applied to him for a rescript, containing particular directions upon this subject; the emperour wrote him an answer, in which the sentiment we have mentioned is beautifully exhibited. "No certain rule," says he, "can be given with regard to the degree of evidence, which will be sufficient in every cause that shall occur. This only I can recommend to you in general; that you by no means confine yourself to any one kind or degree; but that, according to the nature and the circumstances of every case, you estimate, in your own mind, what you believe, and what you do not think to be sufficiently proved."[c]

2. Publius Aelius Traianus Hadrianus, or Hadrian (76–138), was Roman Emperor from 117 to 138.

c. 2. M'D. Ins. 631.

The evidence of the sciences is very different from the evidence of facts. In the sciences, evidence depends on causes which are fixed and immovable, liable to no fluctuation or uncertainty arising from the characters or conduct of men. In the sciences, truths, if selfevident, are instantly known. If their evidence depend on their connexions with other truths, it is evinced by tracing and discovering those connexions. In facts, it is otherwise. They consist not of principles which are selfevident; nor can their existence be traced or discovered by any necessary connexion with selfevident principles. As facts, therefore, are neither principles, nor necessarily connected with principles; the evidence of facts is unsusceptible of a general theory or rules.

Let us then forbear to attempt a graduated scale of this kind of evidence. It is the philosopher's stone of criminal jurisprudence. It is impossible to establish general rules, by which a complete proof may be distinguished from a proof that is incomplete, and presumptions slightly probable may be distinguished from conjectures altogether uncertain.

If, therefore, the evidence of facts can be ascertained, distinguished, and estimated by no system of general rules; the consequence unavoidably is, that, in every case, the evidence of facts must depend upon circumstances, which to that case are peculiar. The farther consequence unavoidably is, that the power of deciding on the evidence of facts must be a discretionary power; for it is a power of deciding on a subject unsusceptible of general principles or rules.

And, after all, is it, at last, come to this? Do we live by discretionary power? Is this the final result of the boasted trial by jury? In Turkey, life and every thing precious in life depend on the nod of one man: here, it seems, on the nod of twelve. There is a difference, indeed, in number: but, in principle, where is the difference?

Such is, and such must be our doom. It is agreed, on all hands, that, in every state, there must be somewhere a power supreme, arbitrary, absolute, uncontrollable: these are strong expressions for discretionary power. There have been, it is true, different opinions concerning the question—where does this power reside?

What security, then, it may next be asked, is there, under any government, for the enjoyment of property, character, freedom, and life; if, under every government, the last resolution of the tedious and expensive process is into arbitrary or discretionary power?

Let us not despair: perhaps, after a little investigation, we may be happy enough to discover some emerging isthmus, on which, amidst this unstable, watery scene that surrounds us, we may be able to find rest for the soles of our feet.

It has been shown, at large, that it is impracticable, by any determinate rules, to ascertain or graduate the force of evidence in facts; and that, consequently, juries, who decide on the evidence of facts, must possess discretionary powers. But though it be impracticable to ascertain this matter by determinate rules; is it, therefore, impracticable also to give and acquire some conception of it by a general reference? Perhaps not.

Let us try: let the reference be as comprehensive as possible: if we must live by discretion, let the exercise of that discretion be universally unanimous. If there must be, in every political society, an absolute and discretionary power over even the lives of the citizens; let the operations of that power be such, as would be sanctioned by unanimous and universal approbation. Suppose then, that, in pursuing this train of thought, we assume the following position—that the evidence, upon which a citizen is condemned, should be such as would govern the judgment of the whole society.

Let us, first, inquire, whether this position be reasonable: let us next inquire, whether, if this position is reasonable, the establishment of it would give, to the citizen, a just degree of security against the improper exercise of discretionary power: let us, in the last place, inquire, whether, if this theory is eligible, it be possible to reduce its principles to practice.

1. I am first to inquire, whether the position—that the evidence, upon which a citizen is condemned, should be such as would govern the judgment of the whole society—be a reasonable position.

We showed, at large, in a former part of these lectures,[d] that, in a society, the act or judgment of a majority is always considered as the act or judgment of the whole.

Before the formation of society, the right of punishment, or, to speak with more propriety, the right of preventing the repetition of crimes, belonged to him who had suffered the injury, arising from the crime which was committed. In a society formed and well constituted, the right of him who has suffered the injury is transferred to the community. To the com-

d. Ante vol. 1. p. 639.

munity, therefore, instead of the injured individual, he who committed the injury is now to answer. To answer to the community for his conduct, was a part of the social contract, which, by becoming a member, he tacitly and voluntarily made.[e] In this manner, a complete right is vested in the society to punish; and a full obligation is laid on the individual offending, to be amenable to punishment.

The social contract is of a peculiar kind: when analyzed into its component parts, it is found to be a composition of agreements, equal in number to the number of all the members, of which the society is composed. To each of those agreements there are two parties. One member of the society is the party on one side: all the other members form the party on the other side.

The punishment of a crime in regulated society presupposes two things. 1. The crime must be authenticated. 2. The penalty must be ascertained. Upon the principles which we have laid down, each of those two prerequisites to punishment must be equally the act of the society—of the whole society.

With regard to each of these prerequisites, the society may act either collectively and personally, or by deputation and representation. If they act by deputation and representation, they may intrust one of the forementioned prerequisites to the management of one class of deputies and representatives; and, to another class, they may commit the management of the other prerequisite. With regard to both, however, the proceedings must be those of the whole society, or, at least, sanctioned by the authority of the whole society: for it must be remembered, that to the whole society the right of punishment was transferred, and with the whole society the engagement to be amenable to its justice was made.

On a nearer and more minute view of things, we shall discover a most material difference between the modes proper for the management of the different prerequisites; because, on a nearer and more minute view of things, we shall discover, in the management of those different prerequi-

e. Upon this principle of consent, all civil penalties are debts to the publick; from whence the Greeks and Romans used λυειν, and "poenas solvere, luere,"[3] for undergoing a punishment, which was a conditional debt contracted by their own consent. Pet. on. Jur. 79.

3. Plague released as punishment.

sites, a most material difference in the situation of the parties to the social contract.

Penalties may be adjusted, graduated, and ascertained by general rules, and against all the members of the society indiscriminately. In the consequences of the regulations made upon this subject, every member may be affected in a double capacity; he may be affected, either as the individual party to one agreement, or as forming one of the numerous party to each of the other agreements, of which we have seen the social contract to be composed. In other words, he may be affected either as the author or as the sufferer of the penalties. Impartiality, therefore, in the conduct of every member, may rationally be expected; and there will be little reason to use strong or numerous precautions against interestedness or its effects. If the society act by representatives, and a difference of sentiment takes place among them concerning any subject; the numbers on the different sides, in the representative body, will probably bear to one another a proportion nearly the same, as would be found if all the members of the society were personally assembled.

But when we attend to the management of the other prerequisite—that of authenticating the commission of a crime—a situation of men and things, extremely different, appears to our view. Here no general rules can be adopted—no measures can be taken, which will equally and indiscriminately affect all the different members of the community in their turn. Here, the parties to one of the agreements, which form the social contract, appear in their original stations—on one side, an individual—on the other, all the members of the society except himself—on one side, those who are to try—on the other, he who is to be tried.

In this isolated situation, in which he necessarily but unfortunately stands; and in which, if all the members of the society were present, his fate must, from the very nature of society, be decided by the voice of the majority—in this situation, if the society act by representatives, it is reasonable to demand, and it is just to grant the reasonable demand, that the unanimous voice of those who represent parties, and who themselves are parties as well as judges, should be necessary to warrant a sentence of condemnation. In such a situation, where the representatives are not indifferent, and, consequently, may not be impartial, their unanimous suffrage may be considered as nothing more, than what is necessary to found a fair presumption concerning the sentiments of a majority of the whole community, had the whole community been personally present. In such a situation, therefore, we may probably be justified in recurring to our position—that the evidence, upon which a citizen is condemned, should be such as would govern the judgment of the whole society: and we may require the unanimous suffrage of the deputed body who try, as the necessary and proper evidence of that judgment.

2. I am next to inquire, whether the establishment of this position would give, to the citizen, a just degree of security against the improper exercise of discretionary power.

In all states, as we have seen, discretionary powers must be placed somewhere. The great body of the people is their proper permanent depository. But on some occasions, and for some purposes, they must be delegated. When they are exercised by the people themselves, a majority, by the very constitution of society, is sufficient for the purpose. When they are exercised by a delegation from the people, in the case of an individual; it would be difficult to suggest, for his security, any provision more efficacious than one, that nothing shall be suffered to operate against him without the unanimous consent of the delegated body.

This provision, however, may still be fortified by a number of additional precautions. Care may be taken in the manner of forming the delegated body. As this body cannot, for reasons which will appear afterwards, be selected, on every occasion, by the great body of the people themselves; they may, on every occasion, be selected by an officer, confidential, impartial, and, by the people themselves, appointed for this very purpose. Notwithstanding this very guarded selection, yet if any improper character appear among the delegated body, every reasonable exception may be allowed against his competency to act. To a necessary exercise of discretionary powers on one hand, the indulgence of a discretionary power may be opposed, on the other. Leave may be given to reject any determinate number of the delegated body, even without disclosing any cause of rejection. Under all these guarded and generous precautions, the person who would undergo a trial might, with an almost literal propriety, be said to try himself.

If, even after all these precautions, conviction might, by possibility, take place improperly; a power might be vested in another body to set the improper conviction aside, and to remit the trial of the cause to a new abstract of the citizens.

Surrounded and fortified by establishments and provisions of this nature, innocence might certainly be secure.

3. I am now, in the last place, to inquire, whether these principles, so beautiful in theory, can possibly be reduced to practice.

Reduced to practice! It cannot have escaped you, that I have been describing the principles of our well known trial by jury.

Those principles, so illustrious in themselves, will receive a new degree of splendour from a more particular investigation concerning the history, the nature, and the properties of this admired institution.

To Athens, to Germany, and to Normandy, the institution of juries has been attempted to be severally traced. From Athens it has been supposed to be transplanted to Rome; from Rome, to England. Those who think it originated in Normandy or Germany, suppose it to have been brought into England from the place of its original establishment.

The great principle of Solon's system was, unquestionably, this noble one—that every citizen should enjoy the inestimable right of being tried by his peers, and bound only by laws to which he had given his consent. His laws were of the most extensive nature. They comprehended rules of right, maxims of morality, precepts of agriculture, and regulations of commerce. His institutions concerning marriage, succession, testaments, the rights of persons and of things, have been disseminated through the jurisprudence of every civilized nation in Europe.[f] The trial by jury, therefore, as well as other establishments, may, it is said, refer, with great propriety, its original to Athens.

In Athens, the citizens were all equally admitted to vote in the publick assembly, and in the courts of justice, whether civil or criminal.[g]

The trial by a jury in Athens was conducted, it is said, with the same forms as those of an English jury, with a few exceptions arising from the difference between the two political constitutions.[h] When the cause was ready for hearing, the jury, who were to try it, were chosen by ballot.[i] It

f. 1. Gill. 461.
g. Pet. on Jur. 57. 58. 1. Gill. 459.
h. Pet. on Jur 27.
i. Id. 69.

was necessary that they should be competent in point of understanding, character, and disinterestedness.[j] The jury was very numerous: it consisted sometimes of five hundred, sometimes of a thousand, sometimes of fifteen hundred members.[k] If the defendant, in a criminal prosecution, had half the number of votes in his favour, he was acquitted.[l] The presiding archon settled the cause for trial, gave the ballot, received the verdict, and published it.[m]

In this mode of trial, we are told, equal law was open to all: it was favourable to liberty, because it could not be influenced by intrigues.[n]

In every particular cause, the jurors were chosen and sworn anew.[o] They were attended by proper officers of the court, that no one might mix with them, or corrupt them, or influence their decisions.[p] They were not obliged to follow testimony in cases immediately within their own knowledge: but when witnesses were the best evidence, they were admitted.[q] They were an important body of men, vested with great powers, patrons of liberty, enemies to tyranny.[r]

The antiquity of this institution among the most civilized people of the world, is urged as an argument, that it is founded in nature and original justice.[s] "The trial by a jury of our own equals seems to grow out of the idea of just government; and is founded in the nature of things."[t]

From this institution, as it was established and observed by the Greeks, we pass to it as established and observed by the Romans.

About sixty years after the expulsion of the Tarquins,[4] the Romans, agitated by the dissensions between the patricians and plebeians, on many

j. Id. 28. 29.
k. Id. 29.
l. Id. ibid.
m. Id. 28. 50. 51.
n. Id. 32.
o. Pet. on Jur. 43.
p. Id. 44.
q. Id. 48. 69. 81.
r. Id. 69.
s. Id. 70.
t. Id. 108.

4. The Tarquins were a powerful political family that ruled Rome prior to the establishment of the Republic. The Tarquins were driven from power after the rape of Lucretia by the son of Tarquinius Superbus, Tarquinius Sextus, in 510 B.C.

subjects, and particularly on that of their judicial government, sent commissioners to Athens to obtain a transcript of the laws of Solon.

Among the Romans, there was a double selection of jurors. On the kalends[5] of January, a number, different at different times, of citizens of best note were chosen by ballot. From these, all the juries were supplied, to the number of eighty one each, upon every new cause.[u] On each side, there was a liberty to challenge fifteen: fifty one remained to give the verdict. This *rejectio judicum*[6] is often mentioned by Cicero.[v]

In Rome as in Athens, the jury were sworn; and the defendant was acquitted on an equality of votes.[w]

Both at Athens and Rome, the time allowed to the counsel for their pleadings, was measured by the dropping of a certain quantity of water.[x] When the counsel, on each side, had finished their arguments by saying, "dixi," the praetor sent out the jury to consult about their verdict. When they returned with their verdict, they delivered it to the praetor; and he published it.[y]

The Roman juries were judges of law as well as of fact.[z] They could give a verdict of condemnation, a verdict of acquittal, or a verdict of *non liquet.*[7] This last has, by some, been considered as a special verdict; but improperly; for a special verdict furnishes the court with a statement of facts, on which they can found a decision of law; whereas a *non liquet* among the Romans immediately adjourned the cause for farther consideration. In some modern tribunals on the continent of Europe, a most scandalous use has, by judges, been made of their power to pronounce a *non liquet.*

In the celebrated cause of Milo,[8] we can trace the vestiges of a special jury. Pompey,[9] who was, at that time, sole consul, with the dictatorial

5. The first day of each month. Roman pontiffs used the day to announce the rest days of the month. It was also used as a day for debtors to pay off their debts.

u. Pet. on Jur. 113. 115.

6. Trial of rejection, or rejection trial.

v. Id. 114. 115. 122.

w. Id. 117.

x. Id. 134.

y. Id. 119. 120.

z. Id. 121.

7. It is not clear.

8. Titus Annius Milo (95–47 B.C.) was a Roman politician and agitator who took part in recalling Cicero from exile. He was later tried and convicted of murder.

9. Pompey (106–48 B.C.) was an important Roman military and political leader.

power, "videre ne quid detrimenti respublica caperet,"[10] appointed a jury, in all respects, of the most able and upright men. Of this jury, the celebrated Cato[11] was one. "Te, M. Cato, testor,"[12] says Cicero, in his animated and particular address. The selection of a jury in this peculiar manner, instead of the usual way by ballot, was, probably, one instance, in which Pompey exercised his dictatorial authority.[a]

Julius Caesar extended the Roman name and power into Gaul and Germany; and reduced those countries into the form of Roman provinces. This is an expression of strong and peculiar import. When a country was reduced into the form of a Roman province, it lost its own laws, and was governed by those of Rome.[b]

Caesar visited Britain: Claudius, one of his successours, achieved the conquest of a considerable part of the island. He planted in it four colonies. One of them—that at Malden[13]—was intended, as we are told by Tacitus,[c] not so much as a check upon the rebel Britons, as to accustom the new conquests to a familiarity with the Roman laws—"imbuendis sociis ad officia legum."[14] His designs were crowned with success. The Britons, who, at first, were disgusted even with the language of Rome, became soon the admirers of her language, her eloquence, and her laws.[d] Under the reign of Severus,[15] the Roman laws were in their meridian splendour in Britain, and were illustrated by the talents and authority of the celebrated Papinian.[e][16]

When the Romans retired from England to guard the vitals of the empire, the Britons resumed, in part, their ancient customs; but blended them with the Roman institutions, with which they had long been familiar. As the trial by jury was a part of the Roman system of judicial polity,

10. To see that the public interest suffered no damage.

11. Likely a reference to Marcus Porcius Cato Uticensis, or Cato the Younger (95–46 B.C.), a Roman statesman who opposed Julius Caesar.

12. One who gives evidence.

a. Pet. on Jur. 133.

b. Id. 140.

13. An area in the Royal Borough of Kingston upon Thames.

c. Ann. l. 12.

14. To accustom the new conquests to a familiarity with the Roman laws.

d. Pet. on Jur. 142.

15. Lucius Septimius Severus (146–211) was Roman Emperor from 193 to 211.

e. Id. 143.

16. Aemilius Papinianus (142–212) was a Roman jurist, author, and friend of Emperor Severus.

when her colonies were established in Britain, it is probable, that this, among other parts, was left and was continued among the Britons.[f]

Such is the train of observations, which has induced an opinion, that the trial by jury was introduced into England from Athens, through the intermediate channel of Rome. Others think they can trace this mode of trial through a different channel.

The very learned Selden is of opinion, that the Saxons derived the institution of juries immediately from the Grecians. The government of the Saxons, about the time of Tiberius, was, in general, as he informs us,[g] so suited to that of the Grecians, that it cannot be imagined but much of the Grecian wisdom was introduced among them, long before the glory of the Romans was exalted to its greatest height. It may be well supposed, he infers, that there is some consanguinity between the Saxons and the Grecians, though the degree of that consanguinity be not known. The people were a free people, because they were a law to themselves. This was a privilege belonging to all the Germans, in the same manner as to the Athenians and the Lacedemonians.

The most ordinary trial among the Saxons was, upon a traverse of the matter in fact, by witnesses before the jurors; their votes made the verdict, and determined the matter in fact. In former times, continues he, it was questionless a confused manner of trial by votes of the whole multitude, which made the verdict hard to be discerned. But time taught them better advice, to bring the voters to a certain number, according to the Grecian way.[h]

The trial *per pares,*[17] we are told by others, was common to all the northern nations, as well as to the Saxons.[i]

It is probable, says an ingenious and well informed writer, that, among the Saxons, every kind of law suit was, at first, determined in full assembly, and by a plurality of voices. But when the duty of these assemblies became burthensome by the increase of business, convenience introduced a practice of selecting a certain number of their members to assist their president

f. Pet. on Jur. 146. 179.
g. Bac. on Gov. 9.
h. Bac. on Gov. 56.
17. By evidence.
i. Millar. 440. Sulliv. 251.

in the determination of each cause. Hence the origin of juries; the precise date of whose establishment is uncertain, because it probably arose from no general or publick regulation, but from the gradual and almost imperceptible changes, authorized by common usage in the several districts of the kingdom. The number of jurymen was, for some time, different upon different occasions; till the advantage of uniform practice introduced a general rule, which determined, that no less than twelve persons should be called in all ordinary causes.[j]

A third class of writers contend, that juries, properly so called, were first introduced into England from Normandy. They admit a near affinity between this institution and that known to the tribunals of the Saxons; but insist, that, among that people, the trial by jury, speaking correctly,[k] did not exist. The trial, say they, *per duodecim juratos,*[18] called *nambda,*[19] was established among the Scandinavians at a very early period; but having fallen into disuse, was revived by a law of Reignerus surnamed Lodbrog,[20] about the year eight hundred and twenty. Seventy years after this time, Rollo[21] made his settlement in Normandy; and, among other customs, carried with him this mode of trial. When the Normans transplanted themselves into England, they were anxious to legitimate this as well as other parts of their jurisprudence, and endeavoured to substitute it in the place of the Saxon *sectatores,*[22] or suitors to the court. The earliest mention, they say, which we find of any thing like a jury, was in the reign of the Conqueror. He had referred a cause to the county, or *sectatores,* to determine in their county court, as the course then was according to the Saxon establishment. That court gave their opinion of the cause. But Odo, the bishop of Baieux,[23] who

j. Millar. 123.

k. 1. Reev. 18. 60.

18. By twelve jurors.

19. Nambda was a form of trial used by early Scandinavians.

20. Ragnor Lodborg, a king of the Danish Isles and one of the most feared marauders of northeast England.

21. Rollo is likely the Frankish-Latin name taken by Hrolf Ganger (c. 860–c. 932), a Viking leader, who with his followers (northmen or Normans) conquered what became known as Normandy in northern France.

22. Suitors of court who, among the Saxons, gave their judgment or verdict in civil suits upon the matter of fact and law.

23. Odo, the bishop of Bayeux (c. 1036–1097), was half-brother of William the Conqueror and a seemingly corrupt statesman.

presided at the hearing of the cause, was dissatisfied with their determination, and directed, that, if they were still sure they spoke truth, they should choose twelve from among themselves, who should confirm it upon their oaths. The old trial by an indefinite number of suitors of court continued, it is added, for many years after the conquest; but the precedent set by the Bishop of Baieux[24] had a great effect towards altering it. It was not, however, till the reign of Henry the second,[25] that the trial by jurors became general.[l]

If this account possessed all the accuracy, with the want of which it contains an implied censure of others, still it would admit the principles and substantial rules of trial by jury, to have subsisted among the Saxons; and would establish, between their institution and that of the Normans, a difference only with regard to the number of jurors, and to their qualification by an oath. But, on farther examination, we shall find, that, in both these respects, the law was the same before as after the conquest—that the suitors of the court, in other words, the freemen, were the judges, or, as we now say, the jury.[m]

Before the conquest, we can discover the clearest vestiges of a jury qualified by an oath, and consisting of twelve men. The most ancient, says Selden,[n] are to be found in a law of King Ethelred.[26] Its original is in the following words—"In singulis centuriis comitia sunto, atque liberae conditionis viri duodeni, aetate superiores, una cum praeposito sacra tenentes juranto se adeo verum aliquem innocentem haud damnaturos, sontemve absoluturos"—In every hundred let there be a court; and let twelve freemen of mature age, together with their foreman, swear, upon the holy relicks, that they will condemn no innocent, and will absolve no guilty person.[o]

Selden, as we find from his notes collected by Bacon, translates the word "praepositus"—the lord of the hundred. If his translation is just; then this is a strict instance of the duodecemviral judgment.[27] I translate the word

24. Possibly Odo of Bayeux (c. 1036–1097), Norman bishop and half-brother of William the Conqueror.

25. Henry II (1133–1189) was king of England from 1154 to 1189.

l. Id. 60. 61.

m. Sulliv. 247.

n. Anal. b. 2. c. 6.

26. Ethelred II (c. 968–1016) was King of England from 978 to 1013 and from 1014 to 1016.

o. Pet. on Jur. 159.

27. A trial by a twelve-man jury.

"praepositus"—the foreman of the jury: if my translation is just; then the jury, in this instance, consisted of thirteen members, including their foreman. I can only say, that, so far as I know, my translation is the usual one of the word, praepositus; that it seems rather unnatural to designate the lord of the hundred by the name of the president of the jury; and that, I apprehend, it was never customary for the judge and jury to be sworn "together"—"una."

There were two Saxon kings of the name of Ethelred. The first was the immediate predecessor of the great Alfred: the second was one of his successours. Selden refers the law which we have mentioned, to the reign of the second Ethelred. Now, there must be some mistake here one way or the other. If this law describes the jury of twelve; it is not the most ancient vestige of it; for, as we shall soon see, it was unquestionably established in the reign of Alfred. The conjecture is far from being improbable, that this law should be referred to the reign of the first Ethelred; and that it describes a jury consisting of thirteen—a foreman and twelve others.

It has been already observed, that, among the Saxons, the number of jurymen was probably different at different times. It may be observed here, that, before the era of which we now speak, we discover not the slightest traces of the principle of unanimity in juries. If a jury was equally divided in a criminal prosecution, we have seen that, in Athens and Rome, the defendant was acquitted: but what was to be done in a civil cause? To avoid frequent dilemmas of this kind, it is probable that juries consisted generally of an uneven number. This number might be fixed by the first Ethelred to thirteen. This, at least, was an improvement upon a larger and more inconvenient number.

But to the penetrating Alfred, this number, and the regulations connected with this number, would, probably, appear to require and to be susceptible of still greater improvement. A jury of thirteen sit on the life of a prisoner. Six vote for his condemnation: six vote for his acquittal: must his life depend on a single vote—perhaps not more to be relied on than the single throw of a die? Is it not probable, that such as this would be the soliloquy of the humane Alfred? If so; is it not probable, that, from this precarious situation, the family of Alfred—for his people were his children—would be relieved by the resources of a mind, no less distinguished by its vigorous exertion, than by its wise and benevolent reflections? We can only conjecture his motives, indeed: but we know his conduct. He fixed the number of jurors at twelve: to a conviction by that number, he rendered a unanimous vote indispensably necessary. To him the world is indebted for the unanimous duodecemviral judgment.

I establish these interesting facts.

I have already mentioned, on the authority of my Lord Coke, that the greatest part of the book called "The Mirrour of Justices," was written long before the conquest. In that book, we find an account of Alfred's acts and judgments, conjectured to have been originally composed by himself. Of that account, I give the following very literal translation from the old French—the language, in which Andrew Horne[28] compiled and published the book. "He hanged Cadwine, because he judged Hackwy to death without the assent of all the jurors, in a case where he had put himself upon a jury of twelve men; and because three were for saving him against nine, Cadwine removed the three for others upon whom Hackwy did not put himself." "He hanged Frebern, because he judged Harpin to death, when the jurors were in doubt as to their verdict; for where there is a doubt, they should save rather than condemn."[p]

These texts are short: but they are pregnant with precious instruction.

1. Each juror may here find a salutary lesson for his conduct, in the most important of all the transactions of a man or a citizen—in voting whether a fellow man and a fellow citizen shall live or die. Does he doubt? he should acquit. It is only when the clearest conviction is in full and undivided possession of the mind, that the voice of conviction ought to be pronounced.

2. All the jurors may, in this transaction, of all human transactions the most important, find a salutary lesson for their conduct, in forming the collected verdict of the whole from the separate judgment of each.

I speak of criminal—I speak of capital cases; because the cases here mentioned were those, in which persons were "judged to death."

Is the judgment of a majority of the members—that the defendant should be convicted—a sufficient foundation for a verdict of conviction by the jury? It is not. That verdict must be composed of each separate judgment. In the case before us, a majority of three to one were for conviction. But the

28. *The Mirrour of Justices* is a book supposedly compiled by Andrew Horne that relates the story of judicial discipline in the time of Alfred the Great.

p. Pet. on Jur. 166, 167.

judge was hanged for pronouncing sentence of death upon the votes of this majority, though it was propped by an adventitious accession of three other votes.

3. Every citizen may here find most comfortable information of the jealous attention, with which the law watches over him, even when he is accused of violating the law. No jury can pass upon him, except that upon which he puts himself. "Hackwy," says the case before us, "did not put himself upon those others." For every trial there must be a new selection. The discretionary powers, which we have described, and which, in one view, appear so formidable, though, in every view, they are so necessary, can never be exercised against him by any body of men, to the exercise of whose powers he does not give his consent. He may suffer, indeed, in another way. He may suffer the pain of contumacy, direful and hard. His contumacy may, by a legislative process, be transformed into a confession of his guilt. But, by his country he can never suffer, unless, in the language of the law, he "put himself upon his country."

In the strictest and most correct meaning of the word, we have unquestionably, I think, traced the trial by jury to the Saxons. Selden thinks they derived it immediately from the Greeks: others think they derived it from the Greeks through the intermediate channel of the Romans. The latter seems the most probable opinion. From the Romans they might receive it, by their immediate intercourse with them in Germany, or they might receive it by still another intermediate channel—that of the Britons.

It has been already mentioned, that the Roman arms were followed constantly and rapidly by the Roman laws. If, therefore, we can trace the conquests of Rome to the Saxons; to them we may expect to trace the institutions of Rome likewise.

The loss of the legions under Varus[29] was one of the most striking events in the reign of Augustus. On the mind of the emperour it made so deep an impression, that he was often heard to cry, in his interrupted slumbers—Varus! restore my legions! This remarkable disaster happened in or near the country of the Cherusci, which was itself a part of Saxony; and was, indeed, the consequence of the extraordinary pains employed

29. Publius Quintilius Varus (c. 46 B.C.– A.D. 9) was a Roman statesman and general who is most famous for losing three legions in the Battle of Teutoburg Forest.

by Varus, to diffuse among the inhabitants the laws and jurisprudence of Rome.

By Velleius Paterculus[30] we are informed, that when Varus commanded the army in Germany, he entertained an opinion, that men, who had nothing human about them but their form and their language, might be civilized by laws much more easily, and much more effectually, than they could be brought under subjection by the sword. Under the influence of this impression, he remained in his camp without military exertion; and, surrounded with enemies, sat in judgment on causes, which were brought before him, in the same manner as if he had been a praetor, presiding in the forum of Rome. Of this propensity, the Germans took an artful advantage. They instituted, before Varus, a continued series of litigation; they expressed, in the strongest terms, their gratitude at beholding their controversies terminated by Roman justice, and at seeing the mild energy of law substituted in the place of decisions by force. They expressed also their hopes, that, by the influence of this new discipline, their own ferocity would be gradually softened, and themselves would be gradually qualified to think and to act as the friends of Rome. The surprise of his legions was the first thing which roused him—but it roused him too late—from his delusive dream.

The Saxons, it is said, might see the benefit and retain the exercise of the Roman institutions, after they had expelled him who introduced them with so much zeal, and so much unguarded confidence.

The Saxons, who invaded and conquered England, might also learn the Roman forms of decision through the medium of the Britons. On a former occasion,[q] I mentioned, that there is, in truth, no reason to suppose that the destruction of the Britons by the Saxons, on their invasion of England, was so great or general as it has been frequently represented. After some time, there was, unquestionably, an intimate and a continued intercommunication of manners, customs, and laws between the two nations. Even an English historian admits, that a more minute and particular account of the Anglo-Saxon constitution might be extracted from the Welch laws of Howell Dha,[31] which were collected in the year eight hundred and

30. Marcus (Gaius?) Velleius Paterculus (c. 19 B.C.– A.D. 31) was a Roman soldier and historian who wrote the *Compendium of Roman History*.

q. Ante. p. 765.

31. Hywel Dda or Howell the Good (880?–950) was king of Wales.

forty two, than even from the Saxon laws themselves. He indeed accounts for this similarity, by supposing that the Welch adopted the regulations of their ancient enemies. A Welch historian would, probably, admit the fact of the similarity, but, as to the inference drawn from it, he might, perhaps, be able to turn the tables upon the historian of England. It is, indeed, highly probable, that the Saxons borrowed more from the Britons, than the Britons borrowed from the Saxons.

I have now traced the trial by jury, in its principle, and in many parts of its practical rules, to the most splendid eras of Rome and Athens: and I have ascertained the reign, in which its present number was fixed, and the principle of unanimity in verdicts of conviction was introduced. On this principle of unanimity, farther attention ought to be bestowed.

We have seen an express and a very awful authority, that, in verdicts of conviction in criminal cases, it must be inviolably observed. Is the rule extended—ought it to be extended to verdicts of acquittal in criminal cases? Is it extended—ought it to be extended to any verdict in civil cases? I state the questions on the double grounds of fact and reason; because, in these lectures, we are entitled to consider the law as citizens as well as jurists. It may be our duty to obey, when it is not our duty, because, without any fault, it is not in our power, to approve.

I shall consider the questions historically and on principle. On this, as on other topicks of common law, we shall probably find that principle is illustrated by history.

I beg leave, before I proceed, to suggest one precaution—that the idea of a unanimous verdict should be carefully distinguished from the idea of a unanimous sentiment in those who give that unanimous verdict. This distinction, perhaps, will be found far from being unworthy of your attention. But let us proceed.

That verdicts in civil causes, as well as verdicts of conviction in criminal causes, must be unanimous in order to be valid, seems to be a rule unknown to the law of England for many ages after that of Alfred. During some reigns after the conquest, the law was, that if some of the jurors were for one party, and some for the other, new jurors were added, till twelve were found, who agreed in opinion for one of the parties.[r] In the reign of

r. 1. Reev. 106.

Henry the third, a unanimous verdict was still not deemed absolutely necessary; but the dissenting jurors were amerced, as guilty of a kind of offence, in obstinately maintaining a difference of opinion.[s]

In the next reign—that of Edward the first—it was laid down for law by a respectable writer,[t] that when the jurors differed in opinion, the judge, before whom the cause was tried, might, at his election, add others, till twelve were found unanimous; or might compel the jury to agree among themselves, by directing the sheriff to keep them without meat or drink, till they agreed on their verdict.[u] There was still another method, which, we are informed by a remarkable case in that reign, was the custom. The verdict of the minority as well as of the majority was ascertained, and distinctly entered on the record; and then judgment was given according to the verdict of the majority.[v]

In the eighth year of Edward the third, when a juror delayed his companions a day and a night, without assenting or giving any good reason why he would not assent, the judge committed him to prison. In the forty first year of the same reign, the point was fully debated in the court of common pleas, and, as has been generally thought, finally settled. All the jurors, except one, were agreed. They were remanded, and remained all that day and the next without eating or drinking. Being then asked if they were agreed, the dissenting juror answered, no; and said that he would die first in prison. On this, the justices took the verdict of the eleven, and committed the single juror to prison. All this happened in an assize. But when judgment was prayed upon this verdict, in the court of common pleas, the justices were unanimously of opinion, "that a verdict from eleven jurors was no verdict at all." When it was urged, that former judges had taken verdicts of eleven both in assize and trespass, and one taken in the twentieth year of the king was particularly mentioned; Thorpe, one of the justices, said, that it was not an example for them to follow, for that judge had been greatly censured for it: and it was said by the bench, that the justices ought to have carried the jurors about with them in carts till they were agreed. Thus it was settled, we are told, that the jurors must be unanimous in the verdict;

s. Id. 242.
t. Fleta.
u. 1. Reev. 480.
v. Id. ibid. 2. Hale. P. C. 297.

and that the justices may put them under restraint, if necessary, to produce such unanimity.[w]

Unanimity produced by restraint! Is this the principle of decision in a trial by jury? Is that trial, which has been so long considered as the palladium of freedom—Is that trial brought to its consummation by tyranny's most direful engine—force upon opinion—upon opinion given under all the sanctions and solemnities of an oath? Every other agreement produced by duress is invalid and unsatisfactory: what contrary principles can govern this?

Let us here make a pause—let us turn round and look back upon the point said to be settled, and the manner of settling it. Useful observations will probably be the result.

We see that, in civil cases, unanimity was not originally required from the jurors: the unanimous verdict of twelve was, indeed, deemed necessary; and, for this reason, new jurors were added, till twelve were found of the same mind. This mode must have been productive of very great inconveniences. It was necessary that the added jurors should be as fully informed concerning the cause, as those who had been impannelled originally. Every new addition, therefore, must have been attended with all the trouble, and expense, and delay of a new trial. With a view, probably, to avoid those inconveniences, a custom was introduced to enter on the record the opinion of the minority as well as that of the majority; and to give judgment upon the latter opinion.[x]

From the record of the case, however, in which this is stated to have been the custom, it appears that another mode was adopted sometimes by the jurors among themselves, and without any communication of it to the court. A large extract of this record, of the twentieth year of Edward the first, is furnished us in one of the valuable notes annexed to my Lord

w. 2. Reev. 191.

x. In the fifty sixth year of Henry the third, we have a precedent of the manner, in which the entry on the record was made—"And all the jury except—say upon their oath, &c. and—says upon his oath, &c. But because the aforesaid eleven say accordingly, &c. therefore it is considered," &c.

In a record of the fourteenth year of Edward the first, the reason is assigned in these words—"quia dicto majoris partis juratorum standum est." To the principle—that a majority is sufficient—and not—that unanimity is necessary—an appeal is made on the record. 2. Hale. P. C. 297.

Hale's history of the pleas of the crown.[y] The history of that case, and the conduct of the jury who tried it, deserve very particular attention.

Certain lands were recovered against a prior before two judges of assize, in the sixteenth year of Edward the first. The prior complained, that injustice had been done him at the assize; and the bishop of Winchester and others were appointed to hear the prior's complaint, and to do justice. The judges appealed, for their justification, to the record of the judgment, which they had given. In that record, the conduct of the jury was stated very minutely. John Pickering, one of the jurors, in narrating the verdict of the jury, was contrary to all the other jurors; for he narrated a different thing from what was agreed upon among them, as appeared by their examination. For this conduct he was amerced, and ordered into the custody of the sheriff, till he made satisfaction for his transgression. The judges, say the bishop and his associates, without specifying on the record, as was the custom in such cases, the opinions of the eleven, or the contradictory opinion of John Pickering, received the verdict, as if all had been of the same sentiment concerning it, and gave judgment accordingly. This judgment was, by the bishop and his associates, declared contrary to the law and custom of the kingdom. From this decision, a writ of errour was brought before the king, by the original plaintiff. But whether any final determination was given, or, if given, what it was, we are not informed.

From the record it appears, that, when the jurors could not agree in a verdict, it was the custom and deemed to be the law to enter the different sentiments upon the record, and give judgment according to those of the majority. But from this record something more appears. It appears, that the jury might agree upon a verdict among themselves, and appoint one of their number to narrate it to the court—that if the person, thus appointed, narrated the verdict in a manner contrary to what was agreed on, he was guilty of a misdemeanor—that the verdict agreed on should not, however, be vitiated by the prevarication of the foreman, but should be received according to what was agreed upon among the jury. Such is the evident import of the record before the judges of assize, and of the judgment which they gave upon the proceedings.

The bishop and his associates are extremely inaccurate in stating the facts, upon which they ground their reprehension of the judges. From their

y. Vol. 2. p. 298.

statement one would be led to imagine, that Pickering narrated one verdict as the voice of the other eleven, and another as his own; and that the judges, without taking any notice of this contradiction, had received and entered the verdict as a unanimous one. But this was very far from being the fact, as it appears upon the record of the two judges of assize. Pickering specified in his narration no difference of sentiment. He, on the contrary, attempted to palm upon the court, as a unanimous verdict, one contradictory to that which had been agreed on among the jury. The other jurors disclosed the verdict agreed on. That verdict was received and entered as a unanimous one. Pickering himself appears not to have either denied or retracted his own agreement to it. The law and custom of the kingdom, therefore, concerning contradictory verdicts, were applied, with great inaccuracy, to the proceedings before the two judges.

Highly probable it is, however, that, before this verdict was formed, much diversity of sentiment was entertained concerning it, among the jurors. The expressions of the record are very remarkable—"inter illos fuit *provisum*"—the verdict was *provided* among them. Consideration, consultation, adjustment are all suggested by this emphatick phrase.

One important subject of their deliberation is mentioned; and it appears, that their sentiments were worthy of the subject, which employed their attention. The prior, it seems, claimed the plaintiff as his villain. The consequence of this claim, if established, would have been, that the plaintiff could not have recovered the lands in question. For a villain could acquire no property in lands or goods; but if he purchased either, the lord might enter upon them, or seize them for his own use.[z]

The jury found, that the father of the plaintiff was a free man, and of free condition; and that although the father and his issue held, of the prior and his predecessors, their tenements in villainage and by villain services, this should not prejudice them as to the freedom of their persons. They assign the reason—because no prescription of time can reduce free blood to a condition of slavery; therefore the plaintiff should recover. This position, indeed, the bishop and his associates declare to be altogether false; and some of the jury themselves, perhaps, entertained a degree of hesitation concerning it, and did not adopt it till after much deliberation and advise-

z. 2. Bl. Com. 93.

ment. They provided, however, a verdict, founded on this position, and instructed one of their number to narrate that verdict to the court.

The conduct of this jury in forming their verdict deserves the attention—perhaps, as we shall afterwards find, the imitation of their successours. Sentiments, somewhat discordant when taken separately, may, by a proper process, be melted down into a unanimous verdict.

Hitherto we have discovered no law or authority, which, in civil causes, requires unanimity in the verdicts, far less in the sentiments, of jurors. In this reign, however, an approach seems, at first sight, to be made towards the rule. The author of Fleta, who wrote in the time of Edward the first, gives, as we have seen, the election to the judges, either to increase the number of jurors till twelve are found unanimous, or to compel the first twelve, by hunger and thirst, to agree.

The author of Fleta was a writer very respectable: great deference is due to his sentiments: but the sentiments of no writer have, on the balance of authority, the weight of judicial determinations. Besides, the practice of withholding from jurors the causes of torpor and the incentives of passion, while they ponder and deliberate concerning their verdict, will, perhaps, be traced to a source and to principles, very different from those assigned by the author of Fleta.

The case decided in the forty first year of the reign of Edward the third may, perhaps, be urged as a leading and governing authority for the principle of unanimity in the verdicts and opinions of jurors. In that case, the court said, that the justices ought to have carried the jurors about with them in carts, till they were agreed. But, as to this saying of the court, I crave the liberty of proposing two questions.

Is it supported by any previous custom or adjudication? Our investigations hitherto lead us to conclude, that it has no such support.

Is it the point of adjudication in this very case? It is not. The question in judgment before the court was this—Is the verdict from eleven jurors only a good verdict? This question the court determined judicially; and their determination was in the negative. But was the other question—what shall be done with a disagreeing jury?—was this question in judgment before them? It was not. Was the answer given to this question a necessary consequence of their adjudication on the point judicially before them? It was not. The verdict of eleven jurors only might be an erroneous verdict.

Does it follow, that the errour can be prevented or rectified only by carting the jury till they agree? According to the practice previous to this saying of the court, it would have been rectified by entering on the record the opinion of the dissenting juror. According to the practice subsequent to this saying, the errour would have been prevented by directing a juror to be withdrawn. According to the principles of jury trial, it might be prevented or rectified by a variety of modes other and more eligible than that of carting the jury. Some of those modes will soon be suggested.

"I would know," says my Lord Chief Justice Vaughan, in the celebrated cause of Bushell,[32][a] "whether any thing be more common, than for two men, students, barristers, or judges, to deduce contrary and opposite conclusions from the same case in law? And is there any difference, that two men should infer distinct conclusions from the same testimony? Is any thing more known, than that the same author, and the same place in that author, is forcibly urged to maintain contrary, conclusions; and the decision is hard which is in the right? Is any thing more frequent in the controversies of religion, than to press the same text for opposite tenets? How then comes it to pass, that two persons may not, with reason and honesty, apprehend what a witness says, to prove one thing in the understanding of one, and a contrary thing clearly in the understanding of the other? Must, therefore, one of these," asks his Lordship, "merit fine and imprisonment?"

Must, therefore, both of these, I beg leave to ask, merit what is worse than imprisonment and fine? Must they be exposed, in carts, to publick derision, because they act a part which is common, innocent, unavoidable? Must they suffer all the extremities of hunger and thirst till, at last, agonizing nature makes the necessary but disgraceful barter of unsufferable punishment for degrading prevarication? Are instruments subscribed by pain, by infamy, and by shame—are these the letters recommendatory, which our law despatches, or wishes to despatch, to the remotest regions of the globe, in order to concentre in the trial by jury the admiration and imitation of all?

32. Edward Bushell, along with four other jurors in the 1670 trial of William Penn and William Meade, voted to acquit. They were imprisoned and fined. Bushell refused to pay the fine and brought suit. In *Bushell's Case* (1670), Lord Chief Justice Vaughan ruled that members of a jury could not be punished for their verdict.

a. Vaughan, 141.

It must, however, be confessed, that though no judicial determinations, so far as I know, are precisely in the point; yet the forms of our law, rendered venerable by the immemorial practice of ages, seem at least to countenance, if not to presuppose, the principle of unanimity in the trial by jury. When the jury retire, a bailiff is sworn to keep them together till they be agreed of their verdict. When they return to the bar, the first question asked of them is—are you agreed of your verdict? This question must be answered in the affirmative, before the verdict can be received. Such are the established forms of the law. They seem to require a unanimous verdict.

Every juror swears that he will give a true verdict according to his evidence. The sacred obligation of this oath demands, that to unanimity truth shall not be made a sacrifice.

In this situation are the jury placed. Truth and unanimity—qualities very distinct—qualities, on some occasions, seemingly irreconcilable—must unite in the composition of their verdict. To extricate them from such a labyrinth, where the law seems to point to one direction, and their oaths seem to point to another, is there no affectionate hand to furnish them a clue?

What is a verdict? It is the joint declaration of twelve jurymen upon their oaths. Littleton[33] calls it "the verdict of twelve men."[b]

"Veredictum," says my Lord Coke, in his valuable Commentary, "quasi dictum veritatis, as judicium is quasi juris dictum. Et sicut ad quaestionem juris non respondent juratores, sed judices; sic ad quaestionem facti, non respondent judices, sed juratores." A verdict is a declaration of the fact: a judgment is a declaration of the law. To a question of law the judges, not the jury, shall answer: so, to a question of fact, the jury, not the judges, shall answer. So far the parallel holds exactly between the duties of judges and of jurors, in their respective provinces of law and of fact. So far the parallel holds between a verdict and a judgment.

We have seen what a verdict is: it is a joint declaration of the jury. What is a judgment? It is, I apprehend, the joint declaration of the court. It is not merely a declaration of a majority of the judges: it is the declation of the

33. Sir Thomas Littleton (c. 1407–1481) was an English legal scholar and judge. He is most famous for his book on property law, *Treatise on Tenures*.

b. 1. Ins. 226.

court. When it is solemnly pronounced, even by a dissenting president, it must be announced as "the judgment of this court"—not as the "judgment of a majority of the judges." Why should not the parallel hold, in this instance too, with regard to a jury, except in a case of conviction, which has been already shown to stand upon its own peculiar foundation?

We have seen, that, in this instance too, the parallel did hold formerly with regard to the jury. We have seen, that the declaration of the majority operated as the verdict of the jury. For some time, indeed, the dissent of the minority was noticed on the record; but was it necessary to notice that dissent? Was it necessary to continue that practice? Every one knows, that judgments are entered as the acts of the court generally, even when there is a dissenting minority. Why should not the same practice prevail—why should we not presume that the same practice has prevailed, with regard to juries? On the record, the transactions of the court bear the same stamps of unanimity with the transactions of the jury: whence, then, can it be inferred, that a degree of unanimity is, in reality, required from the jurors, which, on all hands, is acknowledged to be unnecessary in the judges?

Whether, therefore, we consult the suggestions of the records, or the information of etymology, the inferences of analogy, or the language of adjudications, we shall find no authority to conclude, that, in civil causes, the verdict of a jury must be founded on unanimous opinion.

But recurrence will still be had to those venerable forms, immemorially established, which countenance or presuppose the doctrine of unanimity in the trial by jury. Before a verdict can be received, it will be urged, the jury must declare, that of that verdict they are agreed.

Permit me, on this occasion, to have recourse to a conjecture. I propose it with diffidence: I pursue it with caution: if my expressions concerning it become sanguine, it shall not be till I think I have established it. My conjecture is, that by the phrase, "agreed of a verdict," nothing more is meant, than that the jury are willing and prepared to give a verdict; and by that means, bring to a decision the controversy submitted to them.

In early times, a verdict, as we have seen, could not be prevented by the contrary vote or sentiment of one or of a minority of the jurors. The jury was increased till twelve were unanimous; or the vote of a majority was received as a decision. But the effect of an obstinate refusal to give any vote was very different. We have seen, that all the votes were required to be disposed of on the record; and that though eleven votes on one side, and one on the other, formed materials for a verdict; yet eleven votes, unopposed by the dissenting one, were deemed insufficient for that purpose. Those, therefore, who wished to obstruct the administration of justice in the trial by jury, accomplished their wishes by refusing to give any vote on either side. In turbulent times—and the times I allude to were turbulent—this expedient would be often used, by the friends of a powerful usurper in possession, against a legal recovery by him who had right. To restrain and to prevent the pernicious effects of such a conduct, every juror was sworn to give a verdict; the bailiff was sworn to confine him till he should agree to give it; and no declaration was received by the court, till it was unanimously declared, that, as to the point of *giving* a verdict, they were all agreed.

These observations will throw a new light upon some points, which have been already mentioned. The case of an obstinate juror, of the species now described, happened, as we before noticed, in the eighth year of the reign of Edward the third. Upon that case, my Lord Chief Justice Vaughan makes the following remarks: "This book," says he, "rightly understood, is law: that he staid his fellows a day and a night, without any reason or assenting, may be understood, that he would not, at that time, intend the verdict at all, more than if he had been absent from his fellows; but wilfully not find for either side. In this sense, it was a misdemeanor against his oath; for his oath was truly to try the issue, which he could never do, who resolved not to confer with his fellows." "And in this sense," adds he, "it is the same with the case 34. Ed. III. where twelve being sworn, and put together to treat of their verdict, one secretly withdrew himself, and went away, for which he was justly fined and imprisoned; and it differs not to withdraw from a man's duty, by departing from his fellows; and to withdraw from it though he stay in the same room: and so is that book to be understood."[c] These remarks corroborate what I have mentioned—that the great object seems to have been to secure a decision, not a unanimous decision, by verdict. For both the cases, just now noticed, happened before that which is alleged to have settled the principle of unanimity. I hope, I have now established my conjecture.

c. Vaugh. 151.

I have asked, "since judgments are entered as the acts of the court generally, when there is a dissenting minority; why should not the same practice prevail—why should we not presume that the same practice has prevailed, with regard to juries?" I now go farther, and undertake to evince, that the reason for that practice is much greater, and that, consequently, the presumption in its favour is much stronger, in the case of jurors, than it is in the case of judges. This will appear from a variety of considerations.

In the turbulent times, to which I allude, the jurors, as we are told by Montesquieu, were obliged to fight either of the parties who might give them the lie. When there was no dissent, or which, as to this point, was the same thing—when no dissent appeared, a party who gave the lie to one, must engage in single combat with each. Their number would render him circumspect. A regard, therefore, to the security of jurors would superinduce every prudent appearance of unanimity in their opinions and verdicts. But this reason applied not to the judges.

In times the most civilized and tranquil, it is improper to expose jurors unnecessarily to the concealed resentment of those, who may be affected by the parts they severally take in the juries, of which they are members. This reason is applicable, but not so strongly applicable, to the judges.

In this argument, whatever shows a greater reason for preserving the vestiges of diversity in the sentiments of the judges, than in those of the jurors, will have the same effect, as that which shows a greater reason for preserving the appearance of unanimity in the sentiments of the jurors, than in those of the judges. We have seen,[d] that "a judge, particularly a judge of the common law, should bear a great regard to the sentiments and decisions of those, who have thought and decided before him." We have seen,[e] "that the evidence of facts—and facts are the province of juries—cannot be ascertained, distinguished, or estimated by any system of general rules; and that, for this reason, the evidence of facts must, in every case, depend on circumstances, which to that case are peculiar." The natural consequences from these two positions are, that it might be useful, perhaps material, to preserve, on the record, evidences of the unanimity or diversity of sentiments, with which judgments are given, so that they may

d. Ante. p. 952.
e. Ante. p. 957.

make the slighter or deeper impression on the minds of succeeding judges; and that such a measure, with regard to verdicts, would be altogether useless and immaterial; since every verdict rests on its own peculiar circumstances, without precedent and without example.

The result is, that the reasons for apparent unanimity on the record are not so great, nor the presumption arising from them so strong, in the case of judges as in the case of jurors: an apparent unanimity, however, is preserved, while a real diversity of sentiment subsists, in the case of judges: there is, therefore, much greater reason to presume, that a real diversity of sentiment may subsist, though an apparent unanimity be preserved, in the case of juries.

It may be naturally asked—if this principle of unanimity in the trial by jury be unfounded; how has it happened, that the opinion of its existence has been so general and so permanent, not only among the people at large, but even among professional characters? This has already been accounted for in part. It was prudent to preserve the appearance of unanimity: this uniform appearance would naturally produce and disseminate an opinion that the unanimity was real. Besides, in one species—in the most important species of verdicts—those of conviction in criminal, still more in capital cases—this unanimity, upon the principles which have been explained, was not only apparent, but real and indispensable. Farther; the awful precedents set by Alfred, to establish the principle of unanimity in this species of verdicts, would naturally make a deep and lasting impression upon all—upon professional characters, as well as upon others. Impressions, deep and lasting, are always diffusive: their influence, therefore, extended beyond those causes, which had originally produced them. Unanimity, confined, in its principle, to verdicts of conviction in criminal cases, was applied indiscriminately to cases and verdicts of every kind—to verdicts of acquittal, as well as to those of conviction—to cases civil, as well as to cases criminal.

This subject, so very interesting to juries and to all who, and whose causes, are tried by juries, I have investigated minutely and carefully, historically and upon principle. Of many late *dicta* I have taken no notice, because they are suspended on those of a more early period. To trace matters to their remotest sources, is the most satisfactory and the most successful mode of detecting errours, as well as of discovering truths. In doing both, I hope that, on this subject, I have had some success: if so, I shall have much satisfaction; for I shall have contributed to dispel a cloud, dark and heavy, which has hitherto shaded and hung over the trial by jury, so luminous when beheld in its unintercepted lustre.

If I have been successful, many practical advantages will result to parties, to jurors, and to judges. My theory is shortly this. To the conviction of a crime, the undoubting and the unanimous sentiment of the twelve jurors is of indispensable necessity. In civil causes, the sentiment of a majority of the jurors forms the verdict of the jury, in the same manner as the sentiment of a majority of the judges forms the judgment of the court. In many cases, a verdict may, with great propriety, be composed of the separate sentiments of the several jurors, reduced to what may be called their average result. This will be explained. Hitherto, I have said nothing concerning verdicts of acquittal in criminal cases. After what has been observed, it is unnecessary to say much concerning them. If to a verdict of conviction, the undoubted and the unanimous sentiment of the twelve jurors be of indispensable necessity; the consequence unquestionably is, that a single doubt or a single dissent must produce a verdict of acquittal.

Let us now see whether this theory, short and plain, may not be reduced to practice, with great security and advantage to parties, to juries, and to judges.

In criminal prosecutions, the state or society is always a party. From the necessity of the case, it is also always a judge. For we have seen, that, in the social contract, the party injured transfers to the publick his right of punishment, and that, by the publick, the party injuring agrees to be judged. The state acts by the medium of the selected jury. Can the voice of the state be indicated more strongly, than by the unanimous voice of this selected jury? Again; the state, though a party on one side, has a deep interest in the party on the other side; for to a well organized state, every citizen is precious. According to the theory which we are now trying by its application to practice, the state can lose no precious part of herself, unless on the strongest indication that she herself, if consulted on the occasion, would say,

— immedicabile vulnus
Ense recidendum est; ne pars sincera trahetur.[34]

34. An incurable wound must be cut away with the sword to keep the healthy part from being drawn with it.

By the practice of this theory, the state will lose no member by the malice or resentment of a single individual, who, with a constitution as strong as his heart is hard, can starve his fellow jurors into a reluctant and prevaricating verdict of conviction.

How stands the other party to a criminal prosecution? He stands single and unconnected. He is accused of a crime. For his trial on this accusation, he is brought before those who, if he is guilty, represent his offended judge. If it were possible, the characters of party and judge should be separated altogether. When that is impossible, the greatest security imaginable should be provided against the dangers, which may result from their union. The greatest security is provided by declaring, and by reducing to practice the declaration, that he shall not suffer, unless the selected body who act for his country say unanimously and without hesitation—he deserves to suffer. By this practice, the party accused will be effectually protected from the concealed and poisoned darts of private malice and malignity, and can never suffer but by the voice of his country.

By this practice, we are led to see the beautiful and exquisite propriety and emphasis of a form, which is used every day in criminal trials; but which is the object of little attention, because it is used every day. When the jury are sworn to try a person for a crime, the clerk of the court informs them succinctly of the nature of the charge; that the prisoner has pleaded to it, that he is not guilty; that for trial he has put himself upon his country —"which country," adds he, "you are." Upon the principles which I have stated and explained, a jury, in criminal cases, may, indeed, be called the country of the person accused, and the trial by jury may, indeed, be denominated the trial *per patriam.*[35]

"In a well tempered government," says the Empress of Russia, in the excellent instructions which she gave concerning a code of laws for her extensive empire, "In a well tempered government, no person is deprived of his life, unless his country rise up against him."[f] Let others know, and teach, and publish, and recommend fine political principles: it is ours to reduce them to practice.

We may now conclude, that the practice of the theory, which we have explained, is advantageous and secure for the parties in criminal causes.

35. Literally "by country." In this context the phrase is synonymous with "trial by jury."
f. 3. War. Bib. 67.

Let us next examine it in relation to causes of a civil nature. Here, we say, the sentiment of a majority of the jurors forms the verdict of the jury, in the same manner as the sentiment of a majority of the judges forms the judgment of the court.

That the sentiments of the majority shall govern, is, as we before showed at large,[g] the general rule of society. To this rule we have seen the strongest reason to introduce an exception, with regard to verdicts of conviction in criminal prosecutions. Does the same reason extend to civil causes? We presume not. In civil causes, the jury stand equally indifferent to the parties on either side. As the juridical balance thus hangs in perfect equipoise between them; it is for their security, and for their advantage too, that the scales should clearly indicate the proportional weight of law and truth which is thrown into them, and that a preponderancy on the whole should direct the decision. To insist that a jury should be unanimous, is eventually, in many cases, to ordain, that their verdict shall not be the legitimate offspring of free deliberation and candid discussion; but shall be the spurious brood of strength of constitution and obstinacy of temper. For the advantage and security of the parties this cannot be; the other must.

Let us now consider this subject as it respects juries. From the principle of unanimity, as it has been often understood, he who will be obliged to discharge the important trusts and duties of a juryman has but a comfortless prospect before him. He must perform the most interesting business of society—he must decide upon fortune, upon character, upon liberty, upon life: all this he must perform in conjunction with others, whom he does not choose, whom, perhaps, he does not know, with whom, perhaps, he would not wish to associate; for though jurors are selected, they are not selected by one another: all this, too, he must perform in real or in counterfeited unanimity with eleven others, each of whom is summoned and appears on this business under the same untoward circumstances with himself. What must he do? In the affairs of life, real unanimity among such a number is little to be expected; least of all is it to be expected in matters which are litigated, and concerning which, if there had been no doubt, it is to be presumed there would have been no controversy. If real unanimity cannot be expected, he must either counterfeit it himself, or

g. Ante. vol. 1. p. 639.

he must be an accessory before the fact to the counterfeiting of it by others. The first is the principal, the second is inferiour only to the principal degree of disingenuity. Such a situation can never be desirable: on some occasions, it may be dreadful.

Let us suppose, that matters are brought to the sad alternative—that a juror must ruin his constitution, or, perhaps, literally starve himself; or, to avoid immediate death or a languishing life, he must, contrary to his conscience, doom a fellow man and a fellow citizen to die—what must he do? In this crisis of distress, he prays direction from the laws of his country: the laws of his country, as often understood, tell him—you must starve: for it cannot be insinuated, that the laws will advise him to belie his conscience. He obeys the hard mandate: by the virtue of obedience he loses his life: by his death the jury are discharged: for now there is a natural, as well as a moral impossibility of obtaining the unanimous verdict of twelve men. The former produces what, on every principle of morality and jurisprudence, the latter ought most unquestionably to have produced. But what must be the consequence of the jury's discharge? Does it discharge the person accused? No. A second jury must sit upon him; and before that second jury must be brought all those inextricable difficulties, which produced such calamity in the first.

Where is this to end? By the practice of the principles which I have explained, this can never begin. It is no hardship for each juror to speak his genuine and undisguised sentiment. Is it for conviction? Let him declare it. Let every other, in the same manner, declare his genuine and undisguised sentiment. If the sentiment of every other is for conviction; the verdict of conviction is unanimous. If a single sentiment is not for conviction; then a verdict of acquittal is the immediate consequence. To this verdict of acquittal, every one whose private sentiment was for conviction ought immediately to agree. For by the law, as it has been stated, twelve votes of conviction are necessary to compose a verdict of conviction: but eleven votes of conviction and one against it compose a verdict of acquittal.

Thus it is as to criminal matters. Under this disposition of things, can an honest and conscientious juror dread or suffer any inconvenience, in discharging his important trust, and performing his important duty, honestly and conscientiously? Under this disposition of things, will the citizens discover that strong reluctance, which they often and naturally discover, against serving on juries in criminal, especially in capital cases? Under this disposition of things, will those who have influence with the returning officer, exert that influence to prevent their being returned; and will those who cannot prevent their being returned, but can pay a fine, pay the fine rather than perform the service? Under this disposition, will juries, in criminal, especially in capital cases, be composed—as we have seen them too often composed—chiefly of such as have neither influence enough to avoid being returned, nor money enough to pay a fine for their nonattendance?

In civil causes, the business of the jury will be managed and directed in the same manner as the business of the court, and of every other publick body. Unanimity will always be acceptable: free and candid discussion will always be used: if they produce unanimity, it is well: if they reach not this high aim, acquiescence will be shown in the sentiment of the majority. This is the conduct of legislators: this is the conduct of judges: why should not this be the conduct of jurors?

I mentioned, that, in many cases, a verdict may, with great propriety, be composed of the separate sentiments of the several jurors, reduced to what may be called their average result. This I now explain.

It has been observed—and the observation has been illustrated at great length—that the power of juries is a discretionary power. This discretionary power arises from the nature of their office. Their office is to try the truth of facts: the truth of facts is tried by their evidence: the force of evidence cannot be digested by rules, nor formed into a regular system.

In many causes, there can be but two different sentiments. If, for instance, a suit be brought for the recovery of a horse; there can be, among the jury, only two opinions—that the plaintiff ought, and that he ought not, to recover. If there is a majority on either side, the voice of the majority should govern the verdict. If, on each side, there be an equal number of opinions, the verdict should be in favour of the possessor. "Melior est conditio possidentis."[36]

But there are many other causes, in which twenty different opinions may be entertained, as well as two; and there is no fixed rule, by which the accuracy or inaccuracy of any one of them can be ascertained. An action of slander, for instance, is brought by a young woman to recover damages for

36. The condition of the possessor is the better one.

an injury, which she has sustained by the defamation of her character. A variety of opinions may be formed, without end, concerning the particular sum which she ought to recover. Each of those various opinions may be composed from a variety of combining circumstances, the precise force of any of which can never be liquidated by any known methods of calculation. Those combining circumstances will arise from the situation and character of the plaintiff, from the situation and character of the defendant, from the nature and kind of the injury, and from the nature and extent of the loss. In the mind of each of the jurors, according to his situation and character, each of those combining circumstances may produce an effect, different from that which is produced by them in the mind of every other juror. The opinions, which are composed of those circumstances operating thus differently, must, of necessity, be different. Each juror forms his own. The opinion of each has an equal title to regard. How shall a verdict be collected from twelve opinions, no two of which are the same? Let each pronounce the particular sum, which, he thinks, the plaintiff ought to recover: let the sums be added together: let the amount of the whole be divided by twelve: let the sum produced by this division form the verdict of the jury. In this manner I explain what I mean by a verdict, "composed of the separate sentiments of the several jurors, reduced to what may be called their average result." This mode of forming a verdict will, on many occasions, be found useful and satisfactory.

Let us, in the last place, consider this subject as it regards judges. Judges do not, indeed, undergo, but, with melancholy, sympathetick feelings, they are obliged to witness—nay, they are obliged to be instrumental in—the feelings which jurors undergo, from the principle and the practice of unanimity, as it is frequently understood.

How natural is it for a jury, worn down by thirst, and hunger, and want of sleep, distracted by altercations and debates, bewildered by the difficulties and embarrassments by which those debates and altercations were produced—how natural is it for them to fly, for relief and instruction, to the court! Before the court they appear, pale, anxious, dejected; and beg the court to instruct and relieve them. On the principle of unanimity, as often received, what can the court do or advise? If they are well disposed—and we will presume them well disposed—they will, with every mark of compassionate attention and regard, advise them to do—what, if they could have done, there would have been no application for advice—"gentlemen, we advise you to agree: return to your chamber; confer together; reason together; come to an agreement; for you must agree; otherwise we cannot receive your verdict."

I have presumed the court to be well disposed: for this presumption, there is not always a sufficient ground. In the celebrated trial of William Penn and William Meade, four of the jurors dissented from the others. The recorder of London, before whom the cause was tried, addressing himself to Mr. Bushel, one of the four dissenters, said, Sir, you are the cause of this disturbance, and manifestly show yourself an abettor of faction; I shall set a mark on you, Sir. Gentlemen, said he to the whole jury, you shall not be dismissed, till we have a verdict that the court will accept; and you shall be locked up without meat, drink, fire, and tobacco: we will have a verdict, by the help of God, or you shall starve for it.[h]

But I have presumed the court to be well disposed. If they really are so, their situation is, indeed, a distressful one. They see before them a body of men, intrusted by their country with the greatest and most interesting powers: in the execution of this high trust, they see them suffering, though not offending: from those unmerited sufferings, they feel themselves altogether incapable of affording relief. What, in this situation, is left to the court? The alternate emotions of compassion and regret—compassion for those, whom they cannot aid—regret, because they cannot aid them.

By reducing to practice the theory, which I have stated and explained, the judges will be disburthened of all that uneasiness, under which they otherwise must labour; and will, on every occasion, have it in their power to relieve and advise satisfactorily every jury, who may apply to them for advice and relief.

Is the jury sitting in a criminal cause? Are they at a loss what to do? Do they pray the direction of the court? The court may give them a series of directions, which, one would imagine, must contain a remedy for every complaint.—Gentlemen, each of you must know the state of his own mind. Each of you must be clearly of opinion that the prisoner ought to be convicted, or that he ought to be acquitted; or you must be doubtful what opinion you must form. If the first be the case, you ought to vote for

h. 2. St. Tr. 613. 614.

a conviction: if either of the two last be the case, you ought to vote for an acquittal. What we say in the case of one, we say in the case of every one. Let every one, therefore, govern his own vote by these directions. When the vote of each is formed; the next step is to compose the verdict of all from the vote of each. Let the votes, then, be taken: they must be either unanimous or not unanimous: if they are not unanimous, let all agree to a verdict of acquittal: if they are unanimous, they must be unanimous for acquittal, or for conviction: if the former, the verdict is a verdict of acquittal: if the latter, the verdict is a verdict of conviction.

Is the jury sitting in a civil cause? Are they, in this cause too, at a loss what to do? Do they pray the direction of the court? The court may, in this cause too, give them a series of satisfactory directions.—Gentlemen, can only two opinions be entertained concerning the cause before you? If so; after freely and candidly discussing the matter by friendly conference among yourselves, let each make up his own opinion: let all the opinions be collected: if there be a majority on either side, let all agree to a verdict in favour of that side: if there is an equality of votes on each side, let the verdict be given in favour of possession. May any indefinite number of opinions be entertained concerning the cause before you? Let each juror form his own: let the verdict consist of the average result of all.

I trust, I have now shown, that, by reducing to practice the theory, which I have advanced on the subject of unanimity, in jury trials, many solid advantages would result from it to judges, to juries, and to parties. I trust, I have established this theory on every pillar on which a legal theory can be built—on precedent—on authority—on principle.

To all the nations, which swarmed from the northern hive, the trial by jury was common: to none of them, the principle of unanimity was known.

I here finish what, at present, I propose to say, concerning the doctrine of unanimity in the trial by jury.

Of juries there are two kinds; a grand jury, and a traverse jury. The institution of the grand jury is, at least in the present times, the peculiar boast of the common law. In the annals of the world, there cannot be found an institution so well fitted for avoiding abuses, which might otherwise arise from malice, from rigour, from negligence, or from partiality, in the prosecution of crimes.

In Athens, we can discover the vestiges of an institution, which bears a resemblance, though a very slight one, to that of grand juries. There was among them a previous inquiry before that trial, in which the final sentence was pronounced.

In cases of murder, the relations of the deceased alone had a right to prosecute.[i] There is an evident resemblance between this regulation, and that part of the law of England, which relates to prosecutions by appeal. When crimes were committed immediately against the government of Athens, every citizen might step forward as the prosecutor; for an injury offered to the commonwealth was considered as personal to each of its members.

Among the Romans, too, any one of the citizens was permitted to prosecute a publick offence. With all our predilection, however, for those celebrated republicks, we must admit, that these regulations were extremely injudicious, and produced mischiefs of very dangerous, though of very opposite kinds. Prosecutions were, on some occasions, undertaken from motives of rancour and revenge. On other occasions, a friend, a dependent, perhaps a confederate, of the criminal officiously engaged to prosecute him, with a view to ensure his impunity. Of this we have a remarkable instance, in the case of the infamous Verres.[37] Caecilius,[38] his creature and associate, disputed with Cicero the right of accusing him. The preference was adjudged to Cicero, in a process known by the name of *divination.*

There was a time, says Beccaria, when the crimes of the subjects were the inheritance of the prince.[j] At such a time probably it was, that the judge himself became the prosecutor. In several of the feudal nations, this was, indeed, the case. The gross impropriety of this regulation appears at the first view. The prosecutor is a party: without the last necessity, the prosecutor ought not to be both a party and a judge.

Among the Saxons, as we are informed by Mr. Selden, besides the satisfaction recovered by the party injured, there was a way found out to punish the offender by indictment. The difference, adds he, between former

i. 2. Gog. Or. L. 71.

37. Gaius Verres (c. 120–43 B.C.) was a Roman magistrate who was prosecuted for the misgovernment of Sicily by Cicero in 70 B.C.

38. Quintus Caecilius Niger was the quaestor under Verres.

j. Bec. c. 17

indictments and those in these days, consists in this, that the ancient indictments were in the name of one man; those of the latter sort are in the name of the jury. Time and experience, continues he, refined this way of trial into a more excellent condition.[k]

In the reign of Henry the third, the presentment of offences was made by a jury of twelve, returned for every hundred in the county. But towards the latter end of the reign of Edward the third, another improvement was introduced into the institution of grand juries. Besides the jury for every hundred, the sheriff returned a jury for the county, which was termed "the grand inquest." When this grand inquest inquired for the whole body of the county, the business of the hundred inquest, and the whole trust and duty of making presentments and finding indictments, naturally devolved upon the grand jury.[l]

A presentment is an accusation brought forward by the grand jury of their own mere motion. An indictment is a particular charge laid, by the publick prosecutor, before the grand jury, and found by them to be true.

The trust reposed in grand juries is of great and general concernment. To them is committed the custody of the portals of the law, that into the hallowed dome no injustice may be permitted to enter. They make, in the first instance, the important discrimination between the innocent and the guilty. To the former, they give a passport of security: the latter they consign to a final trial by a traverse jury.

The manner, in which grand juries ought to make their inquiries, well deserves to be attentively considered. It has been declared by some, that grand juries are only to inquire, "whether what they hear be any reason to put the party to answer"—"that a probable cause to call him to answer, is as much as is required by law." But, indeed, such a declaration is very little consonant to the oath—the best evidence of the law—which every grand juryman is obliged to take. He swears, that he will inquire diligently. As little is such a declaration consonant to ancient authority and practice. "In those days," says my Lord Coke,[m] speaking of the reign of Edward the first—"in those days (as yet it ought to be) indictments, taken in the

k. Bac. on Gov. 53, 54, 57.
l. 2. Reev. 210, 211.
m. 2. Ins. 384.

absence of the party, were formed upon plain and direct proof, and not upon probabilities or inferences." Still as little is such a declaration consonant to the voice of reason and sound sense. An indictment has been styled, and with no small degree of propriety, the verdict of the grand jury. "It ought to import all the truth which is requisite by law; and every part material ought to be found by the oath of the indictors." Now, is it consistent with reason or sound sense, that a verdict found upon oath—upon an oath to make diligent inquiry—should be the vague, perhaps the visionary, result merely of probability? Ought not moral certainty to be deemed the necessary basis of what is delivered, under the sanction of an obligation so solemn and so strict?

The doctrine, that a grand jury may rest satisfied merely with probabilities, is a doctrine dangerous as well as unfounded: it is a doctrine, which may be applied to countenance and promote the vilest and most oppressive purposes: it may be used, in pernicious rotation, as a snare, in which the innocent may be entrapped, and as a screen, under the cover of which the guilty may escape.

It has been alleged, that grand juries are confined, in their inquiries, to the bills offered to them, to the crimes given them in charge, and to the evidence brought before them by the prosecutor. But these conceptions are much too contracted: they present but a very imperfect and unsatisfactory view of the duty required from grand jurors, and of the trust reposed in them. They are not appointed for the prosecutor or for the court: they are appointed for the government and for the people: and of both the government and people it is surely the concernment, that, on one hand, all crimes, whether given or not given in charge, whether described or not described with professional skill, should receive the punishment, which the law denounces, and that, on the other hand, innocence, however strongly assailed by accusations drawn up in regular form, and by accusers marshalled in legal array, should, on full investigation, be secure in that protection, which the law engages that she shall enjoy inviolate.

The oath of a grand juryman—and his oath is the commission, under which he acts—assigns no limits, except those marked by diligence itself, to the course of his inquiries: why, then, should it be circumscribed by more contracted boundaries? Shall diligent inquiry be enjoined? And shall the means and opportunities of inquiry be prohibited or restrained?

The grand jury are a great channel of communication, between those who make and administer the laws, and those for whom the laws are made and administered. All the operations of government, and of its ministers and officers, are within the compass of their view and research. They may suggest publick improvements, and the modes of removing publick inconveniences: they may expose to publick inspection, or to publick punishment, publick bad men, and publick bad measures.

The relative powers of courts and juries form an interesting subject of inquiry. Concerning it, different opinions have been entertained; and it is of much consequence, in the study and in the practice too of the law, that it be clearly and fully understood. I shall treat it in the same manner, in which I have treated other questions of great importance: I shall examine it historically and on principle.

From a statute made in the thirteenth year of Edward the first, usually called the statute of Westminster the second,[n] it appears, that the contest between judges and juries concerning their relative powers ran, at that time, in a direction very different from that which it has taken since. The judges, then, were disposed to compel the jury to find the law as well as the fact: the jury were disposed to show the truth of the fact only, and to refer to the court the determination of the law. The statute interposed, and declared the discretionary power of the jury to do which of the two they thought most proper. "It is ordained, that the justices assigned to take assizes shall not compel the jurors to say precisely, whether it is or is not a disseisin." A general verdict of this kind included the question of law as well as the question of fact. "It is sufficient that they show the truth of the fact, and pray the assistance of the justices. But if they will voluntarily say, whether it is or is not a disseisin, their verdict shall be received at their own peril."

This statute recognised the law as it then stood, but introduced no new law. We are informed by my Lord Coke, in his commentary on it,[o] that in all actions, real, personal, and mixed, and upon all issues joined, general or special, the jury might find the special matter of fact pertinent and tending only to the issue joined, and might pray the discretion of the

n. C. 30.
o. 2. Ins. 425.

court for the law. This the jurors might do at the common law, not only in cases between party and party, of which the statute puts an example of the assize; but also in pleas of the crown at the suit of the king. This statute, therefore, like many others of the ancient statutes, is only in affirmance of the common law.[p]

Bracton, who wrote in the reign of Henry the third, tells us,[q] that a distinction was commonly taken between the provinces of the judges and jurors in this manner—truth is to be displayed by the jury; justice and judgment by the court. Yet, says he, it seems that judgment sometimes belongs to the jurors, when they declare upon their oath, whether such a one disseised or did not disseise such a one; according to which declaration, the judgment of the court is rendered. But, adds he, as it belongs to the judges to pronounce a just judgment, it is incumbent on them diligently to weigh and examine what is said by the jury, that they themselves may not be misled by the jury's mistakes.

We have the high authority of Littleton, that, in cases where the jury may give their verdict at large—in other words, a special verdict, stating the facts, and praying the decision of the court as to the law—they may, if they will take upon them the knowledge of the law, give their verdict generally, as is put in their charge.[r]

In a case determined in the reign of Queen Elizabeth, it was objected, that a jury could not give a special verdict upon a special and collateral issue; but that, in such case, the jury ought to give a precise and categorical answer to the question arising from such special issue. It was resolved, however, unanimously by the court, that the law will not compel the jurors to take upon them the knowledge of points in law, either in cases of property, or in those which concern life; and that it will not compel even the judges to give their opinions of questions and doubts in law upon the sudden; but, in such cases, the truth of the facts should be found; and, after consideration and conference, the question should be determined according to the law.[s]

p. 9. Rep. 13.
q. Bract. 186 b.
r. Lit. s. 368. 1. Ins. 228.
s. 9. Rep. 11. b. 13.

In the famous trial of John Lilburne,[39] for publishing a book, entitled, an impeachment of high treason against Oliver Cromwell, we hear a language, very different from that, to which we have hitherto been accustomed.

"Let all the hearers know"—said Mr. Justice Jermin,[40] a judge of the upper bench, as it was called during the commonwealth, and who was one of the commissioners appointed in the extraordinary commission of oyer and terminer for the trial of Mr. Lilburne—"Let all the hearers know, the jury ought to take notice of it, that the judges, that are sworn, that are twelve in number, they have ever been the judges of the law, from the first time that ever we can read or hear that the law was truly expressed in England: and the jury are only judges, whether such a thing were done or no; they are only judges of matter of fact."[t] Lord Commissioner Keble[41] delivers it as the opinion of the court, that "the jury are judges of matter of fact altogether; but that they are not judges of matter of law."[u] The prisoner urged the authority of my Lord Coke, that the jury were judges of the law as well as of the fact; but, by a mistake, mentioned the book as a commentary upon Plowden[42] instead of Littleton. The court told him there was no such book; that they knew it a little better than he did. He pressed to read it; and said that it was an easy matter for an abler man than him, in so many interruptions as he met with, to mistake Plowden for Littleton. "You cannot"—these are the words of Judge Jermin, as mentioned in the report of the trial—"you cannot be suffered to read the law: you have broached an erroneous opinion that the jury are the judges of the law, which is enough to destroy all the law in the land; there was never such a damnable heresy broached in this nation before."[v] Mr. Lilburne persisted, however, and read his authorities.

39. John Lilburne (1614?–1657), also known as "Freeborn John," was an English author and political agitator.

40. Justice Philip Jermin (or Jermyn) (1587–1654) was appointed by parliament to be judge of Superior Court in 1648.

t. 2. St. Tri. 19.

41. Richard Keble was Lord Commissioner under Charles I from 1649 to 1654.

u. Id. 69.

42. Edmund Plowden (1518–1585) was a chronicler of English law.

v. Id. ibid.

"Extremes in nature equal ends produce." As were some of the judges under Cromwell, so were some of the judges under Charles the second. We have had occasion to take some notice of the trial of William Penn and William Meade. The jury, at last, agreed on a verdict of acquittal. This verdict the court could not refuse; but they fined each of the jurors forty marks for giving it, "because it was against the direction of the court in matter of law."[w] The jurors were imprisoned till they should pay the fines. Mr. Bushell, one of them, sued a writ of habeas corpus out of the court of common pleas. His case was heard and determined there; and the cause of commitment was adjudged to be insufficient, and Mr. Bushell was discharged.

To what end—said Lord Chief Justice Vaughan, in delivering the opinion of the court—to what end are jurors challenged so scrupulously to the array and the poll? To what end must they be true and lawful men, and not of affinity with the parties concerned? To what end must they have, in many cases, the view, for their exacter information chiefly? To what end must they undergo the heavy punishment of the villainous judgment; if, after all this, they must implicitly give a verdict by the dictates and authority of another man, under pain of fines and imprisonment, when sworn to do it according to the best of their own knowledge? A man cannot see by another's eye, nor hear by another's ear; no more can a man conclude or infer the thing to be resolved, by another's understanding or reasoning.

Upon all general issues, the jury find not the fact of every case by itself, leaving the law to the court; but find for the plaintiff or defendant upon the issue tried, wherein they resolve both law and fact complicately, and not the fact by itself.[x]

In every case, says the late Sir Michael Foster, where the point turneth upon the question, whether the homicide was committed wilfully and maliciously, or under circumstances justifying, excusing, or alleviating; the matter of fact, to wit, whether the facts alleged by way of justification, excuse, or alleviation be true, is the proper and only province of the jury. But whether, upon a supposition of the truth of the facts, such homicide

w. Vaugh. 136.
x. Vaugh. 148. 150.

be justified, excused, or alleviated, must be submitted to the judgment of the court.[y]

It is of the greatest consequence, says my Lord Hardwicke, to the law of England, that the powers of the judges and jury be kept distinct: that the judges determine the law, and that the jury determine the fact.[z]

This well known division between their provinces has been long recognised and established. When the question of law and the question of fact can be decided separately; there is no doubt or difficulty in saying, by whom the separate decision shall be made. If, between the parties litigant, there is no contention concerning the facts, but an issue is joined upon a question of law, as is the case in a demurrer; the determination of this question, and the trial of this issue, belongs exclusively to the judges. On the other hand, when there is no question concerning the law, and the controversy between the parties depends entirely upon a matter of fact; the determination of this matter, brought to an issue, belongs exclusively to the jury. But, in many cases, the question of law is intimately and inseparably blended with the question of fact: and when this is the case, the decision of one necessarily involves the decision of the other. When this is the case, it is incumbent on the judges to inform the jury concerning the law; and it is incumbent on the jury to pay much regard to the information, which they receive from the judges. But now the difficulty, in this interesting subject, begins to press upon us. Suppose that, after all the precautions taken to avoid it, a difference of sentiment takes place between the judges and the jury, with regard to a point of law: suppose the law and the fact to be so closely interwoven, that a determination of one must, at the same time, embrace the determination of the other: suppose a matter of this description to come in trial before a jury—what must the jury do?—The jury must do their duty, and their whole duty: they must decide the law as well as the fact.

This doctrine is peculiarly applicable to criminal cases; and from them, indeed, derives its peculiar importance. When a person is to be tried for a crime, the accusation charges against him, not only the particular fact which he has committed, but also the motive, to which it owed its origin, and from which it receives its complexion. The first is neither the only, nor

y. Fost. 255.
z. Hardw. 28.

the principal object of examination and discussion. On the second, depends the innocence or criminality of the action. The verdict must decide not only upon the first, but also, and principally, upon the second: for the verdict must be coextensive and commensurate with the charge.

It may seem, at first view, to be somewhat extraordinary, that twelve men, untutored in the study of jurisprudence, should be the ultimate interpreters of the law, with a power to overrule the directions of the judges, who have made it the subject of their long and elaborate researches, and have been raised to the seat of judgment for their professional abilities and skill.

But a deeper examination of the subject will reconcile us to what, at first, may appear incongruous. In criminal cases, the design, as has been already intimated, is closely interwoven with the transaction; and the elucidation of both depends on a collected view of particulars, arising not only from the testimony, but also from the character and conduct of the witnesses, and sometimes also from the character and conduct of the prisoner. Of all these, the jury are fittest to make the proper comparison and estimate; and, therefore, it is most eligible to leave it to them, after receiving the direction of the court in matters of law, to take into their consideration all the circumstances of the case, the intention as well as the facts, and to determine, upon the whole, whether the prisoner has or has not been guilty of the crime, with which he is charged.

Juries undoubtedly may make mistakes: they may commit errours: they may commit gross ones. But changed as they constantly are, their errours and mistakes can never grow into a dangerous system. The native uprightness of their sentiments will not be bent under the weight of precedent and authority. The esprit du corps will not be introduced among them; nor will society experience from them those mischiefs, of which the esprit du corps, unchecked, is sometimes productive. Besides, their mistakes and their errours, except the venial ones on the side of mercy made by traverse juries, are not without redress. Of an indictment found by a grand jury, the person indicted may be acquitted on his trial. If a bill be returned "ignoramus" improperly, the accusation may be renewed before another grand jury. With regard to the traverse jury, the court, if dissatisfied with their verdict, have the power, and will exercise the power, of granting a new trial. This power, while it prevents or corrects the effects of their errours, preserves the jurisdiction of juries unimpaired. The cause is not evoked before a tribunal of another kind. A jury of the country—an abstract, as it has been called, of the citizens at large,—summoned, selected, impannelled, and sworn as the former, must still decide.

One thing, however, must not escape our attention. In the cases and on the principles, which we have mentioned, jurors possess the power of determining legal questions. But they must determine those questions, as judges must determine them, according to law. The discretionary powers of jurors find no place for exertion here. Those powers they possess as triers of facts; because, as we have already observed, the trial of facts depends on evidence; and because the force of evidence cannot be ascertained by any general system of rules. But law, particularly the common law, is governed by precedents, and customs, and authorities, and maxims: those precedents, and customs, and authorities, and maxims are alike obligatory upon jurors as upon judges, in deciding questions of law.

True it is, according to the sentiment of my Lord Hardwicke, that it is of the greatest consequence to preserve the separate and distinct powers of the judges and the juries. But equally true it is, that those separate and distinct powers may be rendered reciprocally beneficial, by the most pleasing and harmonious cooperation.

In favour of a conclusion of this kind, the conduct of juries bears ample testimony. The examples of their resisting the advice of a judge, in points of law, are rare, except where they have been provoked into such an opposition by the grossness of his own misconduct, or betrayed into an unjust suspicion of his integrity by the misrepresentation of others. In civil cases, juries almost universally find a special verdict, as often as the judges recommend it to them. In criminal cases, indeed, special verdicts are less frequent: but this happens, not because juries have an aversion to them, but because such cases depend more on the evidence of facts, than on any difficulties arising in points of law.

Nor is it a small merit in this arrangement, that, by means of it, every one who is accused of a crime may, on his plea of "not guilty," enjoy the advantages of a trial, in which the judges and the jury are to one another a mutual check, and a mutual assistance. This point deserves from us a full illustration.

Some things appear, at the first view, to be alike, which, upon a close inspection, are found to be materially different. To a superficial observer, no very important distinction would seem to arise, between the credibility and the competency of evidence. Between them, however, a most important distinction subsists. They spring from different sources; they run in different directions; and, in the division of power between the court and the jury, they are, with great propriety, allotted to different provinces. In some instances, indeed, the line of division is scarcely perceptible; but, even in those instances, the law points out a proper mode of management.

Evidence is of two kinds, written and oral. In each kind, the important distinction between its competency and its credibility takes place. In oral evidence, however, or the testimony of witnesses, the distinction is the most important; and, for this reason, it should be clearly known and strictly preserved.

The excellency of the trial by jury, says the great and good Lord Chief Justice Hale, is, that they are the triers of the credit of the witnesses, as well as the truth of the fact: it is one thing whether a witness is admissible to be heard: whether, when he is heard, he is to be believed, is another thing.[a]

It is a known distinction, says Lord Chief Justice Willes,[43] in a very celebrated cause, that the evidence, though admitted, must still be left to the persons who try the causes, to give what credit to it they please.[b]

That I may observe it once for all, says Lord Chief Justice Hale, in another place, the exceptions to a witness are of two kinds. 1. Exceptions to the credit of the witness, which do not at all disable him from being sworn, but yet may blemish the credibility of his testimony; in such case, the witness is to be allowed, but the credit of his testimony is left to the jury, who are judges of the fact, and likewise of the probability or improbability, credibility or incredibility of the witness and his testimony; these exceptions are of such great variety and multiplicity, that they cannot easily be reduced under rules or instances. 2. Exceptions to the competency of the witness, which exclude him from giving his testimony: and of these exceptions the court is the judge.[c]

The writers on the civil law, to which the trial by jury has, for many ages, been unknown, have attempted to reduce the credibility and incredibility of testimony under rules and instances: but their attempts have shown,

a. 1. Hale. P. C. 635.

43. Sir John Willes (1685–1761) was Lord Chief Justice of His Majesties Court of Common Pleas.

b. 1. Atk. 45. Omychund v. Barker.

c. 2. Hale. P. C. 276.

what, indeed, has been likewise shown from the nature of the thing, that such a reduction is not only not easy, as my Lord Hale says, but is altogether and absolutely impracticable.

Evidence is, by those civilians, distinguished into different degrees—into full probation; into probation less than full; into half probation. The deficiency in half probation is made up, sometimes by torture, sometimes by the suppletory oath of the party. Concerning circumstantial proofs, rules, unsatisfactory because unfounded, have been heaped upon rules, volumes have been heaped upon volumes, and evidence has been added, and divided, and subtracted, and multiplied, like pounds, and shillings, and pence, and farthings. In the parliament of Toulouse,[44] we are told by Voltaire,[d] [45] they admitted of quarters and eighths of a proof. For instance, one hearsay was considered as a quarter; another hearsay, more vague, as an eighth; so that eight vague hearsays, which, in fact, are no more than the reverberated echos of a report, perhaps originally groundless, constitute a full proof. Upon this principle it was, that poor Calas was condemned to the wheel.

Evidence is that which produces belief. Belief is a simple act of the mind, more easily experienced than described. Its degrees of strength or weakness cannot, like those of heat and cold, be ascertained by the precise scale of an artificial thermometer. Their effects, however, are naturally felt and distinguished by a sound and healthful mind. With great propriety, therefore, the common law forbears to attempt a scale or system of rules, concerning the force or credibility of evidence; it wisely leaves them to the unbiassed and unadulterated sentiments and impressions of the jury. But with regard to the propriety or competency of evidence, the case is very different. This subject is susceptible of system and of rule. This subject, therefore, is wisely committed to the information and experience of the judges.

The most general and the most conspicuous rule with regard to the competency of evidence, is, that the best, of which the nature of the fact in question is capable, must be produced, if it can be produced: if it cannot

44. The parliament created by the French king Charles VII at the beginning of the fifteenth century. It exercised judicial functions that were heavily criticized by Voltaire.

d. Com. on Bec. c. 22.

45. Voltaire was the pseudonym for François-Marie Arouet (1694–1778), a skeptical French writer.

be produced, then the best evidence, which can be obtained, shall be admitted. Both the parts of this rule are founded on the most solid reason. To reject, as incompetent, the strongest evidence which can be procured, would be rigid, and unaccommodating to the various vicissitudes of life and business. To admit an inferiour kind of evidence, when evidence of a superiour nature is withheld, would prevent that degree of satisfaction in the minds of the jurors, which evidence should be fitted to produce. Evidence produces belief: the strongest evidence produces the strongest belief: why is the strongest evidence withheld? The party, in whose power it is, can have no motive for withholding it, unless he is conscious that it would disclose something, which his interest requires to be concealed. The satisfactory administration of justice, therefore, demands, that it should be laid before the jury.

The application of this rule is most extensive. What ought or ought not to be presumed in the power of the party, must be collected by a full and intimate knowledge or information concerning the business and transactions of life. The most authentick materials of information and knowledge are furnished by juridical history—a subject deservedly the professional study of judges of the common law.

Another rule, of high import in the administration of justice, is, that evidence, in order to be admitted, must have a proper degree of connexion with the question to be tried: in legal language, it must be pertinent to the issue. A variety of evidence, unconnected with the point specified by the record for the examination of the jury, would have a tendency to bewilder their minds, and to prevent that strict and undivided attention, which is so indispensable to the satisfactory investigation of that, which they are empowered and intrusted to decide.

The evidence proper to be given in each of the numerous kinds of issues, which come before a jury, forms a very interesting portion of legal knowledge. At present, we can only show the principle and the importance of that accuracy, which the law requires in the admission of evidence. The preservation of this accuracy is fitly committed to the experience of the judges.

With regard to oral evidence, or the testimony of witnesses, the rule of the law is, that proper testimony may be received from the mouth of every intelligent person, who is not infamous or interested. Concerning the points of intelligence, of infamy, and of interestedness, a great variety of rules are established by the law. To apply those rules to cases which occur in the course of practice, is, with obvious propriety, allotted to the judges.

In one of those subjects, however—I mean the interest of witnesses—the line of division, between the province of the judges and that of the jury, is faintly marked, and difficult to be ascertained. The degrees of interest are so numerous, and the effects of the same degree of interest upon different characters and in different situations are so diversified, that it is impracticable, in many instances, to define exactly the precise boundary, at which the question of competency ends, and the question of credibility begins. In doubtful cases of this description, the judges, especially of late years, presume in favour of the province of the jury. This is done with great reason. For an objection, urged, without success, against the competency of a witness, may be urged successfully against the credibility of his testimony; and to the objecting party it is altogether immaterial, whether the testimony of the witness is rejected or disbelieved. When an objection, says my Lord Hardwicke, is made against a witness, it is best to restrain it to his credit, unless it is like to introduce great perjury; because it tends to let in light to the cause.[e]

In arranging and in summing up the evidence, the court, from their knowledge and experience of business, can give great assistance to the jury. In questions of law emerging from the evidence, the assistance of the court is still more necessary and essential. Lord Chief Justice Hale observes, that a judge may be of much advantage to the jury, by showing them his opinion even in matter of fact.[f] Of the sentiment of a judge so exemplary in his delicacy as well as in his candour, I risk not the disapprobation; but I add, that this power can never be exercised with a reserve too cautious.

We have seen, by a number of instances, how, in the administration of justice, the jury receive assistance from the judges. Let us now see how the judges receive assistance from the jury.

"Ex facto oritur jus."[46] The jury lay the foundation of truth, on which the judges erect the superstructure of law. A correct statement of the facts, every professional gentleman knows, is necessary to an accurate report. A

e. Hardw. 360.
f. Hale. Hist. 256.
46. Law arises from fact.

true verdict given by the jury, is an essential prerequisite to a just judgment pronounced by the court. Judgments in supposed cases may abundantly evince professional skill; but they will never have a decisive influence over society—they will never come home to the business and bosoms of the citizens—unless they are practically founded on the manners, and characters, and rights of men. The manners, the characters, and the rights of men are truly and practically reported by the verdicts of juries.

To judges of a proper disposition, the assistance of juries is soothing as well as salutary. In criminal cases, it is unquestionably so. "To say the truth"—I use the language of the humane Lord Chief Justice Hale—"it were the most unhappy case that could be to the judge, if he, at his peril, must take upon him the guilt or innocence of the prisoner, and if the judge's opinion must rule the matter of fact."[g]

Take upon him the guilt or innocence of the prisoner! It may be soothing, indeed, to judges, to be relieved from this mental burthen, of all the most anxious: but upon whom—methinks I hear a citizen ask—upon whom must this most anxious of all mental burthens be laid? How must it be born by those on whom it is laid?

This very serious and momentous question brings before us the trial by jury in a view, the sublimity of which I have often admired in silence; but which now—though I feel myself far inferiour to the task—I must endeavour to describe and explain. I solicit your candid indulgence, while I attempt to delineate the particulars, of which this prospect, magnificent and interesting, is composed; and then try, with unequal efforts, to convey the impression which naturally will result from the combination of the whole.

It will be necessary to review some principles, of which notice has been already taken in the course of my lectures. In a former part of them[h] I observed, that, when society was formed, it possessed jointly all the previously separate and independent powers and rights of the individuals who formed it, and all those other powers and rights which result from the social union. I observed, that all those powers and rights were collected, in order to be enjoyed and exercised; that, in a numerous and extended society, all those powers could not, indeed, be exercised personally; but that they

g. 2. Hale. P. C. 313.
h. Ante. vol. 1. p. 556–558.

might be exercised by representation. I asked, whether one power might not be delegated to one set of men? and whether another power might not be delegated to another set of men? alluding to the legislative and executive departments. I mentioned a third power of society—that of administering justice under the laws. I asked, whether this power might not be partly delegated, and partly retained in personal exercise; because, in the most extended communities, an important part of the administration of justice may be discharged by the people themselves. I mentioned, that all this has been done, as I should have the pleasure of showing, when I should come to examine our governments, and to point out, by an enumeration and comparison of particulars, how beautifully, how regularly, and how usefully, we have established, by our practice in this country, principles concerning the distribution, the arrangement, the reservation, the direction, and the uses of that publick power, of which the just theory is still unknown in other nations.

I have had the pleasure of explaining the powers, legislative, executive, and judicial, which the people have delegated: I come now to that part of the judicial authority, which they retain in personal exercise—I mean, the authority to decide in criminal cases; in cases, especially, of life and death.

This may be considered in two different points of light; as a power, and as a burthen. As a burthen, it is considered as too heavy to be imposed, as a power, it is considered as too great to be conferred, permanently upon any man, or any organized body of men. We have seen it a discretionary—so far it partakes of a legislative power. We have seen that, in large and extended communities, necessity directs the delegation of other legislative power. This is a species of legislative power, which may, and therefore should, be exercised in person. In cases of life and death, the standing jurisdiction remains with the people at large. As emergencies occur, an abstract of the people is selected for the occasional exercise of it. The moment that the occasion is over, the abstracted selection disappears among the general body of the citizens. No one citizen, therefore, any more than any other, can complain of this as an uneasy burthen. Except on particular occasions, and during those occasions, it is imposed on no one.

If jurisdiction in cases of life and death, considered as a burthen, is uneasy to those who bear it; considered as a power, it is tremendous to those who behold it. A man, or a body of men, habitually clothed with a power over the lives of their fellow citizens! These are objects formidable indeed. By an operation, beautiful and sublime, of our juridical system, objects so formidable are withdrawn from before the eyes of our citizens—objects so formidable do not exist. To promote an habitual courage, and dignity, and independence of sentiment and of actions in the citizens, should be the aim of every wise and good government. How much are these principles promoted, by this beautiful and sublime effect of our judicial system. No particular citizen can threaten the exercise of this tremendous power: with the exercise of this tremendous power, no particular citizen can be threatened. Even the unfortunate prisoner, the day of whose trial is come, the jury for whose trial are selected, impannelled, and returned—even this unfortunate prisoner cannot be threatened with the exercise of this tremendous power by any particular citizen. When he comes to the bar and looks upon the prisoner, a single supercilious look will produce a peremptory rejection.

Uncommonly jealous is the constitution of the United States and that of Pennsylvania upon this subject, so interesting to the personal independence of the citizens. The formidable power we have mentioned is interdicted even to the legislatures themselves. Neither congress nor the general assembly of this commonwealth, can pass any act of attainder for treason or felony.[i] Now, an act of attainder is a legislative verdict.

I have said, that this authority remains with the people at large. Potentially, indeed, it does; actually, it cannot be said to remain even with them. The contrivance is so admirably exquisite concerning this tremendous jurisdiction, that, in the general course of things, it exists actually no where. But no sooner does any particular emergency call for its operations, than it starts into immediate existence.

But it remains, that I give satisfaction with regard to the inquiry—how shall this burthen, attended with so much uneasiness, be born by those, upon whom, though only occasionally, it is laid?

It is, we acknowledge, a most weighty burthen. That man must, indeed, be callous to sensibility, who, without emotion and anxiety, can deliberate on the question—whether, by his voice, his fellow man and fellow citizen shall live or die. But while capital punishments continue to be inflicted, the burthen must be born; and while it must be born, every citizen, who,

i. Cons. U. S. Art. 1. s. 9. Cons. Penn. Art. 9. s. 18.

in the service of his country, may be called to bear it, is bound to qualify himself for bearing it in such a manner, as will ensure peace of mind to himself, justice to him whose fate be may determine, and honour to the judicial administration of his country. By so qualifying himself, though, in the discharge of his duty, he will feel strong emotions, he will, from the performance of it, feel no remorse.

I must again enter upon a review of some principles, of which notice has already been taken.

With regard to the law in criminal cases, every citizen, in a government such as ours, should endeavour to acquire a reasonable knowledge of its principles and rules, for the direction of his conduct, when he is called to obey, when he is called to answer, and when he is called to judge. On questions of law, his deficiencies will be supplied by the professional directions of the judges, whose duty and whose business it is professionally to direct him. For, as we have seen, verdicts, in criminal cases, generally determine the question of law, as well as the question of fact. Questions of fact, it is his exclusive province to determine. With the consideration of evidence unconnected with the question which he is to try, his attention will not be distracted; for every thing of that nature, we presume, will be excluded by the court. The collected powers of his mind, therefore, will be fixed, steadily and without interruption, upon the issue which he is sworn to try. This issue is an issue of fact. Its trial will depend upon the evidence. Evidence, in every cause, is that which produces: evidence, in a capital cause, is that which *forces* belief.

Belief, as we have seen, is an act of the mind, not easily described, indeed, but easily felt. Does the juror feel its force? Let him obey the constitution of his nature, and yield to the strong conviction. If the evidence produce, upon the mind of each of his fellow jurors, the same strong conviction, which it produces on his, their sentiments will be unanimous; and the unanimous sentiments of all will still corroborate the strong conviction of each. If a single doubt remain in the mind of any juror, that doubt should produce his dissent, and the dissent of a single juror, according to the principles which we have explained, and, we trust, established, will produce a verdict of acquittal by all.

Considered in this manner, is the duty of a juror, in a capital case, intolerably burthensome? It cannot, indeed, as we have said, be discharged without emotion: but the unbiassed dictates of his own constitution will teach—will force him to discharge it properly.

In criminal—in capital cases, with what sublime majesty does the trial by jury now appear to its ravished beholders! In the first and purest principles of society its foundations are laid: by the most exquisite skill, united with consummate benignity, the grand and finely proportioned edifice has been raised: within its walls, strong and lofty as well as finely proportioned, freedom enjoys protection, and innocence rests secure.

CHAPTER VII.
The Subject Continued. Of Sheriffs and Coroners.

The sheriff is an officer of high respectability in our juridical system, and was known to the most early ages of the common law.

Among the Saxons, his power was very great and extensive—judicial as well as ministerial. In his ministerial character, he executed the writs of the king and the judgments of his courts: in his judicial character, the sheriff presided in the several courts of justice comprehended within the sphere of his jurisdiction. He was chosen in the county court by the votes of the freeholders; and, like the king himself, says Selden,[a] was entitled to his honour by the people's favour.

All the other nations of Gothick and German origin, who, on the ruins of the Roman empire, founded kingdoms in the different parts of Europe, had officers of the same kind with the sheriffs of the Anglo-Saxons. This is a strong evidence of their high antiquity, as well as general respectability.[b] In some of the Gothick constitutions, the sheriffs were elected by the people, but confirmed by the king. The election and appointment were made in this manner: the people chose twelve electors; those electors nominated three persons to the king; from those three the king selected one, who was the confirmed sheriff.[c]

The popular elections of the sheriffs, in England, were lost by the people in the reigns of Edward the second[1] and Edward the third; and a new mode of appointment was substituted in their place.[d] In the time of Lord Chancellor Fortescue, the manner of the election of sheriffs was as follows.

a. Bac. on Gov. 41.

b. 2. Hen. 245.

c. 1. Bl. Com. 340

1. Edward II (1284–1327) was king of England from 1307 to 1327.

d. 4. Bl. Com. 420.

Every year there met, in the court of exchequer, all the king's counsellors, as well lords spiritual and temporal, as all other the king's justices, all the barons of the exchequer, the master of the rolls, and certain other officers. All these, by common consent, nominated of every county three persons of distinction, such as they deemed best qualified for the office of sheriff, and presented them to the king. Of the persons so nominated and returned, the king made choice of one, who, by virtue of the king's letters patent, was constituted high sheriff of that county, for which he was so chosen.[e] This mode of nomination and appointment still continues in England.[f]

It has been usual to appoint them annually. But in the reign of Henry the fifth,[2] we find from this custom a parliamentary exception, rendered very remarkable by the reason assigned for it. The king is permitted to appoint sheriffs for four years; "because by wars and pestilence there are not a sufficient number remaining, in the different counties, to discharge this office from year to year."[g]

By a parliamentary regulation made in the reign of Edward the second, and repeated in that of Edward the third, it was directed that sheriffs should be chosen from such persons as had lands in their shires, and that those lands should be sufficient to answer to the king and his people, if grieved.[h]

By a law of the United States, a marshal is appointed for each district for the term of four years; but is removable from his office at pleasure.[i] As no particular mode is specified by the law for appointing the marshal, his appointment falls, of course, under the general provision made by the national constitution.[j] The president nominates, and, with the advice and consent of the senate, appoints him. His powers and his duties are, in general, coincident with those of a sheriff.[k]

e. Fort. de laud. c. 24.

f. Wood. 70.

2. Henry V (1387–1422) was king of England from 1413 to 1422.

g. Bar. on St. 386.

h. 2. Reev. 78.

i. Laws. U. S. 1. cong. 1. sess. c. 20. s. 27.

j. Art. 2. s. 2.

k. "The marshals of the several districts, and their deputies, shall have the same powers in executing the laws of the United States, as sheriffs and their deputies, in the several states, have by law, in executing the laws of the respective states." Laws U. S. 3. cong. 2. sess. c. 101. s. 9. The same provision was contained in a prior law, repealed by that above cited. Laws U. S. 2. cong. 1. sess. c. 28. s. 9. *Ed.*

By the constitution of Pennsylvania,[l] sheriffs are chosen by the citizens of each county: two persons are chosen for the office; one of the two is appointed by the governour. We observe, here, another instance of the old Saxon and German customs revived in the constitution of this commonwealth.

Our sheriffs are elected and hold their offices for three years, if they behave themselves well; but no person shall be twice chosen or appointed sheriff in any term of six years. The converse of this regulation we find in an act of parliament—No man, who has served the office of sheriff for one year, can be *compelled* to serve it again within three years afterwards.[m] The reason of this converse regulation may be collected from another act of parliament. The expense which custom had introduced in serving the office of high sheriff became so burthensome, that it was enacted, that no sheriff should keep any table at the assizes, except for his own family, or give any presents to the judges or their servants, or have more than forty men in livery: yet, for the sake of safety and decency, he may not have less than twenty men in England and twelve in Wales.[n]

An attention to the powers and duties of the sheriff will disclose, I think, a peculiar propriety in the compound mode of election and appointment, directed by our constitution. He executes the process of courts, and, in his county, is the principal conservator of the peace: so far he is an executive officer, and should be appointed by the governour. He returns jurors: for this reason, he should be chosen by the people. Invested with the double character, he should receive his authority partly from both. As he is elected and appointed for three years, and can serve only once in the period of six years; he is, in a considerable degree, independent, and may, therefore, be presumed impartial in the exercise of his very important duties and powers. Those duties and powers we are now concisely to describe.

The judicial power of the sheriff, which, in former times, was very great and extensive, is, by our juridical system, transferred, with great propriety, to other establishments: for it is obviously incongruous, that executive and judicial authority should be united in the same person.

l. Art. 6. s. 1.
m. St. 1. R. 2. c. 11. 1. Bl. Com. 343.
n. St. 13 and 14. C. 2. c. 21. 1. Bl. Com. 346.

Permit me here to observe, that the accumulation of unnecessary and even inconsistent powers seems to be the principal objection against the old Saxon institutions. In most other respects, they are not more venerable on account of their antiquity, than on account of their matured excellence. Permit me also here to observe, that, in the correct distribution of the powers of government, the constitution of Pennsylvania approaches, if it does not reach, theoretick perfection.

The ministerial power of the sheriff is of great importance to the impartial administration of justice, and to the internal peace and tranquillity of the commonwealth. He is the chief officer, says my Lord Coke, within the shire. To his custody the county is committed. This custody is three-fold. 1. Of the life of justice; for no suit begins, and no process is served, but by the sheriff. It belongs to him also to return indifferent juries, for the trials of men's properties, liberties, and lives. 2. Of the life of the law; for, after suits long and chargeable, he makes execution, which is the life and fruit of the law. 3. Of the life of the republick; for, within the county, he is the principal conservator of the peace, which is the life of the commonwealth.[o]

With regard to process issuing from the courts of justice, the sheriff's power and duty is, to execute it, not to dispute its validity: though the writ be illegal, the sheriff is protected and indemnified in serving it.[p] From this general rule, however, one exception must be taken and allowed. He must judge, at his peril, whether the court, from which the process issued, has or has not jurisdiction of the cause.[q]

The selection and the return of jurors is a most momentous part of the power and duty of a sheriff. It is that part, in which abuses are most fatal: it is that part, in which there is the greatest opportunity and temptation to commit them. Let us speak of former times. In the reign of Edward the first, the parliament was obliged to interpose its authority to give relief to the people against sheriffs, who harassed jurors unnecessarily, by summoning them from a great distance, and who returned such as would not give an impartial verdict. This last abuse, says a modern writer[r] on the English law, was never perfectly removed till the late act was made for

o. 1. Ins. 168. a.
p. 6. Rep. 54. 9. Rep. 68.
q. 10. Rep. 76. 2. Wil. 384.
r. Bar. on St. 185.

balloting juries. In an account of Cornwall, written by Mr. Carew,[3] we are informed, that, in the reign of Henry the seventh,[4] an article of charge for the "friendship of the sheriff," was common in an attorney's bill.[s]

As the principal conservator of the peace in his county, and as the calm but irresistible minister of the law, the authority of a sheriff is important; his duty is proportionably great. To preserve or restore the publick tranquillity, to ensure or enforce the effectual execution of the law, he is invested with the high power of ordering to his assistance the whole strength of the county over which he presides.

The law is mild in its mandates; but it will be obeyed. It knows, it presumes, it will suffer none of its ministers to know or to presume, any power superiour to its own. If any man, says my Lord Coke, however great, might resist the sheriff in executing the king's writs; it would be regular and justifiable in the sheriff to return such resistance: but such a return would redound greatly to the dishonour of the king and his crown: what redounds to the dishonour of the king and his crown, is against the common law: and, therefore, if necessity require it for the due execution of the king's writs, the sheriff may, by the common law, take the *posse comitatus*[5] to suppress such unlawful force and resistance.[t]

When necessity requires it, the sheriff not only may, but must at his peril, employ the strength of his county. In the reign of Edward the second, a sheriff had the king's writ to deliver possession of land: the sheriff returned that he could not execute the writ by reason of resistance. This was considered as an insult upon the authority, with which he was invested; and because he took not the power of the county in aid of the execution, he was amerced at twenty marks.[u]

Besides the warrant of the common law, continues my Lord Coke, the sheriff has his letters patent of assistance, by which the king commands, that all archbishops, bishops, dukes, earls, barons, knights, freemen, and

3. Richard Carew (1555–1620) wrote *The Survey of Cornwall* (1602).

4. Henry VII (1457–1509) was king of England from 1485 to 1509.

s. Bar. on St. 458.

5. The power or force of the county. The entire population of a county above the age of fifteen, which a sheriff may summon to his assistance.

t. 2. Ins. 193.

u. 2. Ins. 194.

all others of the county shall attend, assist, and answer to the sheriff, in every thing which belongs to his office. No man above fifteen and under seventy years of age, ecclesiastical or temporal, is exempted from this service: for so it is by construction of law.

How easily are these cases applied to the United States and to Pennsylvania, under the operation of the fine rule, that the empire of the law is stronger as well as safer than the empire of man!

I proceed to consider the office of coroner. This office, though much neglected, though, perhaps, despised, is an office, both ancient and dignified. It forms no inconsiderable part of a complete juridical system.

In the time of the Saxons, as we are informed by Mr. Selden, he was one of the two chief governours of the county. He was made by election of the freeholders in their county court, as the sheriff was, and from among the men of the chiefest rank in the county.[v]

By the constitution[w] of this commonwealth, sheriffs and coroners are chosen and appointed in the same manner. We see here another revival of the Saxon and German institutions.

To the office of sheriff, that of coroner is, in many instances, a necessary substitute: for if the sheriff is interested in a suit, or if he is of affinity with one of the parties to a suit, the coroner must execute and return the process of the courts of justice.[x]

But the most important duty and business of a coroner is of another nature. When any person is killed, or dies suddenly, or dies in prison, the coroner must hold an inquest concerning the manner of his death. This inquest must be held upon the view of the body; for if the body cannot be found, the coroner cannot sit. He must certify his inquisition to the court of king's bench or to the next assizes.[y]

The lord chief justice of the king's bench is the supreme coroner of all England, and may exercise that jurisdiction in any part of the kingdom.[z]

From the statute of Wales, made in the twelfth year of Edward the first, and which, by the remedies provided for Wales, informs us, at the same

v. Bac. on Gov. 41.
w. Art. 6. s. 1.
x. 4. Ins. 271.
y. 1. Bl. Com. 349.
z. 4. Rep. 57 b.

time, what was the law and practice of England—from this statute we learn, that the coroner was directed to attend and summon a jury, when a man was wounded so dangerously, that his life was despaired. This branch of a coroner's duty is now totally neglected. "It is a regulation, however," says the learned observer upon the ancient statutes, "which deserves much to be revived: and I should conceive that this attendance of the coroner with a jury, when a dangerous wound had been received, was to prevent the dying words of the person murdered from being evidence; as this kind of proof, though allowed at present, cannot be too cautiously admitted. It is presumed, indeed, that the words of a person expiring cannot but be true considering the situation, under which he gives the information. But may not a dying man, though a good christian, deprived of expected happiness in life by a wound, received, perhaps, from an enemy, rather wish his punishment more eagerly than he should do? And may not those about the dying person, who are generally relations, repeat what he said more strongly on the trial, than possibly the words were delivered?"[a]

a. Bar. on St. 124.

CHAPTER VIII.
The Subject Continued.
Of Counsellors and Attornies.

In our courts of justice there are counsellors and attornies. In England, there are two degrees of counsellors—serjeants and barristers. How ancient and honourable the state and degree of a serjeant is, has been the ample theme of many learned and elaborate treatises.

My Lord Coke, in a speech which he made upon a call of serjeants, compares the serjeants' coif—a cap of a particular form—to Minerva's helmet; for Minerva was the goddess of counsel. He also discovers, that the four corners of that cap indicate four excellent qualities—science, experience, observation, recordation.[a]

Pace tanti viri,[1] shall the truth be disclosed? If the origin of coifs is investigated, we shall, perhaps, find that Mercury, and not Minerva, is entitled to the merit of the invention. At one period, the clergy were almost the only lawyers known in England; but, in a fit of resentment, they were banished from the bar. Its sweets—for its profits were sweet—could not be easily relinquished. The clerk still pleaded, but disguised in the serjeant's robe, and, by contriving the coif, concealed his clerical tonsure.

But, like many other things, its first origin was lost in its subsequent splendour. The institution became honourable and venerable; and, as such, is still considered and preserved in England. "A serjeant at law," says my Lord Chancellor Fortescue,[b] "shall not take off his coif, though he be in the royal presence, and talking with his majesty. No one can be made a judge of the courts of king's bench or common pleas, until he is called to

a. Bar. on St. 453.
1. With all due respect to so great a man [Lord Coke].
b. De Laud. c. 50.

the state and dignity of a serjeant." To America, however, it has not been transplanted. We leave it to continue and flourish in its native soil.

In the first ages of Athens, the parties pleaded for themselves; but, in later times, they were allowed to have the benefit of counsel.[c] That the length of their speeches might not exhaust the patience of the judges, or prevent other business equally necessary, it was usual—perhaps the spirit of the custom might be revived with no disadvantage—to measure their allotted portion of time by an hour glass, in which they used water instead of sand. So scrupulously exact were they in this particular, that an officer, whose name denoted his office—Εφυδωρ—was appointed to distribute the water equally to each side. While strict justice was required from the advocates, strict justice was done them: the glass was stopped while the proper officer recited the laws which they quoted. Nay, the water remaining at the conclusion of an argument might be transferred to the use of another speaker. Hence this expression—Let such a one speak till my water be run out.[d]

This custom was practised by the Romans. The time allowed, by the law, for the speeches of the advocates is termed, by Cicero, "legitimae horae."[2] The patient and indulgent Antoninus, who was a philosopher as well as an emperour, ordered, as we are told by his historian, plenty of water for the speakers at the bar; in other words, he allowed them full time for their speeches. "Quoties judico," says the younger Pliny, "quantum quis plurimum postulat aquae do"—when I sit in judgment, I give to every advocate as much water as he desires.[e]

This instance of resemblance between the Athenian and Roman bars is not mentioned on account of its intrinsick importance, but because it proves, more strongly than an important instance could prove, the principle of imitation. The coincident practice could be dictated by no common principle of nature or of society.

Counsellors, or barristers at law, have been long known in England. Formerly they were styled "apprenticii ad legem," apprentices to the law;

c. 1. Pot. Ant. 106.
d. Pet. on Jur. 59. 63. 1. Pot. Ant. 118.
2. Lawful time.
e. Pli. Ep. 1. 6. ep. 2. Pet. on Jur. 134.

because they were considered only as learners, and were not permitted to exercise the full office of an advocate, till they were qualified by the knowledge and experience acquired during the long probationship of sixteen years.[f] Edward the first, it is said, introduced the practice of permitting them to plead in the court of king's bench, before they attained the rank and dignity of serjeants.[g]

Attorney, says my Lord Coke, is an ancient English word, and signifies one who is set in the turn, stead, or place of another. Of these, some are private; and some are publick, as attornies at law.[h] The business of an attorney at law is to manage the practical part of a suit, and to follow the advice of the serjeants or barristers, who are of counsel in it.[i]

At the common law, no person could appear by an attorney, without the king's writ or letters patent.[j] In one part of his works, my Lord Coke admires the policy of this regulation. Its genius was to prevent the increase and multiplication of suits. But when statutes permitted the parties to appear by attorney, it is not credible, says he, how suits at law increased and multiplied. Such ill success has ever had the breach of the maxims and the ancient rules of the common law.[k] In another part of his works, he expresses sentiments more favourable to the appointment of attornies. The act commanding the judges to admit them, he styles "an act of grace," because the king gave his royal assent to a law for the quiet and safety of his subjects, giving them power to make attornies, whereby he lost such profit of the great seal, as he formerly received in such cases.[l]

To correct the abuses, which arose from the admission of attornies, whose heads and whose hearts were equally unqualified for the trust, it was enacted, so early as the reign of Henry the fourth,[m] that all the attornies shall be examined by the judges; and such as are good and virtuous and of good fame shall, by the discretion of the court, be received and

f. Fort. de Laud. c. 50.
g. 1. Reev. 491.
h. 1. Ins. 51. b.
i. 2. Ins. 564. Wood. Ins. 466.
j. Wood. Ins. 466.
k. 2. Ins. 249.
l. 2. Ins. 378.
m. St. 4. H. 4. c. 18.

sworn well and faithfully to serve in their offices; and their names shall be entered on the roll.

A barrister is not sworn.[n]

According to the law of the United States, parties may plead and manage their own causes personally, or by the assistance of such counsel or attornies at law, as, by the rules of the several courts, shall be permitted to manage and conduct causes.[o]

By a rule of the supreme court, it is ordered, that it shall be requisite to the admission of attornies and counsellors to practise in that court, that they shall have been such for three years in the supreme court of the state to which they respectively belong, and that their private and professional character shall appear to be fair. In the circuit court for the Pennsylvania district, the same rule is made with the only difference of "two" instead of "three" years.[p]

By a law of Pennsylvania[q] it is provided, that a competent number of persons, learned in the law, and of an honest disposition, may be admitted by the justices of the several courts to practise as attornies in them. No attorney shall be admitted, without taking an oath or affirmation—that he will behave himself in the office of attorney within the court, according to the best of his learning and ability, and with all good fidelity, as well to the court as to the client; that he will use no falsehood, nor delay any person's cause for lucre or malice.[r]

Attornies at law, on one hand, enjoy privileges on account of their attendance in courts: on the other, they are peculiarly subject to the censure and animadversion of the judges.[s]

n. 2. Ins. 214.

o. Laws U. S. 1. cong. 1. sess. c. 20. s. 35.

p. At April sessions, 1804, the abovementioned rule of the circuit court was rescinded, and the following established. "Ordered, that no person shall be admitted to practise as counsel or attorney of this court, unless he shall have previously studied three years, been admitted two years in a court of common pleas, and in the supreme court of a state: or unless he shall have studied four years, been admitted one year in a court of common pleas, and in the supreme court of a state: or unless he shall have studied five years, and been admitted in the supreme court of a state. Satisfaction also of moral character will be required." *Ed.*

q. 1. Laws. Penn. 185. s. 28.

r. Id. 360. s. 38.

s. 3. Bl. Com. 26.

In all the courts of Pennsylvania, and in all those of the United States, except the supreme court, the same person may act both as counsel and as attorney. In the supreme court, the different offices must be exercised by different persons.

The law has not, in every age, nor in every country, been formed into a separate profession. Doubts have been entertained, whether, in any country, or in any age, it should be so formed. Every man, it has been often said, ought to be his own lawyer.

In a system of lectures, addressed peculiarly, though by no means exclusively, to those who are designed for the profession of the law, this question deserves our particular notice. It deserves our notice more especially as we are told, in a very late and a very sensible performance concerning the revolution in France, that those, who have been most active in this mighty event, mean to destroy the separate profession of the law. An event, so auspicious to man, will diffuse a winning appearance over every thing, with which it seems to be, in the slightest manner, connected. But it is our business to examine the foundations, and not merely the external appearances of things.

It may be asked—when you have taken so much pains, in the introduction to these lectures, and in many parts of them, to persuade us, that the knowledge of the law should, especially among a free people, be disseminated universally; will you now turn suddenly in an opposite direction, and endeavour to persuade us, that a distinct and separate profession should be formed of the law? The result, perhaps, of investigating this subject will be, that unless the law is made the peculiar study and profession of some, it will never become the object of knowledge to all.

We have heard the complaint of my Lord Coke, that the admission of attornies at law into the courts of justice is an innovation upon the practice and the policy of the common law. It must be confessed that this is the case. At the common law, both the plaintiff and the defendant appeared in their proper persons. "The plaintiff offers himself," and "the defendant comes" are the immemorial and authentick forms of entry—"Querens obtulit se"—"Defendens venit." These, on both sides, denote a personal appearance.

In the early and simple periods of society, the personal appearance of the parties was all that was necessary. Such were the periods of which we speak. Among the ancient Saxons, few and plain were the forms and circumstances, under which property was litigated and decided in their courts of justice; uniform and short were the proceedings in those courts. Among the ancient Saxons, therefore, professional characters were not necessary for the management or the determination of suits. The king, or the earl, as the case might be, was qualified to judge; and the parties to plead.

An adherence to principle often dictates a variation in practice. In the progress of society, the business of society became more complex and intricate; and the controversies arising from it became more frequent and embarrassed. This new order of things introduced a new order of professions. To the king were substituted the judges: to the earls, the sheriffs; and to the parties, attornies or counsel learned in the law. "After the Anglo-Saxon laws were committed to writing," says Dr. Henry in his history of Britain, "it became necessary that some persons should read and study them with particular attention, in order to understand their true intent and meaning. This gave rise to lawyers by profession, who, in the language of England in those times, were called *roedboran,* or *lahmen,* and, in latin, *rhetores,* or *causidici.* Some of these law men, after having undergone an examination as to their knowledge of the law, were appointed assessors to the aldermen and hundredaries: others of them acted as advocates and pleaders at the bar."[t]

But it will be replied—and still on the authority of my Lord Coke—that the introduction of lawyers multiplies suits at law. The unnecessary "multiplication of lawyers," rather say: for that is the amount of my Lord Coke's complaint: and, even in the ground of his complaint, he appears not altogether steady or consistent. But elsewhere, my Lord Coke traces the multiplication of law suits to causes very different from the establishment of the law as a profession. Their two general causes, says he, are peace and plenty. Peace is the mother of plenty; and plenty the nurse of suits.[u] Instead of wishing the removal of those general causes, he prays for their continuance.

t. 2. Hen. 245.
u. 4. Ins. 76.

In a country governed by the common law, the separate profession of lawyers ought to be established for a peculiar reason. The common law is the law of experience. Far is it, indeed, from being without its general principles; but these general principles are formed strictly upon the plan of the *regulae philosophandi*,[3] which, in another science, Sir Isaac Newton prescribed and observed with such glorious success—they are formed from the coincidence, or the analogy, or the opposition of numberless experiments, the accurate history of which is contained in records and reports of judicial determinations. To peruse those reports—to consult those records, requires much time and industry. To methodise them under the proper heads, requires much attention and patient sagacity. From a variety of particular cases to draw conclusions, neither too wide nor too narrow, requires a judgment habitually exercised, as well as naturally strong. These are the requisites, by which the common lawyer must be formed. From these requisites we may easily infer the propriety of establishing the law as a separate profession. To acquire these requisites is a sufficient employment.

In the common law, principles are collected slowly and with difficulty; but, when once collected, they may be communicated soon and easily. The principles may be known, and may be reduced to practice too, by men who never heard or witnessed one of the legal experiments, from the lengthened series of which those principles are drawn.

In this manner I reconcile my positions—that the knowledge of the law should be disseminated universally—and—that the law should be formed into a separate profession. In this manner, too, I prove—that unless the law is made the peculiar study and profession of some, it will never become the object of knowledge to all.

Should the profession of the law be merely honorary? Or should it be a source of profit as well as of fame? These questions have undergone ample discussion; and have, at different times, received contrary authoritative resolutions. In a government truly republican, the subject will not admit of dispute.

By the Cincian law,[4] every gratification whatever was interdicted to

3. Rules of philosophy. *Regulae Philosophandi* is a section in Newton's *Philosophiae Naturalis Principia Mathematica* (1687).

4. Cincian law was the lex Cincia, a law that, depending upon the era, forbade the giving of gifts to lawyers.

the Roman advocates. What was the consequence? Between citizen and citizen an inequality inconsistent with the government of a free country. Those who had and those who might have causes depending, and were unqualified for pleading them—this is the description of the many—were kept in a state of vassalage to those, by whom they might be pleaded without a fee—this is the description of the few. Hence the well known relation of client and patron: hence the tyranny and servility, to which that well known relation gave rise. Besides, this regulation was as liable to be eluded as it was certain to be abused. Presents, said to be voluntary, might easily supply the place of stipulated fees. We are told of a lawyer, who practised this art with great address and advantage. A piece of plate, which a client had thrown at his feet, was placed conspicuous in his office,[v] with this inscription—"lucri neglecti lucrum."[5]

What can be more honourable than that gain, which is acquired by virtue and talents? In a state of republican equality, what can be more reasonable, than that one citizen should receive a compensation for the services, which he performs to another? still more so, for those which he performs to the state?

It may be expected, that I should here say something concerning the studies which a lawyer should pursue, the accomplishments which he should acquire, and the character which he should support. Something concerning each of these topicks I mean to say, but with a diffidence proportioned to the delicacy of the subject.

I think I may venture the position—that in no science can richer materials be found, and that, in no science, have rich materials been more neglected or abused, than in the science of law—particularly of the common law. Listen to the sentiments of my Lord Bacon, in his book on the advancement of learning. It is well known, that the vast object of this exalted and most comprehensive genius was, to erect a new and lasting fabrick of philosophy, founded, not on hypothesis or conjecture, but on experience and truth. To the accomplishment of this design, it was necessary that he should previously review, in all its provinces and divisions, the state of learning as it then stood. To do this effectually required knowledge

v. Bar. on St. 415.
5. The profit from ignoring profit.

and discernment, exquisite and universal: such were happily employed in the arduous task. Whatever, in science, is erroneous or defective, he has pointed out. He has done more; he has suggested the proper means of correcting errours and supplying defects. Of the science of law, he thus speaks—Those, who have written concerning laws, have treated the subject like speculative philosophers, or like mere practising lawyers. The philosophers propose many things, which, in appearance, are beautiful, but, in fact, are without utility. They make imaginary laws for imaginary commonwealths; and their discourses are as the stars, which give little light, because they are so high. The lawyers, on the other hand, attached implicitly to the institutions of their country, or to the tenets of their sect, exert not their judgment unbiassed, but harangue as if they were in chains.

But certainly, continues he, the knowledge of this subject properly belongs *ad viros civiles.* Those *viri civiles*—"practical statesmen" is, perhaps, the nearest translation, of which our language will admit—he describes in the following manner. They know what appertains to human society, what, to the publick welfare, what, to natural equity, what, to the manners of nations, what, to the different forms of commonwealths. These are qualified to judge concerning laws, by the principles and rules of genuine policy and natural justice. For there are certain fountains of justice, from which all civil laws should flow like streams. To those fountains of justice and publick utility let us have recourse.[w] He then goes on, according to his plan, to give a specimen of a treatise concerning universal justice, or the fountains of law.

I have said that the law, particularly the common law abounds in rich materials. For the truth of this observation, can I appeal to stronger evidence than to a series—continued, almost without interruption, for five hundred years—of cases which actually happened, and were judicially determined? Many of these cases are related in the most accurate and masterly manner; witness the reports of my Lord Coke, of Mr. Peere Williams,[6] and of Sir James Burrow:[7] others, too, deserve to be mentioned. These are

w. 1. Ld. Bac. 248. 2. Ld. Bac. 537.

6. Peere Williams (1664–1736) reported chancery cases from 1695 to 1736.

7. Sir James Burrow (1701–1780) was a student of natural philosophy and a legal reporter.

the precious materials of the common law. These are authentick experiments, on which a sound system of legal philosophy must be formed. On these experiments, the most indefatigable industry has been frequently employed. But has it been employed in a proper manner? Upon cases, cases have been accumulated: to collections, collections have been superadded: but they have been directed, generally, by no order more eligible than that of the alphabet. To one who is already a lawyer, abridgments may, on particular occasions, be of use: but surely they are not calculated to inspire or to guide the liberal and enlightened study of the law.

The Institutes of my Lord Coke are a cabinet richly stored with the jewels of the law: but are not those jewels strewed about in endless and bewildering confusion?

In expression, as well as in arrangement, the compositions of the law have been glaringly imperfect; and have had an injurious tendency to deter those, whose attachment they should have been fitted to attract. Hear the natural and pathetick description which the celebrated Sir Henry Spelman gives of his situation and feelings, when he commenced his study of the common law: "My mother sent me to London to learn the law: when I entered on its threshold, and encountered a foreign language, a barbarous dialect, an inelegant arrangement, and a collection of matter, not only immense, but disposed in such a manner as to be a perpetual load upon the memory; my spirits, I own it, failed within me."[x]

Since his time, indeed, very considerable assistance has been furnished to young gentlemen, engaged in the acquirement of legal knowledge. Of this assistance, the short but very excellent analysis digested by my Lord Chief Justice Hale forms a most valuable part; whether we consider it in itself, or as the foundation of what has been erected upon it. The distribution of this scientifical performance has, as we are informed by Sir William Blackstone, been principally followed in his celebrated Commentaries on the laws of England. It is but justice to add, that, in those Commentaries, the method of Hale's analysis is improved as well as regarded. I have formerly observed, that, in point of expression, the Commentaries are elegant and pure.

x. 1. Bl. Com. 31. n.

But something more is wanting still. Excellent materials, a correct arrangement of those materials, and a proper expression of the arranged form are all necessary; but they are not all that is necessary to a sound system of the law. For a system founded on principles truly political and philosophical, we still look around us in vain. On such principles alone, can a system solid and permanent be erected. To confirm my sentiments, let me again resort to the high authority, before whose splendour the whole host of sciolists hide their diminished heads. "The reasons of municipal laws," says my Lord Bacon, "severed from the grounds of nature, manners, and policy, are like wall flowers, which, though they grow high upon the crest of states, yet they have no deep root."[y]

Let me again repeat it—that we have no such system of the common law as I have described, is by no means owing to the want of the materials proper for the erection of so noble a fabrick. "I do not a little admire the wisdom of the laws of England," says my Lord Bacon in another place,[z] "and the consent, which they have with the wisdom of philosophy and nature itself."

By this time, you are at no loss to discover my sentiments concerning the studies which a lawyer ought to pursue, and the accomplishments which he ought to acquire. He ought to know men and societies of men, in every state and in every relation in which they can be placed: in every state and in every relation in which men or societies of men can be placed, he ought to know what appertains to justice—to comprehensive morality. From the fountains of justice, we have seen, the civil laws should spring. To that fountain, ever full and ever flowing, let the student of the law intrepidly ascend: he will then, with ease, with pleasure, and with certainty, follow the meandering courses of its numerous streams.

It is an opinion, far from being uncommon, that the only institution necessary for a practising lawyer is, to observe the practice in a lawyer's office. No opinion was ever more unfounded: no opinion, perhaps, ever entailed more mischief upon those, who have been its unfortunate victims. I certainly shall not be misunderstood as if I meant to speak with contempt of the practice, which is to be observed in a lawyer's office. Nothing

y. 4. Ld. Bac. 101.
z. Id. 103.

can be more remote from my intention and from my sentiments. To the most accomplished lawyer, even the *minutiae* of practice are objects of regard; and, in his hands, they can be employed to useful, nay, to splendid purposes. In nature, the greatest bodies, the greatest systems of bodies, are composed of the smallest particles; and the microscope, as well as the telescope, discloses a world of wonders to our view. So in the sciences—so, particularly, in the science of law. But to be confined to microscopick observations is the doom of an insect, not the birthright of a man.

I have said that the opinion just mentioned entails much mischief upon its unfortunate victims. I have said the truth. Law, studied and practised as a science founded in principle, is among the most delightful of occupations: followed as a trade depending merely upon precedent, it becomes and continues a drudgery, severe and insupportable. One, who follows it in this manner, lives in a state of continual distrust and alarm. To such a one, every thing new is something odious: for he has been taught to approve of things, not because they are proper or right, but because he has seen them before. To such a one, the least deviation from even the most unessential form, appears equally fatal with the greatest departure from the most important principles: for they agree in the only circumstance, by which he can distinguish either: they are not within the sphere of his practice. Tied to the centre of precedent, he treads, for life, the same dull, and small, and uniform circle around it, without daring to view or to enjoy a single object on either side.

How very different is the situation of him, who ranges, not without rule, but without restraint, in the rich, the variegated, and the spacious fields of science! To his observation and research every thing is open: he is accustomed to examine and to compare the appearances and the realities of things; to contemplate their beauty, to investigate their utility, and to admire the wonderful harmony, with which beauty and utility coincide. To him an object is not dangerous because it is new: he measures it by the correct standard of his principles: he discovers what purposes it is fitted to answer, and what other purposes it is fitted to destroy: he learns when to use it, and when to lay the use of it aside. The discovery of one improvement leads him to the discovery of another: the discovery of that other leads him, in delightful progression, to another still.

I am now to make some remarks concerning the character which a lawyer ought to support.

Laws and law suits seem, in the apprehension of some, to be synonimous or nearly synonimous terms. In the opinion of such, the business and the character of a lawyer will be, to produce and to manage controversies at law. Part of the opinion may be admitted to be just. To manage controversies at law, when they have been produced by another cause, is part of the business of a lawyer: to produce them is no part of it. Even to manage law suits, though a part, is not the principal part, of a lawyer's business: the principal part of his business is to prevent them. The professional pride of a lawyer is, that no controversy arises from any opinion which he gives, nor from the construction of any instrument which he draws. Like a skilful pilot, he has studied correctly the chart of the law: he has marked the places which are dangerous, as well as those which are safe. Like a pilot, honest and benevolent as well as skilful, he cautiously avoids every danger, and through the channels of security steers the fortunes of those, who intrust them to his care.

One reason, why the association between lawyers and law suits is so strong in the minds of some people, may be this, that they never think of the former, till they are plunged in the latter, or in the necessary causes of the latter. But even in this situation, the association is not a correct one; for when they are in this situation, the tardy recourse to a lawyer is to help them out of it.

To give honest and sound advice in questions of law, to those who ask it in matters relating to their business or conduct, forms the character, which a lawyer ought to support. I speak now of his private character: his publick character and conduct come under a different consideration.

A general prejudice against the professional character of the bar has arisen, I believe, from observing, that the gentlemen of the profession appear equally ready to undertake either side of the same cause. Both sides, it is said, and said with truth, cannot be right: and to undertake either with equal alacrity evinces, it is thought, an insensibility—presumed professional—to the natural and important distinction between right and wrong.

This subject deserves to be placed in its true light. That this insensibility is sometimes found at the bar cannot be denied. That it is often imputed when it is not found, ought also to be admitted. A few observation will easily disclose the origin of this prejudice: and its origin ought to be disclosed; for I deem it of publick importance, especially in a free country, that the professional character of the bar should stand in a respectable point of view.

Let it be observed, that by far the greatest number of law suits originate from disputed facts. Of these a lawyer cannot judge, but from the representation of them, which he receives from his client. A dishonest client will impose upon his counsel: an honest client, from the blindness and partiality of self interest, is often imposed upon himself: the imposition, in this case, operates upon the counsel equally as in the other. In both cases, the lawyer, instead of deserving censure, deserves sympathy; for it is always disagreeable to be engaged in a bad and unsuccessful cause.

Again; even when law suits originate from disputed points of law, they frequently spring from positive institutions, particularly from intricate and artificial regulations concerning property. To such questions, the natural distinction between right and wrong is susceptible of no other application, than that they be decided according to the law of the land.

But further; in such cases, the rule of positive law may be really doubtful; and this doubt may be the true cause of the controversy. How often do we see juries and judges divided, nay equally divided, in opinion? If this is so, a difference of sentiment in two gentlemen of the bar should not be viewed as either pretended or reprehensible. The court frequently direct arguments of counsel on each side: can it be improper for the counsel to obey those directions?

These remarks explain and justify the conduct of counsel in the cases which I have described, and are fitted to remove the prejudice, which, in such cases, is entertained against them. If a lawyer is so lost to a sense of his duty and character, as to advocate a cause which he knows to be morally and certainly unjust, his conduct requires not to be explained; and I mean not to justify it.

To the court, as well as to his client, a duty is owing by a gentleman of the bar: these obligations are, by no means, incompatible: both will be discharged by uniform candour, and by a decent firmness properly blended with a dignified respect.

Thus much concerning counsel and attornies at law. I have been full and particular upon this head, because it personally and immediately concerns the future conduct and prospects of many of my hearers.

CHAPTER IX.
The Subject Continued. Of Constables.

I am now to consider the office of a constable. This officer, and the office which he holds, are often treated with a degree of disrespect; but very improperly and very unwisely. In a government founded on the authority of the people, every publick officer is respectable; for every publick officer is a free citizen: he is more; by other free citizens he is invested with a portion of their power.

Besides; the powers and duties of constables, if properly and effectually exercised and discharged, are of real importance to the community; and their publick utility should rescue them from contempt. The antiquity as well as the usefulness of the office is very great. Of its original it may be said, as we are informed by my Lord Bacon,[a] *caput inter nubila condit;*[1] for its authority was granted upon the ancient laws and customs of the kingdom, practised long before the conquest. It was intended and instituted for the conservation of the peace, and for repressing every kind of annoyance and disturbance of the people. This was done by way of prevention and not of punishment; for a constable has no judicial power to hear or determine any cause.

Upon a probability of a breach of the peace, as when warm words have passed, the constable may command the parties to keep the peace, and depart and forbear. When an affray is made, he may part those engaged in it, and keep them asunder. He may arrest and commit the breakers of the peace; and, if they will not obey, he may call power to his assistance.[b] If an affray is in a house, he may break the doors open to restore and preserve the

a 4. Ld. Bac. 94.
1. Its head is hidden in the clouds.
b 4. Ld. Bac. 96.

peace. If an offender fly into another district or county, the constable may make fresh pursuit and take him. To prevent as well as to quell a breach of the peace, he may command all persons to assist him; and those, who refuse, may be bound over to the sessions and fined.[c]

It is the duty of a constable to execute, with speed and secrecy, all warrants directed to him; and not to dispute the authority of him who issues them; provided the matter in question is within his jurisdiction.[d]

The power and duty of constables are extended to a great variety of instances by a number of acts of assembly, which have been passed in Pennsylvania.

In cases of necessity, a constable has power to appoint a deputy.[e]

There are two kinds of constables; a high constable and a petty constable. Their authority is the same in substance, and differs only in point of extent.[f]

To appoint men of low condition to the office of constable, is, according to my Lord Bacon,[g] a mere abuse and degeneracy from the first institution. They ought, says he, to be chosen from among the better sort of residents.

I have now finished my account of the judicial departments of the United States and Pennsylvania; and, with it, the description of their governments and constitutions. To the government and constitution of every other state in the Union, my remarks and illustrations will, generally, be found applicable. In those instances, in which a strict application cannot be made, still, I flatter myself, my remarks and illustrations will throw some light upon the respective advantages or disadvantages of institutions, which cannot be measured by the same common standard.

c. Wood. Ins. 87.
d. Id. ibid.
e. 4. Ld. Bac. 98.
f. 4. Ld. Bac. 98.
g. Id. 96.

CHAPTER X.
Of Corporations.

In a former part of my lectures,[a] after having described a state, I observed, that, in a state, smaller societies may be formed by a part of its members: that these smaller societies, like states, are deemed to be moral persons, but not in a state of natural liberty; because their actions are cognizable by the superiour power of the state, and are regulated by its laws. I mentioned, that, to these societies, the name of corporations is generally appropriated, though somewhat improperly; for that the term is strictly applicable to supreme as well as to inferiour bodies politick. In obedience, however, to the arbitress of language, I shall designate those smaller societies by the name of corporations; and to the consideration of them I now proceed.

A corporation is described to be a person in a political capacity created by the law, to endure in perpetual succession.[b] Of these artificial persons a great variety is known to the law. They have been formed to promote and to perpetuate the interests of commerce, of learning, and of religion. It must be admitted, however, that, in too many instances, those bodies politick have, in their progress, counteracted the design of their original formation. Monopoly, superstition, and ignorance have been the unnatural offspring of literary, religious, and commercial corporations. This is not mentioned with a view to insinuate, that such establishments ought to be prevented or destroyed: I mean only to intimate, that they should be erected with caution, and inspected with care.

In England, corporations may exist by the common law, by act of parliament, by prescription, and by charter from the king.[c] The king and the parliament are corporations by the force of the common law.[d]

a. Ante. vol. 1. p. 636.
b. Wood. Ins. 111.
c. 10. Rep. 29 b.
d. Wood. Ins. 112.

In the United States, and in Pennsylvania, corporations can only exist by the common law, or by virtue of legislative authority. This authority, however, may be exercised by a power delegated by the legislature; as has been done, in this commonwealth,[e] with regard to churches. Upon the same principle, the king, in England, may communicate to a subject the power of erecting corporations, and may permit him to name the persons of whom they shall be composed, and the authority which they shall enjoy. Still, however, it is the king, who really erects them; the subject is only his instrument; and the act of the instrument becomes the act of its mover, under the well known maxim, "qui facit per alium, facit per se."[f1]

To every corporation a name must be assigned; and by that name alone it can perform legal acts.[g]

When a corporation is duly established, there are many powers, rights, and capacities, which are annexed to it tacitly and of course.

It has perpetual succession, unless a period of limitation be expressed in the instrument of its establishment. This succession is, indeed, the great end of an incorporation; and, for this reason, there is, in all aggregate bodies politick, a power necessarily implied of filling vacancies by the election of new members.[h]

The power of removing any of its members for just cause, is a power incident to a corporation. To the order and good government of corporate bodies, it is adjudged necessary that there should be such a power.[i]

Another and a most important power, tacitly annexed to corporations by the very act of their establishment, is the power of making by-laws.[j] This, indeed, is the principal reason for erecting many of the bodies corporate. Their nature or their circumstances are peculiar; and provisions peculiarly adapted to them cannot be expected from the general law of the land. For this reason, they are invested with authority to make regulations for the management of their own interests and affairs. These regulations, however, must not be contrary to the overruling laws of the state; for it

e. 3. Laws. Penn. 40.
f. 10. Rep. 33b. 1. Bl. Com. 474.
1. Who acts through another acts for himself.
g. 10. Rep. 122.
h. 1. Bl. Com. 475.
i. 1. Burr. 539.
j. Ld. Ray. 498. Hob. 211. 1. Bl. Com. 475.

will be remembered, that these smaller societies, though moral persons, are not in a state of natural liberty. Their private statutes are *leges sub graviore lege.*[2] "Sodales, legem quam volent, dum nequid ex publica lege corrumpant, sibi ferunto,"[3] is a rule as old as the twelve tables of Rome.[k4]

The general duties of every corporation may be collected from the nature and design of its institution: it should act agreeably to its nature, and fulfil the purposes for which it was formed.

But corporations are composed of individuals; those individuals are not exempted from the failings and frailties of humanity; those failings and frailties may lead to a deviation from the end of their establishment. For this reason, as has already been observed, they ought to be inspected with care. The law has provided proper persons with proper powers to visit those institutions, and to correct every irregularity, which may arise within them. In England, it has, by immemorial usage, appointed them to be visited and inspected, in the court of king's bench, according to the rules of the common law.[l] We have formerly seen,[m] that the powers of the court of king's bench are vested in the supreme court of Pennsylvania.

A corporation may surrender its legal existence into the hands of that power, from which it was received. From such a surrender, the dissolution of the body corporate ensues. An aggregate corporation is dissolved by the natural death of all its members.[n] By a judgment of forfeiture against a corporation itself, it may be dissolved; but not by a judgment of ouster against individuals. God forbid—such is the sentiment of Mr. Justice Wilmot[o5]—that the rights of the body should be lost or destroyed by the offences of the members.

Suffice it to have said thus much concerning corporations, or subordinate societies established within the society at large.

2. Laws under a weightier law.

3. The private laws of a corporation cannot conflict with the laws of the state.

k. 1. Bl. Com. 476.

4. The twelve tables of Rome formed the centerpiece of the Roman constitution. They were completed in 449 B.C.

l. Id. 481.

m. Ante. p. 902.

n. 3. Burr. 1867.

o. Id. 1871.

5. Sir John Eardley-Wilmot (1709–1792) was appointed chief justice of Common Pleas in 1755.

CHAPTER XI.
Of Citizens and Aliens.

Let us proceed to investigate still farther the component parts of which civil government and all its subordinate establishments consist. They consist of citizens.

I have already observed[a] that the social contract is a contract of a peculiar kind; that when correctly analyzed, it is found to be an assemblage of agreements equal, in number, to the number of individuals who form the society; and that, to each of those agreements, a single individual is one party, and all the other individuals of the society are the other party.

The latter party I have considered heretofore; and have called it the people. The former party I am now to consider; and, in order to avoid confusion, I call it, in this discussion, the citizen; and when I shall have occasion to refer to more subordinate agreements than one, I shall call the individuals, parties to them, by the name of citizens.

I know that the term *citizen* is often applied to one of the more numerous party—to one of the people: and I shall be obliged to take the description of a citizen from the character which he supports as one of the people. But you will easily perceive, that the same person may, at different times, act or be viewed in different characters; and though his description be taken from one of them, the account of his duties and of his rights too may, on a particular occasion, be referred to the other. This I have chosen to do, rather than to introduce an unknown phrase, or to use a known phrase in a new signification. Besides, the expression is frequently employed also in the sense in which I now use it. "Generally speaking," says the great political authority,[b] Aristotle, "a citizen is one partaking equally of power and of subordination."

a. Ante. p. 641.
b. 1. Rus. Anc. Eur. 362.

A citizen then—to draw his description as *one* of the *people*—I deem him, who acts a personal or a represented part in the legislation of his country. He has other rights; but his legislative I consider as his characteristick right. In this view, a citizen of the United States is he, who is a citizen of at least some one state in the Union: for the members of the house of representatives in the national legislature are chosen, in each state, by electors, who, in that state, have the qualifications requisite for electors of the most numerous branch of the state legislature.[c] In this view, a citizen of Pennsylvania is he, who has resided in the state two years; and, within that time, has paid a state or county tax: or he is between the ages of twenty one and twenty two years, and the son of a citizen.[d]

I have, on another occasion,[e] traced the description of a citizen in every other state of the Union: to your recollection of that investigation, and to the constitutions of the several states, I now refer you.

When a man acts as one of the numerous party to the agreements, of which I have taken notice; it is his right, according to the tenour of his agreements, to govern; he is one of the *people*. When he acts as the single party to that agreement, which he has made with all the other members of the society; it is his duty, according to the tenour of his agreement, to obey; he is a *single citizen*. Of this agreement, indeed, it is impossible to ascertain all the articles. From the most obvious deduction of reason, however, one article may be specified, beyond all possibility of doubt. This article, of prime importance, is—that to the publick will of the society, the private will of every associated member must, in matters respecting the social union, be subordinate and submissive. The publick will of the society is declared by the laws. Obedience, therefore—civil obedience—obedience to the laws and to the administration of the laws—this is a distinguishing feature in the countenance of a citizen, when he is seen from this point of view.

That men ought to be governed, seems to have been agreed on all hands: the reason is, that, without government, they could never attain any high or permanent share of perfection or happiness. But the question has been—by whom should they be governed? And this has been made a

c. Cons. U. S. art. 1. s. 2.
d. Cons. Penn. art. 3. s. 1.
e. Ante. p. 517–520.

question, by reason of two others—by whom *can* they be governed?—are they capable of governing themselves?

To this last question, Mr. Burke,[1] in the spirit of his late creed,[f] has answered in the negative. "Society," says he, "requires not only that the passions of individuals should be subjected, but that even in the mass and body as well as in the individuals, the inclinations of men should frequently be thwarted, their will controlled, and their passions brought into subjection. This can only be done *by a power out of themselves.*" This negative answer has been, from time immemorial, the strong hold of tyranny: and if this negative answer be the true one, the strong hold of tyranny is, in fact, impregnable to all the artillery of freedom. If men should be governed; and if they cannot govern themselves; what is the consequence? They must be governed by other masters.

An opinion, however, has, by some, been entertained, that the question, which I last mentioned, may receive an answer in the affirmative. Men, it has been thought, are capable of governing themselves. In the United States, this opinion, which heretofore rested chiefly on theory, has lately been put in a train of fair practical experiment. That this experiment, to human happiness so interesting, may be crowned with abundant and glorious success, is, of all things in this world, the "consummation most devoutly to be wished."

But to its glorious and abundant success, the obedience of the citizens is of a necessity, absolute and supreme. The question, which has been proposed—the question, in the negative answer to which, tyranny has triumphed so long and so generally—the question, concerning which philosophers and patriots have indulged, and been pleased with indulging, a contrary sentiment—the question, which, in the United States, is now put upon an experiment—this all-important question is—not merely nor chiefly—are men capable of governing? Of this, even tyrants will admit the affirmative; and will point to themselves as living proofs of its truth. But the question is—are men capable of governing *themselves?* In other words; are they qualified—and are they disposed to be their *own* masters? For a moral as well as an intellectual capability is involved in the ques-

1. Edmund Burke (1729–1797) was an Anglo-Irish statesman and author. He is most famous for his book *Reflections on the Revolution in France* (1790).

f. Refl. on Fr. Rev. 47.

tion. In still other words; are they qualified—and are they disposed to *obey themselves?* For to government, the correlative inseparable is obedience. To think, to speak, or to act, as if the former may be exercised, and, at the same time, the latter may not be performed, is to think, to speak, or to act, in a manner the most contradictory and absurd.

By a long and minute deduction, I proved, in a former lecture,[g] that, on the true principles of freedom, a man is the only human power, by whom he himself can be *bound.* It requires but a very small variation of phrase, and none of sentiment, to say, that on the true principles of freedom, man is the only human power, by whom he himself can be *governed.*

Are we made so waywardly, that what, in principle, is true and right, must, in practice, be false and wrong? Surely not.

Is the *safety* of man endangered by obedience? What can be a source of greater security, than to be governed only by a law, which has been made by himself, and by others, with whom he participates a general identity of interest, and a perfect equality of duties and of rights?

Is the *freedom* of man infringed by performing the service of obedience to such a law, made as has been mentioned? This service bears, we think, a resemblance as near as, being human, it can bear, to that service, which, with a propriety truly striking and strong, is denominated "perfect freedom."

Is the *dignity* of man degraded by observing a law? The Supreme of Being!—he himself worketh not without a rule!

In a *moral* view, self government increases, instead of impairing, the security, the liberty, and the dignity of the *man;* in a *political* view, self government increases, instead of impairing, the security, the liberty, and the dignity of the *citizen.*

Attend now to the result of the whole.—In a free and well constituted government, the first duty of its every member is—obedience to the laws. That they be true and faithful to themselves, is the allegiance, which a legitimate republick requires from her citizens: to themselves they cannot be true and faithful, unless they obey as well as make the laws—unless, in the terms in which a citizen has been defined, they partake of subordination as well as of power.

g. Ante. vol. 1. p. 572. et seq.

As a citizen of a republican government owes obedience to the laws; so he owes a decent, though a dignified respect to those who administer the laws. In monarchies, there is a political respect of person: in commonwealths, there should be a political respect to office. In monarchies, there are ranks, preeminences, and dignities, all personal and hereditary. In commonwealths, too, there are ranks, preeminences, and dignities; but all official and successive. In monarchies, respect is paid without a prospect of return. In commonwealths, one may, next year, succeed, as an officer, to the respect, which, this year, he pays as a citizen. The dignities of office are open to all.

You will be pleased to hear, that, with regard to this as well as to many other subjects, we have renewed, in our governments, the principles and the practice of the ancient Saxons. Between dignity and duty, no separation was made by them. In the early period of the Anglo-Saxon state, the allodial proprietors were numerous; their estates were generally small; and all were understood to be of the same rank and condition. Some, indeed, were distinguished above others by their character and their talents; but the superiority derived from this source was accompanied with no legal preeminence or power.[h]

So likewise it was in the heroick ages of Greece: no distinction was then known among men, except the distinction, truly honourable, which arose from a difference of abilities and merit.[i]

Titles of nobility in England, though now merely personal, were, in their origin, altogether official. The heretoch or duke was intrusted with a military department: the marquis was appointed to guard the frontiers or marches of the country: the alderman or earl was, as we formerly saw, the first civil officer of the shire. In the juridical history of England, the first arbitrary title of honour, without the shadow of office or duty annexed to it, makes its appearance so late as the reign of Henry the sixth.[2]

Under a republican government, it is prudent as well as proper—it is the interest as well as the duty of the citizens, to show a political respect for office. In the government they have an interest: in every office and depart-

h. Millar. 236.
i. 1. Gill. 49.
2. Henry VI (1421–1471) was king of England from 1422 to 1461.

ment of the government they have an interest: this interest requires, that every department and every office should be well filled: in a commonwealth; respect attached to office is frequently the principal inducement to its acceptance by those, who are qualified to fill it well.

On the citizen under a republican government, a third duty, more severe, it may be thought, than either of the former, is strictly incumbent. Whenever a competition unavoidably takes place between his interest and that of the publick, to the latter the former must be the devoted sacrifice. By the will and by the interest of the community, every private will and every private interest must be bound and overruled. Unless this maxim be established and observed; it is impossible that civil government could be formed or supported. Fortunate, however, it is, that in a government formed wisely and administered impartially, this unavoidable competition can seldom take place, at least in any very great degree.

If the sacrifice, which I have mentioned, is demanded and enforced by the publick, when the competition does not unavoidably take place; or if it is demanded and enforced farther or longer than the existing competition indispensably requires; it is tyranny; it is not government.

The citizen has rights as well as duties: the latter he is obliged to perform: the former he is entitled to enjoy or recover. To that original contract of association, to which, in our reasonings concerning government, an appeal must so often be made, he is a party; nay, in point of right, a party, voluntary, independent, equal. On one side, indeed, there stands a single individual: on the other side, perhaps, there stand millions: but right is weighed by principle; it is not estimated by numbers. From the necessity of the case, as was shown on a former occasion,[j] if a controversy arises between the parties to the social agreement, the numbers, or a selection from the numbers, must be the judges as well as one of the parties. But, because those of one party must, from the necessity of the peculiar case, be the judges likewise; does it follow, that they are absolved from that strict obligation, by which every judge is sacredly bound to administer impartial justice? Does it follow, that they may, with avidity, listen to all the interested suggestions, the advice of which a party would pursue? When the same person is and must be both judge and party; the character

j. Ante. p. 960.

of the judge ought not to be sunk in that of the party; but the character of the party should be exalted to that of the judge.

When questions—especially pecuniary questions—arise between a state and a citizen—more especially still, when those questions are, as they generally must be, submitted to the decision of those, who are not only parties and judges, but legislators also; the sacred impartiality of the second character, it must be owned, is too frequently lost in the sordid interestedness of the first, and in the arrogant power of the third. This, I repeat it, is tyranny: and tyranny, though it may be more formidable and more oppressive, is neither less odious nor less unjust—is neither less dishonourable to the character of one party, nor less hostile to the rights of the other, because it is proudly prefaced by the epithet—legislative. He, who refuses the payment of an honest demand upon the publick, because it is in his power to refuse it, would refuse the payment of his private debt, if he was equally protected in the refusal. He, who robs as a legislator, *because* he dares, would rob as a highwayman—*if* he dared.

And are the publick gainers by this? Even if they were, it would be no consideration. The paltry gain would be but as dust in the balance, when weighed against the loss of character—for as the world becomes more enlightened, and as the principles of justice become better understood, states as well as individuals have a character to lose—the paltry gain, I say, would be but as dust in the balance, when weighed against the loss of character, and against the many other pernicious effects which must flow from the example of publick injustice. But the truth is, that the publick must be losers, instead of being gainers, by a conduct of this kind. The mouth, which will not utter the sentiments of truth in favour of an honest demand, may be easily taught to repeat the lessons of falsehood in favour of an unjust one. To refuse fair claims, is to encourage fraudulent ones, upon the commonwealth. Little logick is required to show, that the same vicious principles and dispositions, which oppose the former, will exert their selfish, or their worse than selfish, influence to support the latter.

I think I have proved, that if the sacrifice, which has been mentioned, is demanded and enforced by the publick, when the competition between publick and private interest does not take place, it is tyranny, and not government; folly, and not wisdom. I have added, that if this sacrifice is demanded and enforced farther or longer than the competition indispensably requires, this, too, is tyranny, and not government. This likewise it is easy to prove.

There may be times, when, to the interest, perhaps to the liberty of the state, every private interest and regard ought to be devoted. At those times, such may be the situation and the peril of the commonwealth—for it is in perilous and distracted times, that, by the citizens, extraordinary exertions of duty ought to be made—at those times, a citizen obeys his duty's and his country's sacred call; he makes the necessary sacrifices, without expressly stipulating for a recompense: of demanding such a stipulation, the impropriety and the indelicacy may be equally evident. Great sacrifices and great exertions are made with faithfulness and zeal; perhaps, with considerable success. The perils disappear: to distraction and danger, peace and serenity succeed: the commonwealth becomes flourishing and opulent. Ought the sacrifice, which, in the hour of her distress and danger, was made at her call, to be continually enforced and demanded by her, after the danger and distress are over? But this sacrifice is demanded and enforced continually, if this citizen has neither received, nor had it in his power to recover, that recompense, which is just. This case—if such a case has ever happened—may go without any actual redress; but it can never go without well grounded complaint.

There is a sacrifice of another kind, not indeed so great, but, on some occasions, very vexatious, which is required of a citizen under a republican government, unnecessarily, and against his rights. He is frequently pestered with a number of frivolous, ambiguous, perplexed, and contradictory laws. The very best constitutions are liable to some complaints. What may be called the rage of legislation is a distemper prevalent and epidemical among republican governments.

Every article of the social contract cannot be ascertained: some of its leading principles cannot easily be mistaken. One certainly is, that, in a free state, the law should impose no restraint upon the will of the citizen, but such as will be productive of advantage, publick or private, sufficient to overbalance the disadvantages of the restraint: for, after all, we shall find that the *citizen* was made for the sake of the *man*. The proof of this advantage lies upon the legislature. If a law is even harmless; the very circumstance of its being a law, is itself a harm. This remark might be remembered, with profit, in the revision of many codes of law. In a word; government and human laws are necessary; if good, they are inestimable, in the present state. It must be admitted, however, that they are a burthen and a yoke: they should resemble that yoke which is easy, and that burthen which is light.

The citizen under a free government has a right to think, to speak, to write, to print, and to publish freely, but with decency and truth, concerning publick men, publick bodies, and publick measures.

Thus much concerning the duties and the rights of a private citizen.

I am next to treat of aliens.

———homo sum;
Nihil humani alienum a me puto.[3]

If this humane maxim had prevailed, as it ought to have prevailed, in the establishment of government, and the formation of laws; the title, which relates to aliens, would have been of an import very different from what we generally find it to be.

The contracted and debasing spirit of monopoly has not been peculiar to commerce; it has raged, with equal violence, and with equal mischief, in law and politicks.

In ancient times, every alien was considered as an enemy. The rule, I think, should be reversed. None but an enemy should be considered as an alien—I mean—as to the acquisition and the enjoyment of property. The rights of citizenship are the rights of parties to the social compact. Even to these, aliens should be permitted to accede upon easy terms.

This subject is of high importance to the United States; to Pennsylvania, in particular.

When I speak of the contracted rule, which prevailed in ancient times, I mean to speak, and I wish to be understood, with some illustrious exceptions. These deserve to be distinctly pointed out. From them, valuable instruction may be drawn.

The general policy of the Egyptians was unfriendly to strangers. It is even said of them, that they were accustomed to kill, or reduce to slavery, all those whom they found upon their coasts; except at one city only,

3. I am human; therefore nothing human is strange to me.

at which they were allowed to land and trade. But Psammeticus,[4] one of their princes, observed maxims of a more humane and enlightened nature. He favoured navigation in his seas; he opened his ports to the commerce of all nations; and he granted every kind of encouragement to every one, who would settle in Egypt. Amasis,[5] one of his successours, governed, by the same principles, his behaviour towards foreigners. He conferred many benefits upon the Grecians; and even allowed them to erect altars and temples. Under the government of Amasis, it is observed, Egypt was perfectly happy.[k]

Under the famous Theseus, the rival and the friend of Hercules, strangers were invited to participate the privileges of Athens: from all parts the invitation was accepted; and the new citizens were incorporated with the ancient Athenians. Every thing now, it is added, seemed favourable to his views: he governed a free people with moderation and benevolence; he was esteemed and beloved by the neighbouring nations; and he enjoyed a foretaste of that profound veneration, with which succeeding ages gradually honour the memory of great men.[l]

This policy, enlarged and generous, was continued in Attica, during many ages after Theseus; and rendered that celebrated country the most frequent resource of the miserable. On a particular occasion, the descendants of the great Hercules, devested of their possessions and driven into banishment by one of the vicissitudes of the times, enjoyed the advantages of the policy introduced by the friend of their ancestor: they were received by the Athenians.[m]

When it was, in the time of Lysias,[6] attempted to contract the foundation of the Athenian government; this part of their ancient policy is, in his oration against that attempt, mentioned with particular respect. "As to myself, I hold it to be the best security for the state, that all have an equal share in the government. When formerly we built walls, and acquired a

4. Likely refers to Psammeticus II, an Egyptian pharaoh (c. 594–588 B.C.) famous for his invasion of Kush.

5. Amasis II (570–526 B.C.) was a pharaoh of the twenty-sixth dynasty and last great pharaoh before the Persian conquest.

k. 3. Gog Or. Laws. 15. 16.

l. 1. Anac. 31. 32.

m. 1. Gill. 69.

6. Lysias (c. 440–380 B.C.) was an Attic orator.

fleet, and money, and allies; we regarded not these advantages as obtained only for ourselves; we shared them with the Eubaeans,[7] by establishing the right of intermarriage. Such were once our principles: by bestowing on strangers the honours of our country, we rendered them our friends: shall we now, by degrading our fellow citizens, render them our enemies? Never let this take place."[n]

"By those states," says my Lord Bacon, in his book concerning the augmentation of the sciences, "who have easily and liberally communicated the right of citizenship, greatness has been most successfully acquired. No commonwealth opened its bosom so wide for the reception of new citizens, as the commonwealth of Rome. The fortune of the empire was correspondent to the wisdom of the institution; for it became the largest on the face of the earth. It was their custom to confer the right of citizenship in the most speedy manner; and in the highest degree too—I mean not only the right of commerce, the right of marriage, the right of inheritance; but even the right of suffrage, and the right to the offices and the honours of the republick. So that it may be said, not that the Romans extended themselves over the whole globe, but that the inhabitants of the globe poured themselves upon the Romans. This is the most secure method of enlarging an empire."[o]

My Lord Hale, another lawyer of eminent name, speaks in the same spirit. "The shutting out of aliens," says he, "tends to the loss of people, which, laboriously employed, are the true riches of any country."[p]

In the law of England, there is a distinction between two kinds of aliens—those who are friends, and those who are enemies. Among alien enemies a subdivision is made, or at least was made till lately, which must occasion some degree of astonishment. Alien enemies are distinguished into such as are temporary, and such as are perpetual. Nay; what is more; this line of distinction, certainly never drawn by the peaceful spirit of christianity, is attempted to be marked by the progress of the christian system. "All infidels"—these are the expressions of my Lord Coke in the report of Calvin's case—"all infidels are perpetual enemies; the law pre-

7. Likely refers to the inhabitants of Euboea, an island in the Grecian archipelago.
n. Gil. Lys. and Isoc. 319.
o. 1. Ld. Bac. 245.
p. 1. Bac. 76. Vent. 427.

sumes not that they will be converted; between them, as with the devils, whose subjects they are, and the christian, there is perpetual hostility; and can be no peace;"—for he fortifies the favourite sentiment by a pleonasm: he goes farther—he attempts to fortify it by the language, tortured surely, of christianity itself. "Quae autem conventio Christi ad Belial; aut quae pars fideli cum infideli."[q] [8]

"Upon this ground," continues he, "there is a diversity between a conquest of the kingdom of a christian king, and the conquest of that of an infidel. In the former case, the ancient laws of the kingdom remain, till they are altered by the conqueror: in the latter case, they are immediately abrogated; and, till new laws be established, the conqueror shall judge them according to natural equity."[r]

The character of an opinion, like the character of a man, may be illustrated by tracing its history and pedigree. The opinion, that "the common law of England, as such, has no allowance or authority in the American plantations," is the bastard child of this bastard mother, begotten on her body by the Commentaries[s] on the laws of England. This very case of Calvin, and this very part of Calvin's case, is cited—none better could be cited—as the authority for an opinion, which was calculated to cut off the noblest inheritance of the colonies: to use, for once, a language *technically* legal, the colonies were *mulier,* though they were *puisne*—they were legitimate, though they were young.

But to return to the subject of alienage—an alien, according to the notion commonly received as law, is one born in a strange country and in a foreign society, to which he is presumed to have a natural and a necessary allegiance.[t]

Errour, as well as truth, is sometimes connected by a regular chain. A man is deemed a dangerous enemy or a suspicious friend to that country in which he wishes to reside, because he is previously deemed an appurtenant or a slave to that country in which he chanced to be born. Such is *one* of the consequences of "natural and necessary allegiance."

q. 2. Cor. VI. 15.

8. And what agreement, pray, is there of Christ toward Belial; or what part has the faithful person in common with the infidel?

r. 6. Rep. 17.

s. 1. Bl. Com. 107.

t. 1. Bac. 76.

Between alien friends, who are temporary subjects, and subjects naturalized or natural born, a species of subjects intermediate is known to the law of England. They are distinguished by the appellation of denizens. The power of denization is a high and incommunicable portion[u] of the prerogative royal. A denizen is received into the nation, like a person who is dropt from the clouds. He may acquire rights, but he cannot inherit them, not even from his own parent: he may transmit rights to his children, who are born after his letters patent of denization; but not to those who were born before. A denizen may be moulded into a thousand fantastical shapes: he may be a denizen in tail, a denizen for life, a denizen for years, a denizen upon condition, a denizen in one court of justice, and an alien in another.[v] Of those modifications, however, a subject naturalized is unsusceptible; because, we are told, they would be inconsistent with the purity, the absoluteness, and the indelibility of natural allegiance.[w] For a sound rule, we receive an unsound reason.

Between a subject naturalized and a subject natural born, the distinction is merely nominal as to private rights: it applies only to the manner, in which those rights are devolved. On one they are devolved by his birth: on the other, by the consent of the nation, expressed in the parliament. With regard, however, to publick rights, the case is widely different. By statutes made even since the revolution, no subject naturalized can be a member of parliament; and no bill for naturalization can be received in either house of parliament, without such a disabling clause.[x]

Britain seems determined to merit and to perpetuate, in political as well as geographical accuracy, the description, by which it was marked many centuries ago—

— *divisos* toto orbe Britannos.[9]

What a very different spirit animates and pervades her American sons! Indeed it is proper that it should do so. The insulated policy of the British

u. 1. Bl. Com. 374.
v. 1. Ins. 129. a.
w. 1. Ins. 129. a.
x. 1. Bl. Com. 374.
9. The Britons separated from the whole world.

nation would as ill befit the expansive genius of our institutions, as the hills, the ponds, and the rivulets, which are scattered over their island, would adequately represent the mountains, and rivers, and lakes of the United States. "In the new world"—I speak now from one of the finest writers of Britain[y]—"in the new world nature seems to have carried on her operations with a bolder hand, and to have distinguished the features of the country by a peculiar magnificence. The mountains of America are much superiour in height to those in the other divisions of the globe. From those lofty mountains descend rivers proportionably large. Its lakes are no less conspicuous for grandeur, than its mountains and rivers." We imitate, for we ought to imitate, the operations of nature; and the features of our policy, like those of our country, are distinguished by a peculiar magnificence.

In a former lecture,[z] we have seen how easily the essential rights of citizenship can be acquired in the United States, and in every state of the Union. Let us now see, how liberally the doors are thrown open for admission to the publick trusts and honours, as well as to the private rights and privileges, of our country.

At the end of two years from the time, at which a foreigner "of good character"—for numbers without virtue are not our object—a former mode of "*better* peopling his majesty's plantations" is now fallen into disrepute—at the end of two years from the time,[a] at which a foreigner of good character sets his foot in this land of generosity as well as freedom, he is entitled to become, if he chooses,[b] a citizen of our national government. At the end of seven years, a term not longer than that which is frequently required for an apprenticeship to the plainest trade, the citizen may become legislator; for he is eligible as a representative in the congress of the United States.[c] After having, in that capacity, undergone the honourable but short probationship of two years, the doors even of our national senate are opened as far as to receive him.[d]

y. 2. Rob. Amer. 3. 4.

z. Ante. p. 839. et. seq.

a. By the law now in force, a residence of five years is required. Laws U. S. 7. cong. 1. sess. c. 28. *Ed.*

b. Laws U. S. 1. cong. 2. sess. c. 3.

c. Cons. U. S. art. 1. s. 2.

d. Cons. U. S. art. 1. s. 3.

In Pennsylvania, the citizen may become a representative[e] at the end of three, a senator,[f] at the end of four, and governour[g] of the commonwealth, at the end of seven years.

It would be tedious, and it is unnecessary, to multiply particulars, by going through all the sister states. In this, as in other respects, in which we have viewed them, we are still pleased with the

— facies, qualis decet esse sororum.[10]

The rights and the disabilities of aliens with regard to property, especially with regard to landed property, forms a subject of investigation both interesting and nice. But, according to my uniform method, I postpone it until I arrive at the second great division of my system. The examination of general principles should precede that of particular rules.

One opinion, however, I will now mention: it seems to be founded on the authority of Sir Henry Spelman and the Grand Custumier of Normandy.[11] The opinion is, that the law, by which an alien is prohibited from holding lands, is an original branch of the feudal system; because, by that system, no one could purchase lands, unless he did fealty to the lords, of whom they were holden; and because an alien, who owed a previous faith to another prince, could not take an oath of fidelity in a second sovereign's dominions.[h]

e. Cons. Penn. art. 1. s. 3.

f. Cons. Penn. art. 1. s. 8.

g. Art. 2. s. 4.

10. Appearance, such as it befits sisters to have.

11. The "Grand Custumier of Normandy" refers to *A Collection of Laws of Normandyw as they stood before the disjoining of those Islands from the Dutch, viz. before the Time of King Henry III.*

h. 1. Bac. 76. Tit. Alien.

CHAPTER XII.
Of the Natural Rights of Individuals.

We have now viewed the whole structure of government; we have now ranged over its numerous apartments and divisions; and we have examined the materials of which it is formed. For what purpose has this magnificent palace been erected? For the residence and accommodation of the sovereign, Man.

Does man exist for the sake of government? Or is government instituted for the sake of man?

Is it possible, that these questions were ever seriously proposed? Is it possible, that they have been long seriously debated? Is it possible, that a resolution, diametrically opposite to principle, has been frequently and generally given of them in theory? Is it possible, that a decision, diametrically opposite to justice, has been still more frequently and still more generally given concerning them in practice? All this is possible: and I must add, all this is true. It is true in the dark; it is true even in the enlightened portions of the globe.

At, and nearly at the commencement of these lectures, a sense of duty obliged me to enter into a controversial discussion concerning the rights of society: the same sense of duty now obliges me to enter into a similar discussion concerning the rights of the constituent parts of society—concerning the rights of men. To enter upon a discussion of this nature, is neither the most pleasant nor the most easy part of my business. But when the voice of obligation is heard, ease and pleasure must preserve the respectful silence, and show the cheerful acquiescence, which become them.

What was the primary and the principal object in the institution of government? Was it—I speak of the primary and principal object—was it to acquire new rights by a human establishment? Or was it, by a human establishment, to acquire a new security for the possession or the recovery of those rights, to the enjoyment or acquisition of which we were previously entitled by the immediate gift, or by the unerring law, of our all-wise and all-beneficent Creator?

The latter, I presume, was the case: and yet we are told, that, in order to acquire the latter, we must surrender the former; in other words, in order to acquire the security, we must surrender the great objects to be secured. That man "may secure *some* liberty, he makes a surrender in trust of the *whole* of it."—These expressions are copied literally from the late publication of Mr. Burke.[a]

Tyranny, at some times, is uniform in her principles. The feudal system was introduced by a specious and successful maxim, the exact counterpart of that, which has been advanced by Mr. Burke—exact in every particular but one; and, in that one, it was more generous. The free and allodial proprietors of land were told that they must surrender it to the king, and take back—not merely "some," but—the whole of it, under some certain provisions, which, it was said, would procure a valuable object—the very object was security—security for their property. What was the result? They received their land back again, indeed; but they received it, loaded with all the oppressive burthens of the feudal servitude—cruel, indeed; so far as the epithet cruel can be applied to matters merely of property.

But all the other rights of men are in question here. For liberty is frequently used to denote all the absolute rights of men. "The absolute rights of every Englishman," says Sir William Blackstone, "are, in a political and extensive sense, usually called their liberties."[b]

And must we surrender to government the *whole* of those absolute rights? But we are to surrender them only—in *trust*:—another brat of dishonest parentage is now attempted to be imposed upon us: but for what purpose? Has government provided for us a superintending court of equity to compel a faithful performance of the trust? If it had; why should we part with the legal title to our rights?

After all; what is the mighty boon, which is to allure us into this surrender? We are to surrender all that we may secure "some:" and this "some," both as to its quantity and its certainty, is to depend on the pleasure of that

a. Refl. on Fr. Rev. 47.
b. 1. Bl. Com. 127.

power, to which the surrender is made. Is this a bargain to be proposed to those, who are both intelligent and free? No. Freemen, who know and love their rights, will not exchange their armour of pure and massy gold, for one of a baser and lighter metal, however finely it may be blazoned with tinsel: but they will not refuse to make an exchange upon terms, which are honest and honourable—terms, which may be advantageous to all, and injurious to none.

The opinion has been very general, that, in order to obtain the blessings of a good government, a sacrifice must be made of a part of our natural liberty. I am much inclined to believe, that, upon examination, this opinion will prove to be fallacious. It will, I think, be found, that wise and good government—I speak, at present, of no other—instead of contracting, enlarges as well as secures the exercise of the natural liberty of man: and what I say of his natural liberty, I mean to extend, and wish to be understood, through all this argument, as extended, to all his other natural rights.

This investigation will open to our prospect, from a new and striking point of view, the very close and interesting connexion, which subsists between the law of nature and municipal law. This investigation, therefore, will richly repay us for all the pains we may employ, and all the attention we may bestow, in making it.

"The law," says Sir William Blackstone, "which restrains a man from doing mischief to his fellow citizens, though it diminishes the natural, increases the civil liberty of mankind.[c]" Is it a part of natural liberty to do mischief to any one?

In a former part of these lectures, I had occasion to describe what natural liberty is: let us recur to the description, which was then given.[d] "Nature has implanted in man the desire of his own happiness; she has inspired him with many tender affections towards others, especially in the near relations of life; she has endowed him with intellectual and with active powers; she has furnished him with a natural impulse to exercise his powers for his own happiness, and the happiness of those for whom he entertains such tender affections. If all this be true, the undeniable consequence is, that he has a right to exert those powers for the accomplishment of those purposes,

c. 1. Bl. Com. 125. 126.
d. Ante. vol. 1. p. 638.

in such a manner, and upon such objects, as his inclination and judgment shall direct; provided he does no injury to others; and provided some publick interests do not demand his labours. This right is natural liberty."

If this description of natural liberty is a just one, it will teach us, that selfishness and injury are as little countenanced by the law of nature as by the law of man. Positive penalties, indeed, may, by human laws, be annexed to both. But these penalties are a restraint only upon injustice and overweening self-love, not upon the exercise of natural liberty.

In a state of natural liberty, every one is allowed to act according to his own inclination, provided he transgress not those limits, which are assigned to him by the law of nature: in a state of civil liberty, he is allowed to act according to his inclination, provided he transgress not those limits, which are assigned to him by the municipal law. True it is, that, by the municipal law, some things may be prohibited, which are not prohibited by the law of nature: but equally true it is, that, under a government which is wise and good, every citizen will gain more liberty than he can lose by these prohibitions. He will gain more by the limitation of other men's freedom, than he can lose by the diminution of his own. He will gain more by the enlarged and undisturbed exercise of his natural liberty in innumerable instances, than he can lose by the restriction of it in a few.

Upon the whole, therefore, man's natural liberty, instead of being abridged, may be increased and secured in a government, which is good and wise. As it is with regard to his natural liberty, so it is with regard to his other natural rights.

But even if a part was to be given up, does it follow that *all* must be surrendered? "Man," says Mr. Burke,[e] "cannot enjoy the rights of an uncivil and of a civil state together." By an "uncivil" contradistinguished from a "civil" state, he must here mean a state of nature: by the rights of this uncivil state, he must mean the rights of nature: and is it possible that natural and civil rights cannot be enjoyed together? Are they really incompatible? Must our rights be removed from the stable foundation of nature, and placed on the precarious and fluctuating basis of human institution? Such seems to be the sentiment of Mr. Burke: and such too seems to have been the sentiment of a much higher authority than Mr. Burke—Sir William Blackstone.

e. Refl. on Fr. Rev. 47.

In the Analysis of his Commentaries,[f] he mentions "the right of personal security, of personal liberty, and of private property"—not as the natural rights, which, I confess, I should have expected, but—as the "civil liberties" of Englishmen. In his Commentaries, speaking of the same three rights, he admits that they are founded on nature and reason; but adds[g] "their establishment, excellent as it is, is still human." Each of those rights he traces severally and particularly to magna charta, which he justly considers as for the most part declaratory of the principal grounds of the fundamental laws of England.[h] He says indeed,[i] that they are "either that *residuum* of natural liberty, which is not required by the laws of society to be sacrificed to publick convenience; or else those civil privileges, which society has engaged to provide, in lieu of the natural liberties so given up by individuals." He makes no explicit declaration which of the two, in his opinion, they are; but since he traces them to magna charta and the fundamental laws of England; since he calls them "civil liberties;" and since he says expressly, that their establishment is human; we have reason to think, that he viewed them as coming under the latter part of his description—as civil privileges, provided by society, in lieu of the natural liberties given up by individuals. Considered in this view, there is no material difference between the doctrine of Sir William Blackstone, and that delivered by Mr. Burke.

If this view be a just view of things, the consequence, undeniable and unavoidable, is, that, under civil government, individuals have "given up" or "surrendered" their rights, to which they were entitled by nature and by nature's law; and have received, in lieu of them, those "civil privileges, which society has engaged to provide."

If this view be a just view of things, then the consequence, undeniable and unavoidable, is, that, under civil government, the right of individuals to their private property, to their personal liberty, to their health, to their reputation, and to their life, flow from a human establishment, and can be traced to no higher source. The connexion between man and his natural rights is intercepted by the institution of civil society.

f. B. 1. c. 1. s. 8.
g. 1. Bl. Com. 127.
h. Id. 128.
i. Id. 129.

If this view be a just view of things, then, under civil society, man is not only made *for*, but made *by* the government: he is nothing but what the society frames: he can claim nothing but what the society provides. His natural state and his natural rights are withdrawn altogether from notice: "It is the *civil social* man," says Mr. Burke,[k] "and *no other*, whom I have in my contemplation."

If this view be a just view of things, why should we not subscribe the following articles of a political creed, proposed by Mr. Burke.

"We wished, at the period of the revolution, and we now wish to derive all we possess, *as an inheritance from our forefathers.* Upon that body and stock of inheritance, we have taken care not to innoculate any cyon alien to the nature of the original plant. All the reformations we have hitherto made, have proceeded upon the principle of reference to antiquity; and I hope, nay I am persuaded, that all those, which possibly may be made hereafter, will be carefully formed upon analogical precedent, authority, and example."

"Our oldest reformation is that of magna charta. You will see that Sir Edward Coke, that great oracle of our law, and indeed all the great men who follow him, to Blackstone, are industrious to prove the pedigree of our liberties."

Let us observe, by the way, that the only position, relating to this subject, for which I find the authority of my Lord Coke quoted,[l] is a position, to which every one, who knows the history of the common law, will give his immediate and most unreserved assent: the position is—"that magna charta was, for the most part, declaratory of the principal grounds of the fundamental laws of England." But Mr. Burke proceeds.

"They endeavour to prove, that the ancient charter, the magna charta of King John, was connected with another positive charter from Henry the first: and that both the one and the other were nothing more than a reaffirmance of the still more ancient standing law of the kingdom. In the matter of fact, for the greater part, these authors appear to be in the right; perhaps not always: but if the lawyers mistake in some particulars, it proves my position still the more strongly; because it demonstrates the powerful prepossession towards antiquity, with which the minds of all our

k. Refl. on Fr. Rev. 47.
l. 1. Bl. Com. 127. 128.

lawyers and legislators, and of all the people whom they wish to influence, have been always filled; and the stationary policy of this kingdom in considering their most sacred rights and franchises as an *inheritance.*"[m]

It is proper to pause here a little.—If, in tracing the pedigree of our "most sacred rights," one was permitted to indulge the same train of argument and reflection, which would be just and natural in the investigation of inferiour titles, we should be prompted to inquire, how it happens, that "mistakes in some particulars" would prove more strongly the general point to be established. Would mistakes in some particulars respecting a title to land, or the genealogy of a family, prove more strongly the validity of one, or the antiquity of the other?

But I must do Mr. Burke justice. The reason, which he assigns, why the making of those mistakes proves his position the more strongly, is, because it proves the "powerful *prepossession* towards antiquity." Of this prepossession I will controvert neither the existence nor the strength: but I will ask—does it prove the point in question?—Does it prove the truth and correctness of even the *civil* pedigree of the liberties of England? Is predilection an evidence of right? Is property or any thing else, which is in litigation, decided to belong to him, who shows the strongest affection for it? If, in a controversy concerning an inferiour object, the person, who claims it, and who undertakes to substantiate his claim, should own, that, in deducing his chain of title, some mistakes were made; but should urge even those mistakes as an argument in his behalf, because his perseverance in his suit, notwithstanding those mistakes, demonstrates his powerful attachment for the thing in dispute; what would a discerning court—what would an unbiassed jury think of his conduct? I believe they would not think that it paid any extraordinary compliment, either to their impartiality or to their understanding.

I begin now to hesitate, whether we should subscribe the political creed of Mr. Burke. Let us, however, proceed and examine some of its other articles.

Some one, it seems, had been so hardy as to allege, that the king of Great Britain owes his crown to "the choice of his people." This doctrine, says Mr. Burke, "affirms a most unfounded, dangerous, illegal, and

m. Refl. on Fr. Rev. 24.

unconstitutional position." "Nothing can be more untrue, than that the crown of this kingdom is so held by his majesty."[n] To disprove the assertion, "that the king of Great Britain owes his crown to the choice of his people," Mr. Burke has recourse to the declaration of rights, which was made at the accession of King William and Queen Mary. "This declaration of right," says he, "is the corner stone of our constitution, as *reenforced,* explained, improved, and in its fundamental principles *for ever* settled. It is called an 'act for declaring the rights and liberties of the subject, and for *settling* the succession of the crown.' These rights and this succession are declared in one body, and bound indissolubly together."[o] "It is curious," adds he, "with what address the *temporary* solution of continuity in the line of succession"—for it was impossible for Mr. Burke not to admit that from this line a temporary deviation was made—"it is curious with what address this *temporary* solution is kept from the eye; whilst all that could be found in this act of necessity, to countenance the idea of an *hereditary succession* is brought forward, and fostered, and made the most of by the legislature." "The legislature," he proceeds, "had plainly in view the act of recognition of the first of Queen Elizabeth, and that of James the first, both acts strongly declaratory of the inheritable nature of the crown; and, in many parts, they follow, with a nearly literal precision, the words and even the form, which is found in these old declaratory statutes."[p] "They give the most solemn pledge, taken from the act of Queen Elizabeth, as solemn a pledge as ever was or can be given in favour of an hereditary succession. 'The lords spiritual and temporal, and commons, do, in the name of all the people aforesaid, most humbly and faithfully submit *themselves, their heirs and posterities for ever;* and do faithfully promise, that they will stand to, maintain, and defend their said majesties, and also the *limitation of the crown, herein* specified and contained, to the utmost of their power."[q]

I have mentioned above, that tyranny, at some times, is uniform in her principles: I have done her full justice: she is not so at all times. Of truth, liberty, and virtue, it is the exclusive prerogative to be always consistent.

n. Refl. on Fr. Rev. 9.
o. Refl. on Fr. Rev. 12.
p. Id. 13.
q. Id. 14.

Let us, for a moment, adopt the statement, which Mr. Burke has given us. Upon that statement I ask—if the humble and faithful submission of the parliament, in the name of all the people, was sufficient, in the time of Elizabeth, to bind themselves, their heirs and posterity for ever, to the line of hereditary succession; how came it to pass, that, in the time of William and Mary, the parliament, in the name of all the people, was justified in deviating, even for an instant, from the succession in that hereditary line? I ask again—if the humble and faithful submission of the parliament, in the name of all the people, was, in the sixteenth century, insufficient to bind their heirs and posterity in the seventeenth century; how comes it to pass that, in the seventeenth century, the humble and faithful submission of the parliament, in the name of all the people, could bind their heirs and posterity in the eighteenth century? Such a submission was either sufficient or it was not sufficient for that binding purpose: let the disciples of the doctrine, which rests on this dilemma, choose between the alternatives.

I have now no hesitation whether we should or should not subscribe the creed of Mr. Burke: that creed, which is contradictory to itself, cannot, in every part, be sound and orthodox.

But, to say the truth, I should not have given myself the trouble of delivering, nor you, of hearing these annotations upon it; unless it had derived the support, which it claims, from the Commentaries on the laws of England. The principles delivered in those Commentaries are never matters of indifference: I have already mentioned,[r] "that when they are not proper objects of imitation, they furnish excellent materials of contrast."

Government, in my humble opinion, should be formed to secure and to enlarge the exercise of the natural rights of its members; and every government, which has not this in view, as its principal object, is not a government of the legitimate kind.

Those rights result from the natural state of man; from that situation, in which he would find himself, if no civil government was instituted. In such a situation, a man finds himself, in some respects, unrelated to others; in other respects, peculiarly related to some; in still other respects, bearing a general relation to all. From his unrelated state, one class of rights arises: from his peculiar relations, another class of rights arises: from his general

r. Ante. vol. 1. p. 444.

relations, a third class of rights arises. To each class of rights, a class of duties is correspondent; as we had occasion to observe and illustrate, when we treated concerning the general principles of natural law.

In his unrelated state, man has a natural right to his property, to his character, to liberty, and to safety. From his peculiar relations, as a husband, as a father, as a son, he is entitled to the enjoyment of peculiar rights, and obliged to the performance of peculiar duties. These will be specified in their due course. From his general relations, he is entitled to other rights, simple in their principle, but, in their operation, fruitful and extensive. His duties, in their principle and in their operation, may be characterized in the same manner as his rights. In these general relations, his rights are, to be free from injury, and to receive the fulfilment of the engagements, which are made to him: his duties are, to do no injury, and to fulfil the engagements, which he has made. On these two pillars principally and respectively rest the criminal and the civil codes of the municipal law. These are the pillars of justice.

Of municipal law, the rights and the duties of benevolence are sometimes, though rarely, the objects. When they are so, they will receive the pleasing and the merited attention.

You now see the distribution, short, and simple, and plain, which will govern the subsequent part of my system of lectures. From this distribution, short, and simple, and plain as it is, you see the close and very interesting connexion between natural and municipal law. You see, to use again my Lord Bacon's language, how the streams of civil institutions flow from the fountain of justice.

I am first to show, that a man has a natural right to his property, to his character, to liberty, and to safety.

His natural right to his property, you will permit me, at present, to assume as a principle granted. I assume it for this reason; because I wish not to anticipate now what will be introduced, with much greater propriety and advantage, when I come to the second great division of my lectures, in which I am to treat concerning things.

To his character, every one has a natural right. A man's character may, I think, be described as the just result of those opinions, which ought to be formed concerning his talents, his sentiments, and his conduct. Opinions, upon this as upon every other subject, ought to be founded in truth.

Justice, as well as truth, requires, concerning characters, accuracy and impartiality of opinion.

Under some aspects, character may be considered as a species of property; but, of all, the nearest, the dearest, and the most interesting. In this light it is viewed by the Poet of nature—

> The purest treasure mortal times afford
> Is spotless reputation.
> Who steals my purse, steals trash.
> 'Twas mine; 'tis his; and has been slave to thousands;
> But he who filches from me my good name,
> Takes from me that, which not enriches him,
> But makes me poor indeed.[1]

By the exertion of the same talents and virtues, property and character both are often acquired: by vice and indolence, both are often lost or destroyed.

The love of reputation and the fear of dishonour are, by the all-gracious Author of our existence, implanted in our breasts, for purposes the most beneficent and wise. Let not these principles be deemed the growth of dispositions only which are weak or vain; they flourish most luxuriantly in minds, the strongest and, let me add, the most humble. Of the happiness of heaven, a part of the unerring description is—that it is "full of glory."

Well may character, then, be considered as one of the natural rights of man: well may it be classed among those rights, the enjoyment of which it is the design of good government and laws to secure and enlarge: well does it deserve their encouragement and protection; for, in its turn, it assists their operations, and supplies their deficiencies.

I remarked, a little while ago, that the rights and the duties of benevolence are but rarely, though they are at some times, the objects of municipal law. The remark may be extended to rights and duties of many other kinds. To many virtues, legal rewards are not, nor can they be, assigned: with legal impunity, many vices are, and must be, suffered to escape. But before a court of honour those qualities and sentiments and actions are amenable, which despise the subtlest process of the tribunals of law, and

1. Wilson quotes Shakespeare, apparently from memory, with slight inaccuracies. The first two lines of the passage are from *Richard II* (I. i. 177–79); the last five are from *Othello* (III. iii. 161–65).

elude the keenest vigilance of the ministers of justice. This court, powerful in its sentences as well as extensive in its jurisdiction, decrees to virtue, and to the virtuous exertion of talents, a crown of fame, pure and splendid: vice, and idleness, less odious only than vice, it dooms to wear the badges of infamy, dirty and discoloured. This court, therefore, in a government of which virtue is the principle and vice is the bane, ought to receive, from all its institutions, the just degree of favour and regard.

> Honour's a sacred tie—
> The noble mind's distinguishing perfection,
> That aids and strengthens virtue, where it meets her.

The Poet adds—

> And imitates her actions, where she is not.

The moral descriptions of Mr. Addison are seldom inaccurate. On this occasion, however, I must declare that I think him liable to the charge of inaccuracy. The counterfeit of virtue should not be dignified with the appellation of honour.

It is the sentiment of some writers, highly distinguished too by their liberal and manly principles, that honour is peculiar to governments which are monarchical. "In extreme political liberty," says the Marquis of Beccaria, "and in absolute despotism, all ideas of honour disappear, or are confounded with others. In the first case, reputation becomes useless from the despotism of the laws; and, in the second, the despotism of one man, annulling all civil existence, reduces the rest to a precarious temporary personality. Honour, then, is one of the fundamental principles of those monarchies, which are a limited despotism; and in these, like revolutions in despotick states, it is a momentary return to a state of nature and original equality."[s]

How prevalent even among enlightened writers, is the mistaken opinion, that government is subversive of equality and nature! Is it necessarily so? By no means. When I speak thus, I speak confidently, because I speak from principle fortified by fact. Let the constitution of the United States—let that of Pennsylvania be examined from the beginning to the end. No right is conferred, no obligation is laid on any, which is not laid

s. Bec. c. 9.

or conferred on every, citizen of the commonwealth or Union—I think I may defy the world to produce a single exception to the truth of this remark. Now, as I showed at large in a former part of my lectures,[t] the original equality of mankind consists in an equality of their duties and rights.

That honour is the principle of monarchical governments, is the well known doctrine of the celebrated Montesquieu. But let us examine the nature and qualities of that honour which he describes. It is that honour which can subsist without honesty; for he says expressly,[u] that, in well policied monarchies, there are very few honest men. It is that honour which forbids not adulation, nor cunning, nor craft. It is that honour which judges of actions not as they are good, but as they are showy; not as they are just, but as they are grand; not as they are reasonable, but as they are extraordinary. It is, in one word, that honour, which fashions the virtues just as it pleases, and extends or limits our duties by its own whimsical taste. To this honour, indeed, truth in conversation is a necessary point: but is this for the sake of truth? By no means.

For the possession of this honour—vicious in its practice, and, even when right in its practice, vicious in its principle—a republican government will not, I presume, contend. But to that honour, whose connexion with virtue is indissoluble, a republican government produces the most unquestionable title. The principle of virtue is allowed to be hers: if she possesses virtue, she also possesses honour. I admire the fine moral and political instruction, as well as the elegant architectural taste, exhibited by the justly framed structure, in which the temple of honour was accessible only through the temple of virtue.

Viewed in this light, the honour of character is a property, which is, indeed, precious. But let it be remembered, that, in this view, it is a property, which must be purchased. To claim that reputation which we do not deserve, is as absurd, though it is not as barefaced, as to claim that property which is not ours. The only difference is, that, in the former case, we claim generally that which belongs to another, while, in the latter case, we claim that which only does not belong to ourselves. In both cases, the claim is equally unfounded.

t. Ante. vol. 1. p. 636, 638.
u. Sp. L. b. 3. c. 6.

To bestow on another that reputation which he does not deserve, is equally profuse, and, in many instances, is more unjust than to bestow on him that property, to which he is not, on the principles either of justice, or charity, or benevolence, entitled. As it is equally profuse, it is more to be guarded against. In the latter case, we bestow what is our own, and, therefore, are inclined to be cautious: in the former case, we are apt to be inconsiderate, because what we bestow is not ours. Indiscriminate praise is not so odious, but it is as useless and it is as heedless as indiscriminate censure. In one important particular they precisely coincide. They have an equal tendency to destroy and to render inefficacious the great distinction between right and wrong, approbation and disapprobation, virtue and vice.

If it is unwarrantable to bestow reputation where it is not due; what epithet shall we assign to that conduct, which plucks the wreath of honour from those temples, around which it has been meritoriously placed? Robbery itself flows not from a fountain so rankly poisoned as that, which throws out the waters of malicious defamation.

The subject of reputation will again come under your view, when I treat concerning prosecutions for libels and actions of slander: both of which suppose an unjustifiable aggression of character. What I have now said will suffice to point to the general principles, on which those actions and prosecutions should be defended, supported, and determined.

Property must often—reputation must always be purchased: liberty and life are the gratuitous gifts of heaven.

That man is naturally free, was evinced in a former lecture:[v] I will not reiterate what has been advanced.

I shall certainly be excused from adducing any formal arguments to evince, that life, and whatever is necessary for the safety of life, are the natural rights of man. Some things are so difficult; others are so plain, that they cannot be proved. It will be more to our purpose to show the anxiety, with which some legal systems spare and preserve human life; the levity and the cruelty which others discover in destroying or sporting with it; and the inconsistency, with which, in others, it is, at some times, wantonly sacrificed, and, at other times, religiously guarded.

v. Vol. 1. p. 638.

In Sparta, nothing was deemed so precious as the life of a citizen. And yet in Sparta, if an infant, newly born, appeared, to those who were appointed to examine him, ill formed or unhealthy, he was, without any further ceremony, thrown into a gulph near mount Taygetus.[w] Fortunate it was for Mr. Pope—fortunate it was for England, which boasts Mr. Pope—that he was not born in the neighbourhood of mount Taygetus.

At Athens,[x] the parent was empowered, when a child was born, to pronounce on its life or its death. At his feet it was laid: if he took it in his arms, this was received as the gracious signal for its preservation: if he deigned not a look of compassion on the fruit of his loins, it was removed and exposed. Over almost all the rest of Greece,[y] this barbarity was permitted or authorized.

In China, the practice of exposing new born children is said to have prevailed immemorially, and to prevail still. As the institutions of that empire are never changed, its situation is never improved.

Tacitus records it to the honour of the Germans, that, among them, to kill infants newly born was deemed a most flagitious crime. Over them, adds he, good manners have more power, than good laws have over other nations. This shows, that, in his time, the restraints of law began to be imposed on this unnatural practice; but that its inveteracy had rendered them still inefficacious.

Under the Roman commonwealth, no citizen of Rome was liable to suffer a capital punishment by the sentence of the law. But at Rome, the son held his life by the tenure of his father's pleasure. In the forum, the senate, or the camp, the adult son of a Roman citizen enjoyed the publick and private rights of a *person:* in his father's house, he was a mere *thing;*[z] confounded, by the laws, with the cattle, whom the capricious master might alienate or destroy, without being responsible to any tribunal on earth.

The gentle Hindoo is laudably averse to the shedding of blood; but he carries his worn out friend or benefactor to perish on the banks of the Ganges.

w. 4. Anac. 161. 162.
x. 3. Anac. 4.
y. Id. ibid.
z. 8. Gibbon. 52.

With consistency, beautiful and undeviating, human life, from its commencement to its close, is protected by the common law. In the contemplation of law, life begins when the infant is first able to stir in the womb.[a] By the law, life is protected not only from immediate destruction, but from every degree of actual violence, and, in some cases, from every degree of danger.

The grades of solicitude, discovered, by the law, on the subject of life, are marked, in the clearest manner, by the long and regular series of the different degrees of aggression, which it enumerates and describes—threatening, assault, battery, wounding, mayhem, homicide. How those different degrees may be justified, excused, alleviated, aggravated, redressed, or punished, will appear both in the criminal and in the civil code of our municipal law.

Thus much concerning the natural rights of man in what has been termed his unrelated state. I come now to specify and to consider those peculiar relations, by virtue of which a man is entitled to the enjoyment of peculiar rights, and obliged to the performance of peculiar duties.

I begin with marriage, which forms the near relation between husband and wife.

Whether we consult the soundest deductions of reason, or resort to the best information conveyed to us by history, or listen to the undoubted intelligence communicated in holy writ, we shall find, that to the institution of marriage the true origin of society must be traced. By that institution the felicity of Paradise was consummated; and since the unhappy expulsion from thence, to that institution, more than to any other, have mankind been indebted for the share of peace and harmony which has been distributed among them. "Prima societas in ipso conjugio est,"[2] says Cicero in his book of offices;[b] a work which does honour to the human understanding and the human heart.

The most ancient traditions of every country ascribe to its first legislators and founders, the regulations concerning the union between the sexes. The honour of instituting marriage among the Chinese, is assigned to their first sovereign,[c] Fo-hi.[3] In order to render this great foundation of society

a. 1. Bl. Com. 129.

2. The first bond of society is marriage.

b. L. 1. c. 17.

c. 1. Gog. Or. L. 22.

3. Fu Hsi (c. 2852 B.C.) was the mythical first emperor of China.

respectable, he adjusted, as we are told,[d] the ceremonies, with which the contracts of marriage were accompanied.

Among the Egyptians, the law of marriage is said to have been established by Menes,[e4] whose name is transmitted to us as that of their first king. The history of Abraham[f] affords a striking instance of the profound respect, which in his day was paid, in Egypt, to the conjugal union.

Cecrops has been already mentioned as the first great legislator of the Athenians, and as borrowing his institutions from those of the Egyptians. Accordingly we are informed, that he established, at Athens, the laws and ceremonies of marriage, in the same manner as they were observed and practised in Egypt. Polygamy was not permitted.[g] These regulations are described as the sources of virtues and enjoyments. They evinced the advantages of decency, the attractions of modesty, the happiness of loving, and the necessity of constancy in love.[h]

The founder of Rome made, concerning marriages, a law, which, on many accounts, will deserve our particular attention. It was expressed in these words: "let every wife, who by the holy laws of marriage falls into the power of a husband, enter with him into a community of goods and sacrifices."[i]

As marriage has been instituted by the first, it has always been encouraged by the wisest legislators. By the law of Moses,[k] a man, during one year after his marriage, was exempted from publick burthens, and from going to war. A regulation nearly similar, as we are told, was established by the Incas of Peru.[l] The *jus trium liberorum*,[5] introduced by the prudent policy of Augustus, was a permanent inducement to matrimony at Rome.[m]

d. 3. Gog. Or. L. 313.

e. 1. Gog. Or. L. 22.

4. Menes (c. 3100–3000 B.C.), an Egyptian pharaoh who was perhaps the founder of the first dynasty, is credited by many scholars for uniting Upper and Lower Egypt.

f. Gen. xii. 19.

g. 2. Gog. Or. L. 19.

h. 1. Anac. 7.

i. 1. Rol. R. H. 32.

k. Deuter. xxiv. 5.

l. 1. Gog. Or. L. 23.

5. The extraordinary rights, privileges, and immunities that the Roman law accorded a father of three or more children.

m. Mont. Sp. L. b. 23. c. 21.

Legislators have, with great propriety, carried their views still farther; they have provided, as far as municipal laws can provide, against the violation of rights, indispensably essential to the purity and harmony of the matrimonial union. Treachery, upon any occasion, is sufficient to stain a page in the annals of life; but perfidy against the solemn engagements of marriage obliterates the impression of happiness from every subsequent part of the conjugal history. Upon this subject, however, so interesting to the finest sentiments and emotions of the heart, every thing, that might be wished, cannot, we fear, be expected from the operation of human laws. Much must be left to the influence of that legitimate honour, which we have described as the inseparable friend and companion of virtue. From the bastard honour, which we likewise described, it would be ridiculous, in this case, to hope for any assistance. In this case, as in many others, that honour glories in its shame.

Concerning the ancient Germans, Tacitus, in his short but masterly account of their manners,[n] informs us, that among them the laws of marriage were rigidly observed; and that no part of their conduct was more exemplary.

We have seen the first institution of marriage among the Athenians and the Romans: a concise view of its history will be instructive and interesting.

In the heroick ages of Greece, we are told,[o] the rights of beauty and feminine weakness were highly respected and tenderly observed. The simplicity of those ages was equally remote from the cruel tyranny of savages, which condemns the fair sex to servitude, and the sordid selfishness of luxury, which considers them solely as instruments of pleasure. Hence those affecting scenes so exquisitely described by Homer, which, in the interviews of Hector and Andromache, exhibit the most striking image of nuptial felicity and love. But this beautiful picture of ancient manners was soon miserably defaced; and, in the degenerate periods of Greece, the fair sex were as much neglected and despised, as they had been loved and admired in the heroick ages.

In those degraded times, of which I am now obliged to speak, no pains were employed to render the Grecian females agreeable members of society, in any one part of their lives. Education was either entirely withheld

n. C. 18.
o. 1. Gill. 52. 56.

from them; or it was directed to such objects as were fitted to contract and debase, instead of elevating and enlarging the mind. When they were grown up, they were thrown away in marriage, without being consulted in the choice; and by entering into this new state, they found the severe guardianship of a father succeeded by the absolute dominion of a husband. At this period, even the laws of Athens countenanced this unworthy tenour of conduct: to secure the fortune of the husband was deemed an object of greater importance, than to protect the person and honour of the wife, from the outrage so peculiarly dreaded by female virtue.[p]

Let us now turn our attention to Rome. You recollect, that, by a law of Romulus, "the wife fell into the power of the husband." The law, which, on the whole, was very susceptible of a construction mild and generous, received from this part of it an interpretation most unwarrantable and severe. By this interpretation, coloured with the unnatural fiction, that, on a solemn marriage, the wife was adopted by the husband, he acquired over her all the tremendous plenitude of Roman paternal power. This extreme, as is usual, soon produced its opposite; and female servitude was exchanged for female licentiousness. The solemnities of the ancient nuptials were declined, in order to avoid the odious consequences superinduced upon them by the construction and fiction of law; and the parties, without losing, on either side, their independence or their name, subscribed definite and stipulated articles of a marriage contract. Their cohabitation, and the appearances of a common interest which they exhibited, were received, without investigation, as sufficient evidence of a regular and solemn marriage. Hence that detestable train of conjugal vice, infidelity, rage, rancour, and revenge, with which so many volumes of the Roman story are crowded and disgraced.

By the precepts of christianity, and the practice of the christians, the dignity of marriage was, however restored.

In the eye of the common law, marriage appears in no other light than that of a civil contract: and to this contract the agreement of the parties, the essence of every rational contract, is indispensably required. If, therefore, either of the parties is incapable of agreeing, is unwilling to agree, or has not, in fact, as well as in ability and will, concluded the agree-

p. Gill. Lys. and Isoc. Int. c.

ment; the marriage cannot be established by the principles of the common law.

Disability to contract marriage may arise from immature age. A man, as we have seen before,[q] may consent to marriage at fourteen; a woman, at twelve years of age. If, before those respective ages, a marriage take place, either party may, at the age of consent, but not before or after that age, disagree, declare the marriage void, and marry again: but if, at the age of consent, they agree to continue together, there is no occasion for another marriage between them; that which has taken place being deemed a marriage, though only an inchoate and imperfect one. If, at the time of the inchoate marriage, one of the parties is, and the other is not of the age of consent, when the last arrives at that age, the first as well as the last may disagree; for in a contract of marriage, both or neither must be bound.[r]

Disability to contract marriage may arise from the want of reason. Consent, as has been already observed, is essential to this, as to every other contract; but those who enjoy not a competent share of reason, are incapable of giving consent.[s]

By a law of Pennsylvania, certain degrees of consanguinity and affinity, specified in a table subjoined to the law, are disabilities to contract matrimony: and all marriages within those degrees are declared to be void. I refer you to the table specifying the degrees.[t]

One marriage undissolved, forms a disability to contract another. In such a case the second marriage is void as well as criminal.[u]

"Consensus non concubitus facit matrimonium,"[6] is a maxim of our law; marriage, therefore, must be the effect of willingness as well as of capacity to contract it.[v]

When to the ability and will to contract, an actual contract is added; then the marriage is complete.

q. Ante. p. 844.
r. 1. Ins. 79. a. b.
s. 1. Bl. Com. 438.
t. 1. Laws Penn. 46.
u. 1. Bl. Com. 436.
6. A meeting of the minds, and not cohabitation, constitutes a marriage.
v. 1. Ins. 33.

Before the time of Pope Innocent the third,[7] there was no solemnization of marriage in the church; but the man came to the house where the woman inhabited, and led her home to his own house; which was all the ceremony then used.[w]

By an act of the legislature of Pennsylvania, all marriages, not forbidden by the law of God, shall be encouraged.[x] In the construction of legacies, it is a general rule, that all conditions are unlawful, which would operate against the liberty of marriage.[y]

It will be proper, in the next place, to consider the consequences of marriage.

The most important consequence of marriage is, that the husband and the wife become, in law, only one person: the legal existence of the wife is consolidated into that of the husband. Upon this principle of union, almost all the other legal consequences of marriage depend. This principle, sublime and refined, deserves to be viewed and examined on every side. Among human institutions, it seems to be peculiar to the common law. Peculiar as it is, however, among human institutions, it seems not uncongenial to the spirit of a declaration from a source higher than human—"They twain shall be one flesh."

Even of the common law, this was not always a principle. We are told by the learned Selden, that the Saxon wives were never one with their husbands; nor were they, as wives, under the view of the frank-pledge: a Saxon wife was obliged to give pledge by her friends, that she would do no wrong. She passed as an appurtenant to her husband, rather than one in unity with him: and her estate was rather appurtenant to her than to him: for if she failed in her good carriage to her husband, she was to make him amends out of her own estate; and if that was insufficient, then her pledges were to make satisfaction for her.[z] This interposition of friends between husband and wife, in matters respecting either their conduct or their claims, seems alien to the delicacy and nearness of the matrimonial connexion. On very pressing emergencies, indeed, it is necessary that the law

7. Lotario de' Conti di Segni (c. 1161–1216) served as Pope Innocent III from 1198 to 1216.

w. 3. Bac. 575.

x. 1. Laws. Penn. 36.

y. Swin. 266.

z. Bac. on Gov. 65.

should interfere, and on such emergencies we shall see that it does interfere; but the general presumption and the universal wish ought to be, that, between husband and wife, there subsist or may subsist no difference of will or of interest. Such accordingly, during many centuries past, has been the language of the law. Bracton, in the reign of Henry the third, informs us, that "husband and wife are as one person, because they are one flesh and blood."[a] Littleton, whose sayings are of such high authority, tells us repeatedly, "that the husband and the wife are but one person in the law."[b]

In pursuance of this principle, a crime, except treason and murder,[c] committed by the husband and wife, shall be charged against him solely; because the law will suppose that she acted under his influence or coercion. In pursuance of the same principle, a husband and wife cannot be witnesses for or against one another: if they were permitted to give testimony for one another, one maxim of the law would be violated—No one can be a witness in his own cause: if they were permitted to give testimony against one another, another maxim of the law would be violated—No one is obliged to accuse himself.

But, as has before been intimated, whenever urgent emergencies arise; whenever any outrage is threatened or committed against the peace or safety of society, as well as against the refined rules of the conjugal union; the law will interpose its authority, and, though it will not order, because it cannot enforce its orders for observing the latter, it will order, because it can enforce its orders for preserving the former.

The refined delicacy of the maxim—that husband and wife are considered as one person by our law—appears now in a beautiful and striking point of view. The rights, the enjoyments, the obligations, and the infelicities of the matrimonial state are so far removed from her protection or redress, that she will not appear as an arbitress; but, like a candid and benevolent neighbour, will presume, for she wishes, all to be well.

To the other rights and to the other duties of a marriage life, we must extend the observations which we have already applied to one of them. Reliance must be placed on that honour, which is the inseparable friend and companion of virtue.

a. 1. Ins. 187 b.
b. S. 168. 291.
c. 1. Bl. Com. 444.

I have spoken concerning those consequences of marriage, which relate to the persons of the husband and wife: the consequences which relate to their property, will be fully considered under the second great division of my system: you observe, that I carefully avoid the blending of the two divisions.

By that event which closes the scene of all sublunary enjoyments, marriage is dissolved: it may be dissolved sooner—by divorce.

To the law of England, two kinds of divorce are known—a divorce from the bed and the table—and a divorce from the chains—the metaphor is proper on this occasion—a divorce from the chains of matrimony. The propriety of the first kind, I am, I confess, at a loss to explain: that of the second kind is frequently obvious. When, as we have seen, the impression of happiness must be obliterated from every succeeding part of the conjugal history, why should any more blackened pages be added to the inauspicious volume? But of causes which are slight or trivial, a divorce should, by no means, be permitted to be the effect. When divorces can be summoned to the aid of levity, of vanity, or of avarice, a state of marriage becomes frequently a state of war or stratagem; still more frequently, a state of premeditated and active preparation for successful stratgems and war. Such was the case in ancient Rome. "Passion, interest, or caprice," says the Historian of her falling state,[8] "suggested daily motives for the dissolution of marriage; a word, a sign, a message, the mandate of a freeman declared the separation; the most tender of human connexions was degraded to a transient society of profit or pleasure."[d]

—Sic fiunt octo mariti
Quinque per autumnos.[9]
Juv. sat. VI. 20.

Non consulum numero, sed maritorum annos suos computant.[10]
Sen. de. Benef. III. 16.

Both these remarks are levelled particularly at the female sex: but who drew the picture, in which the lion was injuriously represented?

8. Edward Gibbon (1737–1794) was author of *The History of the Decline and Fall of the Roman Empire* (1776).

d. 8. Gibbon. 62

9. Thus eight husbands are made in the space of five autumns.

10. They compute their years not by the number of consuls, but by the number of their husbands.

Cicero, after having said, as we have seen, "prima societas in ipso conjugio est," adds, "proxima in liberis."[11] I consider, in the next place, the relation of parent and child.

The transition is, indeed, a natural one. The sentiments of parental affection are generally warm and tender, in proportion to those of conjugal love. The sentiments of filial duty are generally sincere and respectful, in proportion to those of parental affection.

It is the duty of parents to maintain their children decently, and according to their circumstances; to protect them according to the dictates of prudence; and to educate them according to the suggestions of a judicious and zealous regard for their usefulness, their respectability, and their happiness.

The formidable power of a Roman father is unknown to the common law. But it vests in the parent such authority as is conducive to the advantage of the child. When it is necessary—and a real necessity exists much more rarely than is often imagined—a moderate chastening may be administered; but every milder means should be previously used. Part of his authority he may delegate to the person intrusted with his child's education:[e] that person acts then in the place, and he ought to act with the disposition, of a parent. The legal power of a father ceases, when the child attains the age of twenty one years.

But,—for we now turn to the duties of children—as obedience and subjection to their parents are due from them during their minority; honour and reverence are naturally and justly expected from them ever afterwards. If it become necessary, the child should, according to his circumstances, maintain the parent: 'tis but a natural and grateful return for the maintenance, which the parent has given to the child.

The decent reserve which the common law has shown, with regard to the relation between parent and child, should be admired, and may be accounted for on the same principles, which were observed under the relation of husband and wife. The civil law interposed in the nice feelings and tender transactions of both relations, with a rude and indelicate management. In that law, we find an enumeration of fourteen different reasons,

11. The first bond of society is marriage, the next, our children.
e. 1. Bl. Com. 453.

for which a father may disinherit his child. Would it not have been much more natural, to have left, as the common law has left, this subject to the decision of that judge, which holds its tribunal in every parent's breast?

But, here as on former occasions, I refer the questions of property—and there are very important ones—arising from this relation, to the full discussion, which will be given under the second division of my system.

A bastard is one who is born out of lawful marriage. By law, he is considered *quasi nullius filius*.[12] But surely it is the natural duty of his parents to maintain, to protect, and to educate him.

The rules which govern the relation between a father and his child, govern, but in an inferiour degree, and for a shorter time, that relation, which is substituted in the place of the other, between a guardian and his ward. On this subject, therefore, it will not be necessary to descend into particulars.

I come now to examine the relation between a master and his servants.

Slavery, or an absolute and unlimited power, in the master, over the life and fortune of the slave, is unauthorized by the common law. Indeed, it is repugnant to the principles of natural law, that such a state should subsist in any social system. The reasons, which we sometimes see assigned for the origin and the continuance of slavery, appear, when examined to the bottom, to be built upon a false foundation. In the enjoyment of their persons and of their property, the common law protects all. With regard, however, to any right, which one man may have acquired to the personal service of another, the case is very different. This right the common law will support.[f] He, to whose service this right is acquired, is only in the same state of subjection, to which every servant and apprentice is obliged, and finds it his interest, to submit.

The contract between a master and a servant arises upon the hiring. If a servant is retained generally, without expressing any limited time, the law will construe it to be for a year:[g] the reasonable foundation of this rule is, that, through the revolutions of the seasons, equality shall be preserved in the contract; that the master shall not have it in his power to dismiss the

12. As if no offspring.

f. 1. Bl. Com. 423. 425.

g. 1. Ins. 42. b.

servant when there is little work to be done; nor the servant have it in his power to depart when there is much. The contract, however, may be made for any term longer or shorter than a year.[h] If, during the term of the contract, the servant become sick, this is a condition incident to humanity. In his sickness, the master is bound to take care of him, and provide for him; nor can a deduction of wages be made for the time, during which he is detained from service.[i]

If a servant marry, the marriage dissolves not the contract to serve:[k] if, without any reasonable cause, he depart from his service, within the term, for which he is retained; he can recover no wages.[l] A contract for service is, on both sides, personal, and is discharged by the death of either of the parties.[m] This is the rule at the common law.

A master, we are told, may justify an assault in defence of his servant; and a servant, in defence of his master; the former, because he has an interest in the service of the latter; the latter, because the defence of the former is considered as part of the consideration, for which wages are stipulated and received.[n] The law is unquestionably so as is here stated: the reasons assigned for it, I am inclined to believe, are founded on principles much too narrow. The defence of one's own person is a part of the law of self preservation. The defence of the person of another is, I think, a part of the law of humanity. This point, however, which is of a very general importance to the peace and security of society, will merit an investigation in another place.

The common law, retaining the refined delicacy which we have observed oftener than once, will not, without strong necessity, inspect or interpose in the interiour government of a family. That sufficient authority, however, may exist to preserve order in the domestick department—a department of mighty moment to human happiness—the law invests the master with a power to correct, but moderately, his servant or apprentice, for negligence or for other misbehaviour. We have seen that "sine imperio, nulla domus

h. 1. Bl. Com. 425.
i. 2. Burr. 948.
k. F. N. B. 168.
l. Wood. Ins. 51.
m. Str. 1267. Wood. Ins. 51.
n. 1. Bl. Com. 429.

stare potest."[o13] Besides; in the regulation which the law has drawn concerning an atrocious outrage, in which she found it necessary to interpose, she has with a pencil exquisitely fine, but whose strokes can be traced by a discerning eye, marked a line of general direction for the relative rights and duties of a master and servant. From the latter to the former, she expressly requires a species, though an inferiour species, of allegiance: from the former to the latter, she, by a necessary consequence, strongly inculcates a species, though an inferiour species, of protection. These remarks will receive illustration, when the crime of petty treason shall come under our view.

Apprentices are a species of servants. They are usually bound for a term of years, to serve and to be instructed by their masters in their profession or trade.

Persons under the age of twenty one years cannot, by the common law, bind themselves apprentices, in such a manner as to become liable to an action for departing from their service, or for other breaches of their indentures. For this reason, it is necessary that the parent, guardian, or some friend of the apprentice be bound for the faithful discharge of his duty.[p] But it is not every minor, who has such connexions, willing to be bound for him.

By the custom of London, an infant, unmarried and above the age of fourteen years, may bind himself apprentice to a freeman of London; and the covenants in the indenture of apprenticeship shall be as valid, as if the apprentice had been of full age.[q] The spirit of this custom has been adopted and enlarged by the legislature of Pennsylvania. A minor, bound an apprentice with the assent of the parent, the guardian, or the next friend, or with the assent of the overseers of the poor, and approbation of any two justices, is bound as fully as if of age at the time of making the indentures. But an apprenticeship under this very excellent law must expire, in the case of a male, at twenty one, in the case of a female, at eighteen years of age.[r]

To qualify one for the skilful and successful exercise of a trade or profession, an apprenticeship is certainly useful; but, by the common law, it is not necessary. It was resolved, as we are informed in one of the reports

o. Cic. de leg. l. 3.

13. Without the power to command, no house is able to stand.

p. S. Bac. 547.

q. Id. 347.

r. 1. Laws Penn. 540, s. 1.

of my Lord Coke, that, at the common law, no man can be prohibited from exercising his industry in any lawful occupation; for the law hates idleness, the mother of all evil, and especially in young men, who, in their youth, which is their seed time, ought to learn lawful trades and sciences, which are profitable to the commonwealth, and of which they themselves may reap the harvest in their future years. Besides; the common law abhors all monopolies, which forbid any from working in any lawful trade. If he who undertakes to work is unskilful, his ignorance is his sufficient punishment; for "quilibet quaerit in qualibet arte peritos;"[14] and if, in performing his work, he injures his employer, the law has provided an action to recover damages for the injury done.[s] To every monopoly, we are told by the same book in another place,[t] there are three inseparable incidents against the commonwealth. 1. The price of the commodity is raised. 2. The quality of the commodity is debased. 3. Those who formerly maintained themselves and their families by the same profession or trade, are impoverished, and reduced to a state of beggary and idleness.

Besides apprentices, and those to whom the name of servant is appropriated in the language of common life, the relation of servant is extended, by the language and by many of the rules of the law, to others in a superiour ministerial capacity—to bailiffs, to stewards, to agents, to factors, to attornies, and to the masters of vessels considered in their relation to the owners of them.[u]

Of many acts of the servant, the master is entitled to receive the advantage: of many others, he is obliged to suffer or to compensate for the injury. In each series of cases—it would be, here, improper to attempt an enumeration of particulars—In each series of cases, the principle is the same. Whatever is done by the servant, in the usual course of his business, is presumed, and fairly presumed, to be done by the command, or the authority, tacit or express, of the master; whatever is done by the master's command, is considered, and justly considered, as done by the master in person: "Qui facit per alium, facit per se."[15]

14. Experts are sought in my occupation.

s. 11. Rep. 53. b. 54.

t. Id. 86. b.

u. 3. Bac. 544.

15. He who acts through another, acts by or for himself.

Thus much concerning the relation between master and servant: and thus much concerning the component parts of that important and respectable, though small and sometimes neglected establishment, which is denominated a family. "Id autem est"—says Cicero,[v] in the fine and just passage already cited oftener than once—"id autem est principium urbis, et quasi seminarium reipublicae."[16] It is the principle of the community; it is that seminary, on which the commonwealth, for its manners as well as for its numbers, must ultimately depend. As its establishment is the source, so its happiness is the end, of every institution of government, which is wise and good.

In the introduction to my lectures[w] I told my hearers, that "publick law and publick government were not made for themselves;" but that "they were made for something better;" that "I meant society;" that "I meant particularly domestick society." Perhaps, it was then thought, by some, that all this was introduced merely for the sake of an encomium—but, by the way, an encomium severely just—with which it was accompanied. In the regular course of my system, the sentiment has now undergone a scrutinizing analysis in the most minute detail. I can appeal to such, if any such, who thought otherwise then—I can appeal to all, who have formed their opinion now, whether the sentiment, in all its parts, and in all its objects too, is not founded in sound politicks and genuine philosophy.

In digesting a system of English law a little more than a century ago, it would have been necessary to notice and explain another domestick relation—not, indeed, founded in nature—that of lord and villain. Of the feudal city, however, we can still recollect the exteriour battlements and towers, cumbrous, but disproportioned and insecure, and the interiour buildings and halls, spacious, but comfortless and inconvenient. In ruins it now lies. With sentiments very different from those of regret, we can exclaim over it—*fuit servitus.*[x17]

v. De Off. l. 1. c. 17.

16. Moreover it is the beginning of the city, and the nursery, as it were, of the commonwealth.

w. Vol. 1. p. 452.

x. Fuit Ilium.

17. Slavery is a thing of the past.

I have now done with considering the peculiar relations of man in a state of society, independent of civil government. But in that state, as he bears peculiar relations to some, so he bears a general relation to all. From that general relation, rights and duties result. His rights are, to receive the fulfilment of the engagements which are made to him, and to be free from injury to his peculiar relations, to his property, to his character, to his liberty, to his person. His duties are, to fulfil the engagements, which he has made; and to do no injury, in the same extensive meaning, in which he would wish and has a right to suffer none.

In a former lecture,[y] when I delineated at large the principles and the character of the social man, these rights and duties received their illustration, and were shown to be laid deeply in the human frame. To your recollection of what was then said, I beg leave to refer you. These rights and duties are indeed, as has been observed, great pillars on which chiefly rest the criminal and the civil codes of the municipal law. It would surely be preposterous to undermine their foundation, with a view to give strength or stability to what they support—to unfix what rests on the immovable basis of nature, and to place it on the tottering institutions of man.

I here close my examination into those natural rights, which, in my humble opinion, it is the business of civil government to protect, and not to subvert, and the exercise of which it is the duty of civil government to enlarge, and not to restrain. I go farther; and now proceed to show, that in peculiar instances, in which those rights can receive neither protection nor reparation from civil government, they are, notwithstanding its institution, entitled still to that defence, and to those methods of recovery, which are justified and demanded in a state of nature.

The defence of one's self, justly called the primary law of nature,[z] is not, nor can it be abrogated by any regulation of municipal law.[a] This principle

y. Vol. 1. p. 627. 628.

z. Est igitur, judices, haec non scripta, sed nata lex; quam non dedicimus, accepimus, legimus; verum ex natura ipsa arripuimus, hausimus, expressimus; ad quam non docti, sed facti, non instituti, sed imbuti sumus; ut si vita nostra in aliquas insidias, si in vim, si in tela aut latronum aut inimicorum incidisset, omnis honesta ratio esset expediendae salutis: silent enim leges inter arma; nec se expectari jubent, cum ei qui expectare velit. ante injusta poena luenda sit, quam justa repetenda.[18] Cic. pro Mil.

a. 3. Bl. Com. 4.

18. There exists, Judges, this law which is not written, but inborn; we have not learned it, received it, or read it, but from nature herself we have snatched, imbibed, and extorted it; a law to which we are not trained, but in which we are made; in which we are not instructed, but

of defence is not confined merely to the person; it extends to the liberty and the property of a man: it is not confined merely to his own person; it extends to the persons of all those, to whom he bears a peculiar relation—of his wife, of his parent, of his child, of his master, of his servant:[b] nay, it extends to the person of every one, who is in danger;[c] perhaps, to the liberty of every one, whose liberty is unjustly and forcibly attacked. It becomes humanity as well as justice.

The particular occasions on which the defensive principle may be exercised, and the degrees to which the exercise of it may be carried, will appear in subsequent parts of my lectures: for instead of being disavowed, it is expressly recognised by our municipal institutions.

As a man is justified in defending, so he is justified in retaking, his property, or his peculiar relations, when from him they are unjustly taken and detained. When and how this recaption may be made, will also appear in the proper places. For this redress, dictated by nature, is also recognised by municipal law.

Under the same description, the right of abating or removing nuisances may, in many instances, be classed.

This long investigation concerning natural rights and natural remedies, I conclude by answering the question, with which I introduced it: man does not exist for the sake of government, but government is instituted for the sake of man. The course of it has naturally led me to consider a number of interesting subjects, in a view somewhat different, perhaps, from that, in which we see them considered in some of our law books; but in a view perfectly consonant to the soundest rules and principles of our law.

THE END OF THE SECOND VOLUME.

---

with which we are imbued; the law, namely, that whenever our life falls into some ambush, is attacked, or is set upon by brigands or enemies, there is every honest reason for saving one's self: for amid arms the laws are silent, and they do not order a man to wait around, since he who will wait must suffer an unjust penalty before he obtains a just retribution.

b. Id. 3.

c. 1. Haw. 131.

PART 3.

Lectures on Law.

CHAPTER I.

Of the Nature of Crimes; and the Necessity and Proportion of Punishments.

Hitherto, we have considered the rights of men, of citizens, of publick officers, and of publick bodies: we must now turn our eyes to objects less pleasing—the violations of those rights must be brought under our view. Man is sometimes unjust: sometimes he is even criminal: injuries and crimes must, therefore, find their place in every legal system, calculated for man. One consolatory reflection, however, will greatly support us in our progress through this uninviting part of our journey: we shall be richly compensated when we reach its conclusion. The end of criminal jurisprudence is the *prevention* of crimes.

What is an injury?—What is a crime?—What is reparation?—What is punishment?—These are questions, which ought to be considered in a separate, and also in a connected, point of view. At some times, they have been too much blended. In some instances, the injury and the reparation have been lost in the crime and the punishment. In other instances, the crime and the punishment have, with equal impropriety, been sunk in the reparation and injury. At other times, they have been kept too much apart. The crime has been considered as altogether unconnected with the injury, and the punishment as altogether unconnected with reparation. In other instances, the reparation only has been regarded, and no attention has been given to the punishment: the injury only has been calculated; but no computation has been made concerning the crime.

An injury is a loss arising to an individual, from the violation or infringement of his right.

A reparation is that, which compensates for the loss sustained by an injury.

A crime is an injury, so atrocious in its nature, or so dangerous in its example, that, besides the loss which it occasions to the individual who suffers by it, it affects, in its immediate operation or in its consequences, the interest, the peace, the dignity, or the security of the publick. Offences and misdemeanors denote inferiour crimes.

A punishment is the infliction of that evil, superadded to the reparation, which the crime, superadded to the injury, renders necessary, for the purposes of a wise and good administration of government.

Concerning an injury and a reparation, and the measures by which each of them ought to be estimated, it will not be necessary to say much; because, with regard to them, much confusion or mistake has not been introduced into the theory or practice of the law.

Concerning crimes and punishments, and concerning the relation between a crime and an injury, and between punishment and reparation, the case is widely different indeed. On those subjects, an endless confusion has prevailed, and mistakes innumerable have been committed. On those subjects, therefore, it will be proper to be full; and it will certainly be attempted—I promise not success in the attempt—to be both accurate and perspicuous.

From an inattention or a disregard to the great principle—that government was made for the sake of man, some writers have been led to consider crimes, in their origin and nature as well as in their degrees and effects, as different from injuries; and have, consequently, taught, that without any injury to an individual, a crime might be committed against the government. Suppose, says one of the learned commentators on Grotius, that one has done neither wrong nor injury to any individual, yet if he has committed something which the law has prohibited, it is a crime, which demands reparation; because the right of the superiour is violated, and because an injury is offered to the dignity of his character.[a] How naturally one mistake leads to another! A mistake in legislation produces one in criminal jurisprudence. A law which prohibits what is neither a wrong nor an injury to any one! What name does it deserve? We have seen[b] that a law which

a. 2. War. Bib. 15.
b. Ante. vol. 2. p. 1045.

is merely harmless without being tyrannical, is itself a harm; and should be removed.

But this doctrine is unsupported by sound legal principle. Every crime includes an injury: every offence is also a private wrong: it affects the publick, but it affects the individual likewise. It is true indeed, that, in very gross injuries, we seldom hear of any satisfaction being awarded to the individual, for reasons, the propriety of which will, by and by, be examined. But in offences of an inferiour nature, the distinction, and, at the same time, the connexion between the crime and the injury is most accurately marked and preserved. For a battery, he who commits it may be indicted. Violence against the person of an individual is a disturbance of the publick peace. On this disturbance punishment may be inflicted. But in the crime and the punishment, the injury is not sunk, nor is the reparation lost. The party who has suffered the violence may bring his action against the party who has committed it: and recover in damages a satisfaction for the loss which has been sustained.

The doctrine, that a crime may be committed against the publick, without any injury being done to an individual, is as little consonant to the history, as it is to the principles of criminal jurisprudence. Among the Saxons, as we are informed by Mr. Selden, the most ancient way of proceeding, in criminal causes, was by an appeal of the party complaining. But afterwards, in cases which concerned damage, injury, or violence done to the body of a man or to his estate, the king—who represented the publick—was found to be therein prejudiced, beside the prejudice done immediately to the subject: and upon this ground, a way was found out to punish the offender by indictment, beside the satisfaction done to the party wronged.[c]

In the very early periods of society, those actions, even the most atrocious, which now are viewed and prosecuted as solely crimes against the state, were considered and resented merely as private injuries. In those ages, the conceptions of men were too crude to consider an injury done to an individual, as a crime committed against the publick; they viewed it only as a prejudice to the party, or the relations of the party, who were immediately affected. The privilege of resenting private injuries, in the

c. Bac. on Gov. 53.

opinion of a very ingenious writer on the history of the criminal law,[d] was that private right which was the latest of being surrendered to society. An improvement in government, so opposite to a strong propensity of human nature, could not have been instantaneous. The progressive steps leading to its completion were slow and almost imperceptible.

Coincident, in a very considerable degree, with these sentiments and observations, is a part of the law and practice of England, which at this moment subsists in its full force—I mean the law and practice concerning appeals, particularly appeals of death. An appeal is the party's private action, seeking satisfaction for the injury done him; and at the same time, prosecuting for the crown in respect of the offence against the publick. On an appeal, the benign prerogative of mercy cannot be exercised; because, saith the law,[e] the plaintiff has an interest in the judgment. This interest, however, may be released; and the release will be a bar to the proceedings on an appeal.

These observations, drawn from so many separate sources, combine in the result, that a crime against the publick has its foundation in an injury against an individual. We shall see, in the progress of our investigation, that as, in the rude ages of society, the crime was too much overlooked; so, in times more refined, there has been a disposition, too strong, to overlook the injury.

Concerning the standard, by which crimes should be measured in municipal law, there has been much diversity of sentiment among writers, even the wisest and most enlightened. The law of nature, it is admitted on all hands, measures crimes by the intention, and not by the event. Should a standard, different from that which has been established by unerring wisdom, be adopted by uninformed man? Should not that rule, which is observed by the law divine, be observed, in humble imitation, by laws which are human? It is said, not; and it is said, that this difference must be accounted for by those peculiar attributes of the divine nature, which distinguish the dispensations of supreme wisdom from the proceedings of human tribunals. A being whose all-seeing eye observes the inmost recesses of the heart, and whose outstretched arm no flight or stratagem can

d. Kaims. Hist. L. Tr. 19, 20.
e. 5. Rep. 506.

elude or escape—such a being may consider and may punish every crime in exact proportion to the quantity of intrinsick guilt, which is contained in it. But with those to whom the trust and authority of human government is committed, the case is greatly different. Their power and their knowledge are limited by many imperfections: speed may remove, artifice may cover the object of punishment from their view or their grasp: by them, therefore, crimes must be considered in proportion to the ease and security with which they are committed or concealed, and not in strict proportion to their degrees of inherent criminality. Such, or nearly such, seem to be the sentiments of Mr. Paley.[f]

The Marquis of Beccaria goes farther: he thinks himself authorized to assert, that crimes are to be measured only by the injury done to society. They err, therefore, says he, who imagine that a crime is greater or less according to the intention of the person by whom it is committed; for this will depend on the actual impression of objects on the senses, and on the previous disposition of the mind; and both of these will vary in different persons, and even in the same person at different times, according to the succession of ideas, passions, and circumstances. Upon that system, it would be necessary to form, not only a particular code for every individual, but a new penal law for every crime. Men with the best intentions, do the greatest injury, and with the worst, the most essential services to society. That crimes are to be estimated by the injury done to society, adds he, is one of those palpable truths, which, though evident to the meanest capacity, yet, by a combination of circumstances, are known only to a few thinking men, in every nation and in every age.[g]

Sir William Blackstone, in one part of his Commentaries, seems to adopt these sentiments. All crimes, says he, are to be estimated according to the mischiefs which they produce in civil society.[h]

Mr. Eden,[1] in one part of his book on the principles of penal law, tells us, agreeably to the same sentiments, that crimes are of temporal creation, and to be estimated in proportion to their pernicious effects on

f. 2. Paley, 291. 292.

g. Bac. c. 7. 8.

h. 4. Bl. Com. 41.

1. The first Baron Auckland, Sir William Eden (1745–1814), wrote *Principles of Penal Law* (1771).

society:[i] in another part, he says, that, in some cases, it is necessary to punish the offence without any research into its motive; and that, in every case, it is impracticable for lawgivers to assume the divine attribute of animadverting upon the fact, only according to the internal malice of the intention:[j] in a third place, however, he expresses himself in the following manner: "It is true, that crimes are to be estimated, in some degree, by the actual mischief done to society; because the internal malignity of mankind is not within the cognizance of human tribunals. But if this position were received in its fullest latitude, it would prove too much; it would prove that every act of homicide is equally criminal; and that the intention is, in no case, to be considered:"[k] in a fourth place, he considers its flagitiousness as the standard, by which a crime should be measured; and informs us, that, by its flagitiousness, he means its abstract nature and turpitude, in proportion to which, the criminal should be considered as more or less dangerous to society:[l] in a fifth place, he intimates the same sentiment, that "the malignity of the fact is the true measure of the crime."[m]

Is it not shocking to reason, says Mr. Dagge,[2] and destructive of virtue, to contend, that the ill consequence of an act is more to be considered than its immorality? To disregard a crime, however heinous, because it may be supposed not to have a bad effect on society; and to punish slight offences severely, because they tend more immediately to disturb the publick peace, is to sacrifice moral equity to political expediency. But, in fact, there is no real necessity for making such a sacrifice. If we would effectually provide for the lasting peace of society, we should first regard private offences, which are the sources of publick crimes. The subtle distinctions, which casuists make between moral and political delinquencies, are offensive to common sense.[n]

Concerning the standard by which punishments should be measured in municipal law, there has been, as might be expected, as much diversity of sentiment, as concerning the standard for the measure of crimes.

i. Eden. 89.
j. Id. 12.
k. Eden. 12.
l. Id. 8.
m. Id. 10.
2. Henry Dagge wrote *Considerations on Criminal Law* about 1772.
n. 1. Dag. 335. 343.

Publick utility, says Mr. Eden, is the measure of human punishments; and that utility is proportioned to the efficacy of the example.[o]

Liberty, says Montesquieu,[p] is in its highest perfection, when criminal laws derive each punishment from the particular nature of the crime. Then the punishment does not flow from the capriciousness of the legislator, but from the very nature of the thing; and man uses no violence to man.

Among crimes of different natures, says Sir William Blackstone, those should be most severely punished, which are most destructive to the publick safety and happiness: and, among crimes of an equal malignity, those, which a man has the most frequent and easy opportunities of committing, which cannot be so easily guarded against as others; and which, therefore, the offender has the greatest inducement to commit.[q]

Much to the same purpose are the expressions of Mr. Paley—the punishment should be in a proportion compounded of the mischief of the crime, and the ease with which it is executed.[r]

The end of human punishment, says Mr. Paley, in another place, should regulate the measure of its severity.[s] To the propriety of this rule every one will subscribe; but it throws us back upon another, concerning which there is an equal variety and opposition of sentiment.

Criminals, says Plato in his book concerning laws, are punished, not because they have offended, for what is done can never be undone, but that they may not offend.[t]

The very learned Mr. Selden objects to this doctrine, and says, that the antecedent crime is the essence of punishment.[u]

The amendment of the criminal is assigned by some as the end of punishment. To put it out of his power to do future mischief, is the end proposed by others. To deter from the imitation of his example, is that proposed by a third class of writers. Reparation to the injured, is an end recommended by a fourth class.

o. Eden. 151.
p. Sp. L. b. 12. c. 4.
q. 4. Bl. Com. 16.
r. 2. Paley. 290.
s. Id. 287.
t. 1. Dag. 203. Eden. 6.
u. 1. Dag. 203.

Almost all agree, that between crimes and punishments there ought to be a proportion: but how can this proportion be fixed among those, who are so much at variance with regard to the measure of the objects, between which it confessedly ought to subsist.

If there is so much diversity and contrariety of opinion respecting the principles, how much greater diversity and contrariety of conduct may we expect to find with regard to the execution, of the criminal law. Nay, how often shall we find those rules violated in its practice, the propriety of which is agreed in its theory.

The theory of criminal law has not, till lately, been a subject of much attention or investigation. The Marquis of Beccaria led the way. His performance derives much importance from the sentiments and principles, which it contains: it derives, perhaps, more from those, which its appearance has excited in others. It induced several of the most celebrated literati in Europe to think upon the subject. The science, however, is, as yet, but in a weak and infantine state. To convince you that it is so, I need only refer you to the unsatisfactory, nay, the contradictory sentiments, of which I have given you an account, with regard to the two great heads of crimes and punishments. That account has been extracted from the most celebrated writers on the subject—from writers, indeed, who, on any subject, would deserve celebrity.

To give you a history of the practice of criminal law would be a task, not difficult, because the materials are very copious; but it would be very disgusting both to you and to me. I draw the character of this practice from one, who appears to have a head and a heart well qualified to feel and to judge upon the subject—I mean the Author of the principles of penal law. "The perusal of the first volume of the English State Trials,"[v] says he, "is a most disgustful drudgery." "The proceedings of our criminal courts at this era"—meaning that which preceded the revolution—"are so disgraceful, not only to the nation, but to human nature, that, as they cannot be disbelieved, I wish them to be buried in oblivion. From oblivion, it is neither my duty nor inclination to rescue them."—No; nor to rescue from oblivion the proceedings of other ages and of other countries, equally disgraceful and disgustful. I recite only a single instance.

v. Eden. 199.

Mr. Pope, in his picturesque and interesting retrospect of the barbarous reigns of the Conqueror and his son, asks, alluding to the laws of the forests—

What wonder then, if beast or subject slain
Were equal crimes in a despotick reign?
Both, doom'd alike, for sportive tyrants bled,
But while the subject starv'd, the beast was fed.[w]

Many, I dare say, have considered this as a fine fanciful description of the Poet. It has, however, been exceeded by the strict severity of fact. We are, in the Life of Mr. Turgot,[3] told in plain and sober prose, that so rigorous were the forest laws of France even so lately, that a peasant, charged with having killed a wild boar, alleged as an alleviation of the charge, that he thought it was a man.[x]

In these lectures, I have had frequent occasion to observe and to regret the imperfection and the impropriety, which are seen too plainly in the civil codes and institutions of Europe: it is the remark—it is the just remark of Sir William Blackstone, that, "in every country of Europe, the criminal law is more rude and imperfect than the civil."[y] Instead of being, as it ought to be, an emanation from the law of nature and morality; it has too often been avowedly and systematically the reverse. It has been a combination of the strong against the weak, of the rich against the poor, of pride and interest against justice and humanity. Unfortunate, indeed, it is, that this has been the case; for we may truly say, that on the excellence of the criminal law, the liberty and the happiness of the people chiefly depend.

By this time, you see very clearly, that I was well warranted to announce, even in the summary of my system, that the criminal law greatly needs reformation. I added—In the United States, the seeds of reformation are sown. Those seeds, and the tender plants which from some of them are now beginning to spring, let it be our care to discover and to cultivate.

w. Windsor Forest.

3. Anne Robert Jacques Turgot, Baron de l'Aune (1727–1781), was a French statesman and economist.

x. Pri. Lect. 297.

y. 4. Bl. Com. 3.

From those weeds, luxuriant and strong, with which they are still intermingled, and by which, if they continue so, they will indubitably be choked, let it be our business industriously to separate them. From those beasts of the forest, by whom, if left unguarded, they will unquestionably be devoured, let it be our effort vigorously to defend them.

In the fields of the common law, which, for ages past, have lain waste and neglected, some of those seeds and plants will, on an accurate inquiry, be found. In the gardens of the American constitutions, others, and the most choice of them, have been sown and planted by liberal hands.

The generical term used immemorially by the common law, to denote a crime, is *felony*. True indeed it is, that the idea of felony is now very generally and very strongly connected with capital punishment; so generally and so strongly, that if an act of parliament denominates any new offence a felony, the legal inference drawn from it is, that the offender shall be punished for it capitally. But this inference, whatever legal authority it may now have acquired, is by no means entitled to the merit of critical accuracy. At this moment, every felony does not, in England, receive a punishment which is capital: petit larceny is a felony. At this moment, one felony escapes in England, as it must in all other countries, every degree of punishment that is human: suicide is a felony. At the common law, few felonies, indeed, were punished with death.

Treason is now considered, both in legal and in vernacular language, as a species of crime distinct from that of felony; but originally it was not so considered. "In ancient time," says my Lord Coke,[z] "every treason was comprehended under the name of felony." Indeed it was so, down even to the time of Edward the third; for the famous statute of treasons, made in his reign, uses these expressions—"treason or *other* felony."

It will be very important to ascertain the true meaning of a term, employed so extensively and so long by the common law, to convey the idea of a crime.

In order to ascertain the true meaning, it is frequently of importance to ascertain the true etymology, of a term; and in order to ascertain that of the term *felony*, much learned labour has been bestowed by juridical lexicographers and criticks.

z. 3. Ins. 15.

Sir William Blackstone asserts that its original is undoubtedly feudal; and being so, we ought to look for its derivation in the Teutonick or German language; and he prefers that given by Sir Henry Spelman; according to whom, *felon* is taken from two northern words, *fee,* which signifies, as all know, the fief, feud, or beneficiary estate; and *lon,* which signifies price or value. Felony is, therefore, the same as *pretium feudi,* the consideration, for which a man gives up his fief; as we say, in common speech, such an act is as much as your life or estate is worth. "In this sense," says Sir William, "it will clearly signify the feudal forfeiture, or act, by which an estate is forfeited or escheats to the lord."[a] He mentions two other derivations, and adds—"Sir Edward Coke, as his manner is, has given us a still stranger etymology; that it is, 'crimen animo *fellco* perpetratum,'[4] with a bitter or gallish inclination."[b]

The authority of Sir Henry Spelman, in matters of legal antiquity, is unquestionably respectable: it is unfortunate, on this as on many other occasions, that his Glossary, the work here cited, is not in my power; and, therefore, I cannot examine particularly what he says upon the subject.

Serjeant Hawkins,[5] so noted for his painful accuracy and his guarded caution, cites, in his treatise of the pleas of the crown, both the places which are cited by the Author of the Commentaries. The Serjeant had probably examined both: he follows the description of my Lord Coke. From this, I infer one of the two things—that Mr. Hawkins either found something in the Glossary, which prevented his assent to the conclusion drawn from it, or preferred the authority of my Lord Coke to that of Sir Henry Spelman. Thus, on one side we find Sir Henry Spelman and Sir William Blackstone; on the other, my Lord Coke and Serjeant Hawkins. In each scale of authority the weight is great; but, in both, it is equal: the beam of decision inclines at neither end.

If an estate could be purchased, instead of being forfeited, by a felony, I can easily conceive how the crime might be viewed as the consideration of the purchase: if a fee signified a crime, instead of signifying a fief, I can easily conceive how the estate might be viewed as the value forfeited by

a. 4. Bl. Com. 95. 96.

4. A crime committed with malicious or evil intent.

b. 4. Bl. Com. 95. 1. Ins. 391 a.

5. William Hawkins (1673–1746) wrote *A Treatise of the Pleas of the Crown* (1716).

its commission. But the "pretium feudi,"[6] applied in the manner and arrangement in which the application is made here, appears, in my humble conception, to be etymology inverted. Thus stand the propriety and the authority of the derivation adopted by the Author of the Commentaries.

My Lord Coke, when he refers the meaning and the description of felony to the motive, and not to the event, to the disposition which produced it, and not to the forfeiture which it incurs, cites, in the margin, the authority of Glanville, the oldest book now extant in law, and two very ancient statutes; one made in the reign of Henry the third; the other in that of his son, Edward the first. With regard to Glanville, there must be some numerical mistake in the margin; for it refers us to the fifteenth chapter of the fourteenth book: in that book, there are only eight chapters. The statutes I have examined: you shall judge whether they support that meaning of felony, for the truth of which they are cited.

The first is the twenty fifth chapter of the statute of Marlbridge,[7] which was made in the fifty second year of Henry the third. It is very short. "In future, it shall not, by our justices, be adjudged murder, where it is found misfortune only; but it shall take place as to such as are slain by felony—interfectis per feloniam—and not otherwise." Felony is here put most obviously in a contrasted opposition to misfortune; intention to accident. But what is peculiarly unfortunate for the etymology of Sir William Blackstone, a forfeiture was incurred at that time, and, according to the reprehensible theory retained in England for the sake of fees and not for the sake of justice, a forfeiture is still incurred, where a homicide happens by misfortune,[c] as well as where it is committed feloniously. If felony, therefore, "signifies clearly," as he says, "such a crime as works a forfeiture of the offender's lands or goods," the distinction mentioned in the statute would be absurd and ridiculous; referring felony to the principle, and not to the consequences of the fact, the provision in the statute is just and humane.

The other statute cited by my Lord Coke is the sixteenth chapter of Westminster the first, made in the third year of the first Edward. It distinguishes between those criminals who may be bailed, and those who ought

c. 4. Bl. Com. 188.

6. The price of a fief or fee.

7. The Statute of Marlbridge (or Marlborough) is the oldest British law never to have been repealed. King Henry III of England passed the law in 1267.

not to be bailed. In the latter class are ranked those, who are taken for house burning *feloniously* done—"felonieusement fait."—Does this direct our view to the punishment, or to the intention?

But I am able to produce instances still more ancient and still more strong. The Mirrour of Justices, as has been mentioned oftener than once, contains a collection of the law, chiefly as it stood before the conquest; and consequently before the feudal system was introduced into England. In that collection there is a chapter concerning incendiaries: they are thus described—Incendiaries are those who burn a city, a town, a house, a man, a beast or other chattels *of their felony*—"de leur felony,"—in time of peace for hatred or vengeance. Do the words *of their felony* describe that principle, which gives the 'crime its "body and its form?" or do they relate to a feudal forfeiture, then unknown?

But to put the matter in a light still more striking and clear: in the next sentence, a case is supposed, in which the intention existed, the fact was committed; but the effect did not take place; and, consequently, the punishment was not to be inflicted: yet the action is said to be done feloniously. "If one puts fire to a man *feloniously*—felonieusement—so that he is scorched or hurt, but not killed by the fire; it is not a capital crime."[d]

I suggest another argument, the legal force of which will, by every professional gentleman, be seen immediately to be irresistible. In every indictment for felony, the fact charged must be laid to have been done feloniously. To express this meaning, no other term in our language is legally adequate.[e] The antiquity of indictments, and the high authority of their essential forms, I pretend not to ascertain or to circumscribe.

But Sir William Blackstone, in this passage, is opposed not only by principle, by precedent, and by other authority; he is, I think, clearly opposed by his own. He says here, as we have seen, that felony clearly signifies the feudal forfeiture, or act, by which an estate is *forfeited, or escheats* to the lord. And yet, in another place,[f] he recommends great care in distinguishing between escheat to the lord, and forfeiture to the king; and traces them very properly to different sources. "Forfeiture of lands," says

d. 4. Cou. Ang. Nor. 504.
e. 1. Haw. 65.
f. 2. Bl. Com. 251. 252.

he, "and of whatever else the offender possessed, was the doctrine of the old Saxon law, as a part of the punishment for the offence; and does not at all relate to the feudal system, nor is the consequence of any signiory or lordship paramount; but being a prerogative vested in the crown, was neither superseded nor diminished by the introduction of the Norman tenures; a fruit and consequence of which escheat must undoubtedly be reckoned. Escheat, therefore, operates in subordination to the more ancient and superiour law of forfeiture.

"The doctrine of escheat upon attainder, taken singly, is this, that the blood of the tenant, by the commission of any felony (under which denomination all treasons were formerly comprised) is corrupted and stained, and the original donation of the feud is thereby determined, it being always granted to the vassal on the implied condition of *dum bene se gesscrit.*[8] Upon the thorough demonstration of which guilt by legal attainder, the feudal covenant and mutual bond of fealty are held to be broken, the estate instantly falls back from the offender to the lord of the fee, and the inheritable quality of his blood is extinguished and blotted out for ever. In this situation the law of feudal escheat was brought into England at the conquest, and in general superadded to the ancient law of forfeiture. In consequence of which corruption and extinction of hereditary blood, the land of all felons would immediately revest in the lord, but that the superiour law of forfeiture intervenes, and intercepts it in its passage; in case of treason for ever; in case of other felony, for only a year and a day; after which time, it goes to the lord in a regular course of escheat, as it would have done to the heir of the felon, in case the feudal tenures had never been introduced. And that this is the true operation and genuine history of escheats, will most evidently appear from this incident to gavelkind lands (which seem to be the old Saxon tenure) that they are in no case subject to escheat for felony, though they are liable to forfeiture for treason."

Instead, therefore, of considering felony as a feudal forfeiture or escheat, we are here taught, and properly taught, to view them as flowing from different sources, and, in their operations, not only distinct, but incompatible.

8. As long as he should well behave himself—during good behavior.

Having thus traced the true meaning of felony, not to the event or part of the punishment, but to the principle and disposition from which it proceeds; our next step will be to ascertain, as plainly and as correctly as possible, the nature and character of that principle and disposition. It is characterized by the epithet *felleo.* Some derive it from the Latin verb *fallo,* which signifies, to deceive, others from the Greek word φηλος, which signifies an impostor or deceiver. In language, these derivations are different: in sentiment, they are the same. Perhaps they may lead us to as just a conception as can well be formed of felony—the generical term employed by the common law to denote a crime.

Without mutual confidence between its members, society, it is evident, could not exist. This mutual and pervading confidence may well be considered as the attractive principle of the associating contract. To place that confidence in all the others is the social right, to deserve that confidence from all the others is the social duty, of every member. To entertain a disposition, in which that confidence cannot with propriety be placed, is a breach of the social duty, and a violation of the social right: it is a crime inchoate. When an injury, atrocious in its nature, or evil in its example, is committed voluntarily against any one member, the author of that voluntary injury has, by his conduct, shown to all, that their right is violated; that his duty is broken; that they cannot enjoy any longer their right of placing confidence in him; that he entertains a disposition unworthy of this confidence; that he is false, deceitful, and treacherous: the crime is now completed.

A disposition, regardless of social duty to all, and discovered by an injury, voluntary, and atrocious or dangerous, committed against one—this is a crime against society. Neither the disposition separated from the injury, nor the injury separated from the disposition, constitutes a crime. But though both the ingredients are necessary, they have not an equal operation in forming that character, from which a crime receives its denomination. In the consideration of crimes, the intention is chiefly to be regarded.

As the injuries, and the breaches of social trust and confidence, which we have mentioned, may relate to a great variety of objects, and, in their own nature, may be more or less aggravated, it follows, that crimes may be distinguished into many different species, and are susceptible of many different degrees.

Some think, that, at common law, the disposition, separated from the injury, constituted a crime. The saying, that "voluntas reputabitur pro facto,"[9] seems to have given rise to this opinion. On a close examination, however, it will, I imagine, appear, that, in all the cases, on which the opinion is founded, and from which the saying is drawn, an injury was done, though not the injury intended to be done.

A very ancient case is reported in the following manner. A man's wife went away with her adulterer; and they compassed the death of the husband; and as he was riding towards the sessions of oyer and terminer and gaol delivery, they assaulted and beat him with weapons, so that he fell down as dead: upon this they fled. The husband recovered, and made hue and cry, and came to the sessions; and showed all this matter to the justices; and, upon the warrant of the justices, the woman and her adulterer were taken, indicted, and arraigned. All this special matter was found by a verdict; and it was adjudged, that the man should be hanged, and the woman burnt.[g] Here, indeed, the injury intended and compassed—for to compass is, in legal understanding, to intend—was not carried into complete execution: an atrocious injury, however, was perpetrated.

Another case is mentioned to the following purpose. A young man was arraigned, because he intended to have stolen his master's goods, and came to his master's bed, where he lay asleep, and, with a knife, attempted, with all his force, to have cut his throat; and, thinking that he had indeed cut it, fled; upon this, the master cried out; and his neighbours apprehended the young man. All this matter was found by a special verdict; and, in the end, the young man was adjudged to be hanged. Quia voluntas reputabitur pro facto.[10] But upon this case it is to be observed, that there was much more than mere intention: a barbarous outrage was committed on the person of a man; and was even thought by the aggressor to have been fully completed in its most extreme extent. For the young man, it is said, thought that he had indeed cut his master's throat. Accordingly, my Lord

9. The will is regarded as the deed.

g. 3. Ins. 5.

10. Because the will is regarded as the deed.

Coke says upon this subject, that it was not a bare compassing or plotting of the death of a man, either by word, or even by writing; but that some overt deed to manifest that compassing or plotting was necessary.

In a species of high treason, and in a species of felony, the rule is still observed—that the intention manifested by a degree of injury, though not the degree intended, constitutes the crime. This is the case in compassing the death of the king. Though this intention be not completed by his death; the crime is completed by what is called an *overt act,* manifesting that intention by injurious and disloyal conduct. Indeed this rule is so strictly observed in this species of treason, that, even when the intention is carried into full effect by putting the king to death, this completion itself, connected with the intention, is not considered as constituting the crime: it is viewed only as the injurious and overt act which manifests that intention. Agreeably to these principles, the regicides of Charles the first were indicted as compassing his death, and the fact of beheading him was specified and made use of as one of the overt acts to prove this compassing.[h]

The species of felony, in which the rule above mentioned still governs, is burglary. A burglar, says my Lord Coke, is, by the common law, a felon, who, in the night, breaketh and entereth into a mansion house of another, with intent to commit some felony within it.[i] The intention in this crime is to commit a felony; but, in order to constitute the crime, it is not necessary that the intention should be executed; the injurious acts done at the time and the place and in the manner described are sufficient: nay more; if the intention be completed by committing the felony, yet, if it be not committed at the time and the place, and in the manner described, it is not a burglary, though it is a felony of another species.

The foregoing cases, the view under which I have stated them, and the observations which I have drawn from them, show strongly the spirit of the common law in its estimation of crimes. In those cases, the felony or treason is traced to the malignity of the principle, not to the mischief of the consequences: the crime is constituted, though the event fail.

In other cases, indeed, the completion of the event is necessary to the constitution of the crime; but even in these, the intention is much more

h. Kel. 8.
i. 3. Ins. 63.

considered than the act. "Actus non facit reum, nisi mens sit rea,"[j][11] is, I believe, a rule of immemorial antiquity in the common law. If, indeed, it is an errour, as the Marquis of Beccaria alleges it to be, to think a crime greater or less according to the intention of him by whom it is committed, it is, in the common law, an errour of the most inveterate kind; it is an errour which the experience of ages has not been able to correct. "Justitia," said Bracton many hundred years ago, "est voluntarium bonum; nec enim potest dici bonum proprie, nisi intercedente voluntate: tolle enim voluntatem; et erit omnis actus indifferens. Affectio quidem tua nomen imponit operi tuo. Crimen non contrahitur nisi voluntas nocendi[k] intercedat. Voluntas et propositum distinguunt maleficia. Furtum omnino non committitur sine affectu furandi. In maleficiis spectatur *voluntas* et non *exitus*."[l][12]

But, on one hand as well as on the other, there is an extreme. The intention governs; the intention communicates its colours to the act: but the act—the *injurious* act must be done. Abstract turpitude is not, I apprehend, a subject of cognizance in a human forum. The breach of our duty to man and to society alone is the object of municipal reprehension. For those sentiments, for those principles, nay for those actions, by which no other member of society can be affected, no one member is accountable to the others. For such sentiments, for such principles, and for such actions, he is amenable only to the tribunal within, and the tribunal above him. In the human code we have seen it to be a rule, that without an injury there is no crime.

Let us not, however, confine our conceptions of injury to the loss or to the risk merely of property. Of injury, all our rights, natural and civil, absolute and relative, are susceptible. Every injurious violation, therefore,

j. 3. Ins. 6.

11. An act does not render one guilty, unless the mind is guilty. At common law, a crime possessed the element of an evil intention together with an unlawful intent and, consonant with the maxim, a crime is not committed if the mind of the person doing the unlawful act is innocent, and therefore a guilty intent must be proved.

k. Brac. 26.

12. Justice is a voluntary good, for it cannot be strictly called good, unless with the will interceding; for take away the will, and every act will become neither good nor evil. Your desire gives the name to your act. No crime is committed unless the desire of doing wrong enter in. Desire and purpose distinguish crimes. No theft is ever committed without the desire to steal. In wrongdoings the desire is to be scrutinized and not the result.

l. Id. 136 b.

of any of those rights may lay the foundation of a crime. The strings of society are sometimes stretched in the nicest unison: strike one, and all emit a complaining tone. Is a single member of society menaced? He who threatens is bound in a recognisance to keep the peace towards every other citizen, as well as towards him, to whom the immediate cause of alarm was given.[m]

I have now traced and described the principles of the common law with regard to the measure of crimes. We have seen with what wise and experienced caution its rules are guarded from every extreme. The result seems to be, that the common law estimates crimes by the design chiefly, but pays a proportionate attention to the fact—by the malignity, without overlooking the injury, of the transaction. After ideal perfection in her calculations concerning those amounts and proportions she aspires not; she is satisfied with that practical degree of accuracy, which a long and careful experience can attain.

From the consideration of crimes I pass to the consideration of punishments. On this subject some rules, and some valuable ones too, may be gleaned from the principles and the practice of the common law; but we must have recourse chiefly to those which are founded on our new but improved political establishments, and to those which result from the general principles of criminal jurisprudence.

Every crime, we have seen, includes an injury: this I consider as a leading maxim in the doctrine of crimes. In the punishment of every crime, reparation for the included injury ought to be involved: this I consider as a leading maxim in the doctrine of punishments.

In this particular, the law of England is defective to a degree both gross and cruel. The father of a family, whose subsistance depends on his personal industry, is, in the arms of his wife, and amidst his surrounding children, stabbed by the order of an insolent and barbarous neighbour. The miserable sufferers by the event are the miserable witnesses of the crime. The assassin, who has ordered it, is opulent and powerful. To the honour of the English law and of its administration be it said, that no degree of opulence or power will purchase or command impunity to the guilty: this assassin will feel its avenging arm. But to the honour of the English law

m. 4. Bl. Com. 250.

and of its administration can it be added, that every degree of injury shall find its proportioned degree of reparation; and that as the assassin is not above its power, so those who suffer by the assassination are not beneath its care? No. This addition cannot be made. The widow and the orphans, who were the witnesses of the crime and the sufferers by the loss, are recognized in the former, but not in the latter character. They attend to give their testimony on the trial. The rich culprit is condemned as he ought to be. They apply to obtain reparation for the loss—of the life? That is irreparable—of the industry of their husband and father, from the ample patrimony of the criminal, who occasioned the loss? To this application, reasonable and just, what is the answer which must be given in the spirit of the law? His property is forfeited by the crime; no funds remain to make you reparation for your loss. They are dismissed, without being reimbursed the expense of their attendance in consequence of their duty and the order of the law; for the king pays no costs. Can this be right?

It was, in ancient times, ordered otherwise and better. In the early part of our juridical history, we find that a part of the composition or forfeiture for homicide was given to the relations of the person deceased.[n] We find likewise, that, in those times, penalties in cases of personal injury had so far the nature of a civil redress, that they were given as a compensation to the person injured.[p] Thus it was among the ancient Saxons. Reparation, indeed, was one great object in the Anglo-Saxon system of criminal law. The principle may be traced to the Germans as described by Tacitus.[q] "Recipitque satisfactionem universa domus."[13] In one of the very early laws of Pennsylvania, it is directed that "those next of kin shall be considered in the loss occasioned by the death of the party killed."[r]

Another quality of the Saxon jurisprudence in criminal matters deserves our attention—I add, our imitation: they inflicted very few capital punishments.[s] Such was the case, we are told, formerly in Scotland; such was it originally in Ireland; and such was it anciently in Wales.[t]

n. 2. Henry 289. 2. Dag. 90. Eden. 217.
p. 1. Reev. 12.
q. De. Mor. Germ. c. 21. 2. Dag. 77.
13. The entire household receives satisfaction.
r. R. O. Book A. p. 49.
s. 4. Bl. Com. 406.
t. 1. Whitak. 278.

In every case before judgment, the Romans allowed an accused citizen to withdraw himself from the consequences of conviction into a voluntary exile. To this institution, the former practice of abjuration in England bore a strong resemblance. This was permitted, as my Lord Coke says, when the criminal chose rather "perdere patriam, quam vitam."[u] [14] On the same principles, a liberty was given, in Greece,to a person accused to disappear after his first defence, and retire into voluntary banishment—in the language of the English law, to abjure the realm after the indictment was found.[v]

Sabacos,[15] one of the legislators of Egypt, went still further. He abolished capital punishments, and ordained, that such criminals as were judged worthy of death should be employed in the publick works. Egypt, he thought, would derive more advantage from this kind of punishment; which, being imposed for life, appeared equally adapted to punish and to repress crimes.[w]

Punishments ought unquestionably to be moderate and mild. I know the opinion advanced by some writers, that the number of crimes is diminished by the severity of punishments: I know, that if we inspect the greatest part of the criminal codes, their unwieldy size and their ensanguined hue will force us to acknowledge, that the opinion has been general and prevalent. On accurate and unbiassed examination, however, it will appear to be an opinion unfounded and pernicious, inconsistent with the principles of our nature, and, by a necessary consequence, with those of wise and good government.

So far as any sentiment of generous sympathy is suffered, by a merciless code, to remain among the citizens, their abhorrence of crimes is, by the barbarous exhibitions of human agony, sunk in the commiseration of criminals. These barbarous exhibitions are productive of another bad effect—a latent and gradual, but a powerful, because a natural, aversion to the laws. Can laws, which are a natural and a just object of aversion, receive a cheerful obedience, or secure a regular and uniform execution? The expectation is forbidden by some of the strongest principles in the human

u. Eden. 31.
14. To lose his fatherland, than his life.
v. 2. Gog. Or. L. 72.
15. Shabaka (Sabacos) ruled Egypt from 721 to 707 B.C.
w. 3. Gog. Or. L. 15.

frame. Such laws, while they excite the compassion of society for those who suffer, rouse its indignation against those who are active in the steps preparatory to their sufferings.

The result of those combined emotions, operating vigorously in concert, may be easily conjectured. The criminal will probably be dismissed without prosecution, by those whom he has injured. If prosecuted and tried, the jury will probably find, or think they find, some decent ground, on which they may be justified or, at least, excused in giving a verdict of acquittal. If convicted, the judges will, with avidity, receive and support every, the nicest, exception to the proceedings against him; and, if all other things should fail, will have recourse to the last expedient within their reach for exempting him from rigorous punishment—that of recommending him to the mercy of the pardoning power. In this manner the acerbity of punishment deadens the execution of the law.

The criminal, pardoned, repeats the crime, under the expectation that the impunity also will be repeated. The habits of vice and depravity are gradually formed within him. Those habits acquire, by exercise, continued accessions of strength and inveteracy. In the progress of his course, he is led to engage in some desperate attempt. From one desperate attempt he boldly proceeds to another; till, at last, he necessarily becomes the victim of that preposterous rigour, which repeated impunity had taught him to despise, because it had persuaded him that he might always escape.

When, on the other hand, punishments are moderate and mild, every one will, from a sense of interest and of duty, take his proper part in detecting, in exposing, in trying, and in passing sentence on crimes. The consequence will be, that criminals will seldom elude the vigilance, or baffle the energy of publick justice.

True it is, that, on some emergencies, excesses of a temporary nature may receive a sudden check from rigorous penalties: but their continuance and their frequency introduce and diffuse a hardened insensibility among the citizens; and this insensibility, in its turn, gives occasion or pretence to the further extension and multiplication of those penalties. Thus one degree of severity opens and smooths the way for another, till, at length, under the specious appearance of necessary justice, a system of cruelty is established by law. Such a system is calculated to eradicate all the manly sentiments of the soul, and to substitute in their place dispositions of the most depraved and degrading kind.

The principles both of utility and of justice require, that the commission of a crime should be followed by a speedy infliction of the punishment.

The association of ideas has vast power over the sentiments, the passions, and the conduct of men. When a penalty marches close in the rear of the offence, against which it is denounced, an association, strong and striking, is produced between them, and they are viewed in the inseparable relation of cause and effect. When, on the contrary, the punishment is procrastinated to a remote period, this connexion is considered as weak and precarious, and the execution of the law is beheld and suffered as a detached instance of severity, warranted by no cogent reason, and springing from no laudable motive.

It is just, as well as useful, that the punishment should be inflicted soon after the commission of the crime. It should never be forgotten, that imprisonment, though often necessary for the safe custody of the person accused, is, nevertheless, in itself a punishment—a punishment galling to some of the finest feelings of the heart—a punishment, too, which, as it precedes conviction, may be as undeserved as it is distressing.

But imprisonment is not the only penalty, which an accused person undergoes before his trial. He undergoes also the corroding torment of suspense—the keenest agony, perhaps, which falls to the lot of suffering humanity. This agony is by no means to be estimated by the real probability or danger of conviction: it bears a compound proportion to the delicacy of sentiment and the strength of imagination possessed by him, who is doomed to become its prey.

These observations show, that those accused of crimes should be speedily tried; and that those convicted of them should be speedily punished. But with regard to this, as with regard to almost every other subject, there is an extreme on one hand as well as on the other; and the extremes on each hand should be avoided with equal care. In some cases, at some times, and under some circumstances, a delay of the trial and of the punishment, instead of being hurtful or pernicious, may, in the highest degree, be salutary and beneficial, both to the publick and to him who is accused or convicted.

Prejudices may naturally arise, or may be artfully fomented, against the crime, or against the man who is charged with having committed it. A delay should be allowed, that those prejudices may subside, and that neither the judges nor jurors may, at the trial, act under the fascinating impressions of sentiments conceived before the evidence is heard, instead of the calm influence of those which should be its impartial and deliberate result. A sufficient time should be given to prepare the prosecution on the part of the state, and the defence of it on the part of the prisoner. This time must vary according to different persons, different crimes, and different situations.

After conviction, the punishment assigned to an inferiour offence should be inflicted with much expedition. This will strengthen the useful association between them; one appearing as the immediate and unavoidable consequence of the other. When a sentence of death is pronounced, such an interval should be permitted to elapse before its execution, as will render the language of political expediency consonant to the language of religion.

Under these qualifications, the speedy punishment of crimes should form a part in every system of criminal jurisprudence. The constitution of Pennsylvania[x] declares, that in all criminal prosecutions, the accused has a "right to a speedy trial."

The certainty of punishments is a quality of the greatest importance. This quality is, in its operation, most merciful as well as most powerful. When a criminal determines on the commission of a crime, he is not so much influenced by the lenity of the punishment, as by the expectation, that, in some way or other, he may be fortunate enough to avoid it. This is particularly the case with him, when this expectation is cherished by the example or by the experience of impunity. It was the saying of Solon, that he had completed his system of laws by the combined energy of justice and strength. By this expression he meant to denote, that laws, of themselves, would be of very little service, unless they were enforced by a faithful and an effectual execution of them. The strict execution of every criminal law is the dictate of humanity as well as of wisdom.

By this rule, important as well as general, I mean not to exclude the pardoning power from my system of criminal jurisprudence. That power ought to continue till the system and the proceedings under it become absolutely perfect—in other words—it ought to continue while laws are made and administered by men. But I mean that the exercise of the par-

x. Art. 9. s. 9.

doning power should be confined to exceptions, well ascertained, from the general rule. Confined in this manner, instead of shaking the truth or diminishing the force of the rule, the exercise of the power to pardon will confirm the former and increase the latter.

Need I mention it as a rule, that punishments ought to be inflicted upon those persons only, who have committed crimes—that the innocent ought not to be blended in cruel and ruinous confusion with the guilty?

Yes; it is necessary to mention this as a rule: for, however plain and straight it is, when viewed through the pure and clear ether of reason and humanity, it has not been seen by those whom pride and avarice have blinded; nay, it has been represented as a rule, crooked and distorted, by those who have beheld it through the gross and refracting atmosphere of false policy and false philosophy. The doctrines of forfeiture and corruption of blood have found their ingenious advocates, as well as their powerful patrons.

There have been countries and times—there still are countries and times, when and where the rule, founded in justice and nature, that the property of the parent is the inheritance of his children, has been intercepted in its benign operation by the cruel interference of another rule, founded in tyranny and avarice—the crimes of the subject are the inheritance of the prince. At those times, and in those countries, an insult to society becomes a pecuniary favour to the crown; the appointed guardian of the publick security becomes interested in the violation of the law; and the hallowed ministers of justice become the rapacious agents of the treasury.

A poisoned fountain throws out its bitter waters in every direction. This rule, hostile to the nearest domestick connexions, was unfriendly also to the safety of the publick. If the inheritance was reaped by the prince; it was, by him, deemed a matter of small moment, that impunity was stipulated for the crime. Accordingly, we are told, that, in the thirteenth century, one of the methods, by which the kings of England and of other parts of Europe supplied their exchequers, was the sale of pardons for crimes.[y] When crimes were the sources of princely wealth, it is no wonder if they were objects of princely indulgence. In this manner we may naturally

y. Bar. on St. 27.

account for the disorder and violence, which, in those ages, prevailed so universally over Europe.

The law of forfeiture it has been attempted to defend by considerations drawn from utility, and also from natural justice. The high authority of Cicero is also[z] produced upon this occasion—"Nec vero me fugit, quam sit acerbum, parentum scelera filiorum poenis lui; sed hoc praeclare legibus comparatum est, ut caritas liberorum amiciores parentes reipublicae redderet."[a] Amicus Cicero—sed magis amica veritas.[16] For the high authority of Cicero, I certainly entertain a proportionate degree of respect; but implicit deference should be paid to none. Besides; in the passage quoted, Cicero does not speak in a character of authority. He decides not as a judge: he pleads his own cause as a culprit; he defends, before Brutus, a rigorous vote, which he had given in the senate, against the sons of Lepidus.[17]

But farther; upon a closer investigation, it will, perhaps, be found, that the principle of policy, on which Cicero rests his defence, as it certainly is not of the most generous, neither is it of the most enlarged kind; since forfeitures, far from preventing publick crimes and publick dangers, may have the strongest tendency to multiply and to perpetuate both. When the law says, that the children of him, who has been guilty of crimes, shall be bereaved of all their hopes and all their rights of inheritance; that they shall languish in perpetual indigence and distress; that their whole life shall be one dark scene of punishment, unintermitted and unabating; and that death alone shall provide for them an asylum from their misery—when such is the language, or such is the effect of the law; with what sentiments must it inspire those, who are doomed to become its unfortunate though unoffending victims?—with what sentiments must it inspire those, who from humanity feel, or by nature are bound to take, an interest in the fortunes and in the fate of those victims, unfortunate though unoffending? With sentiments of pain and disgust—with sentiments of irritation and

z. 4. Bl. Com. 375.

a. Ep. ad Brut. 12.

16. Nor indeed has it escaped my notice, what a harsh thing it is to pay for the crimes of parents through the punishment of their sons. But this has most plainly been provided for by the laws, that the love for their children might render parents more loving toward the commonwealth. "Dear is Cicero, but dearer Truth."

17. Likely refers to Marcus Aemilius Lepidus (?–12 B.C.), a political ally of Julius Caesar and triumvir with Marcus Antonius and Octvanianus.

disappointment—with sentiments of a deadly feud against the state which has adopted, and, perhaps, against the citizens also who have enforced it.

Vain is the attempt to range the cold and timid suggestions of policy against the vivid and the indelible feelings of nature, and against the warm though impartial dictates of humanity. Who will undertake to satisfy an innocent son, that he is the victim—who will undertake to persuade his relations—his virtuous—his patriotick—his meritoriously patriotick relations, that one so nearly connected with them is the victim, whom the publick good indispensably demands to be offered up as a sacrifice to atone for the guilt of his father? The sons of Lepidus were the children of the sister of Brutus. "Contra patrem Lepidum Brutus avunculus,"[18] says he very naturally in his answer to Cicero.

An attempt has been likewise made to support the law of forfeiture on the foundation of natural justice.[b] "All property," says Sir William Blackstone,[c] "is derived from society, being one of those civil[d] rights which are conferred upon individuals, in exchange for that degree of natural freedom, which every man must sacrifice when he enters into social communities. If therefore a member of any national community violates the fundamental contract of his association, by transgressing the municipal law, he forfeits his right to such privileges as he claims by that contract; and the state may very justly resume that portion of property, or any part of it, which the laws have before assigned him. Hence in every offence of an atrocious kind, the laws of England have exacted a total confiscation of the movables or personal estate; and in many cases a perpetual, in others only a temporary, loss of the offender's immovables or landed property; and have vested them both in the king, who is the person supposed to be offended, being the only visible magistrate in whom the majesty of the publick resides."

It has often been said, that, at elections, the people of England sell their liberty for their own money; but this, I presume, is the first time that this kind of exchange has been brought forward as a fundamental article of their *original* contract.

18. In contrast to their father Lepidus, Brutus is their uncle.
b. 4. Bl. Com. 375.
c. 1. Bl. Com. 299.
d. 4. Bl. Com. 9.

A philosophizing is, on some occasions, an unfortunate turn. It was, we are told, an opinion long received in China, that the globe of the earth was supported on the back of an elephant. The people were satisfied and inquired no farther. An ingenious philosopher, however, was not satisfied so easily. If the earth, reasoned he, must be supported on the back of an elephant, *pari ratione*,[19] the elephant must stand on the back of something else. Exactly fitted for his design, he found a broad backed tortoise. He placed the elephant upon it, and published his new theory of the manner in which the globe was supported. Unfortunately, the spirit of his *ars philosophandi*[20] caught; and he was asked—on whose back will you place the tortoise? To this a satisfactory answer is not yet found in the history of this Chinese philosophy.

The sceptres of princes required a support: the political creed of Europe rested them on forfeitures. The people paid and inquired not. But the attempt is now made to find a rational foundation for forfeitures: they are rested on property as a civil, and not as a natural right.

In both instances, the mistake was made, and the wrong direction was pursued, in the first step which was taken. Forfeitures for crimes, according to the true principles of political philosophy, were a foundation as improper for the revenue of princes, as an elephant, according to the true principles of natural philosophy, was inadequate to sustain the weight of the globe.

But the investigation of the doctrine—that property is a civil right—will, as I have already mentioned, find its appropriated place in the second division of my system.

The observations which we have made are equally applicable to the forfeiture of dower, as to the forfeiture of inheritance.

Corruption of blood is another principle, ruinous and unjust, by which the innocent are involved in the punishment of the guilty. It extends both upwards and downwards. A person attainted cannot inherit lands from his ancestors: he cannot transmit them to any heir: he even obstructs all descents to his posterity, whenever they must, through him, deduce their right from a more remote ancestor.[e]

19. For like reason; by the same reasoning.
20. Philosophical art or science.
e. 4. Bl. Com. 381.

This unnatural principle—I call it unnatural, because it dissolves, as far as human laws can dissolve, the closest and the dearest ties of nature—this unnatural principle was introduced by the feudal system, pregnant with so many other principles of the most mischievous kind: and it still continues to disgrace the criminal jurisprudence of England. It begins now, however, to be very generally deserted as to its principle. The ingenious and elegant Mr. Eden, who seems to cling to forfeiture, at least in a qualified degree, as "to a branch of the penal system, which will not be suffered to fall from the body of our law, without serious consideration,"[f] admits very freely, that it is not so easy to reconcile, either to reason or benevolence, that corruption of blood, by which the inheritable quality is for ever extinguished.[g] Sir William Blackstone intimates a very laudable wish, that the whole doctrine may, in England, be antiquated by one undistinguishing law.[h]

This subject of extending punishments beyond the guilty, I conclude with a passage from one of the laws of Arcadius[21] and Honorius,[22] the Roman emperours. "Sancimus ibi esse paenam, ubi et noxa est; propinquos, natos, familiares, procul a calumnia submovemus, quos reos sceleris societas non facit. Nec enim affinitas, vel amicitia, nefarium crimen admittunt; peccato igitur suos teneant auctores; nec ulterius progrediatur metus quam reperiatur delictum."[i23]

As the punishment ought to be confined to the criminal; so it ought to bear a proportion, it ought, if possible, to bear even an analogy, to the crime.[j] This is a principle, the truth of which requires little proof; but the application of which requires much illustration.

f. Eden 48.

g. Id. 39.

h. 4. Bl. Com. 382.

21. Flavius Arcadius (377/78–408) was the Eastern Roman Emperor from 395 to 408.

22. Flavius Augustus Honorius (384–423) was the Western Roman Emperor from 395 to 423. It was during his reign that the Visigoths sacked Rome (410).

i. Eden. 49.

23. We deem it sanctioned that the punishment should lie where the guilt is; relations, children, friends we keep far removed from any calumny, whom mere social intercourse does not make guilty of the crime; for neither blood relationship nor friendship incurs a nefarious charge. Therefore let sins bind only their own doers, and let fear proceed no further than wrongdoing is proved.

j. Id. 83.

"It is not only," says the Marquis of Beccaria, "the common interest of mankind that crimes should not be committed; but it is their interest also that crimes of every kind should be less frequent, in proportion to the mischief which they produce in society. The means, therefore, which the legislature use to prevent crimes, should be more powerful in proportion as they are destructive of the publick safety and happiness. Therefore there ought to be a fixed proportion between punishments and crimes." "A scale of crimes," adds he, "may be formed, of which the first degree should consist of such as tend immediately to the dissolution of society; and the last, of the smallest possible injustice done to a private member of that society."[k]

To a scale of crimes, a corresponding scale of punishments should be added, each of which ought to be modified, as far as possible, according to the nature, the kind, and the degree of the crime, to which it is annexed. To select, where it can be done, a punishment analogous to the crime, is an excellent method to strengthen that association of ideas, which it is very important to establish between them.

In the graduation of reach of these scales, and in the relative adjustment between them, a perfect accuracy is unquestionably unattainable. The different shades both of crimes and of punishments are so numerous, and run so much into one another, that it is impossible for human skill to mark them, in every instance, distinctly and correctly. How many intervening degrees of criminality are there between a larceny of the petty kind and a robbery committed with every degree of personal insult and outrage—between a private slander and a publick inflammatory libel—between a simple menace and a premeditated murder—between an unfounded murmur and a daring rebellion against the government?

But though every thing cannot, much may be done. If a complete detail cannot be accomplished; certain leading rules may be established: if every minute grade cannot be precisely ascertained; yet the principal divisions may be marked by wise and sagacious legislation. Crimes and punishments too may be distributed into their proper classes; and the general principles of proportion and analogy may be maintained without any gross or flagrant violation.

k. Bec. c. 6. p. 17. 19.

To maintain them is a matter of the first moment in criminal jurisprudence. Every citizen ought to know when he is guilty: every citizen ought to know, as far as possible, the degree of his guilt. This knowledge is as necessary to regulate the verdicts of jurors and the decisions of judges, as it is to regulate the conduct of citizens. This knowledge ought certainly to be in the possession of those who make laws to regulate all.

"Optima est lex," says my Lord Bacon, "quae minimum relinquit arbitrio judicis."[l][24] If this is true with regard to law in general; it must be very true, and very important too, with regard to the law of crimes and punishments. What kind of legislation must that have been, by which "not only ignorant and rude unlearned people, but also learned and expert people, minding honesty, were often and many times trapped and snared!" Yet such is the character of the criminal legislation under Henry the eighth, given by the first parliament assembled in the reign of his daughter Mary;[m] which could well describe, for it still smarted under the legislative rod. The *candour*, at least, of legislation should be inviolable.

"Misera est servitus, ubi jus est incognitum."[25] When a citizen first knows the law from the jury who convict, or from the judges who condemn him; it appears as if his life and his liberty were laid prostrate before a new and arbitrary power; and the sense of general safety, so necessary to the enjoyment of general happiness, is weakened or destroyed. But a law uncertain is, so far, a law unknown. To punish by a law indefinite and unintelligible!—Is it better than to punish without any law?

A laudable, though, perhaps, an improvable degree of accuracy has been attained by the common law, in its descriptions of crimes and punishments. On this subject, I now enter into a particular detail. To the description of each crime, I shall subjoin that of its punishment; and shall mention, as I proceed, the alterations introduced by the constitution and laws of the United States and of Pennsylvania. The laws of other nations will frequently be considered in a comparative view.

l. 1. Ld. Bac. 249.

24. That law is best which leaves the least to the decision of the judge.

m. St. 1. Mary. c. 1.

25. Wretched is the thraldom where the law is either uncertain or unknown.

CHAPTER II.
Of Crimes Against the Right of Individuals to Their Property.

Every crime includes an injury: every injury includes a violation of a right. The investigations, which we have hitherto made concerning rights, will direct our course in that which we are now to make concerning wrongs.

I assumed, though, for the reasons assigned, I have not yet proved, that a man has a right to his property. I begin my enumeration of crimes with those which infringe this right.

I have observed that every injurious violation of our rights, natural and civil, absolute and relative, *may* lay the foundation of a crime.[a] I did not mean, however, to insinuate, by this observation, that every injury *ought* to be considered by the law in a criminal point of view. For every injury let reparation be made by the civil code, in proportion to the loss sustained; but let those injuries alone, which become formidable to society by their intrinsick atrocity, or by their dangerous example, be resented by society and prosecuted as crimes. Agreeably to this principle, a private injury done without actual violence, cannot be prosecuted by an indictment.[b] It is not considered as affecting the community.

This principle, however, seems to have gained its full establishment only by the liberality of modern times. It is remarkable, that a law made on this liberal principle, in an early period of Pennsylvania, was repealed by the king in council.[c] But this is not the only instance, in which the improving spirit of our legislation has been at first checked, but has received subsequent countenance by late decisions in England.

a. Ante. p. 1104.
b. 3. Burr. 1703. 1733.
c. R. O. book A. vol. 1. p. 14.

With the enjoyment and security of property, the security and the authenticity of its evidences is intimately connected. For this reason, dangerous and deliberate attacks upon that security or authenticity are crimes by the common law.

Forgery, at the common law, may be described "the fraudulent making or alteration of a writing, to the prejudice of another man's right." For this crime, the punishment of fine, imprisonment, and pillory may, by the common law, be inflicted on the criminal.[d]

Among the Egyptians, publick notaries, who forged false deeds, or who suppressed or added any thing to the writings, which they had received to copy, were condemned to lose both their hands. They were punished in that part, which had been particularly instrumental in the crime.[e] In Lorrain, so long ago as the fourteenth century, forgery was punished with banishment.[f]

The first act of parliament, which appears against it, was made in the reign of Henry the fifth. This act punishes it by satisfaction to the party injured, and by a fine to the king.[g] But this first statute has been the fruitful mother of a thousand more. True it is, that the increase of commerce, the invention of negotiable and even current paper, the institution of national funds, and the many complex securities and evidences of real property have justly rendered the crime of forgery, beside its intrinsick baseness—for it is a species of the *crimen falsi*[1]—a consideration of great importance and extent. But is it equally true, that all this is a sufficient reason, why, in almost all cases possible to be conceived, every forgery, which *tends* to defraud, either in the name of a real or of a fictitious person, should be made, as in England it is now made, a capital crime?[h] "Pluet super populum laqueos."[2] There is a learned civilian, says my Lord Bacon, who expounds this curse of the prophet, of a multitude of penal laws; which are worse than showers of hail or tempest upon cattle; for they fall upon men.[i]

d. 4. Bl. Com. 245.
e. 1. Gog. Or. L. 59.
f. Bar. on St. 380.
g. Id. ib.
1. The crime of falsifying.
h. 4. Bl. Com. 247.
2. A noose hangs over the heads of the people.
i. 4. Ld. Bac. 3.

By a law of Pennsylvania, whoever shall forge, deface, corrupt, or embezzle deeds and other instruments of writing, shall forfeit double the value of the damage sustained, one half of which shall go to the party injured; and shall in the pillory, or otherwise, be disgraced as a false person.[j]

By a law of the United States it is enacted, that if any person shall falsely make, alter, forge, or counterfeit, or cause or procure to be falsely made, altered, forged, or counterfeited, or willingly act or assist in the false making, altering, forging, or counterfeiting any certificate, indent, or other publick security of the United States; or shall utter, put off, or offer, or cause to be uttered, put off, or offered in payment or for sale, any such false, forged, altered, or counterfeited certificate, indent, or other publick security, with intent to defraud any person, knowing the same to be false, altered, forged, or counterfeited, and shall be thereof convicted; every such person shall suffer death.[k]

To forge, says my Lord Coke, is metaphorically taken from the smith, who beateth upon his anvil, and forgeth what fashion or shape he will. The offence is called *crimen falsi,* and the offender *falsarius;* and the Latin word to forge is *falsare* or *fabricare.* And this is properly taken when the act is done in the name of another person.[l] "Falsely to make," says he, are larger words than "to forge;" for one may make a false writing within this act (he speaks of the 5th. Eliz. c. 14. in which, as to the present point, the words used are substantially the same with the words of the law now under consideration) though it be not forged in the name of another, nor his seal nor hand counterfeited. As if a man make a true deed of feoffment under his hand and seal of the manor of Dale unto B.; and B. or some other rase out D and put in S, and then when the true deed was of the manor of Dale, now it is falsely altered and made the manor of Sale; this is a false writing within the purview of the statute.[m]

Another crime against the right of property is larceny. Larceny is described—the felonious and fraudulent taking and carrying away of the personal goods of another.[n] The Mirrour describes the crime as committed,

j. 1. Laws Penn. 5.
k. Laws U. S. 1. cong. 2. sess. c. 9. s. 14.
l. 3. Ins. 169.
m. 3. Ins. 169.
n. Id. 107. 4. Bl. Com. 230.

"treacherousement."[o] More indictments are to be found for larceny, among the records of England, than for all the other crimes known to the law. It is computed that nineteen criminals out of twenty are prosecuted for this crime.[p]

According as the opinions and sentiments of men concerning property have been more or less correct, their notions concerning larceny have been more or less pure. Indeed, in the nature of things, this must be the case. Theft, or the secret acquisition of property, was, at Sparta, thought neither a crime nor a shame. Why? Because at Sparta, Lycurgus had established a community of goods; and when one got hold of a larger share than his neighbours, especially among the young people, it was considered merely as an instance of juvenile address, and as indicating a superiour degree of future dexterity. The senatorial order at Rome, we are told, enjoyed the distinguished privilege of being exempted from every prosecution for larceny.[q] What is still more remarkable, a similar claim of privilege was, in the time of Charles the second, insisted on by the house of lords in England, when a bill was sent to them from the commons, to punish—wood stealers![r] This anecdote we have on the authority of my Lord Clarendon, a peer, the chancellor, and the speaker of the house of lords.

Much has been said, in the English law books, concerning the distinction between grand and petit larceny. The distinction, however ancient, was never founded upon any rational principle; and the farther it flowed from its original source, the more unreasonable and cruel it became. Well might Sir Henry Spelman complain, that, while every thing else became daily dearer, the life of a man became more and more cheap.[s] But, what is more, this distinction, irrational and really oppressive, appears never to have been established with any degree of accuracy. The Author of Fleta says, if a person steals the value of twelve pence *and* more, he shall be punished capitally. Britton, in one place, says, if it is twelve pence *or* more. At this time, therefore—that is, in the reign of Edward the first—it was unsettled whether twelve pence was sufficient, or more than twelve pence

o. C. 1. s. 10. 2. Reev. 42.
p. Bar. on St. 443.
q. Bar. on St. 491.
r. Id. ibid.
s. 4. Bl. Com. 238.

was necessary, to superinduce the capital punishment.[t] A similar diversity and uncertainty of opinion appears in the reign of Edward the third.[u]

In the description of larceny, the taking is an essential part. For every felony includes a trespass; and if the person is guilty of no trespass in taking the goods, he can be guilty of no felony in carrying them away.[v] This is precisely the law language, conveying the doctrine, which I have illustrated generally and fully—that, without an injury, there can be no crime. A real trespass must be committed; but a real trespass will not be covered or excused by any artful stratagem to prevent the appearance of it. If one, who intends to steal the goods of another, obtains, with that intention, the process of the law to get them into his possession, in a manner apparently legal; this contrivance—an abuse of the law—will not excuse him from a charge of a felonious taking.[w]

To a larceny it is as necessary that the goods be carried away, as that they be taken. But the least removal of the goods is sufficient to satisfy this part of the description. To remove them from one place to another, even in the same room, is, in legal understanding, to carry them away. One, who intended to steal plate, took it out of a trunk, and laid it upon the floor, but was surprised before he could do more; he was adjudged guilty of larceny.[x]

The taking and carrying away, says Sir William Blackstone, and very truly, must also be *felonious,* that is, done *animo furandi.*[3] This, by the way, is a clear and decided instance, that, in the meaning of the common law, felony is referred to the intention, and not to the event. As we saw in the former part of the description, that the crime could not exist without the injury; we see now, that the injury will not constitute the crime without the criminal intention. For, as the Author of the Commentaries next observes, this requisite indemnifies mere trespassers, and other petty offenders.[y]

The last part of the description of larceny at the common law is, that the goods must be personal. Land, or any thing that is adhering to the soil or to the freehold, cannot in one transaction be made the subject of larceny.

t. 1. Reev. 485.
u. 2. Reev. 204.
v. 1. Haw. 89. Kel. 24.
w. 1. Haw. 90.
x. Kel. 31. 1. Haw. 93.
3. With intent to steal.
y. 4. Bl. Com. 232.

But if any thing of this kind is, at one time, separated from the freehold, so as to become a chattel; and is, at another time, taken and carried away; larceny is now committed.[z]

In different nations, and in the same nation at different times, larceny or theft has received very different punishments. It would be tedious minutely to recite them. On no subject has there been more fluctuation in the criminal laws both of Greece and Rome. Seldom, however, was larceny punished capitally at Athens; never among the Romans. In the early part of the Anglo-Saxon period in England, theft of the worst kind did not expose the thief to any corporal punishment. But the compensation which he was obliged by law to make, rendered larceny a very unprofitable business when it was detected. Ina, the king of Wessex, declared stealing to be a capital crime; but allowed the offender or his friends to redeem his life, by paying the price at which it was valued by the law.[a]

The distinction between punishing theft as a crime, and exacting compensation for it as an injury, is strongly marked in a law of Howel Dha, the celebrated legislator of Wales: "If a thief is condemned to death, he shall not suffer in his goods; for it is unreasonable both to exact compensation, and to inflict punishment."

In the ninth year of Henry the first, larceny above the value of twelve pence was, in England, made a capital crime, and continues so to this day; and, in a vast number of instances, it is, by modern statutes, deprived of the benefit of clergy. These statutes, says Mr. Eden, are so complicated in their limitations, and so intricate in their distinctions, that it would be painful, on many accounts, to attempt the detail of them. It is a melancholy truth, but it may, without exaggeration, be asserted, that, exclusive of those who are obliged by their profession to be conversant in the niceties of the law, there are not ten subjects in England, who have any clear conception of the several sanguinary restrictions, to which, on this point, they are made liable.[b]

By a law of the United States, larceny is punished with a fine not exceeding the fourfold value of the property stolen, and with publick whipping not exceeding thirty nine stripes.[c] In Pennsylvania, a person convicted

z. 1. Haw. 93.
a. 2. Henry 290.
b. Eden. 289.

of larceny to the value of twenty shillings and upwards, shall restore the goods or pay their value to the owner, shall also forfeit to the commonwealth the value of the goods, shall undergo a servitude for any term not exceeding three years, and shall be confined and kept to hard labour: a person convicted of larceny under twenty shillings, shall restore the goods or pay their value to the owner, shall forfeit the same value to the commonwealth, shall undergo a servitude not exceeding one year, and shall be confined and kept to hard labour.[d]

Forgery and larceny seem to be the only crimes against the right of private property known to the common law.

Robbery is generally classed among the crimes against the right of private property; but somewhat improperly, in my opinion. Robbery receives its deep dye from outrage committed on the person; but as property also enters into the description of this crime, I shall consider it here.

Robbery, at the common law, is a violent and felonious taking from the person of another, of money or goods to any value, putting him in fear.[e] From this description it appears, that, to constitute a robbery, the three following ingredients are indispensable: 1. a felonious intention, or *animus furandi.* 2. Some degree of violence and putting in fear. 3. A taking from the person of another.

1. There must be a felonious intention to steal: larceny is a necessary, though by no means the most important ingredient, which enters into the composition of a robbery. The circumstances which are calculated and proper to evince this felonious intention, it is impossible to describe or recount: they must, in this as in other crimes, be left to the attentive consideration of those, by whom the person accused is tried. The value, however, of the property on which the larceny is committed, is, as to the robbery, totally immaterial. In this respect, a penny is equivalent to a pound.[f]

2. There must be some degree of violence and putting in fear. This indeed is the characteristick circumstance, which distinguishes robbery from other larcenies. If one assault another with such circumstances of terrour as put him in fear, and he, in consequence of this fear, deliver his money;

c. Laws U. S. 1. cong. 2. sess. c. 9. s. 16.
d. 2. Laws. Penn. 803. s. 3. 4.
e. 3. Ins. 68. 1. Haw. 95.
f. 3. Ins. 69.

this is a sufficient degree of violence; for he was put in fear by the assault; and gave his money to escape the danger.[g] To constitute a robbery, it is sufficient that the force used be such as might create an apprehension of danger, or oblige one to part with his property against his consent. Thus, if a man be knocked down without any previous warning, and stripped of his money while he lies senseless; this, though he cannot strictly be said to be *put in fear*, is undoubtedly a robbery.[h]

3. There must be a taking from the person of another. The thief must be in the possession of the thing stolen. If he go even so far as to cut the girdle, by which a purse hangs, so that it fall to the ground; yet if he do not take it up, he has not completed the robbery, because the purse was not in his possession.[i] The taking must be from the person; but this part of the description is answered, not only by taking the money out of one's pocket, or forcing from him the horse on which he actually rides, but by taking from him, openly and before his face, any thing which is under his immediate and personal care and protection. If one, wishing to save his money, throw it into a bush, and the thief take it up; this is a taking from the person.[j]

We are told by Mr. Selden, that, before the conquest, robbery was punished differently, by the different nations who came from the continent of Europe. By the Saxons, it was punished with death: by the Angles, and by the Danes, it was punished only with fine.[k] After the conquest, these different laws were settled by the Normans in the more merciful way; and if the delinquent fled, his pledge satisfied the law for him. But in the times of Henry the first, the law was again reduced to the punishment of this crime by death: and so it has continued ever since.[l]

In the ancient laws of Wales, it is expressly declared, that robbery shall never be punished with death; "because (say these laws) it is a sufficient satisfaction for this crime, if the goods taken be restored, and a fine paid to the person from whom they were taken, according to his station, for

g. 1. Haw. 96, 97.
h. Fost. 128. 4. Bl. Com. 242.
i. 3. Ins. 69.
j. 3. Ins. 69. 1. Haw. 96.
k. Bac. on Gov. 63.
l. Id. 88.

the violence offered him, and another to the king for the breach of the peace."[m]

Robbery, by a law of the United States, is punished capitally.[n] By a law of Pennsylvania, a person convicted of robbery forfeits to the commonwealth his lands and goods, and undergoes a servitude not exceeding ten years, in the gaol or house of correction.[o]

I proceed now to the consideration of two other crimes at the common law, which, though property, as in the case of robbery, enters into their description, yet receive their deep dye from outrages against personal security. This cannot be enjoyed without a legal guard around the *residence* of the person.

"A man's house is his castle" was the expression, in times rude and boisterous, when the idea of security was found only on its association with the idea of strength; and in such times, no expression more emphatical could have been used. In happier times, when the blessings of peace and law are expected and due—in such times, a man's house is entitled to an appellation more emphatick still—in such times, a man's house is his *sanctuary.* "Quid enim sanctius, quid omni religione munitius, quam domus uniuscujusque civium?"[p3] Into this sanctuary, the law herself, unless upon the most urgent emergencies, presumes not to look or enter. We have seen, on many occasions, with what a delicate—I may add, with what a respectful—reserve, she treats the near and dear domestick connexions. We may well suppose, that she will guard, with peculiar vigilance, the favoured spot in which a family reside. Even those who endeavour clandestinely to pry into its recesses—such are[q] eaves-droppers—receive her reprehension: and unless the peace or security of the publick require it, she will not suffer its doors to be broken, to execute even her own imperial mandates. When she thus solicitously protects the residence of a family from inferiour

m. 2. Henry 292.

n. Laws U. S. 1. con. 2. sess. c. 9. s. 8.

o. 2. Laws Penn. 802. s. 2.

p. Cic. pro dom. 41.

3. For what is more protected in any religion than the home of each and every one of the citizens?

q. 4. Bl. Com. 169.

insults, we may rely, that she will zealously defend it from atrocious crimes. Such are arson and burglary.

Arson is a felony at common law, in maliciously and voluntarily burning the house of another.[r] This is not intended merely of the dwelling house itself, but extends to the outhouses; as the barn, the stable, the cow house, the dairy house, the mill house, the sheep house; which are parcel of the mansion house.[s]

This crime may be committed by wilfully burning one's own house, if the house of another is also burnt; but if no mischief is done to that of another, it is not felony, though the fire was kindled with an intention to burn the house of that other.[t] But if the intention is to burn the house of another person, and by the burning of this the house of a third person is also burned; the burning of the house of this third person is felony; because the pernicious event shall be coupled with the felonious intention.[u]

Neither the mere intention to burn a house, nor even an actual attempt to burn it, by putting fire to it, will, if no part of it be burnt, amount to felony; but if any part of the house be burnt, it is arson, though the fire afterwards go out of itself, or be extinguished.[v] No misfortune, nor even culpable negligence or imprudence, will amount to arson: it must be voluntary and malicious. A person, by shooting with a gun, set fire to the roof of a house; this was determined not to be felony.[w]

Arson is a crime of deep malignity. The object of other felonies against the right to property, is merely to give it a new master; the object of arson is to destroy it—to lose it to society, as well as to its owner. The confusion and terrour which attend arson, and the continued apprehension which follows it, are mischiefs frequently more distressing than even the loss of the property.

The crime of arson was one of the very few punished capitally by the Saxon law. In the reign of Edward the first, those who perpetrated this crime were burnt, that they might suffer in the same manner, in which

r. 3. Ins. 66. 1. Haw. 105.
s. 3. Ins. 67.
t. Cro. Car. 376.
u. 3. Ins. 67.
v. 1. Haw. 106.
w. 1. Hale. P. C. 569.

they had been criminal.[x] This crime is also one of the very few still punished capitally in Pennsylvania.[yz]

Burglary is a felony at the common law, in breaking and entering, by night, the mansion house of another, with intent to commit a felony.[a]

There have been some opinions, that this crime, on a construction of the phrase "by night," may be committed at any time after the setting and before the rising of the sun; because the day was deemed to begin at the end, and to end at the beginning of those times; but the later and better opinion is, that if there be day light enough to discern the countenance of a man when the crime is committed, it cannot amount to a burglary.[b]

To a burglary it is necessary, that the house be both broken and entered. The breaking must be actual, and not merely such as the law implies in every unlawful entry on the possession of another. To open a window; to unlock the door; to break a hole in the wall; to enter an open door and unlatch a chamber door; to come down the chimney; to knock at the door and rush in when it is opened; to gain admittance by an abuse of legal process, or by the means of a conspiring servant; all these are actual breaches. The least degree of entry with any part of the body, or with an instrument held in the hand, or even a load discharged from a gun, is sufficient to satisfy that entry, which the law deems necessary to constitute the crime of burglary.[c]

In a dwelling house only burglary can be committed. But a house in which one sometimes resides, and has left with an intention to return; a house which one has hired, and into which he has brought part of his goods, though he has not lodged in it; a chamber in a college; a room occupied in a private house by a lodger; the out houses *adjoining* to the principal house; all these are mansion houses within the meaning of the law.[d] A shop may be parcel of a mansion house; but if it is severed by a lease to

x. 1. Reev. 485.

y. 1. Laws. Penn. 137. 476.

z. By an act of assembly passed 22d April, 1794, arson is punished by imprisonment at hard labour, for a period not less than five, nor more than twelve years. 3. Laws. Penn. 600. *Ed.*

a. 3. Ins. 63. 1. Haw. 101.

b. 1. Haw. 101.

c. 1. Haw. 103.

d. 3. Ins. 64. 1. Haw. 103. 104. 4. Bl. Com. 226.

one who works in it by day only, and does not lodge in it, it is not burglary to break and enter it in the night time.[e]

To a burglary, an intention to commit some felony, and not merely a trespass, is indispensable; but, as was shown on another occasion,[f] it is not necessary that the felony intended be committed; and it is immaterial whether that felony be by common or by statute law.[g]

By the law of Athens, burglary was a capital crime.[h] Among the Saxons also, *burgessours*[4] were to be punished with death.[i] In Pennsylvania, burglary and robbery receive precisely the same punishment.[j] The punishment for robbery has been already mentioned.

e. Wood. Ins. 388.
f. Ante. p. 1103.
g. 4. Bl. Com. 227.
h. 1. Pot. Ant. c. 26.
4. Burglars.
i. 1. Reev. 485.
j. 2. Laws. Penn. 802. s. 2.

CHAPTER III.
Of Crimes Against the Right of Individuals to Liberty, and to Reputation.

Liberty, as we have seen on former occasions, is one of the natural rights of man; and one of the most important of those natural rights. This right, as well as others, may be violated; and its violations, like those of other rights, ought to be punished, in order to be prevented. Yet these violations are scarcely discernible in our code of criminal law.

This we must ascribe to one of two causes. Either this right has been enjoyed inviolably: or the law has suffered the violations of it to escape with shameful impunity. The latter is the truth: I am compelled to add, that the latter, bad as it is, is not the *whole* truth. Violations of liberty have not only been overlooked: they have also been protected; they have also been encouraged; they have also been made; they have also been enjoined by the law. I speak this not only concerning the statute law; I am compelled to speak it also concerning the common law of England: I speak this not only concerning the law as it was received in the American States before their revolution; I am compelled to speak it also concerning the law as it is received in them still: I speak this not only concerning the law as it is received generally in the other sister states; I am compelled to speak it also concerning the law as it is received in Pennsylvania: nay, I am farther compelled to speak it also of the law as it is recently received in our national government.

Our *publick* liberty we have indeed secured;—*esto perpetua*—But, notwithstanding all our boasted improvements—and they are improvements of which we may well boast—the most formidable enemy to *private* liberty is, at this moment, the law of the land.

In some former parts of my lectures,[a] I have had occasion to remark, and I have remarked with pleasure, that solicitous degree of attention which

a. Ante. vol. 2. p. 384. et. seq.

the law gives to personal security. Its most distant avenues are watchfully guarded. To decide questions, by which it may be affected in the highest, or even in inferiour degrees, I have shown, in a sublime part of our system, to be the incommunicable prerogative of sovereignty or selected sovereignty itself. I have shown, that, by an operation inexpressibly fine, personal safety never sees the arm which holds the sword of justice, but at the moment when it is found necessary that its stroke should be made. Inferiour to personal safety only, if indeed inferiour even to that, is the consideration of personal liberty. And yet, while personal safety can be authoritatively affected only by the community, or a body selected from the community impartially and for the occasion, the law implicitly, causelessly, unconditionally, and continually prostrates personal liberty at the feet of every wretch who is unprincipled enough to trample upon it. I say, unprincipled; because a citizen, who has principle, will not wound it by using the authority of the law. In every state of the union—in every county of every state, there are shops opened, nay licensed, nay established by the law, at which its authority may be purchased, for a trifle, by the worst citizen, in order to infringe the personal liberty of the best.

From the disgrace of these enormities against the rights of liberty, I gladly rescue the character and principles of the common law. The history of the several processes of capias, and orders and rules of commitment will show, when we come to it, that this part of our municipal law is of statute original; and that it was produced in the darkest and rudest, though its existence has continued in the most enlightened and the most refined times.

With another part of these enormities against the rights of liberty, however, impartiality obliges me to charge the common law. Man is composed of a soul and of a body. To mental as well as to bodily freedom, he has a natural and an unquestionable right. The former was grossly violated by the common law. Witness the many overgrown titles, by which the volumes of the law are still distended: witness, in particular, the customs *de modo decimandi,*[1] and the writs *de excommunicate capiendo*[2] and *de heretico*

1. Of the manner of tithing. A prescription de non decimando is a claim to be entirely discharged of tithes and pay no compensation in lieu of them.

2. A writ issued out of a common-law court for the arrest of a person who after having been excommunicated refused to obey the sentence of the ecclesiastical court.

comburendo.[b3] These parts I only mention; because from these parts we are happily relieved: they are parts of the common law, which did not suit those who emigrated to America: they were, therefore, left behind them.

But, in some respects, private liberty is still the orphan neglected; in others, she is still the victim devoted by our municipal law. So inveterate, indeed, is the vice of the law in this particular, that it has infected its very language. The terms, which denote the diminution or the destruction of personal safety—homicide, wounding, battery, assault—are all *prima facie*[4] understood in an unfavourable meaning; though they are sometimes excused, or justified, or even enjoined, as well as sometimes prohibited and punished by the law: but to imprisonment, the idea of legal authority seems, in legal understanding, to be *prima facie* annexed: and when it speaks of the unauthorized kind, it is obliged to distinguish it by adding the epithets *false* or *unlawful.*

But legislators should bear in their minds, and should practically observe—and well persuaded I am, that our American legislators bear in their minds, and, whenever the necessary resettlement of things after a revolution can possibly admit of it, will practically observe, with regard to this interesting subject—the following great and important political maxim:—Every wanton, or causeless, or unnecessary act of authority, exerted, or authorized, or encouraged by the legislature over the citizens, is wrong, and unjustifiable, and tyrannical: for every citizen is, of right, entitled to liberty, personal as well as mental, in the highest possible degree, which can consist with the safety and welfare of the state. "Legum"—I repeat it—"servi sumus, ut *liberi* esse possimus."[5] In the course of my future investigations into this point, I shall be able to evince, in the clearest manner, that our municipal regulations concerning it are not less hostile to the true principles of utility, than they are to those of the superiour law of liberty.

Having made these preliminary observations on a subject, which so greatly needs, and so richly deserves them, I proceed to search the little

b. 4. Bl. Com. 46.

3. For burning a heretic. This writ issued by special direction of the king caused one convicted of heresy to be burned to death.

4. At first view; self-evident.

5. We are slaves to the law in order that we may be able to be free.

that is said in some of our systems of criminal law—in others nothing is said—concerning it.

False imprisonment is punishable by indictment, like assaults and batteries; and the delinquent may be fined and imprisoned.[c]

Thus much concerning the crime of violating the personal liberty of man.

Reputation, except that of official characters, seems not, of late times, any more than personal liberty, to have attracted the distinguished regard of our publick law: and even when it deigns a little degree of regard to it, that regard flows from a wrong principle, and is referred to a wrong end. Libels are considered as objects of publick cognizance, not because the character, but because the tranquillity of the citizens is precious to the publick; and therefore, crimes of this nature are classed and prosecuted and punished as breaches of the peace, and as much resembling challenges to fight.[d] But it was not always so.

I said, on a former occasion,[e] that robbery itself does not flow from a fountain more rankly poisoned, than that which throws out the waters of calumny and defamation. In saying so, I was warranted by authority respectable and ancient. By the laws of the Saxons, the felon, who robbed, was punished less severely than the wretch who calumniated. By a law, made, towards the end of the seventh century, by Lothere, one of the kings of Kent,[6] a calumniator was obliged to pay one shilling to him in whose house or lands he uttered the calumny. It was conceived, it seems, to diffuse a degree of contamination over things inanimate. He was obliged to pay six shillings to the person whom he calumniated, and twelve shillings to the king. When we recollect, that, long *after* this time, a shilling could purchase a fatted ox; we may judge concerning the light, in which defamation was viewed *at* this time. But Edgar the peaceable, who flourished about two centuries afterwards, made, against this crime, a law much more severe: it decreed, that a person convicted of gross and dangerous

c. 4. Bl. Com. 218. 2. Haw. 90.

d. 4. Bl. Com. 150.

e. Vol. 2. p. 1066.

6. Lothere (or Hlothere) was one of the kings of Kent and ruled the Jute kingdom of Kent (now a county in the Southeast of England) from 673 to 685.

defamation should have his tongue cut out, unless he redeemed it by paying his full *were,* as it was called, or the price of his life. This law was confirmed by Canute[7] the great.[f]

By the laws of Egypt, a defamer was condemned to the same punishment, which would have been inflicted on the defamed, if the defamation had been true.[g] Solon, in one of his laws, ordained, that a delinquent in slander should make reparation in money to the party injured; and should also pay a fine into the publick treasury.[h]

A libel may be described—a malicious defamation of any person, published by writing, or printing, or signs, or pictures, and tending to expose him to publick hatred, contempt, or ridicule.[i] It is clearly a crime at the common law.[j]

It has been often observed in the course of these lectures, that one extreme naturally produces its opposite. An unwarrantable attempt made in the star chamber, during the reign of James the first, to wrest the law of libels to the purposes of ministers, and an effort continued ever since to carry that attempt into execution, and even to go beyond some of its worst principles, have, in England, lost to the community the benefits of that law, wise and salutary when administered properly, and by the proper persons. The decision in that case has ever since been considered, in England, as the foundation of the law on this subject. It will be proper, therefore, to examine the parts of that decision with some degree of minuteness.

The libel, prosecuted and condemned, was a satyrical ballad on a deceased archbishop of Canterbury and his living successour.[k]

The first resolution is, that a libel against a magistrate, or other publick person, is a greater offence than one against a private man. This, in the unqualified manner here expressed, cannot be rationally admitted. Other circumstances being equal, that of office ought to incline the beam, if the libel refer to his official character or conduct; because an officer is a citizen

7. Canute (or Cnut) (994/995–1035) was king of England, Denmark, and Norway.
f. 2. Henry. 293.
g. 1. Gog. Or. L. 58.
h. 1. Pot. Ant. 179.
i. 1. Haw. 193.
j. 3. Ins. 174.
k. 5. Rep. 125 a.

and more. But a libel of one kind against a private citizen, may certainly be more atrocious, and of example more atrociously evil, than a libel of another kind against a publick officer.

Another and a more important resolution in that case is—that it is immaterial whether the libel be false or true. This resolution is clearly extrajudicial, because it appears, from the state of the case, that the author of the libel was proceeded against on his own confession. The rule, however, has been followed by more modern determinations; and reasons have been offered to support it on the principles of law. The provocation and not the falsity, says Sir William Blackstone, is the thing to be punished criminally. In a civil action, he admits, a libel must appear to be false as well as scandalous; for, if the charge be true, the plaintiff has received no private injury, and has no ground to demand a compensation for himself, whatever offence it may be against the publick peace; and, therefore, upon a civil action, the truth of the accusation may be pleaded in bar of the suit. But in a criminal prosecution, the tendency which all libels have to create animosities, and to disturb the publick peace, is the sole consideration of the law.[l]

Upon this passage, I observe, in the first place, that a libel is a violation of the right of character, and not of the right of personal safety. It is no wonder if the reasonings on this crime are inaccurate, when its very principle is mistaken.

I observe, in the second place, that these inaccurate reasonings are attempted to be established by a gross inconsistency. When they refer to the *effects* of the libel, they suppose the tendency to produce disturbances of the peace: when they refer to the *causes* of the libel, they say to him who is actuated by them—you ought, in a settled government, to complain for every injury in the ordinary course of law, and by no means to revenge yourself.[m] Why is not this advice given consistently, to the person provoked by the libel? If he has received an injury—if on that injury a crime is superinduced; the law will repair the former, and punish the latter: if no injury has been sustained, no foundation has been laid for a crime.

l. 4. Bl. Com. 150.
m. 5. Rep. 125 b.

I observe, in the third place, that Sir William Blackstone here seems not to have been sufficiently attentive to a principle, which he properly subscribes in another part of his Commentaries:[n] the crime includes an injury: every publick offence is also a private wrong, and somewhat more: it affects the individual, and it likewise affects the community.

The only points, it is said, to be considered in the prosecution for a libel, are, first, the making or publishing of the book or writing: secondly, whether the matter be criminal.[o]

On the last of these two points, a celebrated controversy has subsisted between judges and juries; the former claiming its decision as a question of law; the latter claiming it as a question of fact, or, at least, necessarily involved in the decision of a question of fact. After what I have said, in a former lecture,[p] concerning the general duties and powers of juries, you will be at no loss to know my sentiments on this controverted subject. I only remark, at present, that if a libel be, as I think it is, a crime against the right of reputation; the trial on a libel must be the trial of a character; or some part of a character. Of all questions, almost, which can be proposed, I think this the most remote from a question of law.

The constitution of Pennsylvania has put this matter upon an explicit footing, consonant, or nearly consonant in my opinion, to the true principles of the common law: "in all indictments for libels, the jury shall have a right to determine the law and the facts, under the direction of the court, as in other cases."[q]

The punishment of a libel is a fine, or a fine and corporal punishment.[r]

n. 4. Bl. Com. 5.
o. Id. 151.
p. Vol. 2. p. 975. et seq.
q. Art. 9. s. 7.
r. 1. Haw. 196.

CHAPTER IV.
Of Crimes Against the Right of Individuals to Personal Safety.

The crimes which are next to be enumerated and considered are those against the right of personal safety. On this subject, the common law has been peculiarly accurate and attentive.

An assault is an attempt or offer, with force and violence, to do a corporal hurt to another; as by striking at him; by holding up the fist at him; by pointing a pitchfork at him, if he be within its reach; by presenting a gun at him, if he be within the distance to which it will carry; or by any other act of a similar kind, done in an angry and threatening manner.[a] An assault is violence inchoate.[b]

A battery is violence completed by beating another. Any injury done to the person of a man, in an angry, or revengeful, or rude, or insolent manner, as by touching him in any manner, or by spitting in his face, is a battery in the eye of the law.[c] In that eye, the person of every man is sacred: between the different degrees of violence it is impossible to draw a line: with great propriety, therefore, its very first degree is prohibited.[d]

Wounding is a dangerous hurt given to another; and is an aggravated species of battery.[e]

These offences may unquestionably be considered as private injuries, for which compensation ought to be decreed to those who suffer them. But viewed in a publick light, they are breaches of the publick peace: as such

a. 1. Haw. 133.
b. 3. Bl. Com. 120.
c. 1. Haw. 134.
d. 3. Bl. Com. 120.
e. Id. 121.

they may be prosecuted; and as such they may be punished. The punishment is fine, or fine and imprisonment.[f]

A battery or an assault, violence or an offer of violence, is susceptible of deep criminality from the atrocious intention, with which it is sometimes offered or done. An assault with a design to murder, to perpetrate the last outrage upon the honour of the fair sex, or to commit the crime which ought not to be even named—these are instances of what I mention: in these instances, to a heavy fine and imprisonment, it is usual to add the judgment of the pillory.[g]

Assaults, batteries, and woundings may be sometimes excused, and sometimes justified. The particular cases in which this may be done, will be explained with more propriety, when we come to consider them as private injuries, and not as publick offences.

Affrays are crimes against the personal safety of the citizens; for in their personal safety, their personal security and peace are undoubtedly comprehended. An affray is a fighting of persons in a publick place, to the terrour of the citizens. They are considered as common nuisances. They may, and ought to be suppressed by every person present; and the law, as it gives authority, so it gives protection, to those who obey its authority in suppressing them, and in apprehending such as are engaged in them; if by every person present; then still more strongly by the officers of peace and justice.[h] In some cases, there may be an affray, where there is no actual violence; as where a man arms himself with dangerous and unusual weapons, in such a manner, as will naturally diffuse a terrour among the people.[i]

To challenge another, by word or letter, to fight a duel, or to be the messenger of such a challenge, or to provoke, or even to endeavour to provoke, another to send such a challenge, is a crime of a very high nature, and is severely reprehended by the law:[j] duels are direct and insolent contempts of the justice of the state.[k]

f. 1. Haw. 134. 4. Bl. Com. 217.
g. 4. Bl. Com. 217.
h. 3. Ins. 158. 4. Bl. Com. 145.
i. 1. Haw. 135.
j. 3. Ins. 158. 1. Haw. 135.
k. 1. Haw. 138.

Affrays are punished by fine and imprisonment, the measure of which must be regulated by the circumstances of the case.[1] For sending a challenge, the offenders have been adjudged to pay a fine, to be imprisoned, to make a publick acknowledgment of their offence, and to be bound to their good behaviour.

It cannot have escaped your observation, with what a judicious mixture of poignant contempt the common law seasons its indignation against those, who are so lost to true sentiment as to deem it honourable to insult the justice of their country. They are not treated as criminals of dignity: they are considered in the very degraded view of common nuisances: the putrid offals of the shambles are viewed, as we shall see, in the same light.

Neither can it have escaped your observation, with what a deep knowledge of human nature, the common law traces and pursues duels to what is frequently their cowardly as well as their cruel source. Many are vain and base enough to wish and aspire at that importance, which, in their perverted notions, arises from being even the second in a quarrel of this nature, who have not spirit enough to face that danger, which arises from being the first. Hence often the officious and the insidious offers of friendship, as it is called, on these occasions, by those who, with hearts pusillanimous and malignant, inflame, instead of endeavouring, as those possessed of bravery and humanity would endeavour, to extinguish an unhappy dispute—a dispute, perhaps, unpremeditated as well as unhappy—regretted as well as unintended by the immediate parties—and to rescue them from the consequences of which, without any violation of the rules of true honour, and even without any departure from the rules of false honour, which every one has not the calm courage to violate, nothing is wanting but a conduct diametrically opposite to that of these pretended friends—a conduct which will prevent extremities, without wounding a sentiment which, without necessity, ought not to be wounded, because it is delicate though it be mistaken.

Animated with a just degree of blended resentment and disdain against the conduct first described, the common law wisely and humanely extends disgrace and censure and punishment to those who provoke, even to those who *endeavour* to provoke, another to send a challenge.

1. Id. ibid.

On the same principles on which affrays are prohibited and punished, riots, routs, and unlawful assemblies are also prohibited and punished by the common law. Two persons may commit an affray; but to a riot, a rout, or an unlawful assembly, three are necessary. A riot is a tumultuous disturbance of the peace by persons unlawfully assembled with a view to execute, and actually executing, some unlawful act, in a violent and turbulent manner, to the terrour of the people.[m] A rout is a riot unfinished; and is committed by persons unlawfully assembled with a view to execute, and actually making a *motion* to execute, an unlawful act, the execution of which would render the riot complete. An unlawful assembly is an unfinished rout; and is committed by persons unlawfully assembled with a view, but without actually making a motion, to execute an unlawful act, to the execution of which, if they had made an actual motion, they would have been guilty of a rout.[n] The punishment of these offences, at the common law, has generally been by fine and imprisonment only: cases, however, very enormous have been punished by the pillory also.[o]

Mayhem is a crime committed by violently depriving one of the use of any part of his body, by losing the use of which he becomes less able, in fighting, to annoy his adversary or to defend himself.[p] This is an atrocious breach of the publick peace and security. By it, one of the citizens is disabled from defending himself; by it, his fellow citizens are debarred from receiving that social aid which they are obliged to give; by it, the state loses those services, which it had a right to exact and expect. In ancient times, this crime was punished according to the law of retaliation: it is now punished with fine and imprisonment.[q]

The forcible abduction or stealing of a person from his country, is a gross violation of the right of personal safety. To this crime the term *kidnapping* is appropriated by the law. It robs the state of a citizen; it banishes the citizen from his country; and it may be productive of mischiefs of the most lasting and humiliating kind. By the common law, it is punished with fine, with imprisonment, and with the pillory.[r]

m. 1. Haw. 155. Salk. 594. 3. Ins. 176.
n. 1. Haw. 158.
o. Id. 159.
p. 1. Haw. 111.
q. 4. Bl. Com. 206.
r. Id. 219.

A rape is an irreparable and a most atrocious aggression on the right of personal safety. Besides the thousand excruciating, but nameless circumstances by which it is aggravated, some may be mentioned with propriety. It is a crime committed not only against the citizen, but against the woman; not only against the common rights of society, but against the peculiar rights of the sex: it is committed by one from whom, on every virtuous and manly principle, her sex is entitled to inviolable protection, and her honour to the most sacred regard. This crime is one of the selected few, which, by the laws of the Saxons, were punished with death. The same punishment[s] it still undergoes in the commonwealth of Pennsylvania.[t] On this subject, for an obvious reason, particular observations will not be expected from a lecture in the hall: they are fit for the book and the closet only: for even the book and the closet they are fit, only because they are necessary.

The crime not to be named, I pass in a total silence.

I now proceed to consider homicide, and all its different species. Homicide is the generical term used by the law to denote every human act, by which a man is deprived of his life. It may be arranged under the following divisions—enjoined homicide—justifiable homicide—homicide by misfortune—excusable homicide—alleviated homicide—malicious homicide—treasonable homicide.

I. 1. Homicide is enjoined, when it is necessary for the defence of the United States, or of Pennsylvania. At present, it is not necessary for me, and, therefore, I decline to examine the general and very important subject concerning the rights of war. I confine myself merely to that kind of war, which is defensive: and even that kind I now consider solely as a municipal regulation, established by the constitution of the nation, and that of this commonwealth.

The constitution of the nation is ordained to "provide for the common defence." In order to make "provision" for that defence, congress have the power to "provide for arming the militia," and "for calling them forth," "to repel invasions:" they have power "to provide a navy," "to raise and support

s. 1. Laws Penn. 135.

t. By the act of assembly of 22d. April 1794, the punishment of this crime is changed into imprisonment at hard labour, for a period not less than ten, nor more than twenty one years. 3. Laws Penn. 600. *Ed.*

armies," "to declare war."[u] Whenever the primary object, "the common defence," renders it necessary, the power becomes the duty of congress: and it requires no formal deduction of logick to point to the duty, when necessity shall require, of military bodies, "raised, supported, and armed." In Pennsylvania, it is explicitly declared upon the very point, that "the freemen of this commonwealth shall be armed for its defence."[v]

2. Homicide is enjoined, when it is necessary for the defence of one's person or house.

With regard to the first, it is the great natural law of self preservation, which, as we have seen,[w] cannot be repealed, or superseded, or suspended by any human institution. This law, however, is expressly recognised in the constitution of Pennsylvania.[x] "The right of the citizens to bear arms in the defence of themselves shall not be questioned." This is one of our many renewals of the Saxon regulations. "They were bound," says Mr. Selden, "to keep arms for the preservation of the kingdom, and of their own persons."[y]

With regard to the second; every man's house is deemed, by the law, to be his castle; and the law, while it invests him with the power, enjoins on him the duty, of the commanding officer. "Every man's house is his castle," says my Lord Coke, in one of his reports, "and he ought to keep and defend it at his peril; and if any one be robbed in it, it shall be esteemed his own default and negligence."[z] For this reason, one may assemble people together in order to protect and defend his house.[a]

3. Homicide is frequently enjoined by the judgment of courts agreeably to the directions of the law. This is the case in all capital punishments. This species of homicide is usually classed with those kinds which are justifiable. The epithet is true so far as it goes. But it goes not far enough to characterize the conduct of the officer to whom it relates. One may be justifiable in doing a thing, in omitting to do which he may be equally justified. But this is not the case with a sheriff, or other ministerial officer of justice. He is *commanded* to do execution.

u. Cons. U.S. art. 1. s. 8.
v. Cons. Penn. art. 6. s. 2.
w. Ante. vol. 2. p. 1083.
x. Art. 9. s. 21.
y. Bac. on Gov. 40.
z. 7. Rep. 6.
a. 1. Hale. P. C. 547. 4. Bl. Com. 223.

II. As homicide is enjoined, when a sentence of death is to be executed; so it is sometimes justified in the execution of other process from the courts of justice. When persons, who have authority to arrest, and who use the proper means for that purpose, are resisted in doing so, and the party making resistance is killed in the struggle; this homicide is justifiable.[b] If a person, who interposes to part the combatants in an affray, and gives notice to them of his friendly intention, is assaulted by any of them, and, in the struggle, happens to kill; this is justifiable homicide. For, in such cases, it is the duty of every man to interpose, that mischief may be prevented, and the peace may be preserved. This rule is founded in the principles of social duty.[c] If a woman, in defence of her honour, kill him who attempts the last outrage against it; this homicide is justifiable.[d] In the same manner, the husband or father may justify the killing of one, who makes a similar attempt upon his daughter or wife.[e] In these instances of justifiable homicide, the person who has done it is to be acquitted and discharged, with commendation rather than censure.[f]

III. Homicide by misfortune happens, when a man, in the execution of a lawful act, and without intending any harm, unfortunately kills another.[g] The act must not only be lawful, but must also be done in a lawful manner. If a master, correcting his servant moderately, happens to occasion his death, it is only misadventure; for the act of correction was lawful: but it is much otherwise, if he exceed in the manner, the instrument, or the quantity of the correction.[h]

This species of homicide, if found by a jury, still, in strict law, as it is received in England, subjects the unfortunate—I cannot call him the guilty—party, to a forfeiture of his personal estate; or, as some say, only a part of it. He has, it is true, his pardon, and a writ for restoring his goods, as a matter of course, when he pays the fees for them.[i] Sir William Blackstone seems to make an apology for this forfeiture, by observing, that, in

b. Eden. 209. Fost. 270. 1. Hale. P. C. 494.
c. Fost. 272. Eden. 209.
d. Fost. 274. Eden. 210.
e. 4. Bl. Com. 181.
f. Id. 182. Fost. 279.
g. Fost. 258.
h. 4. Bl. Com. 182. Fost. 262.
i. 4. Bl. Com. 188.

the case of homicide by misadventure, the law presumes negligence, or, at least, a want of sufficient caution, in him who was so unfortunate as to commit it; who, therefore, is not altogether faultless.[j] The law itself is severe in this instance—confessedly so: but the apology for it seems to be founded on a principle, rigorous and totally inadmissible.

Shall the unfortunate be necessarily viewed as also incautious? Shall negligence be presumed by the law, when misadventure has been found by the jury? No. The doctrine is inadmissible. It is rigorous. Accidents of this lamentable kind may be the lot of the wisest and most cautious, and of the best and most humane among men: they most frequently happen among those who are relations or friends; because those associate most frquently together. In such cases, to ascribe the calamity to a conduct "not altogether faultless;" to "presume negligence," when nothing existed but bitter misfortune, would, indeed, be to "heap affliction upon the head of the afflicted," and to stab afresh a heart still bleeding with its former wound. It would be to aggravate the loss of even a brother, a parent, a child, a wife; if of aggravation such a loss, in such circumstances, is susceptible.[k]

The law itself, in this instance, is, as has been mentioned, severe—confessedly so. The fees of office have probably, in this as in too many other instances, prevented improvement. "I therefore think," to use the expressions of a great master of criminal law, "those judges, who have taken general verdicts of acquittal in plain cases of homicide by misfortune, have not been to blame. They have, to say the worst, deviated from ancient practice in favour of innocence, and have prevented an expense of time and money, with which an application to the great seal, though in a matter of course, as this undoubtedly is, must be constantly attended."[l] It is proper to observe that this late practice of the judges is mentioned by Sir William Blackstone, in terms which intimate his approbation.[m]

IV. Excusable homicide is that which, on a sudden affray[n] between parties, is given in the necessary defence of him who wishes and endeavours to quit the combat. This is carefully to be distinguished, because it

j. Id. 186.
k. Fost. 264.
l. Fost. 288.
m. 4. Bl. Com. 188.
n. Fost. 276.

is materially different, from that kind of self defence which is justified or enjoined to prevent the perpetration of the most atrocious outrage upon one's person or habitation.[o]

The species of homicide, which we are now to consider, though excusable by the benignity of the law, is still culpable. It is done, when a person, engaged in a sudden affray, quits the combat before a mortal wound is given, and retreats or flies as far as he can with safety; and then, urged by mere necessity, kills his adversary for the preservation of his own life.[p] This species approaches near to manslaughter; and, in experience, the boundary between them is, in some places, difficult to be discerned: it is marked, however, in the consideration of law. In both species, it is supposed that passion has kindled on each side; and that blows have passed between the parties. But in the case of manslaughter, either the combat on both sides continues till the mortal stroke is given, or the party giving it is not in imminent danger: whereas, in the case of excusable homicide, he who is excused declines, before a mortal stroke given, any further combat, and retreats as far as he can with safety; and then, through mere necessity, and to avoid immediate death, kills his adversary.[q]

Though this species of homicide is very different from that which happens by misfortune; yet the judges, in one as well as the other, permit, if not direct, a general verdict of acquittal.[r]

V. To alleviated homicide, the term *manslaughter* is appropriated. When the epithet *alleviated* is applied to this species of homicide, it must be understood only as compared with that which is malicious; for manslaughter, though in this view an alleviated, is a felonious homicide. It is the unlawful killing of another, without malice; and may be either voluntarily, upon a sudden heat or provocation; or involuntarily, but in the commission of some unlawful act. When manslaughter is voluntary, it is distinguished from excusable homicide by this criterion—that, in the latter case, the killing is through necessity, and to avoid immediate death; whereas, in the former, there is no necessity at all; it being a sudden act of revenge. When manslaughter is involuntary, it is distinguished from homicide by

o. 4. Bl. Com. 183.
p. Fost. 275.
q. Fost. 275. 277. 4. Bl. Com. 185.
r. 4. Bl. Com. 188.

misfortune by this criterion—that the latter always happens in consequence of a lawful, the former, in consequence of an unlawful act. Manslaughter, both voluntary and involuntary, is distinguished from malicious homicide by this criterion—that the latter is with, the former without, malice.

In England, manslaughter is punished by burning in the hand, and by the forfeiture of goods and chattels.[s] In the United States, it is punished by a fine not exceeding one thousand dollars, and by imprisonment not exceeding three years.[t] In Pennsylvania,[u] it is punished by a fine at the discretion of the court, and by imprisonment not exceeding two years; and the offender shall find security for his good behaviour during life.[v]

VI. To malicious homicide the term *murder* is appropriated by the law. This name was, in ancient times, applied only to the *secret* killing of another; for which the vill or hundred where it was committed was heavily amerced. This amercement was called *murdrum.* This expression is now applied to the crime; and the crime is now considered in a very different, and much more extensive point of view, without regarding whether the person killed was killed openly or secretly.[w]

Murder is the unlawful killing of another with malice aforethought, express or implied.[x] The distinction, you observe, which is strongly marked between manslaughter and murder is, that the former is committed without, the latter with malice aforethought. It is essential, therefore, to know, clearly and accurately, the true and legal import of this characteristick distinction.

s. 4. Bl. Com. 193.

t. Laws U. S. 1. cong. 2. sess. c. 9. s. 7.

u. 1. Laws. Penn. 846.

v. The punishment of *voluntary* manslaughter, by the act of 22d April, 1794, (3. Laws. Penn. 601. s. 7.) is, for the first offence, imprisonment at hard labour, not less than two, nor more than ten years; and the offender shall be sentenced likewise to give security for his good behaviour during life, or for any less time, according to the nature and enormity of the offence. For the second offence, he shall be imprisoned as aforesaid not less than six, nor more than fourteen years. In cases of *involuntary* manslaughter, the prosecutor for the commonwealth may, with the leave of the court, wave the felony, and charge the person with a misdemeanor; who, on conviction, shall be fined and imprisoned as in cases of misdemeanor; or the prosecutor may charge both offences in the indictment; and the jury may in such case acquit the party of one, and find him guilty of the other charge. 3. Laws. Penn. 601. s. 8. *Ed.*

w. 4. Bl. Com. 195.

x. 3. Ins. 47.

There is a very great difference between that sense which is conveyed by the expression *malice* in common language, and that to which the term is appropriated by the law. In common language, it is most frequently used to denote a sentiment or passion of strong malevolence to a particular person; or a settled anger and desire of revenge in one person against another. In law, it means the dictate of a wicked and malignant heart; of a depraved, perverse, and incorrigible disposition. Agreeably to this last meaning, many of the cases, which are arranged under the head of implied malice, will be found to turn upon this single point, that the fact has been attended with such circumstances—particularly the circumstances of deliberation and cruelty concurring—as betray the plain indications and genuine symptoms of a mind grievously depraved, and acting from motives highly criminal; of a heart regardless of social duty, and deliberately bent upon mischief. This is the true notion of malice, in the legal sense of the word. The mischievous and vindictive spirit denoted by it, must always be collected and inferred from the circumstances of the transaction. On the circumstances of the transaction, the closest attention should, for this reason, be bestowed. Every circumstance may weigh something in the scale of justice.

In England, in the United States, in Pennsylvania, and almost universally throughout the world, the crime of wilful and premeditated murder is and has been punished with death. Indeed it seems agreed by all, that, if a capital punishment ought to be inflicted for any crimes, this is unquestionably a crime for which it ought to be inflicted. Those who think that a capital punishment is enjoined against this crime by the law which is divine, will not imitate the conduct of that Polish monarch, who remitted to the nobility the penalties of murder, in a charter of pardon beginning arrogantly thus[y]—"Nos divini juris rigorem moderantes, &c."[z][1]

y. 4. Bl. Com. 194.

z. Murder, by the act of 22d April, 1794, is distinguished into two degrees. Murder of the first degree alone is punished with death, and is the only capital crime now known to the laws of Pennsylvania. Murder perpetrated by means of poison, or by lying in wait, or by any other kind of wilful, deliberate, and premeditated killing, or committed in the perpetration, or attempt to perpetrate, any arson, rape, robbery, or burglary, is deemed murder of the first degree. All other kinds of murder are deemed murder in the second degree. The punishment of this is imprisonment at hard labour, for a period not less than five, nor more than eighteen years. 3. Laws. Penn. 599. 600. s. 1. 2. 4. *Ed.*

1. We, moderating the rigor of divine law . . .

VII. Treasonable homicide is committed by a servant who kills his master, and a wife, who kills her husband. Petit treason is the name appropriated, by the law, to this crime. It arises from the relation which subsists between the person killing and the person killed. The crime which, committed by another, would be murder, is petit treason when committed by the wife, or by a servant.

The punishment of this crime, in England, is, that the man is drawn and hanged; and the woman is drawn and burned.[a] By a law[b] still in force in Pennsylvania, persons convicted of this crime, or of murder, shall suffer as the laws of Great Britain now do or hereafter shall direct and require in such cases respectively.[c]

a. 4. Bl. Com. 204.

b. 1. Laws. Penn. 135.

c. "Every person liable to be prosecuted for petit treason shall in future be indicted, proceeded against, and punished, as is directed in other kinds of murder." Act of 22d April, 1794. s. 3. 3. Laws Penn. 600. *Ed.*

CHAPTER V.
Of Crimes, Immediately Against the Community.

I have hitherto considered crimes, which wound the community through the sides of individuals: I now come to consider one which directly and immediately aims a stab at the vitals of the community herself. I mean treason against the United States, and against the state of Pennsylvania.

Treason is unquestionably a crime most dangerous to the society, and most repugnant to the first principles of the social compact. It must, however, be observed, that as the crime itself is dangerous and hostile to the state, so the imputation of it has been and may be dangerous and oppressive to the citizens. To the freest governments this observation is by no means inapplicable; as might be shown at large by a deduction, historical and political, which would be both interesting and instructive. But, at present, we have not time for it.

To secure the state, and at the same time to secure the citizens—and, according to our principles, the last is the end, and the first is the means—the law of treason should possess the two following qualities. 1. It should be determinate. 2. It should be stable.

It is the observation of the celebrated Montesquieu,[a] that if the crime of treason be indeterminate, this alone is sufficient to make any government degenerate into arbitrary power. In monarchies, and in republicks, it furnishes an opportunity to unprincipled courtiers, and to demagogues equally unprincipled, to harass the independent citizen, and the faithful subject, by treasons, and by prosecutions for treasons, constructive, capricious, and oppressive.

a. Sp. L. b. 12. c. 7.

In point of precision and accuracy with regard to this crime, the common law, it must be owned, was grossly deficient. Its description was uncertain and ambiguous; and its denomination and penalties were wastefully communicated to offences of a different and inferiour kind. To lop off these numerous and dangerous excrescences, and to reduce the law on this important subject to a designated and convenient form, the famous statute of treasons was made in the reign of Edward the third, on the application of the lords and commons. This statute has been in England, except during times remarkably tyrannical or turbulent, the governing rule with regard to treasons ever since. Like a rock, strong by nature, and fortified, as successive occasions required, by the able and the honest assistance of art, it has been impregnable by all the rude and boistrous assaults, which have been made upon it, at different quarters, by ministers and by judges; and as an object of national security, as well as of national pride, it may well be styled the legal Gibraltar of England.

Little of this statute, however, demands our minute attention now: as the great changes in our constitutions have superceded all its monarchical parts. One clause of it, indeed, merits our strictest investigation; because it is transcribed into the constitution of the United States. Another clause in it merits our strongest regard; because it contains and holds forth a principle and an example, worthy of our observance and imitation.

After having enumerated and declared all the different species of treason, which it was thought proper to establish, the statute proceeds in this manner: "and because many other cases of like treason may happen in time to come, which, at present, a man cannot think or declare; it is assented, that if any other case, supposed treason, which is not specified above, happen before any judges, they shall not go to judgment in such case; but shall tarry, till it be shown and declared before the king and his parliament, whether it ought to be judged treason or other felony."

The great and the good Lord Hale observes[b] upon this clause, "the great wisdom and care of the parliament, to keep judges within the bounds and express limits of this statute, and not to suffer them to run out, upon their own opinions, into constructive treasons, though in cases which seem to have a parity of reason"—cases of like treason—"but reserves them to the

b. 1. Hale. P. C. 259.

decision of parliament. This," he justly says, "is a great security as well as direction to judges; and a great safeguard even to this sacred act itself."

It is so. And it was all the safeguard which the parliament, by the constitution, as it is called, of England, could give. It was a safeguard from the arbitrary constructions of courts: it was a shelter from judicial storms: but it was no security against legislative tempests. No parliament, however omnipotent, could bind its successours, possessed of equal omnipotence; and no power, higher than the power of parliament, was then or is yet recognised in the juridical system of England. What was the consequence? In the very next reign, the fluctuating and capricious one of Richard the second, the parliaments were profuse, even to ridicule—if, in such a serious subject, ridicule could find a place—in enacting new, tyrannical, and even contradictory treasons. This they did to such an abominable degree, that, as we are told by the first parliament which met under his successour, "there was no man who knew how he ought to behave himself, to do, speak, or say, for doubt of the pains of such treasons."[c]

In the furious and sanguinary reign of Henry the eighth, the malignant spirit of inventing treasons revived, and was carried to such a height of mad extravagance, that, as we have seen on another occasion, the learned as well as the unlearned, the cautious as well as the unwary, the honest as well as the vicious, were entrapped in the snares. How impotent, as well as cruel and inconsistent, is tyranny in the extreme! His savage rage recoiled, at some times, upon those who were most near to him; at other times, with more justice, upon himself. The beautiful and amiable Boleyn became the victim of that very law, which her husband, in his fit of lustful passion—for the monster was callous to *love*—made for her security. When the enormities of his life and reign were drawing towards their end, his physicians saw their tyrant in their patient; and they refused to apprize him of his situation, because he had made it treason to predict his death.

Admonished by the history of such times and transactions as these, when legislators are tyrants or tools of tyrants; establishing, under their own control, a power superiour to that of the legislature; and availing themselves of that power, more permanent as well as superiour; the people of the United States have wisely and humanely ordained, that "treason

c. St. 1. Hen. 4. c. 10.

against the United States shall consist only in levying war against them, or in adhering to their enemies, giving them aid and comfort."[d]

In this manner, the citizens of the Union are secured effectually from even legislative tyranny: and in this instance, as in many others, the happiest and most approved example of other times has not only been imitated, but excelled. This single sentence comprehends our whole of national treason; and, as I mentioned before, is transcribed from a part of the statute of Edward the third. By those who proposed the national constitution, this was done, that, in a subject so essentially interesting to each and to all, not a single expression should be introduced, but such as could show in its favour, that it was recommended by the mature experience, and ascertained by the legal interpretation, of numerous revolving centuries.

To the examination, and construction, and well designated force of those expressions, I now solicit your strict attention.

"Treason consists in levying war against the United States." In order to understand this proposition accurately and in all its parts, it may be necessary to give a full and precise answer to all the following questions. 1. What is meant by the expression "levying war?" 2. By whom may the war be levied? 3. Against whom must it be levied?

To each of these questions I mean to give an answer—if possible, a satisfactory answer; but not in the order, in which they are proposed. I begin with the second—by whom may the war spoken of be levied? It is such a war as constitutes treason. The answer then is this: the war must be levied by those who, while they levy it, are at the same time guilty of treason. This throws us back necessarily upon another question—who may commit treason against the United States? To this the answer is—those who owe obedience to their authority. But still another question rises before us—who are they that owe obedience to that authority? I answer—those who receive protection from it. In the monarchy of Great Britain, protection and allegiance are universally acknowledged to be rights and duties reciprocal. The same principle reigns in governments of every kind. I use here the expression *obedience* instead of the expression *allegiance;* because, in England, allegiance is considered as due to the natural,[e] as well as to the

d. Con. U. S. art. 3. s. 2.
e. 1. Bl. Com. 371.

moral person of the king; to the man, as well as to the represented authority of the nation. In the United States, the authority of the nation is the sole object on one side. An object strictly corresponding to that, should be the only one required on the other side. The object strictly corresponding to authority is, obedience to that authority. I speak, therefore, with propriety and accuracy unexceptionable, when I say, that those who owe obedience to the authority, are such as receive the protection, of the United States.

This close series of investigation has led us to a standard, which is plain and easy, as well as proper and accurate—a standard, which every one can, without the possibility of a mistake, discover by his experience, as well as by his understanding—by what he enjoys, as well as by what he sees. Every one has a monitor within him, which can tell whether he feels protection from the authority of the United States: if he does, to that authority he owes obedience. On the political, as well as on the natural globe, every point must have its antipode. Of obedience the antipode is treason.

I have now shown, by whom the war may be levied. On this subject, a great deal of learning, historical, legal, and political, might be displayed; and changes might easily be rung on the doctrines of natural, and local, and temporary, and perpetual allegiance. I purposely avoid them. The reason is, that so much false is blended with so little genuine intelligence, as to render any discovery you would make an inadequate compensation for your trouble in searching for it. The rights and duties of protection and obedience may, I think, in a much more plain and direct road, be brought home to the bosom and the business of every one.

I now proceed to another question—what is meant by the expression "levying war?" From what has been said in answer to the former question, an answer to this is so far prepared as to inform us, that the term *war* cannot, in this place, mean such a one as is carried on between independent powers. The parties on one side are those who owe obedience. All the curious and extensive learning, therefore, concerning the laws of war as carried on between separate nations, must be thrown out of this question. This is such a war as is levied by those who owe obedience—by citizens; and therefore must be such a war, as, in the nature of things, citizens can levy.

The indictments for this treason generally describe the persons indicted as "arrayed in a warlike manner." As where people are assembled in great numbers, armed with offensive weapons, or weapons of war, if they march thus armed in a body, if they have chosen commanders or officers, if they march with banners displayed, or with drums or trumpets: whether the greatness of their numbers and their continuance together doing these acts may not amount to being arrayed in a warlike manner,[f] deserves consideration. If they have no military arms, nor march or continue together in the posture of war; they may be great rioters, but their conduct does not always amount to a levying of war.[g]

If one, with force and weapons invasive or defensive, hold and defend a castle or fort against the publick power; this is to levy war. So an actual insurrection or rebellion is a levying of war, and by that name must be expressed in the indictment.[h]

But this question will receive a farther illustration from the answer to the third question; because the fact of levying war is often evinced more clearly from the purpose for which, than from the manner in which, the parties assemble. I therefore proceed to examine the last question—against whom must the war be levied? It must be levied against the United States.

The words of the statute of treasons are, "If any one levy war against the king." I have before observed that, in England, allegiance is considered as due to the natural, as well as to the moral person of the king. This part of the statute of treasons has been always understood as extending to a violation of allegiance in both those points of view—to the levying of war not only against his person, but also against his authority or laws.[i] The levying of war against the United States can, for the reasons already suggested, be considered only in the latter view.

The question now arising is the following—Is such or such a war levied against the United States? This question, as was already intimated, will be best answered by considering the intention with which it was levied.[j] If it is levied on account of some *private* quarrel, or to take revenge of particular persons, it is not a war levied against the United States.[k] A rising to maintain a *private* claim of right; to break prisons for the release of *particular* persons, without any other circumstance of aggravation; or to re-

f. 1. Hale. P. C. 131. 150.
g. Id. 131.
h. 3. Ins. 10.
i. 1. Haw. 37. 4. Bl. Com. 81. Fost. 211.
j. Fost. 208.
k. Fost. 209.

move nuisances which affect, or are thought to affect, in point of interest, the parties who assemble—this is not a levying of war against the United States.[l] Insurrections in order to throw down *all* inclosures, to open *all* prisons, to enhance the price of *all* labour, to expel foreigners in general, or those from any single nation living under the protection of government, to alter the established law, or to render it ineffectual—insurrections to accomplish these ends, by numbers and an open and armed force, are a levying of war against the United States.[m]

The line of division between this species of treason and an aggravated riot is sometimes very fine and difficult to he distinguished. In such instances, it is safest and most prudent to consider the case in question as lying on the side of the inferiour crime.[n]

Treason consists in "adhering to the enemies of the United States, giving them aid and comfort." By enemies, are here understood the citizens or subjects of foreign princes or states, with whom the United States are at open war. But the subjects or citizens of such states or princes, in actual hostility, though no war be solemnly declared, are such enemies.[o] The expressions "giving them aid and comfort" are explanatory of what is meant by adherence. To give intelligence to enemies, to send provisions to them, to sell arms to them, treacherously to surrender a fort to them, to cruise in a ship with them against the United States—these are acts of adherence, aid, and comfort.[p]

To join with rebels in a rebellion, or with enemies in acts of hostility, is treason in a citizen, by adhering to those enemies, or levying war with those rebels. But if this be done from apprehension of death, and while the party is under actual force, and he take the first opportunity which offers to make his escape; this fear and compulsion will excuse him.[q]

In England, the punishment of treason is terrible indeed. The criminal is drawn to the gallows, and is not suffered to walk or be carried; though usually a hurdle is allowed to preserve him from the torment of being dragged on the ground. He is hanged by the neck, and is then cut down

l. Id. 210.
m. Id. 211. 213.
n. 1. Hale. P. C. 146.
o. Fost. 219.
p. Fost. 217. 1. Haw. 38. 4. Bl. Com. 82.
q. Fost. 216.

alive. His entrails are taken out and burned, while he is yet alive. His head is cut off. His body is divided into four parts. His head and quarters are at the disposal of the king.[r]

In the United States and in Pennsylvania,[s] treason is punished in the same manner as other capital crimes.

A traitor is hostile to his country: a pirate is the enemy of mankind—*hostis humani generis.*

Piracy is robbery and depredation on the high seas; and is a crime against the universal law of society. By declaring war against the whole human race, the pirate has laid the whole human race under the necessity of declaring war against him. He has renounced the benefits of society and government: he has abandoned himself to the most savage state of nature. The consequence is, that, by the laws of self defence, every community has a right to inflict upon him that punishment, which in a state of nature, every individual would be entitled to inflict for any invasion of his person or his personal property.[t]

"If any person," says a law of the United States, "shall commit, upon the high seas, or in any river, haven, basin, or bay, out of the jurisdiction of any particular state, murder or robbery, or any other offence, which, if committed within the body of a county, would, by the laws of the United States, be punished with death; every such offender shall be deemed, taken and adjudged to be a pirate and felon, and being thereof convicted shall suffer death."[u]

By the ancient common law, piracy committed by a subject was deemed a species of treason.[v] According to that law, it consists of such acts of robbery and depredation upon the high seas, as, committed on the land, would amount to a felony there.[w] The law of general society, as well as the law of nations, is a part of the common law.[x]

r. 4. Bl. Com. 92.

s. Treason against the state is now punished by imprisonment at hard labour, for a period not less than six, nor more than twelve years. 3. Laws Penn. 600. For the description of treason against the state, see 1. Laws Penn. 726. 2. Laws Penn. 83. *Ed.*

t. 4. Bl. Com. 71.

u. Laws U. S. 1. con. 1. sess. c. 9. s. 8.

v. 4. Bl. Com. 71.

w. 4. Bl. Com. 72.

x. Id. 73.

CHAPTER VI.

Of Crimes, Affecting Several of the Natural Rights of Individuals.

Those crimes and offences of which I have already treated, attack some *one* of the natural rights of man or of society: there are other crimes and offences, which attack *several* of those natural rights. Of these, nuisances are the most extensive and diversified.

A nuisance denotes any thing, which produces mischief, injury, or inconvenience. It is divided into two kinds—common and private.[a] The latter will be treated under the second division of my system: it is a damage to property. Common nuisances are a collection of personal injuries, which annoy the citizens generally and indiscriminately—so generally and indiscriminately, that it would be difficult to assign to each citizen his just proportion of redress; and yet, on the whole, so "noisome," that publick peace, and order, and tranquillity, and safety require them to be punished or abated.

On this subject, and, I believe, on this subject alone, the common law makes no distinction between a person and a thing. The exquisite propriety, with which the distinction is lost in this subject, proves strongly the importance of preserving it in every other. The exception establishes the rule.

How degraded are persons when they deserve to be classed with things! We have seen, on a former occasion,[b] that—1. The duellists and the promoters of duels are ranked with the offals of the shambles. The station is, indeed, a most humiliating one. Let no station, however, yield to absolute despair. From the very lowest depression, as well as from the very highest exaltation, there is a return in a contrary course. In pure compassion

a. 3. Bl. Com. 216. 4. Bl. Com. 166.
b. Ante. p. 1139.

for the degraded hero, let us give him at least one grade of promotion. Perhaps, by vigorous exertion, he may become qualified for his advanced dignity. The quarreller or promoter of quarrels of one sex, may behave so as to reflect no great disgrace on the common scold of the other. She, too, is a common nuisance.

2. A common scold, says the law, is a publick nuisance to her neighbourhood: as such she may be indicted, and, if convicted, shall be placed in a certain engine of correction, called the trebucket, castigatory, or *cucking* stool; which, in the Saxon language, signifies the scolding stool; though now it is frequently corrupted into *ducking* stool; because the residue of the sentence against her is, that when she is thus placed, she shall be plunged in the water[c]—for the purpose of prevention, it is presumed, as well as of punishment.

Our modern man of gallantry would not surely decline the honour of her company. I therefore propose humbly, that, in future, the cucking stools shall be made to hold double.

3. Eaves droppers too, another set of honourable associates—such as listen under walls, or windows, or eaves of a house, in order to hear the discourse of the family, and from that discourse to frame tales, mischievous and slanderous—these are common nuisances: they may be indicted as such; and as such may be punished by fine and finding sureties for their good behaviour.[d]

It is whispered to me, that the expression "eaves droppers" must refer to a very early and a very simple state of society, when people lived in cabins or huts: because, when people live in three story houses, it would be rather awkward to listen at their eaves in order to learn the secrets of families. It is therefore suggested, that, as the common law is remarkable for its adroitness in accommodating itself to the successive manners of succeeding ages, a small alteration should be made in the description of this nuisance, in order to suit it to the present times; and that the tea table should be substituted in the place of the eaves of the house. I declare I have not the remotest objection to the proposal; provided the wine tables, whenever they merit it, be of the party.

c. 4. Bl. Com. 169.
d. Id. ibid.

4. To keep hogs in any city or market town is a common nuisance.[e]

5. Disorderly houses are publick nuisances; and, upon indictment, may be suppressed and fined.[f]

6. Every thing offensive and injurious to the health of a neighbourhood is a common nuisance; is liable to a publick prosecution; and may be punished by fine according to the quantity of the misdemeanor.[g]

7. Annoyances in highways, bridges, and publick rivers are likewise common nuisances.[h] Other kinds might be enumerated.

Indecency, publick and grossly scandalous, may well be considered as a species of common nuisance: it is certainly an offence, which may be indicted and punished at the common law.[i]

Profaneness and blasphemy are offences, punishable by fine and by imprisonment. Christianity is a part of the common law.[j]

e. 4. Bl. Com. 167.
f. Id. ibid.
g. Id. ibid.
h. Id. ibid.
i. 1. Haw. 7. 1. Sid. 168. Wood. Ins. 412.
j. 2. Str. 834. 4. Bl. Com. 59.

CHAPTER VII.

Of Crimes Against the Rights of Individuals Acquired Under Civil Government.

Under civil government, one is entitled not only to those rights which are natural; he is entitled to others which are acquired. He is entitled to the honest administration of the government in general: he is entitled, in particular, to the impartial administration of justice. Those rights may be infringed: the infringements of them are crimes. These we next consider.

1. Extortion is the taking of money by any officer, by colour of his office, either where none is due, or where less is due, or before it is due. At common law, this crime may be severely punished by fine and imprisonment, and by a removal from the office, in the execution of which it was committed.[a]

2. Oppression under colour of office is a crime of still more extensive and of still more malignant import. Tyrannical partiality is generally its infamous associate. These, at the common law, may be punished with fine, with imprisonment, with forfeiture of office, and with other discretionary censure regulated by the nature and the aggravations of the crimes.[b]

By a law of the United States, it is enacted, that if any supervisor or other officer of inspection of the excise shall be convicted of extortion or oppression in the execution of his office; he shall be fined not exceeding five hundred dollars, or imprisoned not exceeding six months, or both, at the discretion of the court; and shall also forfeit his office.[c]

3. Even negligence in publick offices, if gross, will expose the negligent officers to a fine; and, in very notorious cases, to a forfeiture of office.[d]

a. 1. Haw. 170. 171.
b. 4. Bl. Com. 140.
c. Laws U. S. 1. cong. 3. sess. c. 15. s. 39.
d. 1. Haw. 168.

4. Embracery is an attempt to influence a jury corruptly, by promises, persuasions, entreaties, money, or entertainments. The person embracing is punished by fine and imprisonment. The yielding juror is distinguished by superiour punishment.[e]

5. Bribery is, when a judge, or other person employed in the administration of justice, takes any undue reward to influence his behaviour in office. At common law, bribery, in him who offers, in him who gives, and in him who takes the bribe, is punished with fine and imprisonment. In high offices, the punishment has deservedly been higher still.[f]

Bribery also signifies sometimes the taking or the giving of a reward for an office of a publick nature. Nothing, indeed, can be more palpably pernicious to the publick, than that places of high power and high trust should be filled, not by those who are wise and good enough to execute them, but by those who are unprincipled and rich enough to purchase them.[g]

By a law of the United States, if any person shall give a bribe to a judge for his judgment in a cause depending before him; both shall be fined and imprisoned at the discretion of the court; and shall for ever be disqualified to hold any office of honour, trust, or profit under the United States.[h]

6. Perjury is a crime committed, when a lawful oath is administered in some judicial proceeding, by one who has authority, to a person who swears absolutely and falsely, in a matter material to the issue or cause in question.[i]

An oath, says my Lord Coke, is so sacred, and so deeply concerns the consciences of men, that it cannot be administered to any one, unless it be allowed by the common law, or by act of parliament; nor by any one, who has not authority by common law, or by act of parliament: neither can any oath allowed by the common law, or by act of parliament, be altered, unless by act of parliament.[k] For these reasons, it is much to be doubted whether any magistrate is justifiable in administering voluntary affidavits, unsupported by the authority of law. It is more than possible, that, by such

e. 4. Bl. Com. 140.
f. 4. Bl. Com. 139.
g. 1. Haw. 168.
h. Laws U. S. 1. cong. 2. sess. c. 9. s. 21.
i. 3. Ins. 164.
k. 3. Ins. 165.

idle oaths, a man may frequently incur the guilt, though he evade the temporal penalties of perjury.

It is a part of the foregoing definition of perjury, that it must be when the person swears *absolutely.* In addition to this, it has been said, that the oath must be direct, and not as the deponent thinks, or remembers, or believes.[l] This doctrine has, however, been lately questioned; and, it seems, on solid principles. When a man swears, that he believes what, in truth, he does not believe, he pronounces a falsehood as much, as when he swears absolutely that a thing is true, which he knows not to be true. My Lord Chief Justice De Grey, in a late case, said, that it was a mistake, which mankind had fallen into, that a person could not be convicted of perjury for deposing on oath according to his belief.[m] It is certainly true, says my Lord Mansfield, that a man may be indicted for perjury, in swearing that he believes a fact to be true, which he must know to be false.[n]

At common law, the punishment of perjury has been very various. Anciently it was punished with death; afterwards with banishment, or cutting out the tongue; afterwards by forfeiture; now by fine and imprisonment, and incapacity to give testimony.[o] To these last mentioned punishments, that of the pillory is added by a law of the[p] United States.[q]

7. Subornation of perjury is the crime of procuring another to take such a false oath as constitutes perjury. It is punished as perjury.[r]

8. Conspiracy is a crime of deep malignity against the administration of justice. Not only those, who falsely and maliciously cause an innocent man to be indicted and tried, are properly conspirators; but those also are such, who *conspire* to indict a man falsely and maliciously, whether they do

l. Id. 166. 1. Haw. 175.

m. Leach 304.

n. Leach 304.

o. 4. Bl. Com. 137.

p. 1. cong. 2. sess. c. 9. s. 18.

q. By a late act of assembly in Pennsylvania (6. Laws Penn. 513.) it is provided, that persons convicted of perjury, or subornation of perjury, shall forfeit and pay any sum not exceeding five hundred dollars, and suffer imprisonment and be kept at hard labour during any term not exceeding seven years; and further, shall thereafter be disqualified from holding any office of honour, trust, or profit in the commonwealth, and from being admitted as a legal witness in any cause. *Ed.*

r. 4. Bl. Com. 137.

or do not any act in the prosecution of the conspiracy.[s] From the description of this crime it is obvious, that at least two persons are necessary to constitute it.[t]

He who is convicted of a conspiracy to accuse another of a crime which may touch his life, shall have the following judgment pronounced against him: that he shall lose *liberam legem,* the freedom and franchise of the law, by which he is disqualified to be a juror or a witness, or even to appear in a court of justice: that his houses and lands and goods shall be forfeited during his life: that his trees shall be rooted up, his lands shall be wasted, his houses shall be rased, and his body shall be imprisoned. This is commonly called the villainous judgment: and is given by the common law.[u] By that law, all confederacies whatever wrongfully to prejudice a third person are highly criminal.[v]

9. Common barratry is another offence against the administration of justice. A common barrator is a common mover, or exciter, or maintainer of suits or quarrels, either in courts, or in the country. One act only will not constitute a barrator. He must be charged as a common barrator.[w] He is the common nuisance of society under a civil government.

A common barrator is to be fined, imprisoned, and bound to his good behaviour: if he be of the profession of the law, he is also to be further punished by being disabled, in future, to practise.[x]

10. At common law, the embezzling, defacing, or altering of any record, without due authority, was a crime highly punishable by fine and imprisonment.[y]

By a law of the United States, if any person shall feloniously steal, take away, alter, falsify, or otherwise avoid any record, writ, process, or other proceedings in any of the courts of the United States, by means of which any judgment shall be reversed, made void, or not take effect; such person

s. 1. Haw. 189.
t. Id. 192.
u. 1. Haw. 193.
v. Id. 190.
w. Id. 243.
x. Id. 244.
y. Id. 112.

shall be fined not exceeding five thousand dollars, or imprisoned not exceeding seven years, and whipped not exceeding thirty nine stripes.[z]

11. To obstruct the execution of lawful process, is a crime of a very high and presumptuous nature: to obstruct an arrest upon criminal process, is more particularly so. It has been holden, that the party opposing such an arrest becomes a partner in the crime—an accessory in felony, and a principal in treason.[a]

By a law of the United States, if any person shall knowingly and wilfully obstruct, resist, or oppose any officer of the United States in serving or attempting to serve any mesne process or warrant, or any rule or order of any of the courts of the United States, or any other legal or judicial writ or process whatsoever; or shall assault, beat, or wound any officer, or other person duly authorized, in serving or executing any such writ, rule, order, process, or warrant; he shall be imprisoned not exceeding twelve months, and fined not exceeding three hundred dollars.[b]

12. When one is arrested upon a criminal process, it is an offence even to escape from custody; and this offence may be punished by fine and imprisonment.[c] But if an officer, or a private person,[d] who has the custody of another, permits him to escape, either by negligence, or, still more, by connivance; such officer or private person is culpable in a much higher degree. He has not the natural desire of liberty to tempt—he has official obligations to prevent it. If he permits it through negligence, he may be punished by fine: if he permits it by consent or connivance, his conduct is generally agreed to amount to the same kind of crime, and to deserve the same degree of punishment, as the crime of which the prisoner is guilty, and for which he is committed; whether trespass, or felony, or treason.[e]

13. To break a prison was, at the common law, a capital crime, whatever might have been the cause, for which the person breaking it was committed. The reason assigned was—interest reipublicae ut carceres sint in

z. Laws U. S. 1. cong. 2. sess. c. 9. s. 15.
a. 4. Bl. Com. 129. 2. Haw. 121.
b. Laws U. S. 1. cong. 2. sess. c. 9. s. 22.
c. 2. Haw. 122.
d. 2. Haw. 138.
e. Id. 134. 1. Hale. P. C. 590.

tuto.[f] Seldom is there reason to complain of the common, as of a rigorous law. In this instance, however, there is unquestionably reason for complaint. The Mirrour complains of it as a hard law. Its severity was moderated by a statute made in the reign of Edward the second.[g] By that statute, the breaking of a prison is not a capital crime, unless the party breaking it was committed for a capital crime. But to break prison, when lawfully committed for an inferiour offence, is a misdemeanor, and may be punished with fine and imprisonment.[h]

14. A rescue is the freeing of another, by force, from imprisonment, or from an arrest. In the person rescuing, it is generally the same crime, as a breach of prison would have been in the person breaking it. There is, however, one exception: a person, who is committed for treason and breaks the prison, is guilty of felony only: he, who rescues him, is guilty of treason.[i]

By a law of the United States,[j] if any person rescue one convicted of a capital crime, the person rescuing shall be punished capitally: if he rescue one committed, for, but not convicted of a capital crime, or one committed for, or convicted of a crime not capital; he shall be fined not exceeding five hundred dollars, and imprisoned not exceeding one year.

15. Offences against the courts, have always been considered as offences against the administration of justice. By the ancient common law before the conquest, to strike or to draw a sword in them, was a capital crime:[k] and the law still retains so much of the ancient severity, as only to exchange the loss of life for that of the offending limb.

If, while the courts in Westminster hall are sitting; or if, before justices of assize, or justices of oyer and terminer, any one shall draw a weapon upon any judge, though he strike not; or if he strike a juror or any other person, with or without a weapon; he shall lose his right hand, shall forfeit all his goods and all the profits of his lands during his life, and shall suffer perpetual imprisonment.[l]

f. 2. Ins. 589. "It concerns the state that prisons be safe places of confinement."
g. Id. ib. St. 1. Ed. 2. s. 2.
h. 2. Haw. 128. 4. Bl. Com. 131.
i. 2. Haw. 139. 140.
j. 1. Cong. 2. sess. c. 9. s. 23.
k. 3. Ins. 140.
l. 1. Haw. 57. 3. Ins. 140.

CHAPTER VIII.

Of the Persons Capable of Committing Crimes; and of the Different Degrees of Guilt Incurred in the Commission of the Same Crime.

I have now enumerated the crimes and offences known to the common law; and have stated their punishments, as inflicted either by that law, or by positive statutes of the United States or of Pennsylvania.

When we come to a retrospect of this enumeration of crimes and punishments, we shall find that it is fruitful of much instruction, both of the speculative and of the practical kind. At present, let us consider who are capable and who are not capable of committing crimes. The general rule is, that all are capable of committing them. This general rule will be best illustrated and proved by ascertaining its exceptions. We have seen already, that the common law measures crimes chiefly by the intention. The intention necessarily supposes the joint operations of the understanding and the will. If the operation of either is wanting, no crime can exist. In ideots, at all times; in lunaticks, except during their lucid intervals; and in infants, till they arrive at the age of discretion, the operation of the understanding is wanting. In ministerial officers, in wives, in persons under duress, the operation of the will is frequently presumed, by the law, to be wanting. In all such cases, the law imputes not criminality of intention.

On this subject, I cannot now enter into a detail: suffice it to have mentioned the general principles, according to which the particular cases are classed and determined.

In the commission of the same crime, the law often distinguishes different degrees of guilt. One may be a principal or an accessory: a principal may be so in the first or in the second degree: an accessory may be so before or after the fact. In some crimes, there are no accessories; in others, there are none before the fact.

The part acted by a principal is coexistent with the commission of the crime: the part acted by an accessory is antecedent or subsequent to it.

A principal in the first degree, is he who personally perpetrates the crime: a principal in the second degree, is he who is present, aiding and abetting it.[a]

An accessory before the fact is he who, though absent when the crime was committed, yet procured, counselled, commanded, or abetted the commission of it:[b] an accessory after the fact is he who, knowing a crime to be committed, receives, relieves, comforts, or assists the criminal.[c]

In treason, there are no accessories either before or after the fact; for all consenters, aiders, abettors, and knowing receivers and comforters of traitors, are themselves principals. As to the course of proceeding, however, those who actually committed the treasonable fact, should be tried before those who consented or aided: for, in a contrary course of proceeding, this inconvenience might follow, that those who, in other crimes, would be principals in the second degree, might be convicted, and afterwards those who, in other crimes, would be principals in the first degree, might be acquitted. This most evidently would be absurd.[d]

In trespass, and in crimes not felonious, all those who, in felonious crimes, would be accessories before the fact, are deemed principals; and those who, in felonious crimes, would be accessories after the fact, are not considered as having committed any offence.[e]

The distinction between accessories after and accessories before the fact, and between accessories and principals, ought to be carefully and accurately preserved: for in many cases, there is a real difference between the degrees of guilt, and a proportioned difference ought to be established, where it is not already established, between the degrees of punishment.

The distinction between principals in the first and those in the second degree, though preserved in theory, and sometimes in the course of proceedings on the trial, is, nevertheless, lost universally in the scale of punishments. He who watches, at a distance, to prevent a surprise, which might

a. 1. Hale. P. C. 615.
b. Id. ibid.
c. 1. Hale. P. C. 613.
d. Id. 613.
e. Id. ibid.

defeat the execution of a concerted plan, is punished equally with him, who, in the execution of it, uses the assassinating poignard, not necessary, not generally intended, but deemed solely by him who uses it as, in some measure, contributing to the principal and the concerted purpose. In such an immense disparity of guilt, there ought to be a disparity of punishment.

These reflections receive support from considerations of utility, as well as from those of intrinsick justice. When a number confederate in a common enterprise, whose supposed advantages are to be equally participated, it is their effort to share only an equal proportion of the danger, as they are to receive only an equal proportion of the gain. This effort, instead of being countenanced by measuring the same punishment to all who act any part in the concerted enterprise, should be counterworked by graduating the punishment according to the part which each has acted. If the principal, who personally perpetrates the crime—for there is generally a capital part to be acted by some one—is distinguished, in punishment, from those who are only present, aiding and abetting the common adventure; this will increase the difficulty of finding one, who will act this capital and conspicuous part; as his danger will become greater in proportion to the greater severity of his punishment.

Besides; where there is society in danger, there is society in exertion; for even in criminal enterprises the social nature is not lost. Let one be selected, solitary, to perpetrate a crime and to suffer a punishment, in the pain and guilt of which none are to be involved but himself; he will no longer be buoyed up on a fluid surrounding him at an equal level; and as it sinks down from him, he will sink down to it. Among associates in crimes, the law should sow the seeds of dissension.

Misprision consists in the concealment of a crime, which ought to be revealed.[f]

By a law of the United States, misprision of treason is punished with a fine not exceeding a thousand dollars, and imprisonment not exceeding seven years;[g] and misprision of felony, with imprisonment not exceeding three years, and a fine not exceeding five hundred dollars.[h]

f. 3. Ins. 36. 4. Bl. Com. 119.
g. Laws U. S. 1. con. 2. sess. c. 9. s. 2.
h. Id. s. 6.

The receiving of goods, known to be stolen, is a high misdemeanor at the common law. By a law of the United States, it is punished in the same manner as larceny.[i]

Theft-bote, or the receiving again of one's goods which have been stolen, or other amends, upon an agreement not to prosecute, was formerly held to render one an accessory to the larceny: it is now punished only with fine and imprisonment. But merely to receive the goods again is no offence, unless some favour be shown to the thief.[j]

On the subject, concerning principals and accessories, as well as on the former, concerning the incapacity of guilt, I cannot now enter into a detail: suffice it here, as it sufficed there, to mention the general principles which will govern and illustrate the particular instances.

i. Id. s. 17.
j. 1. Haw. 125.

CHAPTER IX.
Of the Direct Means Used by the Law to Prevent Offences.

I should now, according to my general plan, "point out the different steps, prescribed by the law, for apprehending, detaining, trying, and punishing offenders." But it will be proper first to consider a short, though a very interesting, title of the criminal law—the direct means which it uses to prevent offences.

These are, security for the peace; security for the good behaviour; and the peaceful, but active and authoritative interposition of every citizen, much more of every publick officer of peace, to prevent the commission of threatened, or the completion of inchoate crimes.

1. Security for the peace consists in being bound, alone, or with one or more sureties, in an obligation for an ascertained sum, with a condition subjoined that the obligation shall be void, if the party shall, during the time limited, keep the peace towards all the citizens, and particularly towards him, on whose application the security is taken.[a]

Whenever a person has just cause to fear that another will kill, or beat, or imprison him, or burn his house, or will procure others to do such mischief to his person or habitation; he may, against such person, demand security for the peace; and every justice of the peace is bound to grant it, when he is satisfied, upon oath, that the party demanding it is, and has just reason to be, under such fear; and that the security is not demanded from malice, nor for vexation.[b] Upon many occasions, a justice of the peace may officially take security for the peace, though no one demand it. He may take it of those who, in his presence, shall make an affray, or shall threaten

a. 1. Haw. 129. 4. Bl. Com. 249.
b. 1. Haw. 127.

to kill or beat any person, or shall contend together with hot words, or shall go about with unusual weapons or attendants, to the terrour of the citizens.[c]

If the party to be bound is in the presence of the justice, and will not find such sureties as are required; he may be immediately committed for his disobedience, and until he find them: but if he is absent, he cannot be committed without a warrant to find sureties. This warrant should be under seal, and should mention on whose application, and for what cause, it is granted.[d]

The obligation or recognisance to keep the peace may be forfeited by any actual violence to the person of another, whether done by the party himself, or by others through his procurement: it may be forfeited by any unlawful assembly to the terrour of the citizens; and even by words tending directly to a breach of the peace, as by challenging one to fight, or, in his presence, threatening to beat him. But it is not forfeited by words merely of heat and choler; nor by a bare trespass on the lands or goods of another, unaccompanied with violence to his person.[e]

2. Security for the good behaviour includes security for the peace and more; but they are of great affinity with each other; and both may be contained in the same recognisance. It is not easy, upon this subject, to find precise rules for the direction of the magistrate: much is left to his own discretion. It seems, however, that he may be justified in demanding this security from those, whose characters he shall have just reason to suspect as scandalous, quarrelsome, or dangerous.

It has been said, that whatever is a good cause for binding a man to his good behaviour, will be a good cause likewise to forfeit his recognisance for it. But this rule is too large. One is bound, to prevent what may never happen: he is bound for giving cause of alarm; not for having done any mischief. His recognisance, however, may certainly be broken by the commission of any actual misbehaviour, for the prevention of which it was taken.[f]

3. I have mentioned the peaceful, but active and authoritative interposition of every citizen, much more of every publick officer of the peace, as a

c. Id. 126.
d. Id. 128.
e. 1. Haw. 130. 131.
f. Id. 129. 131.

means for preventing the commission of threatened, and the completion of inchoate crimes. This subject has not received the attention, which it undoubtedly merits; nor has it been viewed in that striking light, in which it ought to be considered.

In every citizen, much more in every publick officer of peace and justice, the whole authority of the law is vested—to every citizen, much more to every publick officer of peace and justice, the whole protection of the law is extended, for the all-important purpose of preventing crimes. From every citizen, much more from every publick officer of peace and justice, the law demands the performance of that duty, in performing which they are clothed with legal authority, and shielded by legal protection.

The preservation of the peace and the security of society has, in every stage of it, been an object peculiarly favoured by the common law. To accomplish this object, we can trace, through the different periods of society, regulations suited to its different degrees of simplicity, or of rudeness, or of refinement.

The much famed law of decennaries, by which, in small districts, all were reciprocally bound for the good behaviour of all, was well adapted to the age of the great Alfred, when commerce was little known, and the habits and rules of enlarged society were not introduced.

In times more turbulent, precautions for the security of the citizens were taken, more fitted to those turbulent times. The statute of Winchester, made in the thirteenth year of the reign of Edward the first, contains many regulations upon this subject; but they were regulations for enforcing the "ancient police" of the kingdom;[g] and their design is expressly declared to have been, to prevent the increase of crimes; or, in the language of that day, "to abate the power of felons."

For the purposes of prevention, it was directed, that, in great walled towns, the gates should be shut from the setting to the rising of the sun: that, during that time, watches, as had been *formerly* used, should, in proportion to the number of inhabitants, watch continually: that if any stranger passed by, these watches should arrest and detain him till the morning: and that if any one resisted the arrest, hue and cry should be raised; and those, who kept watch, should follow the hue and cry from town to town, till the

g. 1. Reev. 442.

offender was taken. Every week, or at least every fifteenth day, the bailiffs of towns were obliged to make inquiry concerning all who lodged in the suburbs; and if they found any who lodged or received persons, of whom it was suspected that they were "persons against the peace," they were to do what was right in the matter.[h]

The hue and cry was an institution of the common law: the Mirrour, speaking of the ancient laws before the conquest, makes express mention of pursuit from town to town at the hue and cry. The passage is very remarkable, and deserves, on many accounts, to be transcribed at large. It is a part of that section which has for its title—"the first constitutions ordained by the ancient kings, from King Alfred." Among others are introduced the following articles—"Every one of the age of fourteen years and upwards shall be ready to kill capital offenders in their notorious crimes, or to pursue them from town to town at hue and cry." "If they can neither kill nor apprehend them, they shall take care to have them put in the exigent, in order that they may outlaw or banish them in the following manner," &c.[i]

If a man, who is under a recognisance to keep the peace, beat or fight with one who attempts to kill *any* stranger; it is not a forfeiture of his recognisance.[j]

If, as we have seen upon a former occasion,[k] a person who interposes to part the combatants in a sudden affray, and gives notice to them of his friendly intention, be assaulted by them or either of them, and, in the struggle, should happen to kill; this will be justifiable homicide. On the other hand, if this person be killed by the combatants, or either of them, it will be murder. To preserve the publick peace, and to prevent mischief, it is the duty of every man, in such cases, to interpose.[l]

When the law enjoins a duty, it both protects and authorizes the discharge of it. Ministers of justice, it will be admitted on all hands, are, while in the execution of their offices, under the peculiar protection of the law. Without such protection, the publick peace and tranquillity could not,

h. St. 13. Ed. 1. c. 4.
i. 4. Cou. Ang. Norm. 487.
j. 1. Haw. 131.
k. Ante. p. 1143.
l. Fost. 272.

by any means, be preserved. But this peculiar protection of the law is not confined personally to one, who is a minister of justice: it is extended to all those who come in aid of him, and afford their assistance for the preservation of the peace. Even all those who *attend* for that purpose are under the same protection. It is immaterial whether they were or were not commanded to render their service upon the occasion. This peculiar protection of the law extends still farther. It reaches to private persons who, though no minister of justice be present, interpose for preventing mischief in the case of an affray. They are in the discharge of a duty which the law requires. The law is their warrant; and they may justly be considered as persons employed in the publick service, and in the advancement of justice.[m]

If so, in the case of an affray, in which, on each side, the same disposition is shown; much more so, in a case of premeditated, concerted, planned, prepared, riotous, felonious, and treasonable outrage, on one side—connived at, perhaps countenanced, by those in the administration of the government. In such a case, the legal duty, the legal authority, and the legal protection operate with tenfold energy and force. In such a case, the law may well be said to throw herself, without reserve, upon the arms of the citizens. In such cases, the citizens, with open arms, are bound to receive her, and to give her that protection, which, in return, she confers upon them.

The application of this important principle of preventive justice is admirably fitted to small, as well as to the greatest occasions. If it was strictly made upon all occasions, the benefits redounding to society would be immense. The petulant ill nature of the boy, the quarrelsome temper of the man, the rapacious aim of the robber, and the malignant disposition of the assassin, would be immediately checked in their operations. The principles themselves, unsupplied with fuel to inflame them, would, at last, be extinguished.

Thus much for the means, which the law employs directly for the benevolent purpose of preventing crimes.

m. Fost. 309.

CHAPTER X.

Of the Different Steps Prescribed by the Law, for Apprehending, Detaining, Trying, and Punishing Offenders.

I now proceed to the different steps which the law prescribes for apprehending, detaining, trying, and punishing criminals.

A warrant is the first step usually taken for their apprehension.

A warrant is a precept from a judicial to a ministerial officer of justice, commanding him to bring the person mentioned in it, before him who issues it, or before some other officer having judicial authority in the cause.[a] This warrant should be under the hand and seal of the magistrate issuing it: it should mention the time and place of making it, and the cause for which it is granted. It may be either to bring the party generally before any magistrate, or specially to bring him before the magistrate only who grants it. It may be directed to the sheriff, constable, or to a private person; for the warrant constitutes him, for this purpose, an authorized officer.[b]

By the constitution of Pennsylvania,[c] no warrant to seize persons shall issue without describing them as nearly as may be, nor without probable cause supported by oath or affirmation. Such warrant may be granted, even by any justice of the peace, for treason, felony, or any other offence against the peace.[d]

When the warrant is received by the person to whom it is directed, he is authorized, and, if a publick officer, obliged to execute it, so far as the jurisdiction of the magistrate and himself extends.[e] A sheriff may depute

a. Wood. Ins. 81. 1.Bl. Com. 137. 4. Bl. Com. 287.
b. 2. Haw. 85.
c. Art. 9. s. 8.
d. 2. Haw. 84.
e. 4. Bl. Com. 288.

others; but every other person is obliged himself to execute it; though others may lawfully assist him. A warrant directed to all constables generally can be executed by each only in his own precinct: but a warrant directed to a particular constable by name, may be executed by him any where within the jurisdiction of the magistrate.[f]

The execution of the warrant is commenced by an arrest; which is the apprehending or restraining of the person, whom it mentions or describes.[g] But, besides those arrests which are made in the execution of warrants, there are others enjoined or justified by the law.

All, of age, who are present when a felony is committed, or when a dangerous wound is given, are, on pain of fine and imprisonment, bound to apprehend the person who has done the mischief.[h] If the crime has been committed out of their view, they are, upon a hue and cry, obliged to pursue with the utmost diligence, and endeavour to apprehend him who has committed it. Hue and cry is the pursuit of an offender from place to place, till he is taken: all who are present when he commits the crime, are bound to raise it against him on his flying for it. Every one is obliged to assist an officer demanding his assistance, in order to apprehend a felon, to suppress an affray, or to secure the persons of affrayers.[i] In all these cases, the doors of houses may, if necessary, be broken open for the apprehension of the offenders, if admittance is refused on signifying the cause of demanding it.[j]

It is a general rule, that, at any time, and in any place, every private person is justified in arresting a traitor or a felon; and, if a treason or a felony has been committed, he is justified in arresting even an innocent person, upon his reasonable suspicion that by such person it has been committed.[k] If one see another upon the point of committing a treason or a felony, or doing any act which would manifestly endanger the life of another; he may lay hold on him, and detain him till it may be presumed reasonably that he has altered his design.[l] In the case of a mere breach of the peace, no private person can arrest one for it after it is over.[m]

f. 2. Haw. 86.
g. 4. Bl. Com. 286.
h. 2. Haw.74.
i. Id. 75.
j. Id. 86. 4. Bl. Com. 289.
k. 2. Haw. 76.
l. Id. 77.
m. Id. ibid.

Whenever an arrest may be justified by a private person, it may *a fortiori* be justified by an officer of justice.[n] In addition to their own personal exertions, they have a right to demand the assistance of others.[o] A constable may not only arrest affrayers, but may also detain them till they find security for the peace.[p] A justice of the peace may, by parol, authorize any one to arrest another, who, in his presence, is guilty of an actual breach of the peace, or, in his absence, is engaged in a riot.[q]

Whenever a person is arrested for a crime, he ought to be brought before a justice of the peace, or other judicial magistrate. This magistrate is obliged immediately to examine into the circumstances of the crime alleged; and according to the result of this examination, the person accused should be either discharged, or bailed, or committed to prison.

If it clearly appear that no crime was committed, or, if committed, that the suspicion conceived against the prisoner is entirely unfounded; he should be restored to his liberty.[r]

To bail a person is to deliver him to his sureties, who give sufficient security for his appearance: he is intrusted to their friendly custody, instead of being committed to the confinement of the gaol. At the common law, every man accused or even indicted of treason or of any felony whatever, might be bailed upon good surety: for at the common law, says my Lord Coke,[s] the gaol was his pledge, who could find no other: he could be bailed, till he was convicted.

This part of the common law, however, is, in England, greatly altered by parliamentary provisions, which restrict, in numerous instances, the power of admitting to bail. Indeed it is obvious, that between the law of capital punishments and that of commitments, the connexion must be intimate and inseparable. In capital offences, no bail can be a security equal to the actual custody of the person: for what is there, which a man may not be induced to forfeit to save his life?[t] One court in England, and only one—the court of king's bench, or, in the time of the vacation, any judge of that court—still possesses the discretionary power of bailing in any

n. 2. Haw. 80.
o. Id. 81.
p. Id. ibid.
q. Id. 83.
r. Id. 87.
s. 2. Ins. 189.
t. 4. Bl. Com. 294.

case, according to its circumstances; excepting only such persons as are committed by either house of parliament, while the session lasts, and such as are committed for contempts by any of the superiour courts of justice.[u]

To refuse or to delay bail, where it ought to be granted, is a misdemeanor at the common law,[v] and may be punished on an indictment. By the constitution of Pennsylvania,[w] it is declared, as an inviolable rule, "that excessive bail shall not be required;" and "that all prisoners shall be bailable by sufficient sureties; unless for capital offences, when the proof is evident or presumption great."

If the crime is not bailable, or if the prisoner cannot find sureties, the magistrate is under the disagreeable necessity of ordering, by a warrant under his hand and seal and containing the cause of the order, that he shall be imprisoned in the publick gaol, till he be thence delivered by the due course of law.[x] This is a commitment.

This imprisonment, it ought to be remembered, is for the purpose only of keeping, not for that of punishing the prisoner: he ought, for this reason, to be treated with every degree of tenderness, of which his safe custody will possibly admit. In particular, a gaoler is not justified, by the law, in fettering a prisoner, unless where he is unruly, or where it is absolutely necessary to prevent an escape.[y] "Solent praesides in carcere continendos damnare ut in vinculis contineantur; sed hujusmodi interdicta sunt a lege, quia carcer ad continendos, et non puniendos, haberi debeat."[z] "Custodes vero gaolarum paenam sibi commissis non augeant, nec eos torqueant; sed, omni saevitia remota, pietateque adhibita, judicia in ipsos promulgata debite exequantur."[a1] Such is the law of imprisonment, ancient and approved.

u. Id. 296.
v. 2. Haw. 90.
w. Art. 9. s. 13, 14.
x. 4. Bl. Com. 297.
y. 3. Ins. 34.
z. Bract. 105. a.
a. Fleta. l. 1. c. 26.

1. Guards are accustomed to condemn those who are to be held in prison to being confined in chains; but things of this sort are forbidden by law, because a prison ought to be regarded as confining men, not punishing them. Indeed, the guards of jails should not increase the punishment for those committed to their care, nor should they torture them. But, with all cruelty removed, and with piety brought to bear, they ought to execute the judgments promulgated against their prisoners.

When the party is taken, and bailed or imprisoned; the next step in order is, to institute a prosecution against him. This may be done by four different methods—by appeal; by information; by presentment; by indictment.

1. An appeal is an accusation by one private person against another for some crime: it is a private action of the party injured, demanding punishment for the injury which he has suffered: it is also a prosecution for the state, on account of the crime committed against the publick.[b]

In ancient times there were appeals for a breach of the peace, for a battery, and for false imprisonment, as well as for more aggravated injuries and crimes; but they have been out of use, and converted into actions of trespass, for many hundred years.[c]

An appeal lies for mayhem, for larceny, for arson, for rape, for death. It is brought by the party ravished, robbed, maimed, or whose house was burned; or by the wife, or, if no wife, by the heir, of the person killed.[d] An appeal may be brought previous to an indictment; and if the defendant be acquitted, he cannot afterwards be indicted for the same crime: if he is found guilty, he shall suffer the same punishment as if he had been convicted on a prosecution by an indictment.[e] An appeal may be discharged by the concurrence of all the parties interested—by the pardon of the crown, and by the release of the appellant.[f]

The appeal can be traced to the ancient forests of Germany. "Luitur homicidium," says Tacitus,[g] "certo armentorum ac pecorum numero; recipitque satisfactionem universa domus."[2]

On this subject there is, in our law books, an immense profusion of professional learning. As the appeal is now but little used, I decline any minute inquiry concerning it: as it is still in force, it would have been improper wholly to have omitted it.

2. A second mode of prosecuting crimes and offences is by information. Some informations are brought partly at the suit of the state, and partly

b. 4. Bl. Com. 308. 2. Haw. 155.

c. 2. Haw. 157.

d. 2. Haw. 164. 4. Bl. Com. 310.

e. 4. Bl. Com. 311.

f. 1. Hale. P.C. 9.

g. De mor. Ger. c. 21.

2. Homicide is atoned for by a certain number of cattle and sheep; and the entire family receives satisfaction.

at the suit of a citizen. These are a species of *qui tam*[h] actions; and will be considered when we treat concerning civil suits.

Informations in the name of the state or of the crown alone are of two kinds: those which are filed *ex officio* by the publick prosecutor, and are properly at the suit of the publick; and those which are carried on in the name, indeed, of the commonwealth or crown, but, in fact, at the instance of some private person or common informer. The first have been the source of much; the second have been the source of intolerable vexation: both were the ready tools, by using which Empson and Dudley,[3] and an arbitrary star chamber, fashioned the proceedings of the law into a thousand tyrannical forms. Neither, indeed, extended to capital crimes: but ingenious tyranny can torture in a thousand shapes, without depriving the person tortured of his life.

Restraints have, in England, been imposed upon the last species: but the first—those at the king's own suit, filed by his attorney general—are still unrestrained.[i] By the constitution of Pennsylvania, both kinds are effectually removed. By that constitution, however, informations are still suffered to live: but they are bound and gagged. They are confined to official misdemeanors; and even against those, they cannot be slipt but by leave of the court. By that constitution, "no person shall, for any indictable offence, be proceeded against criminally by information"—"unless by leave of the court, for oppression and misdemeanor in office." Military cases are also excepted.[j]

3. Presentment is a third species of prosecution. A presentment, in its most extensive signification, comprehends inquisitions of office, of which the coroner's inquest is one: it comprehends likewise regular indictments, which are preferred and found. But, in its proper sense, it is an accusation found by a grand jury, of their own motion, and from their own knowledge and observation, without any bill being laid before them by the prosecutor for the publick. This presentment is afterwards reduced into proper form by the publick prosecutor; and in this form is sent to the grand

h. 4. Bl. Com. 303.

3. Richard Empson (?–1510) and Edmund Dudley (c. 1462–1510) were members of Henry VII's controversial tribunal called Council Learned in the Law. After Henry VII's death they were both executed for treason.

i. Id. 307.

j. Art 9. s. 10.

jury, in the same manner as bills which are originally preferred to them by that officer. These bills and this presentment, found in form; are indictments.

When the grand jury, after having heard the evidence adduced to support a bill, think it insufficient for this purpose, they endorse on the bill "ignoramus," and direct the foreman to sign this endorsement. By this endorsement it is meant, that though the matters charged in the bill may be true, their truth is not sufficiently evinced to the jury. If the charge in the bill appears to be supported, it is then endorsed "a true bill," and as such is signed by the foreman.

A grand jury must consist of at least twelve members, because twelve are necessary—it must not consist of more than twenty three members, because twelve are sufficient, to find an indictment; and twelve would not be a majority of a greater number.

At the common law, a grand jury cannot find an indictment for any crime, but such as has been committed within the county or precinct, for which they are returned.[k]

A bill cannot be returned true in part, and false in part; it must be returned "a true bill" or "ignoramus" for the whole. Nor can it be returned specially or conditionally.[l]

Much might be said concerning the form of indictments generally, and also concerning the particular form of the indictment for each particular species of crimes: but this kind of learning, which, by the by, ought neither to be overlooked nor disregarded by the professional lawyer, is found in full and minute detail in the numerous books and treatises of the criminal law. To these I beg leave to refer you. To go fully into particulars would employ too great a proportion of my lectures: to go imperfectly would convey no information that could be deemed regular or satisfactory.

Suffice it to observe, as a general and important principle with regard to indictments, that as to persons, times, and places, and, above all, as to the descriptions of crimes, the most precise certainty which can be reasonably expected is indispensably required. Certainty, indeed, is a governing and a pervading quality in all good legislation, and in all good administration of

k. 2. Haw. 220.
l. Id. 210.

law. In this very important quality, the common law, pure and unadulterated, has attained a very uncommon degree of perfection. I add, that the common law is equally remarkable for the simplicity as for the accuracy of its forms. I repeat it—they deserve the close study and attention of every lawyer by profession. Even to others, who have leisure and a taste to inspect minute as well as splendid beauties, the forms of the common law will afford entertainment and instruction.

The principles of the great institution of grand juries have been explained fully in another place.

When a person is indicted, and is not already committed or under bail, the next step in the legal arrangement is, to issue process against him, in order that he may be obliged to answer the charge, of which he stands indicted.

On an indictment for any crime under the degree of treason or felony, the process proper to be first awarded, at the common law, is a *venire facias,*[4] which, from the very name of it, is only in the nature of a summons to require the appearance of the party.[m] If this process is not obeyed, and it is seen by the return that he has lands in the county by which he may be distrained; then a distress shall be awarded against him, from time to time, till he appear. But if the return shows that he has no lands in the county; then a writ of *capias* is awarded against him. By this writ, as is intimated from its name, the sheriff is commanded to take the body of the person accused, and have him before the court at the time and place specified in the writ itself. If he cannot be taken: on the first capias, a second, and so on, shall be issued:[n] On an indictment for felony or treason, a capias is always the first process.[o]

We are told that, in the case of misdemeanors in England, it is now the usual practice for any judge of the court of king's bench, upon certificate of an indictment found, to award a writ of capias immediately against the defendant.[p]

4. That you cause to come. This writ caused the sheriff to summon persons for jury service or to summon one charged with a petit misdemeanor or on a penal statute.

m. 2. Haw. 283.

n. 2. Haw. 283.

o. Id. 284.

p. 4. Bl. Com. 314.

If the party abscond, and cannot be taken; then, after the several writs have been issued against him in regular number according to the nature of the crime with which he is charged, he is, at five county courts, proclaimed and required to surrender himself; and if he does not appear at the fifth requisition, he is then adjudged to be outlawed—put out of the protection of the law.[q]

When one is outlawed on an indictment for a misdemeanor, he forfeits his goods and chattels. In felony or treason, outlawry is a conviction and an attainder of the crime charged in the indictment.[r] Any one may arrest an outlaw for those crimes, in order to bring him to execution. He was formerly said "gerere caput lupinum," and might be knocked on the head like a wolf, by everyone who met him. But the law is now very justly holden to be otherwise. As to the security of his person, the greatest and the most notorious criminal is still under the protection, though liable to the punishment, of the law. It is lawful, as has been said, to apprehend him, in order to bring him to legal punishment. But to kill him wantonly, wilfully, or deliberately, merely because he is an outlaw, is murder.[s]

The proceedings necessary to an outlawry are uncommonly circumstantial, and must be exact to the minutest degree. Indeed, it is proper that they should be so. The consequence is, that an outlawry may, in most instances, be reversed on a writ of errour. When this is done, the person indicted is admitted to his defence against the indictment.

When a person indicted comes or is brought before the proper court, he is arraigned; in other words, he is called upon by his name, the indictment is read to him, and he is asked what he has to say in answer to the indictment.

At this important crisis of his fate, when his life may depend upon a word, and when, for this reason, every word should, as far as possible, be the result of perfect recollection and freedom, he must not be loaded with fetters or chains; he must not be brought to the bar in a contumelious manner; he ought to be used with all the humanity and gentleness consistent with the situation, in which he unfortunately stands; and he should suffer

q. 4. Bl. Com. 314.
r. Id. ibid. 2. Hale. P. C. 205.
s. 1. Hale. P. C. 497.

no uneasiness, except that which proceeds from internal causes.[t] The judge should exhort him to answer without fear; and should give him assurance that justice shall be duly administered.[u] "Cum captus coram justiciariis producendus fuerit, produci non debet ligatis manibus (quamvis aliquando compedibus propter periculum evasionis) et hoc ideo, ne videatur coactus ad aliquam purgationem suscipiendam".[v 5]

Is it necessary to fortify, by authority, the law of humanity? Sometimes it is. Sometimes the law of humanity, even when fortified by authority, has been pleaded in vain. The cruel violation, as well as the benign observance, of the principles of goodness and law ought to be known and marked. The last should be approved and imitated: the first should be detested and avoided. In the present enlightened century—and humanity should surely attend knowledge—a chief justice of the court of king's bench suffered a person in irons to be arraigned for treason, before him, though he was informed, that they were so grievous as to prevent the prisoner's sleeping except in a single posture, and that even while he was before the court, he would be unable to stand, unless the gaoler—for the gaoler had more bowels than the judge—unless the gaoler assisted him to hold up his chains.[w]

It is usual to desire the prisoner to hold up his hand when he is arraigned. This formality is not improper, because it serves to identify the person: it is not necessary, because the person may be identified in another manner. My Lord Bacon mentions a Welshman, who put a curious construction on this ceremony. Having been at a court, where he saw the prisoners hold up their hands at the bar as they severally received their sentences, he told one of his acquaintances that the judge was an excellent fortune teller; for if he only looked upon the hand of a person, he could immediately declare what would be his fate.[x]

A person, upon being arraigned, must stand mute, or give an answer.

t. 2. Haw. 308.

u. 2. Ins. 316.

v. Bract. 137. a.

5. When the prisoner is to be brought into the presence of his judges, he should not be led forth with hands tied (although sometimes with foot-fetters on account of the danger of escape) and that for this reason, lest he seem forced to undergo some ordeal.

w. 6. St. Tri. 231.

x. 3. Ld. Bac. 270.

One is considered as standing mute, when he gives no answer at all; when he gives such an answer as cannot be received; and when he pleads not guilty, but, on being asked how he will be tried, either refuses to say any thing, or will not put himself upon the country.[y]

On standing mute, the judgment was indeed a terrible one—"that he be sent to the prison from whence he came, and put into a dark lower room, and there be laid naked upon the bare ground, upon his back, without any clothes or rushes under him, or to cover him, his legs and arms drawn and extended with cords to the four corners of the room, and upon his body laid as great a weight of iron as he can bear, and more. The first day he shall have three morsels of barley bread without drink; the next day he shall have three draughts of standing water next the door of the prison, without bread; and this to be his diet till he die."[z] To the execution even of this terrible judgment some have submitted, that from forfeiture their estates might be rescued for the benefit of their children; for by standing mute, forfeiture and the corruption of blood are prevented.

The origin of the *peine fort et dure*[6] it is exceedingly difficult to trace: it seems, however, to be no legitimate offspring of the ancient common law: by that law, the standing mute amounted to a confession of the charge.[a]

By the law of Scotland, if the pannel stands mute and will not plead, the trial shall proceed as usual; and it is left to him to manage his own defence, as he shall think proper.[b] The spirit of this law is adopted by the legislature of the United States.[c] "If a person indicted shall stand mute, the court shall proceed to his trial, as if he had pleaded not guilty, and shall render judgment accordingly."[d]

To an indictment, the prisoner may give an answer, or plead, as the law terms it, in a great variety of ways.

I. He may admit the facts, as stated in the indictment, to be true; but, at the same time, may deny that the facts, thus stated and admitted, amount

y. 2. Hale. P. C. 316.

z. Id. 319.

6. A cruel and relentless punishment.

a. 4. Bl. Com. 323.

b. Bar. on St. 87.

c. Laws U. S. 1. con. 2. sess. c. 9. s. 30.

d. A similar provision is contained in an act of assembly of Pennsylvania. 3. Laws Penn. 119. *Ed.*

in law to the crime charged in the indictment. This is a demurrer. Thus, if one is indicted for larceny committed by stealing apples growing on a tree, he may demur to this indictment; in other words, he may admit that he took the apples from the tree, but deny that the fact of taking them amounts in law to the crime of larceny; because apples, unsevered from the tree, are not personal goods; and because of personal goods only larceny can be committed. This demurrer brings regularly before the court the legal question, whether the facts stated constitute the crime charged in the indictment. When the prosecutor joins in this demurrer—when he avers that the facts stated constitute the crime charged; then an issue is said to be joined. An issue is the result of the pleadings in a single point, denied on one side and affirmed on the other. It is either an issue in law, such as has now been mentioned; or it is an issue in fact, such as will be mentioned hereafter.

It seems to be taken for granted, by many respectable writers on the criminal law, that if, on a demurrer to an indictment, the point of law is determined against the prisoner, he shall have the same judgment pronounced against him as if he had been convicted by a verdict. With regard to crimes not capital this seems to be the case: but with regard to capital crimes, no adjudication is produced in support of the opinion. My Lord Hale indeed says, in one place of his valuable history of the pleas of the crown, that if a person be indicted of felony, and demur to the indictment, and it be judged against him, he shall have judgment to be hanged; for it is a confession, and, indeed, a wilful confession of the indictment.[e] In another place, however, he takes a distinction between this kind of confession, which, though voluntary, is still extrajudicial, and that full and solemn confession, which will by and by be mentioned. An extrajudicial confession, says he, though it be in court, as where the prisoner freely discloses the fact, and demands the opinion of the court whether it be felony, will not be recorded by the court, even if, upon the fact thus disclosed, it appear to be felony; but he will still be admitted to plead *not guilty* to the indictment.[f] There seems to be a solid reason for this distinction: for though a demurrer admits the truth of the facts as stated in the indict-

e. 2. Hale. P. C. 257.
f. 2. Hale. P. C. 225.

ment, yet it cannot be considered as an explicit and solemn confession of what is more material—the criminal and felonious intention, with which the facts were done. This criminal and felonious intention is the very point or *gist,* as the law calls it, of the indictment; and should be answered explicitly and directly.

II. This answer may be given by a solemn and judicial confession, not only of the fact, but of the *crime*—in the language of the law, it may be done by pleading *guilty.*

Upon this subject of confession on the part of the criminal, three very interesting questions arise with respect to capital crimes: for of those only I now speak. 1. Is a confession necessary? 2. Ought it to be made? 3. Ought it to be received as a sufficient foundation for a conviction, and judgment against life?

1. In many countries, his confession is considered as absolutely indispensable to the condemnation of the criminal. The Marquis of Beccaria conjectures that this rule has been taken from the mysterious tribunal of penitence, in which the confession of sins is a necessary part of the sacrament: thus, says he, have men abused the unerring light of revelation.[g] This confession they endeavour to obtain by the oath, and by the torture, of the person accused. He is obliged to answer interrogatories. These interrogatories—we are told; for of experience on this subject we are happily ignorant—these interrogatories are reduced to a system, captious, uncandid, and ensnaring; and terrour is frequently added to fraud.[h] The practice of demanding the oath of the accused is said, by the famous President de Lamoignon,[7] to have derived its origin from the customs of the inquisition.[i]

Very opposite, upon this subject, is the genius of the Gentoo code.[8] In that very ancient body of law, we find it expressly declared, that wherever

g. Bec. c. 16.

h. 5. War. Bib. 321.

7. Could refer to either (1) Guillaume de Lamoignon (1617–1677), a French lawyer and president of the parlement of France (1658), or (2), Guillaume-Chrétien de Lamoignon de Malesherbes (1721–1794), president of the cour des aides in the parlement of France and counsel to Louis XVI.

i. 8. War. Bib. 195.

8. The Anglo-Brahmanical body of law that resulted from Warren Hastings's attempt to codify Hindu law. It was published under the title *A Code of Gentoo Laws* (1776).

a true testimony would deprive a man of his life; if a false testimony would be the preservation of it, such false testimony is lawful.[j]

Between those extremes the constitution of Pennsylvania[k] observes the temperate mean. "In prosecutions by indictment or information, a man cannot be compelled to give evidence against himself." This is likewise an immemorial and an established principle of the common law.

In the case of oaths, says Beccaria, which are administered to a criminal to make him speak the truth, when the contrary is his greatest interest, there is a palpable contradiction between the laws and the natural sentiments of mankind. Can a man think himself obliged to contribute to his own destruction? Why should he be reduced to the terrible alternative of doing this, or of offending against God? For the law, which, in such a case, requires an oath, leaves him only the choice of being a bad christian, or of being a martyr. Such laws, continues he, are useless as well as unnatural: they are like a dike opposed directly to the course of the torrent: it is either immediately overwhelmed, or, by a whirlpool which itself forms, it is gradually undermined and destroyed.[l]

If it is useless, unjust, and unnatural, to attempt the extracting of truth by means of the oath; what is it, to make this attempt by means of the torture? This, like the former, is happily unknown to the common law. This, like the former, can be traced to the merciless tribunals of the inquisition. This, like the former, has been a practice both general and destructive.

To the civil law, its origin has been frequently ascribed. My Lord Coke, in his third Institute, declares himself explicitly of this opinion. He says, that in the reign of Henry the sixth, the Duke of Exeter and the Duke of Suffolk intended to have brought the civil laws into England; and, for a beginning, first brought into the tower the rack or brake allowed in many cases by the civil law.[m] To systems, as well as to men, justice should be done. From the imputation of a sanguinary as well as of a tyrannical spirit, the Roman law, at least in its brighter ages, deserves to be rescued. The different periods in the history of that celebrated law should be case-

j. Gent. Laws. 115.
k. Art. 9. s. 9.
l. Bec. c. 18.
m. 3. Ins. 35.

fully distinguished; and the redness or the blackness of one era ought not to shade or stain the purity and the splendour of another.

In the times of the republick, torture was known at Rome; and this, it must be owned, was too much to be known any where. It was confined, however, to the slaves. The whole torrent of Cicero's eloquence was poured indignant upon the infamous Verres,[9] because he had the audacity as well as cruelty to torture a Roman citizen, with his eyes turned towards Rome. "Caedebatur virgis in medio foro Messanae civis Romanus, judices; cum interea nullus gemitus, nulla vox alia istius miseri, inter dolorem crepitumque plagarum, audebatur, nisi haec, civis Romanus sum."—"O nomen dulce libertatis! O jus eximium nostrae civitatis! O lex Porcia, legesque Semproniae! O graviter desiderata, et aliquando reddita plebi Romanae tribunicia potestas! Huccine tandem omnia reciderunt, ut civis Romanus, in provincia populi Romani, in oppido faederatorum, abreo qui beneficio populi Romani fasces et secures haberet, deligatus in foro virgis caederetur? Quid, cum ignes ardentesque laminae caeterique cruciatus admovebantur?"[n]—"Non fuit his omnibus iste contentus. Spectet, inquit, patriam: in conspectu legum libertatisque moriatur."[o][10]

In another place, the same exquisite judge of human nature and of law describes, in the most masterly manner, the futility of that kind of proof, which arose from the torture of slaves. "Quaestiones nobis servorum, ac tormenta accusator minitatur; in quibus quanquam nihil periculi suspicamur, tamen illa tormenta gubernat dolor, moderatur natura cujusque

9. Gaius Verres (c. 120–43 B.C.) was a Roman magistrate notorious for his misgovernment of Sicily.

n. Cic. in Ver. V. 62. 63.

o. Id. 66.

10. "A Roman citizen, Judges, was scourged with whips in the middle of the forum of Messana. When all the while no other groan, no other word, was heard from that poor wretch amid the pain and noise of the lashes but this: I am a Roman citizen"—"O sweet name of liberty! O most excellent law of our state! O porcian Law and the Sempronian Laws! O power of the tribunate, urgently longed for and finally restored to the Roman People! Have then all things regressed to this point, that a Roman citizen, in a province of the Roman People and in a town of the allies, should be bound and lashed in the forum by a man who held the insignia of office by the beneficence of the Roman People? And what about when fires, burning plates, and other tortures were brought to bear?"—"But he [i.e., Verres] was not content with all this. He will, he says, gaze upon his Fatherland; may he die in the gaze of her laws and liberty!"

tum animi tum corporis; regit quaesitor, flectit libido, corrumpit spes, infirmat metus, ut in tot rerum angustiis nihil veritati loci relinquatur."[p11]

About three hundred years after Cicero, the celebrated Ulpian,[12] characterized as "the friend of the laws and of the people,"[q] speaks of torture in the same strain—"Res est fragilis et periculosa, et quae veritatem fallat. Nam plerique patientia sive duritia tormentorum ita tormenta contemnunt, ut exprimi eis veritas nullo modo possit: alii tanta sunt impatientia, ut in quovis mentiri, quam pati tormenta velint. Ita fit, ut etiam vario modo fateantur, ut non tantum se, verum etiam alios comminentur."[r13]

The early christians also bore their testimony against the cruel and absurd practice. "Cum quaeritur," says St. Augustine,[14] "utrum vir sit nocens, cruciatur; et innocens luit pro incerto scelere certissimas paenas; non quia illud commisisse detegitur, sed quia non commisisse nescitur; ignorantia judicis calamitas innocentis"—"judex torquit accusatum, ne occidat, nesciens, innocentem; tortum et innocentem occidit, quem, ne innocentem occiderit, torserat."[s15]

Among the moderns, says a sensible French writer, the practice of torture has been adopted and carried to the last degree of atrocity, in those countries in which human nature has been most debased and most op-

p. Cic. pro. P. Syl. c. 28.

11. The accuser threatens us with investigations and tortures of our slaves; although we suspect not the slightest danger to ourselves in such matters, even so those torturings are controlled by pain, moderated by the nature of the mind and body of the individual, ruled by the investigator, bent by desire, corrupted by hope, weakened by fear—so that, in short, in so many exigencies no place is left for the truth.

12. Domitius Ulpianus (?–228) was a Roman jurist and legal writer.

q. 1. Gib. 249.

r. 2. War. Bib. 23.

13. It is a treacherous and dangerous thing, and such as to delude the truth. For many, whether through capacity to suffer or toughness, so defy the torments of torturers that it is impossible to extort the truth from them. Others are so little able to suffer that they are willing to lie in any way to avoid undergoing torture. Thus it happens that they even confess inconsistently, so that not only do they inform against themselves, but implicate others.

14. Augustine of Hippo, or St. Augustine (354–430), was an important early Christian theologian.

s. Id. 22.

15. When one wishes to know whether a man is guilty, he is tortured; and an innocent man suffers most definite punishments for an indefinite offense; not because he is discovered to have committed that offense, but because it is not known that he did not commit it; the judge's lack of knowledge is the innocent man's misfortune. The judge tortures the accused lest unknowingly he should kill an innocent man; he kills the tortured and innocent man whom he had tortured in order that he not kill an innocent man.

pressed—I mean those of the inquisition: on the contrary, it has been abolished or moderated in those, in which the human mind has reassumed her liberty—in Geneva, in England, in France under Lewis the sixteenth.[t] [16]

From what has been observed, the inference is clear, that the confession of the criminal is not necessary to a conviction or sentence in the case of a capital crime.

2. In the case of a capital crime, ought this confession to be made?

I think not. When I say this, I speak with a reference to the effect, which this confession is allowed to have by the common law. I am justified by authority in what I say. From tenderness to life, the court is usually very averse to the receiving and recording of such a confession; and will advise the prisoner to retract it, and plead another plea to the indictment.[u] If a person under the age of twenty one years make this confession, the court in justice ought not to record it, but should put him to plead *not guilty;* or, at least, ought to inquire by an inquest of office concerning the truth, and circumstances of the fact.[v] A confession, refused altogether, or received with reluctance, ought not to be made.

3. Ought this confession to be received, and considered as a sufficient foundation for a conviction and judgment against life?

By the common law, as it now is and as it always has been received, such a confession is deemed a sufficient foundation for a conviction and judgment against life. This express, judicial, and direct confession is considered as the highest possible conviction;[w] and after it is made and received, the court does and can do nothing but pronounce the judgment of the law.[x]

It now, I apprehend, appears from principle, as it appeared a little while ago from authority, that, on an indictment for a capital crime, this express, judicial, and direct confession of it ought not to be made. He who makes it undertakes to be the arbiter of his own life: for, as we now see, the judgment of death follows as a consequence, necessary and unavoidable. A decision of this very solemn kind ought to be a decision of the

t. 8. War. Bib. 197.

16. Louis XVI (1754–1793) was king of France from 1774 to 1793. He was executed during the French Revolution.

u. 2. Hale. P. C. 225. 4. Bl. Com. 324.

v. 1. Hale. P. C. 24.

w. 2. Haw. 333.

x. 4. Bl. Com. 324.

society, upon the principles formerly explained, and not a decision of the party himself. For such a decision he may be unqualified, sometimes on account of his understanding, sometimes on account of his disposition. He may not be apprized of every legal ingredient, which ought to form a part in the composition of the crime which he confesses: human conduct is sometimes influenced by an irresolute impatience, as well as, at other times, by an overweening fondness of life.

It is certainly true, that persons have confessed themselves guilty of crimes, of which, indeed, they were innocent. A remarkable case of this nature is mentioned in our law books. A gentleman of the name of Harrison appeared alive, many years after three persons had been hanged for his murder; one of whom confessed it.[y] Many persons accused have confessed themselves guilty of witchcraft, and of other crimes equally problematical.

By the civil law, the confession of the person accused is not sufficient to convict him of a capital crime, without other proofs: for it may so happen, that such a confession is dictated only by the inquietude or despair of a troubled mind.[z] Another reason may likewise be assigned: he may, by a mistaken as well as by a disordered understanding, acknowledge that to be a crime, which in law is not that crime.

Thus much for confession, or the plea of *guilty* to an indictment.

III. An indictment may be answered by a plea to the jurisdiction of the court, in which it is found. This plea is proper when an indictment for any particular crime is found in a court, which has no authority to hear, try, or determine that particular crime: as if a court of quarter sessions should arraign one on an indictment for treason, of which that court has no jurisdiction.[a]

IV. An indictment may be answered by a plea in abatement—in other words, a plea, the design of which is to destroy the indictment, without answering the crime which it charges. This, in some cases, may be very proper; as when one is indicted and called to answer by a wrong name. If he suffer this mistake to pass unnoticed, it is doubtful whether he may not afterwards be indicted for the same crime by his right name. If the

y. Tr. per Pais. 603.
z. 1. Domat. 460.
a. 2. Hale. P. C. 256.

plea be supported, the indictment will be abated; but he may be immediately indicted anew, by the name which he has averred to be his true one. For in all pleas in abatement it is a rule, that he who would take advantage of a mistake, must show, at the same time, how that mistake may be rectified.

V. An indictment may be answered by a plea in bar. A plea in bar does not directly deny the commission of the crime charged; but it adduces and relies on some reason calculated to show, that the prisoner cannot be tried or punished for it, either on that or on any other indictment.

A former acquittal of the same charge is a plea of this kind: for it is a maxim firmly established by the common law, that no one can be brought in danger oftener than once on account of the same crime.

A former conviction of the same crime is also a plea of this kind; and depends on the same principle.

An attainder of any capital crime is a good plea in bar of an indictment for the same, or for any other crime. The reason is, that by the attainder the prisoner is dead in law; his blood is corrupted; and his estate is forfeited; so that an attempt to attaint him a second time would be altogether nugatory and superfluous.

It is natural and obvious to remark here, how the severity of punishment becomes the parent of impunity for crimes. When one is punished, or condemned to be punished, as far as he can be punished, for one crime, he may commit another, without any fear or risk of additional punishment.

In proportion as the criminal code becomes less severe, the operation of the plea of a former attainder becomes less powerful; for it is never proper, unless when a second trial could answer no purpose.

A pardon is another plea in bar of an indictment; for, by remitting the punishment of the crime, it destroys the end which is proposed by the prosecution. In England, an advantage is gained by pleading a pardon, which cannot be obtained by it after an attainder. A pardon prevents the corruption, but cannot restore the purity of blood.

If any one of these pleas in bar is successful, the party pleading it is discharged from farther prosecution; but if they should all fail, a resource is still left.

VI. An indictment may be answered by pleading *not guilty* of the crime which it charges. An issue, you recollect, is a point denied on one side and affirmed on the other. The plea of *not guilty* is called the general issue; because, on that plea, the whole charge comes regularly and fully under examination. It is averred by the indictment: it is denied by the plea. On this plea alone—such, as we have seen from the foregoing deduction, is the benignity of the common law—on this plea alone, the prisoner can receive a final judgment against him. A judgment of acquittal may be produced by many different causes: but a sentence of condemnation can be founded only on a conviction of guilt.

When the prisoner pleads that he is not guilty; he, for the trial of his plea, puts himself upon his country. The extensive and the emphatick import of this expression, neglected because it is common, was fully illustrated on another occasion.[b]

In ancient times, a variety of methods, by which crimes might be tried, was known to the common law. A trial might be had by ordeal; and this species of trial was either by fire or by water. The corsned, or morsel of execration, was another kind of trial. The trial by battle was a third kind. A fourth kind still remains and is our boast—the trial by jury. This trial, both in the United States and in this commonwealth, is a part of the constitution as well as of the law.

The history and the general principles of this institution, celebrated so long and so justly, have already been explained to you at large. I shall, therefore, confine myself at present to such remarks, chiefly of a practical nature, as will arise from the usual course of proceedings in trials for crimes.

By the constitution of Pennsylvania,[c] persons accused of crimes shall be tried by an impartial jury of the vicinage: or, in legal interpretation, of the county.[d] By the national constitution,[e] crimes committed in any state shall be tried in that state: and by a law of the United States,[f] twelve, at least, of the jurors must be summoned from the very county, in which the crime was committed.

In the court of king's bench, there is time allowed between the arraignment and the trial, for a jury to be impanelled by a writ of *venire facias*

b. Ante. vol. 2. p. 958. 986.
c. Art. 9. s. 9.
d. 2. Hale. P. C. 264.
e. Art. 3. s. 3.
f. 1. cong. 1. sess. c. 20. s. 29.

directed to the sheriff. But justices of oyer and terminer and general gaol delivery, and justices of the quarter sessions[g] of the peace, may, by a bare award and without any writ or precept, have a panel returned by that officer: for, in consequence of a general precept directed to him beforehand, he returns to the court a panel of jurors to try all persons, who may be called upon for their trial at that session. Before such justices, it is usual, for this reason, to try criminals immediately or soon after their arraignment.[h]

Jurors must be "*homines liberi et legales,*" men free and superiour to every legal exception; for every legal exception is a cause of challenge. My Lord Coke[i] enumerates four such causes—propter honoris respectum—propter defectum—propter delictum—propter affectum. The first cause relates to the peerage solely: the second is an exception against aliens and minors: the third is an exception against persons convicted of infamous crimes: the fourth is an exception which arises from bias or partiality. When this bias is apparent, the challenge founded on it is a *principal* one, and takes effect immediately: when the bias is only probable, the challenge is only to *the favour;* and its validity must be decided by triers, selected by the court for this purpose, till two are sworn of the jury. These two, as they are acknowledged or found to be impartial, become the triers of all the others.

Besides these challenges for cause, which operate as frequently as they exist, the benignity of the common law allows, as we saw before, every person indicted for a capital crime to challenge peremptorily, or without cause, any number of jurors under thirty six—the number of three juries.[j] In every capital crime, except treason, this number is, by a law of the United States,[k] reduced to twenty jurors. A person who challenges more than the number allowed, is, by the same law, to be treated as one who stands mute. That treatment we have already seen. By a law of Pennsylvania, a similar deduction is made in the number of peremptory challenges: but he, who challenges more than the number allowed, shall suffer as a criminal convicted.[l] There is a great difference between the two provisions: by that of

g. Wood. Ins. 666.
h. 4. Bl. Com. 344, 345. 2. Haw. 405.
i. 1. Ins. 156. b.
j. 2. Haw. 413.
k. 1. cong. 2. sess. c. 9. s. 30.
l. 1. Laws. Penn. 134.

the United States, the person indicted is treated as one who must be *tried:* by that of Pennsylvania, he is treated as one, who is *already convicted.*[m]

When an alien is tried, one half of his jury should be aliens, if he require it.[n]

On this subject of challenges it is proper to observe, that it seems to have been very familiar in the Roman law, during the existence of the commonwealth. In a criminal process, before the court of the praetor, the accuser and the accused were each allowed to except against fifteen of those returned to try the cause. This exception was denominated "*rejectio judicum*"—in the phraseology of our law, the challenge of the jury. Whenever Cicero uses the expression—judices; its legal translation is—Gentlemen of the jury.

Concerning the celebrated trial of Milo,[17] we have a number of particular facts transmitted to us, which deserve our particular notice and attention. On the first day of the trial, or, as we would say, on the return of the *venire facias,* the *judices*—we would say the jury—were produced, that they might be balloted. The next day, they balloted eighty one persons to make up the jury. But the accuser had the liberty to challenge fifteen; and the accused could challenge as many. By these challenges on both sides, the number of those who were to give the verdict was reduced to fifty one. In another place we have a particular account of the votes given for, and of those given against, Milo: added together, they amount to the precise number of fifty one.[o]

At Rome, as we have seen on more occasions than one, prosecutions were considered as the causes of the accusers, rather than as the causes of the commonwealth. The proceedings were regulated by this supposition. Accordingly, in a criminal prosecution, the challenge extended to such persons as either party—the accuser as well as the accused—had reason, or thought he had reason, to suspect might be influenced in their verdict by favour, affection, consanguinity, malice, or any other passion, which might lead to partiality or a corrupt judgment.[p]

m. The law of Pennsylvania is now similar to that of the United States. 3. Laws Penn. 119. *Ed.*

n. 3. Bl. Com. 360. 4. Bl. Com. 346. 2. Haw. 420. 1. Dall. 73.

17. A famous trial in 52 B.C. in which T. Annius Milo, who was represented by Cicero, was convicted for the murder of Publius Clodius.

o. Pet. on Jur. 114.

p. Id. 180.

When a prosecution, as well as the defence of it, was viewed as the cause of an individual, it might be reasonable enough that, in this view, the power of challenging jurors should, on both sides, be equal. But when a prosecution is considered as the cause of the community, by a part of which community this very cause is to be tried; matters now assume a very different appearance. This important difference was fully explained in the account which I gave of the radical principles, as I may call them, of the trial by jury.[q] The accused stands alone on one side: on the other side stand the whole community: the jury are indeed a *selected* part; but still they are a *part* of the whole community: the power of challenging, therefore, ought not, on both sides, to be equal.

True it is, that, at the common law, the king might challenge peremptorily, as well as the prisoner. The distinction between a publick and a private prosecutor was not sufficiently regarded. From this characteristick feature, by the way, a strong intrinsick evidence appears of the lineage of juries. But equally true it is, that the distinction was perceived at an early period, was then established—I mean in the reign of Edward the first—and has been since uniformly observed.[r] In consequence of this distinction, it has been the law, for many centuries past, that the privilege of peremptory challenges, though enjoyed by the prisoner, is refused to the king.

If, on account of the number of challenges, or the non-attendance of the jurors, so many of the panel returned as are necessary to make a jury cannot be had, the court may award a *tales*—others qualified in the same manner—to be added to the panel, till twelve are sworn to try the cause.[s]

Their oath is—that they will well and truly try and true deliverance make between the—United States—and the prisoner at the bar, and a true verdict give according to their evidence. After they are sworn, the indictment is read, and the issue which they are sworn to try is stated to them: and then the publick prosecutor opens the cause, and arranges, in such order as he thinks most proper, the evidence which is to be offered in support of the prosecution.

q. Ante. vol. 2. p. 960.
r. 2. Haw. 412.
s. 4. Bl. Com. 348.

But it is a settled rule at the common law, as it is *now* received in England, that, in a trial for a capital crime, upon the general issue, no counsel shall be allowed the prisoner, unless some point of law, proper to be debated, shall arise. By a statute, however, made in the reign of William the third, and by another made in that of George the second,[18] an exception to this general and severe rule is introduced, for the benefit of those who are indicted or impeached for treason.[t] This practice in England is admitted to be a hard one, and not to be very consonant to the rest of the humane treatment of prisoners by the English law. Indeed the judges themselves are so sensible of this defect in their modern practice, that they generally allow a prisoner counsel to stand by him at the bar, and instruct him what questions to ask, or even to ask questions for him.

This practice of refusing counsel to those who are indicted for a capital crime, is not agreeable to the common law as it was formerly received in England. The ancient Mirrour tells us, that, in civil causes, counsel are necessary to manage and to defend them, by the rules of law and the customs of the realm. He adds, with irresistible force, that they are still more necessary to defend indictments of felony, than causes of a less important nature.[u] On this, as on many other great and interesting subjects, we have renewed the ancient common law. It is enacted by a law of the United States,[v] that persons indicted for crimes shall be allowed to make their full defence by counsel learned in the law. It is declared by the constitution of Pennsylvania,[w] that, in all criminal prosecutions, the accused has a right to be heard by himself and his counsel.

In England, it has been an ancient and commonly received practice, that, as counsel was not allowed to any prisoner accused of a capital crime, so neither should he be suffered to exculpate himself by the testimony of witnesses. This doctrine was so unreasonable and severe, that the courts became ashamed of it, and gradually introduced a practice of examining witnesses for the prisoner: but they stopped in the middle of the road to redress—they would not examine the witnesses upon their oaths. The con-

18. George II (1683–1760) was king of England from 1727 to 1760.
t. 4. Bl. Com. 349, 350.
u. Mir. c. 3.
v. 1. cong. 2. sess. c. 9. s. 29.
w. Art. 9. s.

sequence was, that juries gave less credit to witnesses produced on the part of the prisoners, than to witnesses produced on the part of the crown.[x]

This practice, however, like the last, is not agreeable to the common law, as it was in ancient times received in England. To say the truth, says my Lord Coke,[y] we never read in any act of parliament, ancient author, bookcase, or record, that in criminal cases, the party accused should not have witnesses sworn for him; and therefore there is not so much as a *scintilla juris*[19] against it. By a statute made in the reign of Queen Anne, the ancient common law on this point is renewed in England; and witnesses for the prisoner shall be examined upon oath, in the same manner as witnesses against him.[z]

On this subject, the ancient common law, as might have been expected, is renewed in the United States and in Pennsylvania. By a law of the former[a] it is provided, that persons indicted for crimes shall be allowed to make proof in their defence by lawful witnesses; and that, to compel the appearance of their witnesses, the court shall grant the same process as is granted to compel witnesses to appear on the prosecution. By the constitution of Pennsylvania,[b] it is declared, that, in all criminal prosecutions, the accused has a right to have compulsory process for obtaining witnesses in his favour.

The compulsory process for obtaining witnesses is a subpoena *ad testificandum*,[20] which commands them to appear at the trial. If this command is disobeyed, an attachment issues for the contempt.[c]

In honour of the Founder of Pennsylvania it ought to be observed, that, in the charter of privileges[d] which he granted to its inhabitants, he declared, "that all criminals shall have the same privileges of witnesses and counsel as their prosecutors." On this as on many other subjects, Pennsylvania preceded England in point of liberal and enlightened improvement.

x. 4. Bl. Com. 352.

y. 3. Ins. 79.

19. A particle of right; a spark of interest.

z. St. 2. An. st. 2. c. 9.

a. 1. cong. 2. sess. c. 9. s. 29.

b. Art. 9. s. 9.

20. To testify. This type of habeas corpus writ was used to bring a prisoner to testify in court.

c. 3. Bl. Com. 369.

d. S. 5.

The constitution of Pennsylvania[e] declares, that, in all criminal prosecutions, the accused has a right to meet the witnesses face to face. Those who know the nature and the mischiefs of secret accusations, know the importance of this provision, and the security which it produces.

By the constitution of the United States,[f] no person shall be convicted of treason, unless on the testimony of two witnesses to the same overt act, or on confession in open court. The subject of confession has been already treated.

The courts of justice, in almost every age, and in almost every country, have had recourse to oaths, or appeals to heaven, as the most universal and the most powerful means to engage men to declare the truth. By the common law, before the testimony of a witness can be received, he is obliged to swear, that it shall be the truth, the whole truth, and nothing but the truth.

The testimony of witnesses is one species of evidence, as we formerly saw in those lectures,[g] in which the great subject of evidence was opened, and but just opened. The general principles, upon which testimony is received and believed, were then stated in a short and summary manner, as connected with some native propensities of the human mind. The important distinction between the credibility of witnesses and their competency was explained at large,[h] when I discoursed concerning the separate provinces of courts and juries. I observed, that every intelligent person, who is not infamous or interested, is a competent witness. The common law coincides, in this point, with the law of Athens: for, by that law, no man could be a witness in his own cause; and he who, by his ill behaviour, had rendered himself infamous—ατιμος—was deemed unworthy of credit.[i]

The Marquis of Beccaria is of opinion, that the objection against the competency of a witness should be confined altogether to his interest; and that his infamy should not exclude him. Every man of common sense, says he, every one whose ideas have some connexion with each other, and whose sensations are conformable to those of other men, may be a witness;

e. Art. 9. s. 9.
f. Art. 3. s. 3.
g. Ante. vol. 2. p. 807. et seq.
h. Ante. vol. 2. p. 1002–1006.
i. 1. Pot. Ant. 117.

but the credibility of his testimony will be in proportion as he is interested in declaring or concealing the truth. Hence it appears how irrational it is to exclude persons branded with infamy; for they ought to be credited when they have no interest in giving false testimony.[j]

If this subject is investigated upon principle, it will, perhaps, be found, that the practice of the law is more congenial to the native sentiments of our mind, than are the speculations of the ingenious philosopher.

Belief is the end proposed by evidence of every kind. Belief in testimony is produced by the supposed veracity of him who delivers it. The opinion of his veracity, as we saw when we examined the general principles of testimony,[k] is shaken, either when, in former instances, we have known him to deliver testimony which has been false; or when, in the present instance, we discover some strong inducement which may prevail on him to deceive. The latter part of this observation applies to interested witnesses; and the application to them is admitted to be a proper one, and to be sufficient to exclude them from testimony. But who is a person infamous in the eye of the common law? He who has been convicted of an infamous crime. What, in the eye of the common law, is an infamous crime? When we investigated the true meaning of the *felleus animus,*[21] according to the common law, we found that it indicated a disposition, deceitful, false, and treacherous.[l] He who is convicted of an infamous crime, is one who has been proved guilty of some conduct, which evinced him to have been false—to have committed the *crimen falsi;* of which so many different grades—from treason to a cheat, and both included—are known to the law.

It may, however, be urged, on the principles of Beccaria, that to the conduct of which he has been convicted, he was probably drawn by a motive of interest; and that, if no such motive exists in the present instance, the inference from the past to the present is without foundation. To this it may be justly answered, that the reason why interest excludes a witness is not, because it certainly will, but because it possibly may, occasion a deviation from the truth; and because this deviation may be produced

j. Bec. c. 13.
k. Ante. vol. 2. p. 811. 812.
21. A deceitful, false, or treacherous disposition.
l. Ante. p. 1101.

even by an involuntary and imperceptible bias, which interest will sometimes impress upon minds intentionally honest. That this last consideration has great weight in the judgment of the law, is evident from one of the modes which it adopts to discover the existence of interest—a mode, which, I believe, can be rationally accounted for only by this last consideration. A witness, who is suspected to be interested, may be examined upon his *voir dire*[22]—in other words, he may be required to declare, upon oath, whether he is interested or not. This mode of proceeding obviously supposes him honest as well as interested. For if it supposed him dishonest, would not the conclusion be irresistible—that he who ought not to be believed when he gives his testimony *in chief,* as it is called, ought as little to be believed, when he gives his testimony on his *voir dire*? That involuntary and unavoidable bias which interest sometimes impresses on the mind, and which, of consequence, may affect the testimony of the offered witness, is deemed by the law a sufficient reason for his exclusion from testimony.

If he whose testimony may deceive, merely because he is interested, though he be honest, shall for this reason be excluded; shall we admit the testimony of one who is false, though he be disinterested? The former is rejected, because he *may be* biassed involuntarily; for the danger of even an involuntary bias is, for this purpose, sufficient: and shall one, whom interest *has* biassed voluntarily and infamously—shall such a one be received? On good grounds, therefore, are persons infamous excluded from giving testimony.

That evidence which arises from testimony is, in the law, denominated positive. There is another kind, which the law terms presumptive. When the fact itself cannot be proved by witnesses, that which comes nearest to such proof is, the proof of such circumstances, with which the fact is either necessarily or usually attended. This is presumptive evidence. When those circumstances are proved, with which the fact is *necessarily* attended, the presumption is said to be violent: when those circumstances only are proved with which the fact is *usually* attended, the presumption is said to be only probable.[m]

22. To speak the truth.
m. 3. Bl. Com. 371.

Presumptive proof, as described by the common law, coincides with that species which, in our general view of the sources of evidence, we saw rising from experience. On that occasion,[n] it was observed, that if an object is remembered to have been frequently, still more, if it is remembered to have been constantly succeeded by certain particular consequences, the conception of the object naturally associates to itself the conception of the consequences; and on the actual appearance of the object, the mind naturally anticipates the appearance of the consequences also: that if the consequences have followed the object *constantly,* and the observations of this constant connexion have been sufficiently numerous; the evidence produced by experience amounts to a moral certainty: that, if it has been *frequent,* but not entirely uniform; the evidence amounts only to probability, and is more or less probable, as the connexion has been more or less frequent. Violent presumption, as it is termed by the law, or moral certainty, as it is denominated by philosophy, amounts to full proof:[o] probability, or probable presumption, has also its due weight.[p] The coincidence between philosophy and law is a coincidence which, to the friends of both, always gives pleasure.

It ought to be observed here, that, in cases of a capital nature, all presumptive proof should be received with caution: for the law benignly holds that it is more eligible that ten guilty persons should escape, than that one innocent person should suffer a capital punishment.

After the evidence is heard, the jury are next to consider what verdict they ought to give upon it; for they are sworn, as we have seen, to give a true verdict according to their evidence. To give a verdict is the great purpose for which they are summoned and empanelled. Till they give a verdict, therefore, they cannot be discharged.[q] This verdict may either be special—in other words, it may state particularly the facts arising in the cause, and leave to the court the decision of the law resulting from those facts; or it may be general—in other words, it may determine both the facts and the law. A general verdict is either guilty or not guilty: on a verdict of not

n. Ante vol. 2. p. 815.
o. 1. Ins. 6. b.
p. 3. Bl. Com. 372.
q. 4. Bl. Com. 354.

guilty, the prisoner is discharged: by a verdict of guilty, he is convicted: on a conviction the judgment and the punishment pronounced and inflicted by the law regularly follow, unless they are intercepted by errour in the proceedings, by a reprieve, or by a pardon.

When a sentence of death is pronounced, the immediate and inseparable consequence, by the common law, is attainder. The law puts him out of its protection, considers him as a bane to human society, and takes no farther care of him than barely to see him executed: he is already considered as dead in law. There is, in capital cases, a great difference between a man convicted and one attainted. Till judgment is given, there is, in such cases, still a possibility of innocence in the contemplation of the law.[r]

In England the consequences of attainder are forfeiture, escheat, and corruption of blood. Concerning these subjects we have already treated fully.

I have now enumerated and described the several crimes, the several punishments, and the modes of prosecuting criminals. In doing this, I have conformed myself to the common law and to the improvements made upon it by the constitutions and laws of the United States and of Pennsylvania.

THE END OF THE LECTURES ON LAW.

r. 4. Bl. Com. 373.

BIBLIOGRAPHICAL GLOSSARY

The purpose of this glossary is to identify the works Wilson referred to. The editions listed are not necessarily the particular ones Wilson used. In general, where multiple editions existed, I have cited an early edition, usually the first. In a few cases this did not seem advisable (e.g. Hooker's *Ecclesiastical Polity,* which was first published in embryonic form many years before the cited full-length edition which Wilson probably used), and I have then cited the earliest available full-length edition. Except for such completely self-explanatory references as those to the Bible, the United States Constitution, and national statutes, I have identified them all, even at some risk of explaining the obvious. A reader of these volumes is not likely to wonder what "Bl. Com." refers to, but "Ld. Ray." might slow him down a little, and the simplest course was to gloss everything. This has the additional advantage, as I said in the Introduction, of providing us with a compendious list of Wilson's scholarly sources.

In his classical citations, Wilson consistently uses the abbreviations l. for liber (book) and c. for capitulum (chapter).

(Addison) Tatler: Sir Richard Steele, Joseph Addison and others, *The Tatler.* London, 1709–1710.

Anac.: Jean Jacques Barthélemy, *Travels of Anacharsis the Younger in Greece . . .* First published in English in London, 1790–1791.

Anal. Rev.: *The Analytical Review.* London, 1788–1799.

Atk.: John Tracy Atkyns, *Reports of Cases Argued and Determined in the High Court of Chancery in the Time of Lord Chancellor Hardwicke.* 3 vols. London, 1765–1768.

Bac. on Gov.: See (Bacon) Discourses on Government.

(Bacon) Discourses on Government: Nathaniel Bacon, *An Historical and Political Discourse of the Laws and Government of England . . .* London, 1682.

Bar. on St.: Daines Barrington, *Observations on the More Ancient Statutes . . .* London, 1746.

(Barbeyrac) Pref. to Puff.: See Puff.

(Beccaria) C.: Cesare Beccaria, *An Essay on Crimes and Punishments. With a Commentary Attributed to Voltaire.* London, 1767.

Bever: Thomas Bever, *The History of the Legal Polity of the Roman State; and of the Rise, Progress, and Extent of the Roman Laws.* London, 1781.

Bl. Com.: Sir William Blackstone, *Commentaries on the Laws of England.* 4 vols. Oxford, 1765–1769.

Boh. Ins. Leg.: William Bohun, *Institutio Legalis; or, Introduction to the Study and Practice of the Laws of England . . .* London, 1708–1709.

Bol. Rem.: Henry St. John, Viscount Bolingbroke, *Remarks on the History of England.* London, 1743.

(Bolingbroke) Diss. on Part.: Henry St. John, Viscount Bolingbroke, *A Dissertation upon Parties . . .* London, 1735.

(Bolingbroke) Patriot King: Henry St. John, Viscount Bolingbroke, *Letters on the Spirit of Patriotism, on the Idea of a Patriotic King . . .* London, 1749.

Bol. Tracts: Henry St. John, Viscount Bolingbroke, *A Collection of Political Tracts.* London, 1748.

Bouch. The. Com.: Mathieu Antoine Bouchaud, *Théories des traites de commerce entre des nations . . .* Paris, 1777.

Bracton: Henry de Bracton, *De Legibus.* London, 1569.

Burgh Pol. Dis.: James Burgh, *Political Disquisitions; or, An Enquiry into Public Errors, Defects, and Abuses.* 3 vols. London, 1774–1775.

Burke, Reflections on French Rev.: Edmund Burke, *Reflections on the Revolution in France.* London, 1790.

Burl.: Jean Jacques Burlamaqui, *The Principles of Natural and Political Law . . .* 2 vols. London, 1763.

Burn's Ecc. Law: Richard Burn, *Ecclesiastical Law.* 2 vols. London, 1763.

Burr.: Sir James Burrow, *Reports of Cases Adjudged in the Court of King's Bench . . .* 5 vols. [London] 1766–1780.

Caes.: Caesar, *Commentarii Belli Gallici.*

(Caesar) de Bel. Gal.: Caesar, *Commentarii Belli Gallici.*

Chal.: George Chalmers, *Political Annals of the Present United Colonies.* London, 1780.

Cic. de Amic.: Cicero, *Laelius de Amicitia.*

Cic. de clar. orat.: Cicero, *Brutus.*

Cic. de fin.: Cicero, *De Finibus Bonorum et Malorum.*

Cic. de leg.: Cicero, *De Legibus.*
Cic. de leg. agr.: Cicero, *De Lege Agraria Oratio.*
Cic. de Nat. Deo.: Cicero, *De Natura Deorum.*
Cic. de off.: Cicero, *De Officiis.*
Cic. de orat.: Cicero, *De Oratore.*
Cic. Ep. ad Brut.: Cicero, *Epistulae ad Brutum.*
Cic. pro. Balb.: Cicero, *Pro Balbo.*
Cic. pro. Caec.: Cicero, *Pro A. Caecina.*
Cic. pro Cluent.: Cicero, *Pro Cluentio.*
Cic. pro dom.: Cicero, *De Domo Sua ad Pontifices Oratio.*
Cic. pro Mil.: Cicero, *Pro Milone.*
Cic. pro P. Syl.: Cicero, *Pro Publio Sulla.*
Cic. pro Rosc. Am.: Cicero, *Pro Sexto Roscio Amerino.*
Cic. Somn. Scip.: Cicero, *Somnium Scipionis* (in *De Re Publica* 6, 13).
Cic. Ver. V.: Cicero, *Actionis Secundae in C. Verrem Liber V.*
(Cicero) De Rep.: Cicero, *De Re Publica.*
(Cicero) Frag. de rep.: Cicero, *De Re Publica.* (Except for the *Somnium Scipionis,* this work was known in Wilson's time only in fragments quoted by other authors.)
(Coke) Ins.: Sir Edward Coke, *The Institutes of the Laws of England.* 4 parts. London, 1628–1644.
(Coke) Rep.: Sir Edward Coke, *The Reports of Sir Edward Coke . . . of Divers Resolutions and Judgements . . . of Cases in Law . . .* First published in its entirety in English in London, 1658.
Col. Jur.: Frances Hargrave, *Collectanea Juridica . . .* 2 vols. London, 1791–1792.
Com. Per.: See Stu. V.
Cou. Ang. Norm.: David Houard, *Traités sur les coutumes anglo-normandes.* 4 vols. Paris, 1776.
Cro. Car.: Sir George Croke, *Reports, King's Bench and Common Bench* (1582–1641). Written in French; revised and published in English by Sir Harbottle Grimston. London, 1661–1667.
D.: See Dig.
Dag.: Henry Dagge, *Considerations on Criminal Law . . .* 3 vols. London, 1774.
Daws. Orig. Laws: George Dawson, *Origo Legum.* London, 1694.
de Bel. Gal.: See (Caesar) de Bel. Gal.
de leg.: See Cic. de leg.
De orat.: See Cic. de orat.
De Rep.: See (Cicero) De Rep.

Dig.: Corpus Juris Civilis. *Digesta.*

Domat: Jean Domat, *The Civil Law in Its Natural Order* . . . Translated by William Strahan. 2 vols. London, 1727.

Eden: William Eden, Baron Auckland, *Principles of Penal Law.* London, 1771.

Edin. Phil. Trans.: Royal Society of Edinburgh, *Transactions.* Vol. 1. Edinburgh, 1788.

El. Jur.: Richard Wooddeson, *Elements of Jurisprudence* . . . London, 1783.

Elem. Crit.: Henry Home, Lord Kames, *Elements of Criticism.* 3 vols. Edinburgh, 1762.

Encyc. Tit. Jurisprudence: *Encyclopédie méthodique: Jurisprudence.* 8 vols. Paris and Liège, 1782–1789.

F. N. B.: Sir Anthony Fitzherbert, *The New Natural Brevium* . . . (Translated into English) London, 1704.

Finch: Sir Henry Finch, *Laws, or a Discourse Thereof.* London, 1627.

Fleta: A treatise subtitled *seu Commentarius juris Anglicani,* written by an unknown author in about 1290. Wilson probably knew it only through Selden (q.v.).

(Fortescue) De Laud.: Sir John Fortescue, *De Laudibus* . . . London, 1616.

Fost.: Sir Michael Foster, *A Report of Some Proceedings . . . and of Other Cases* . . . Oxford, 1762.

Fr. Rev.: John Talbot Dillon, *Historical and Critical Memoirs of the General Revolution in France* . . . London, 1790.

Frag. de rep.: See (Cicero) Frag. de rep.

(Frederic of Prussia) K. Prus. works.: *Posthumous Works of Frederic II* . . . 13 vols. London, 1789.

Gen. Dict.: Pierre Bayle, *A General Dictionary . . . in which a New and Accurate Translation of that of Mr. Bayle is included . . . by John Peter Bernard . . . and Other Hands* . . . 10 vols. London, 1734–1741.

Gent. Laws: Nathaniel Brassey Halhed, tr., *A Code of Gentoo Laws . . . Written in the Shanscrit Language.* London, 1776.

Gib.: See Gibbon.

Gibbon: Edward Gibbon, *The History of the Decline and Fall of the Roman Empire.* 12 vols. London, 1783–1790.

Gil.: See Gill.

Gil. Lys. and Isoc.: John Gillies, *Orations of Lysias and Isocrates.* London, 1778.

Gilb. Ev.: Sir Geoffrey Gilbert, *Law of Evidence.* Dublin, 1754.

Gill.: John Gillies, *The History of Ancient Greece, Its Colonies and Conquests.* 2 vols. London, 1786.

Gog. Or. Laws: Antoine Yves Goguet, *The Origin of Laws, Arts, and Sciences* . . . 3 vols. Edinburgh, 1761.

Grant's Ess.: James Grant, *Essays on the Origin of Society, Language, Property . . .* London, 1785.

Gro.: Hugo Grotius. *Of the Law of Warre and Peace.* London, 1654.

Guth.: William Guthrie, *A General History of England . . .* 4 vols. London, 1744–1751.

Hale P. C.: Sir Matthew Hale, *Historia Placitorum Coronae.* 2 vols. London, 1736.

Hale's Hist.: Sir Matthew Hale, *History and Analysis of the Common Law of England . . .* London, 1713.

Hardw.: Thomas Lee, *Cases Argued and Adjudged in the Court of King's Bench . . . ; During Which Time the Late Lord Chief Justice Hardwicke Presided in That Court* [1733–1738]. 2nd ed. London, 1815. (Wilson, of course, must have used the first edition, but the pagination seems to have been identical. The standard modern citation for this work is Cas. T. Hard.)

Haw.: William Hawkins, *A Treatise of Pleas of the Crown.* 2 vols. in one. London, 1716–1721.

Hein.: Johann Gottlieb Heineccius, *System of Universal Law.* 2 vols. London, 1741.

Henry: Robert Henry, *The History of Great Britain . . .* 6 vols. London, 1771–1793.

Hob.: Sir Henry Hobart, *Reports* (King's Bench, 1603–1625). London, 1641.

(Hobbes) De Cive: Thomas Hobbes, *De Cive.* [London] 1642. (It is probable that Wilson knew this work only through Pufendorf [q.v.].)

(Hobbes) Lev.: Thomas Hobbes, *Leviathan . . .* London, 1651.

Hooker: Richard Hooker, *Of the Laws of Ecclesiastical Polity.* First published in eight books with a life of the author by Isaak Walton. London, 1666.

(Hume) Ess.: David Hume, *Essays and Treatises on Several Subjects.* 2 vols. London, 1753.

(Hume) Tr. on hum. nat.: David Hume, *A Treatise of Human Nature.* London, 1739–1740.

Hutch.: Francis Hutcheson, *A System of Moral Philosophy.* 2 vols. London, 1755.

Ins.: See Just. Ins. or (Coke) Ins. depending on context.

Jenk.: David Jenkins, *Eight Centuries of Reports . . .* London, 1734.

Jour. Rep. (and) Jour. Sen.: *Annals of Congress.*

Just. Ins.: *Corpus Juris Civilis. Institutiones* (Institutes of Justinian).

Kaims, Hist. L. Tr.: Henry Home, Lord Kames, *Historical Law Tracts.* 2 vols. Edinburgh, 1758.

Kaims Pr. Eq.: Henry Home, Lord Kames, *Principles of Equity.* Edinburgh, 1760.

Kel.: Sir John Kelyng, *A Report of Divers Cases in Pleas of the Crown . . .* London, 1708. (The standard modern citation for this work is Kel. J.)

Ld. Bac.: Francis Bacon, *Works.* 4 vols. London, 1740. (Wilson may have used more than one edition of Bacon's works, but this seems the likely source for most of his citations.)

Ld. Ray.: Sir Robert Raymond, First Baron, *Reports, King's Bench and Common Pleas* [1694–1732]. 2 vols. London, 1775.

Leach: Thomas Leach, *Cases in Crown Law* . . . [1730–1789]. London, 1789.

Lel. Dem. Int. to oration de corona: Thomas Leland, translator, *The Orations of Aeschines and Demosthenes on the Crown . . . Volume the Third* . . . London, 1777. ("Int." refers to the translator's introduction to this volume.)

Lel. L. P. Prel.: See Lel. L. Phil. (The reference is to a "Preliminary Dissertation on the Council of Amphyctyons.")

Lel. L. Phil.: Thomas Leland, *The History of the Life and Reign of Philip, King of Macedon* . . . London, 1758.

Litt.: Sir Thomas Littleton, *Tenures in Englysshe.* London, 1544.

Liv.: Livy, *Ab Urbe Condita.*

Lock. Gov.: John Locke, *Two Treatises of Government.* London, 1690.

Locke on Hum. Und.: John Locke, *An Essay Concerning Human Understanding.* London, 1689.

M'D Ins.: Andrew MacDowell, *Institute of the Laws of Scotland* . . . 3 vols. Edinburgh, 1751–1753.

Mil.: See Millar.

Millar: John Millar, *An Historical View of the English Government, from the Settlement of the Saxons in Britain to the Accession of the House of Stewart.* London, 1787.

Milt.: John Milton, *The Works of Mr. John Milton* . . . 1697. (Wilson's reference is to this somewhat rare one-volume edition of Milton's prose, publisher unknown. The quotation in Wilson's footnote is a slight paraphrase of a sentence in *The Readie and Easie Way to Establish a Free Commonwealth.*)

Mir.: Andrew Horne, *The . . . Mirrour of Justices* . . . translated . . . by W.H. . . . London, 1646.

Mod.: *Modern Reports: or Select Cases, King's Bench.* 12 vols. London, 1698–1769.

Mod. Ent.: John Mallory, *Modern Entries in English* . . . 2 vols. London, 1734.

Molloy: Charles Molloy, *De Jure Maritimo et Navili; or, A Treatise of Affaires Maritime, and of Commerce.* London, 1676.

(Montesquieu) Sp. Laws: Charles Louis de Secondat, Baron de la Brède et de Montesquieu, *The Spirit of Laws.* 2 vols. London, 1750.

(Necker) Pref.: Jacques Necker, *Of the Importance of Religious Opinions.* London, 1788.

P. Wms.: William Peere Williams, *Reports of Cases, Court of Chancery* . . . (1695–1735) . . . by his son William Peere Williams. 3 vols. London, 1740–1749.

Paley: William Paley, *The Principles of Moral and Political Philosophy.* 2 vols. London, 1787.

Parl. Hist.: *The Parliamentary or Constitutional History of England* . . . 24 vols. London, 1751–1761.

Pett. (or Pet.) on Jur.: John Pettingal, *An Inquiry into the Use and Practice of Juries* . . . London, 1769.

Plin. Ep.: Pliny the Younger, *Epistulae.*

(Pope) Ess. on Man: Alexander Pope, *An Essay on Man.* London, 1733.

Pot. Ant.: John Potter, *Archaeologiae Graecae; or the Antiquities of Greece.* 2 vols. Oxford, 1697–1699.

Pri. Lect.: Joseph Priestley, *Lectures on History and General Policy* . . . London, 1788.

Pub.: *The Federalist* . . . 2 vols. New York, 1788.

Puff.: Samuel Pufendorf, *Of the Law of Nature and Nations* . . . carefully corrected, and compared with Mr. Barbeyrac's French translation, with the addition of his notes . . . Oxford, 1710.

R. O. Book. This refers to the Rolls Office books Wilson had himself compiled and which are referred to on p. 60 of the Preface.

Rapin: Paul de Rapin-Thoyras, . . . *An Historical Dissertation upon Whig and Tory* . . . London, 1717.

Reev.: John Reeves, *History of the English Law* . . . 4 vols. London, 1783–1784.

Reid Ess. Act.: Thomas Reid, *Essays on the Active Powers of Man.* Edinburgh, 1788.

Reid Ess. Int.: Thomas Reid, *Essays on the Intellectual Powers of Man.* Edinburgh, 1785.

(Reid) Inq.: Thomas Reid, *An Inquiry into the Human Mind, on the Principles of Common Sense.* Edinburgh, 1764.

Rep.: See (Coke) Rep.

Rob. Amer.: William Robertson, *The History of America.* 2 vols. London, 1777.

Rol. An. Hist.: Charles Rollin, *The Ancient History of the Egyptians, Carthaginians* [*etc*] . . . 10 vols. London, 1734–1736.

Rol. R. H.: Charles Rollin, *The Roman History from the Foundation of Rome to the Battle of Actium* . . . Translated from the French. 2 vols. London, 1739.

Roll. Pref.: Perhaps Charles Rollin, *The Method of Teaching and Studying the Belles Lettres* . . . 4 vols. London, 1734.

(Rousseau) Or. Com. (and) Orig. Com.: Jean Jacques Rousseau, *The Social Contract.* (Wilson's references are to this work, probably to an English translation; but his abbreviations of the title fit no edition I have found.)

Rus. Anc. Eur.: William Russell, *The History of Ancient Europe* . . . 2 vols. London, 1793. (Manifestly Wilson could not have used this edition in 1790–91, yet it seems to be the first. This suggests that he may have made revisions of the lectures between 1791 and his death.)

Ruth.: Thomas Rutherforth, *Institutes of Natural Law.* 2 vols. Cambridge, 1754–1756.

Salk.: William Salkeld, *Reports of Cases Adjudged in the Court of King's Bench* . . . [1689–1712]. 2 vols. London, 1717.

(Saunderson) Prael.: Robert Sanderson, [probably] *De Obligatione Conscientiae* . . . London, 1660.

(Selden) Anal.: John Selden, *Analecton Anglo-Britannicon* . . . Francfurti, 1615.

(Selden) dissertation on Fleta: John Selden, *Fleta.* London, 1685.

(Selden) Table talk: John Selden, *Table Talk.* London, 1689.

Shaft.: Anthony Ashley Cooper, Earl of Shaftesbury, *Characteristicks of Men, Manners, Opinions, and Times.* 3 vols. London, 1711.

Sid.: Thomas Siderfin, *Les Reports des Divers Special Cases* . . . (1647–1670) 2 vols. in one. London, 1683–1684.

(Smith) Wealth of Nations: Adam Smith, *Wealth of Nations.* 2 vols. London and Edinburgh, 1776.

Spel. Rel.: Sir Henry Spelman, *Reliquiae Spelmannianae.* London, 1698.

St.: refers to British statutes, which were in Wilson's time usually cited as chapters of the statutes of the session of a particular regnal year; e.g. St. 13 Edw. 1 c. 24.

St. Tr.: *A Complete Collection of State-Trials* . . . 6 vols. London, 1730.

(Stewart) Pol. Ec.: Sir James Steuart, *An Inquiry into the Principles of Political Economy.* 2 vols. London, 1767.

Stith: William Stith, *The History of the First Discovery and Settlement of Virginia.* Williamsburg, 1747.

Str.: Sir John Strange, *Reports of Adjudged Cases* . . . [1713–1748]. 2 vols. London, 1755.

Stu. V.: Gilbert Stuart, *A View of Society in Europe* . . . Edinburgh, 1778. (The "Mr. Adair" referred to by Wilson was James Adair, author of *History of the American Indians,* London, 1775. "Com. Per." cited by Stuart refers to Garsilaso de la Vega, the Inca, *Los Comentarios Reales de los Incas,* Madrid, 1723.)

Sulliv.: Francis S. Sullivan, *Historical Treatise on the Feudal Law and the Constitution and Laws of England.* Dublin, 1772.

Swin.: Henry Swinburne, *Treatise of Testaments and Last Wills* . . . London, 1590.

Tac. Agric.: Tacitus, *Agricola.*

Tac. Ann.: Tacitus, *Annales.*

Tac. de mor. Germ.: Tacitus, *Germania* (the title *De Moribus Germanorum* appears in certain manuscripts).

(Taylor) Rule of Conscience: [probably] Jeremy Taylor, *The Rule and Exercises of Holy Living* . . . London, 1650.

Thom. Works: James Thomson, *The Works of Mr. Thomson.* 3 vols. London, 1738–1748.

Tibul. 1.1 Eleg.: Albius Tibullus, *Elegies.*

Tr. per Pais: Giles Duncombe, *Trials per Pais; or the Law Concerning Juries by Nisi Prius* . . . London, 1665.

Tr. on hum. nat.: David Hume, *Treatise of Human Nature.* London, 1739–1740.

Ub. Em.: Emmius Ubbo, *Graecorum Res Publicae* . . . *Lugduni Batavorum,* Ex Officina Elzeviriana, 1632.

Vat.: Emmerich de Vattel, *The Law of Nature.* Translated from the French. 2 vols. in one. London, 1759.

Vaugh.: Edward Vaughan, ed., *Reports and Arguments of* . . . *Sir John Vaughan Kt. Late Chief Justice of His Majesties Court of Common Pleas* . . . [1665–1674]. London, 1677.

Vent.: Sir Peyton Ventris, *Reports* . . . London, 1696.

War. Bib.: Jacques Pierre Brissot de Warville, *Bibliothèque philosophique du législateur, du politique, du jurisconsulte* . . . 10 vols. Berlin and Paris, 1782–1785.

War. The. L. Crim.: Jacques Pierre Brissot de Warville, *Théorie des laix criminelles.* 2 vols. Berlin, 1781.

Warv.: See War. The. L. Crim.

Whitak.: John Whitaker, *The History of Manchester.* 2 vols. London, 1771–1775.

Whitl.: Sir Bulstrode Whitelocke, *Notes Upon the King's Writ for Choosing Members of Parliament* . . . 2 vols. London, 1766.

Wils.: George Wilson, *Reports of Cases Argued and Adjudged in the King's Courts at Westminster* [1742–1774]. 2 vols. London, 1770–1775. (The standard modern citation for this work is Wils. K. B.)

Wood Ins.: Thomas Wood, *An Institute of the Laws of England.* 2 vols. London, 1720.

AFTERWORD

The *Collected Works of James Wilson* was originally to be edited solely by Kermit Hall, a distinguished scholar of constitutional law and president of the State University of New York at Albany. Because of my previous work on Wilson, I had consulted with Liberty Fund on the project and agreed to write a bibliographical essay for the volume. After Kermit Hall's tragic death in 2006, Liberty Fund asked me to help bring the project to completion. Although we share the same surname, Kermit Hall and I are related only by our interest in constitutional law and in James Wilson.

Kermit Hall had made significant progress on these volumes, but much work remained. I found it necessary to add and rearrange documents and to write and revise numerous headnotes and annotations. I made only minor stylistic and grammatical revisions to Kermit Hall's original introduction.

Joining a project of this magnitude at a relatively late stage would have been extremely difficult without the excellent work of editors at Liberty Fund—notably Laura Goetz and Dan Kirklin. As well, I am grateful for support provided by George Fox University, particularly my student assistants Deanne Kastine and Janna McKee. Master librarian Alex Rolfe provided expert assistance tracking down obscure figures for annotations. Joshua W. D. Smith of Veritas School made last-minute translations of approximately two dozen obscure Latin phrases. Finally, as noted above, these volumes exist because of Maynard Garrison, to whom all students of Wilson owe a debt of gratitude.

I would like to dedicate my contributions to these volumes to the founders, teachers, board members, and students of Veritas School in Newberg, Oregon.

Mark David Hall
Herbert Hoover Distinguished Professor of Political Science
George Fox University
May 25, 2007

INDEX

Works referenced by James Wilson are listed under their authors. See the bibliographical glossary for a key to the abbreviations used in Wilson's footnotes.

The typeface used in this book is Adobe Caslon, a 1990 interpretation by Carol Twombly of the classic face cut in the 1720s by the English typographer William Caslon (1692–1766). Trained as an engraver, Caslon turned to type design and cutting, setting up his own type foundry in 1720. Caslon became the first major native English typeface to achieve wide popularity. It displays the small lowercase height and the restrained contrast typical of what are now called old-style fonts. The modern version smooths out many of the idiosyncrasies of William Caslon's original cutting, while retaining the warmth and honesty that have made Caslon a friend of the typographer for centuries.

Book design by Erin Kirk New, Watkinsville, Georgia
Typography by G&S Typesetters, Austin, Texas

www.ingramcontent.com/pod-product-compliance
Lightning Source LLC
La Vergne TN
LVHW051542310726
844171LV00003B/14
* 9 7 8 0 8 6 5 9 7 6 8 7 0 *